❦ ERRATA ❦

The Magic of Numbers & Motion

1991 • ISBN 0-88135-098-2 • LC 89-10813

Page 169, note 15 : read 101 instead of 000.

Page 284, note 12 : read art. 148 instead of 1448.

❧ ❧ ❧ ❧ ❧

The MAGIC *of* NUMBERS *and* MOTION

The Scientific Career of René Descartes

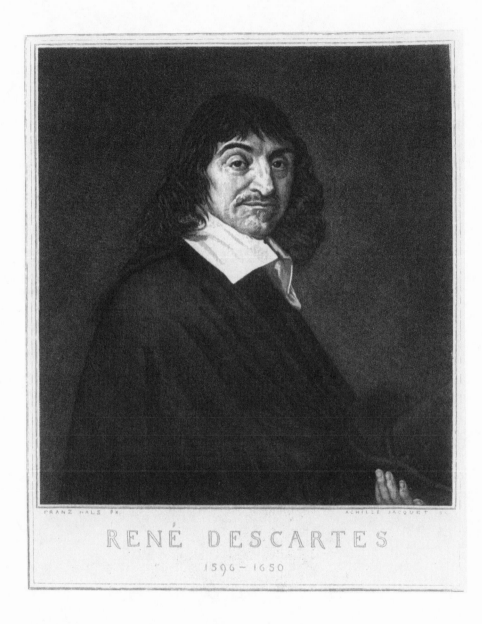

FRANZ HALS PX.   ACHILLE JACQUET SC.

RENÉ DESCARTES
1596 — 1650

The MAGIC of NUMBERS and MOTION

The Scientific Career of René Descartes

WILLIAM R. SHEA

Science History Publications, U.S.A.
1991

First published in the United States of America by
Science History Publications, U.S.A.
a division of
Watson Publishing International
Post Office Box 493, Canton, MA 02021

©Watson Publishing International 1991

First Edition

Library of Congress Cataloging-in-Publication Data
Shea, William R.
  The magic of numbers and motion: the scientific career of René
Descartes/William R. Shea.
    p. cm.
  Includes bibliographical references.
  ISBN 0-88135-098-2
  1. Descartes, René, 1596–1650—Knowledge—Science.   2. Science,
Renaissance.   3. Science—Philosophy.   4. Scientists—France—
Biography.   I. Title.
Q125.2.S54 1990
509.2—dc20
[B]   89-10813
                                                                          CIP

Design & Typesetting by Crane Design, Inc.
Manufactured in the U.S.A.

Contents

To the memory of
Pierre Costabel (1912–1989)
Priest, Scholar, and Historian of Science

Preface

AFTER HIS UNTIMELY DEATH in Stockholm on 11 February 1650, Descartes' private papers were handed over to the French ambassador, Pierre Chanut, who shipped them to his brother-in-law, Claude Clerselier, in France. The cargo reached Rouen safely and was loaded on a boat that went up the Seine. On the outskirts of Paris, the boat sank, and the chest containing Descartes' manuscripts spent three days and three nights on the waters before Clerselier was able to rescue them. With the aid of his servants (who knew little and cared less about Cartesian natural philosophy), he spread out the sheets in various rooms to dry. Over the next seventeen years, Clerselier was to patiently order the faded pages and publish three volumes of Descartes' correspondence as well as his *Treatise on Man*, *The World*, and the *Treatise on the Formation of the Foetus*.

Clerselier is usually thought to have been reasonably successful in his reconstruction of Descartes' dismembered papers, but I cannot help seeing in his labors a symbol of the difficulty of fitting together the various parts of Descartes' varied activity as philosopher, mathematician, theologian, and natural scientist. There is always the danger that the fit may be more apparent than real. Descartes himself tried to hide the seams in a garment of knowledge that he would have liked us to believe to be all of one piece. In the brilliant autobiographical fragment that he published at the age of 41 in his *Discourse on Method*, he reconstructed his past in an attempt to persuade his readers that they should adopt his new scientific method. His own life became the prime exemplar of a well-organized pilgrimage from darkness to light upon a road that may have been narrow but was always straight . . . .

My goal has been to follow Descartes in his journey, and to provide a comprehensive, but by no means exhaustive, survey of his scientific career from his student days at the Jesuit College of La Flèche to his departure for Sweden where he had been summoned by Queen Christina. I have tried to follow Descartes' injunction to be clear (but not clear at all costs), and I am sanguine enough to hope that the reader will be sufficiently stimulated and intrigued by what he finds in this book to turn to Descartes' own works. I have kept my discussion of mathematics in Chapter Three as simple as possible, but anyone who wishes to skip this section at first reading has not only my sympathy, but the assurance that the gist is summarized in a few pages at the end. A chronology of the main events of Descartes' life will be found in the Appendix.

My work could not have been undertaken without the pioneering efforts of Gaston Milhaud (*Descartes Savant*, 1921), Paul Mouy (*Le Développement de la Physique Cartésienne*, 1934), and J. F. Scott, *The Scientific Work of René Descartes*, 1952). I am deeply indebted to these forerunners, and to the numerous friends, colleagues, and students, who have helped me with their advice and constructive criticism. Readers familiar with the works of Eric Aiton, Gerd Buchdahl, I. Bernard Cohen, Paolo Rossi, and R. S. Westfall will immediately realize on whose shoulders I am standing. I thank them most warmly, as well as Robert E. Butts, Catherine Chevalley, Paolo Galluzzi, Marcello Pera, and René Taton, who have remonstrated with me over the years and saved me from many an egregious error. I am especially grateful to Pierre Costabel, who subjected parts of the typescript to his meticulous scrutiny and was kind enough to make me feel that I was not completely wrong. He died as this book was going to press, and it is appreciatively dedicated to his memory. I was also privileged to learn from Neale Watson and Gerald Lombardi, and I thank them for their patience and dedication. I am also grateful to the Social Sciences and Humanities Research Council of Canada, the Department of Philosophy, and the Centre for Medicine, Ethics, and the Law of McGill University for their continued support of my research.

I had the pleasure of writing this book at the Wissenschaftskolleg (Institute for Advance Study) in Berlin, and I wish to thank the Rector, the Librarian and their staff for their invaluable assistance. I am much in the debt of Beata Gallay, who prepared the index, and Firooza Kraft and Iris Hardinge, who typed the manuscript. I am also grateful to Rolf Selbach and John Honeyman of McGill for their help with the illustrations, which are mainly taken from the standard edition of Descartes' *Oeuvres*, edited by Charles Adam and Paul Tannery. This book would never have been completed without the encouragement of my wife, Evelyn, who commented on the typescript and tried to make me live up to Descartes' ideal of clarity and conciseness. It is a pleasure to thank her, and to express my gratitude to our children, Herbert, Joan-Emma, Louisa, Cecilia, and Michael for their probing questions and their unwillingness to let me get away with easy answers.

August 1990
McGill University
Montreal

The MAGIC of NUMBERS and MOTION

The Scientific Career of René Descartes

Chapter One

The Young Man
from Poitou

D ESCARTES WAS BORN on 31 March 1596 at La Haye (now La Haye-Descartes) in the Touraine. The date is known from an inscription around his portrait in the posthumous Latin edition of his *Geometry*.

The portrait and the inscription were made during his lifetime, but Descartes objected to having the date of his birth disclosed lest it should fall into the hands of horoscope-makers.[1] This may be explained by a legitimate desire for privacy, but I believe it also reveals a vestigial fear of the power of astrology. As we shall see when discussing Descartes' juvenile enthusiasm for the Rosicrucians, it is misleading to believe that he was always clothed in the shining armor of pure rationality.

---

[1] The portrait was made in 1644 by Frans van Schooten the Younger, who toyed with the idea of publishing it in the first Latin edition of the *Geometry* that appeared in 1649. In a letter to van Schooten on 9 April 1649, Descartes praised the portrait, "although the beard and the clothes bear no resemblance to reality," but requested that it not be printed. Should van Schooten insist on using it, then he should at least remove the inscription, "A nobleman of the Perron, born on the last day of March 1596." He objected to the first words "because I dislike all titles," and to the remaining "because I also dislike horoscope-makers, whose error we seem to encourage when we publish the date of someone's birth" (René Descartes, *Oeuvres*, Charles Adam and Paul Tannery, eds., 11 vols. (Paris: Leopold Cerf, 1897–1913). This is the standard edition of Descartes' works and was reprinted with additions, (Paris: Vrin, 1964–1979). It will subsequently be referred to as A.T., followed by the volume in Roman and the page in Arabic numbers. The present reference is to volume V, page 338, i.e., A.T., V, p. 338).

Descartes' father, Joachim Descartes, was a member of the Parlement of Brittany in Rennes, and his mother, Jeanne Brochard, the daughter of the Lieutenant General of the Presidial of Poitiers. René may be said to have belonged to the minor nobility, and as a young man, he styled himself Sieur du Perron, from the small *seigneurie* he had inherited. His mother died on 16 May 1597, three days after giving birth to a child who did not survive. Descartes was brought up by his maternal grandmother, Jeanne Sain, who died in 1610, and by a wet nurse to whom he remained attached and to whom he paid an annual pension, as well as making provisions for her in his will.[2]

The College of La Flèche

In 1603, an event occurred that was to exert a profound influence on the young Descartes' education. The Jesuits, who had been expelled from France in 1594, were allowed to return and to found a College at La Flèche in the same part of the country as La Haye.[3] The College opened its doors in 1604, and in 1606 Fr. Etienne Charlet (1570–1652), a cousin of Descartes, became a member of the staff. Charlet was appointed Rector in 1608. The presence of a relative may have induced Descartes' family to send him to the new school, which he entered, in all likelihood, in 1606 at the age of ten and left in 1615 at the age of nineteen, after completing the normal cycle of studies that comprised six years of high school followed by three years of college.[4]

When Descartes arrived at La Flèche the buildings were not completed, and the students were boarded in neighboring houses until the dormitories were ready in 1609. The students numbered about 60 at the time. The College had been richly endowed by its founder, Guillaume Fouquet, Sieur

---

[2] Adrien Baillet, *La Vie de Monsieur Des-Cartes*, 2 vols. (Paris, 1691). Facsimile (Geneva: Slatkine, 1970), vol. II, p. 458. Baillet remains our main source for Descartes' life.

[3] See Camille de Rochemonteix, *Un Collège des Jésuites au XVIIᵉ et au XVIIIᵉ Siècle. Le Collège Henri IV de La Flèche*, 4 vols. (Le Mans: Leguicheux, 1889). The Jesuits enjoyed a high reputation even among Protestants. In 1623, Francis Bacon could say of them: "As far as teaching is concerned, it can be put very briefly: Look at the schools of the Jesuits, there is nothing better" (*De Dignitate et augmentiis scientiarum*, Book VII, Chapter 4, in Francis Bacon, *Works*, J. Spedding, R. L. Ellis, *et alii*, eds., 14 vols. (London 1857–1874). Reprint (Stuttgart-Bad Cannstatt: Frommann, 1963), vol. I, p. 709.

[4] On Descartes at La Flèche, see J. Sirven, *Les années d'apprentissage de Descartes* (Albi: Imprimerie Coopérative de l'Ouest, 1928), pp. 25–52. Descartes could have entered La Flèche as early as 1604 or as late as 1607, and might have left in 1613, 1614, or 1615. Sirven argues for 1607–1615 (pp. 41–48). On the current state of the question, see the lucid account of Geneviève Rodis-Lewis, *Idées et vérités éternelles chez Descartes et ses successeurs* (Paris; Vrin, 1985), pp. 165–181. All Descartes himself said was that he had spent at La Flèche "eight or nine years" (letter to Fr. Grandamy, 2 May 1644, A.T., IV, p. 122), or "almost nine years" (letter to Fr. Hayneuve, 22 July 1640, A.T. III, p. 100).

de la Varenne, and there was no tuition fee. Twenty-four scholarships for students from low-income families had been made available, and this may explain how Marin Mersenne, the son of a modest farmer, was able to attend La Flèche from 1604 to 1609. He was Descartes' senior by eight years, and the two boys could not have been more than mere acquaintances at school. Their friendship dates from 1623 when they met again in Paris and were drawn together by their common scientific interests. Mersenne was to become his most important and stimulating correspondent when Descartes settled in the Netherlands. Virtually all Jesuit colleges encouraged a mix of high and low born, and friendships of this kind were not rare. Attending a Jesuit institution was a way of acquiring a kind of vicarious title. It opened the doors of the best houses of France.

The only classmate that Descartes mentions in his correspondence is François Chauveau, who became a Jesuit and taught at La Flèche.[5] Although fees were not required of students, those who could pay could get a private room. Descartes' family saw to it that he enjoyed this privilege, and because his health was frail, he received permission to rise late, a habit that he was to keep all his life, until he was compelled to rise at 4.00 a.m. to instruct Queen Christina of Sweden.

The most important political event during Descartes' student days was the assassination of King Henri IV by a demented monk on 14 May 1610. The King's heart was solemnly brought to La Flèche on 4 June 1610, and Descartes was one of the 24 young noblemen chosen to form the funeral procession. A year later, the first anniversary of the arrival of the King's heart was duly celebrated, and a sonnet was read in which Galileo's recent discovery of four satellites of Jupiter was commemorated.[6] The fact that Galileo's most sensational telescopic observation was mentioned shows that the Jesuits kept abreast of scientific developments. It also reveals their political acumen, since Galileo had christened the four satellites "Medicean stars" in honour of Cosimo II, the Grand Duke of Tuscany and cousin of the Queen Regent of France, Marie de Medici. The Jesuits could also have known that before the King's death Galileo had been asked by the French court to name the next planet he discovered after Henri IV.[7]

---

[5] Letter of Descartes to Mersenne, 28 January 1641, A.T., III, p. 296, and notes pp. 299 and 873.

[6] See Rochemonteix, *Un Collège des Jésuites*, vol. I, pp. 144–152.

[7] See Galileo's letter to Vincenzo Giugni, 25 June 1610, in Galileo Galilei, *Opere*, Antonio Favaro, ed., 20 vols. (Florence: G. Barbèra, 1890–1909), vol. X, p. 381. In their desire to flatter royalty by raising it to the heavens, two amateur astronomers, the French priest, Jean Tarde, and the Austrian Jesuit, Charles Malapert, later dedicated to the reigning families of France and Austria sunspots that they insisted were planets: J. Tarde, *Borbonia Sidera, id est planetae qui solis limina circumvolitant motu proprio ac regulari, falso hactenus ab helioscopis maculae solis nuncupati* (Paris, 1620), and C. Malapert, *Austriaca Sidera Heliocyclica astronomicis hypothesibus illigata* (Douay, 1633).

Jesuit Education

Teaching in Jesuit Colleges was governed by the *Ratio Studiorum* drafted by St. Ignatius of Loyola and published for the first time in France in 1603, the year the College of La Flèche was founded. Jesuits did not aim at training theologians but lay Christians who would bear witness to the Gospel in the world. They stressed orthodoxy in matters of Faith but encouraged freedom of thought on disputed questions.

Education was based on the Latin classics, and the *Metamorphoses* of Ovid were particularly popular. Descartes mastered Latin and later wrote both his *Meditations* and his *Principles of Philosophy* in that language. He also learned some Greek and acquired a working knowledge of Italian, which was frequently used at the court of Marie de Medici. He enjoyed novels and later recalled his fondness and enthusiasm for the *Amadis*, a lengthy romance that recounts the chivalrous deeds of a knight who is a model of constancy to his loved one.[8]

Musing on the education he had received at La Flèche, Descartes wrote in his *Discourse on Method* that "fables have a charm that awakens the mind," and that "memorable deeds told in histories uplift it and help to form one's judgment." "Reading good books," he added, "is like having a conversation with the most distinguished men of the past—a studied conversation in which they reveal only the best of their thoughts."[9] Descartes was always to feel that books should only contain carefully selected material, and he only revealed what he thought would be considered his best. As a consequence, he was neither a precocious nor a prolific writer. He waited until he was 41 before publishing his first book in 1637. This consisted of the *Optics*, the *Meteors*, and the *Geometry*, and a Preface, the *Discourse on Method*, destined to become more famous than the scientific treatises it introduced. This was followed by three other books, the *Meditations* in 1641, the *Principles of Philosophy* in 1644, and the *Passions of the Soul* in 1649.

The last three years of High School included poetry and rhetoric. "Oratory," we read in the *Discourse on Method*, "has incomparable powers and beauties; poetry has quite ravishing delicacy and sweetness."[10] Descartes wrote verse, and he was always to place poetic inspiration above mere philosophical reasoning.[11]

---

[8] Letter of Descartes to Constantin Huygens, 8 September 1637, A.T., I, p. 396, and note p. 397.

[9] *Discourse on Method*, Part One, A.T., VI, p. 5.

[10] *Ibid.*, p. 6.

[11] Descartes told Huygens that he had composed poems (see letter of Constantin Huygens to Descartes, 14 March 1644, A.T., IV, p. 102). On the superiority of poetic inspiration, see Descartes' *Cogitationes Privatae*, A.T., X, p. 217. One aspect of student life that is not mentioned by Descartes is recorded in a Royal Edict of 1604: "Innkeepers enticed them, women of loose morals laid snares for them, and charlatans corrupted them under the guise of teaching them the science of magic" (Rochemonteix, *Un Collège des Jésuites*, vol. II, p. 90).

The three years of College, or "philosophy" as they were called, were divided into logic, physics and mathematics, and metaphysics. The *Ratio Studiorum* recommended that the teachers follow Aristotle, as interpreted by Thomas Aquinas (1227–1274), who had been proclaimed a Doctor of the Church as recently as 1569 and whose teaching was considered the embodiment of Catholic orthodoxy. It would seem, however, that the Jesuit professors relied on textbooks rather than on the text of Aristotle himself. The students attended two hours of lecture in the morning and in the afternoon. They also had one hour of discussion, generally entrusted to a "repetitor" or graduate student who acted somewhat like a teaching assistant in American universities. On Saturdays, the evening lectures were replaced by a public debate at which students took turns attacking or defending a philosophical position.

The professor of logic was expected to explain Porphyry and the following works of Aristotle: the *Categories, On Interpretation*, the first four chapters of the *Prior Analytics*, the *Topics*, and the section on demonstration in the *Posterior Analytics*. The *Ratio Studiorum* recommended the commentaries of the Jesuits Francesco Toledo (1533–1596) and Pedro de Fonseca (1528–1599), both competent but uninspiring authors. In the second year, physics comprised a survey of Aristotle's *Physics, On the Heavens*, and the first book of *On Generation*. It is more difficult to know what was taught in mathematics. In all likelihood, the Jesuits used the manuals of their greatest mathematician and scientist, Christopher Clavius, who had just died in Rome in 1612, after a distinguished career at the Roman College, the Jesuits' foremost institution of higher learning. In their teaching of mathematics, which was broadly conceived to include the art of fortification as well as musical theory, the Jesuits stressed practical applications and discussed such matters as military and civil engineering that were of interest to young noblemen who would later become officers and administrators. The third year of College was devoted to Aristotle's *Metaphysics*, his treatise *On the Soul*, and the second book of *On Generation*. All these works were interpreted in the light of Thomas Aquinas' *Summa Theologiae*, one of the few works, along with the Bible, that Descartes took with him to Holland.[12]

When Descartes was preparing the *Meditations* for print in 1640, he wrote to Mersenne in Paris for a list of authors who had written textbooks of philosophy since he left school: "I only remember the Conimbricenses, Toletus and Rubius. I should also like to know whether someone has written a popular summary of scholastic philosophy. This would spare me the labor of having to read their ponderous tomes. I seem to remember that a Carthusian or a Feuillant monk did this, but his name escapes me."[13] This is the only explicit reference in the whole of Descartes' correspondence to authors he studied at school. Toletus is Francesco Toledo, the sixteenth-century Jesuit whom the *Ratio Studiorum* recommended. Antonius Rubius or

[12] Letter of Descartes to Mersenne, 25 December 1639, A.T., II, p. 630.

[13] Letter of Descartes to Mersenne, 30 September 1640, A.T., III, p. 185.

Ruvio (1548–1615 was a Jesuit missionary who taught philosophy in Mexico and published a *Mexican Logic or Commentary on the Whole of Aristotle's Logic*, as well as commentaries on other parts of Aristotle's philosophy.[14] The Conimbricenses were a group of professors who published commentaries on the works of Aristotle in Coimbra from 1592 onwards.

The *Nicomachean Ethics* of Aristotle was also on the program of the third year of philosophy at *La Flèche*, and the professor could have used the relevant Coimbra commentary that appeared in 1594. The author of the philosophical summary that Descartes remembered was Eustache de Saint Paul, known as the Feuillant from the name of his convent in Paris. His *Summa Philosophiae* appeared in 1609 and was reprinted eight times between 1611 and 1626. This shows that the Jesuits who taught Descartes made use of the most recent and successful textbook on the market.

How deeply all this scholastic philosophy impressed Descartes is difficult to assess. Twenty years later, he declared that he had "delighted in mathematics," but he patronizingly dismissed philosophy as merely "giving the means of speaking plausibly about any subject and of winning the admiration of the less learned."[15]

Descartes' Professors

Students usually had the same professor for their three years of philosophy. Because of the uncertainty surrounding the exact date of Descartes' arrival at La Flèche, this could have been one of three Jesuits: François Véron (1578–1649), if Descartes graduated in 1613; François Fournet, if he graduated a year later, or Etienne Noël (1581–1660), if he left the College in 1615, as seems more likely. Fr. François Véron acquired some notoriety as the author of a *Method of Controversy* for Catholics when dealing with Protestants, a work that ran into 22 editions between 1615 and 1638. He also wrote an influential *Handbook* for the Sodality of the Blessed Virgin Mary, which had a chapter at La Flèche. We do not know whether Descartes belonged to this pious association, but he was always to be devoted to Mary. The first thing he did after his famous dream of 10 November 1619 was to vow to go to the shrine of Loretto to thank the Blessed Mother. During his 20-year residence in the Netherlands, he intervened only once in disputes between Protestant theologians, and this was to defend an interdenominational confraternity of the Blessed Virgin at Bois-le-Duc.

Fr. Etienne Noël, who is most likely to have been Descartes' professor of philosophy, was Rector of the College when the *Discourse on Method* appeared in 1637, and Descartes sent him one of the first copies. In his letter of transmittal, he described his book as "a fruit that belongs to you, since you

---

[14] Rubius' *Commentaries* are listed, *ibid.*, pp. 195–196, where the works of Tolelus, the Conimbricenses, and the Feuillant (Frère Eustache de Saint Paul) are also given.

[15] *Discourse on Method*, Part One, A.T., VI, pp. 6–7.

sowed the first seeds in my mind."[16] The following year, Descartes was to advise a friend to send his son to La Flèche: "I believe it is useful to have followed a general course in philosophy, the way it is taught in the schools of the Jesuits . . . . I must say, in praise of my masters, that there is no place in the world where philosophy is better taught than at La Flèche."[17] Fr. Noël was interested in physics and astronomy, and he later entered into a lively controversy with Pascal over the interpretation of the vacuum. He remained on good terms with his former pupil, and in 1646 he sent Descartes his two new books, one on Aristotelian physics and the other on the nature of the sun. In the dedication to the first work, a leading Jesuit, Fr. Jean de Riennes, described Noël's achievement as "putting together the ascertained results of the philosophy of Aristotle, René Descartes, and the chemists."[18]

Descartes' professor of mathematics was Jean François (1582–1668), a theology student who was later to publish several books on mathematics and a learned disquisition on the influence of heavenly bodies. But since his first book only appeared in 1652, two years after Descartes' death, we cannot be specific about what he actually taught around 1614.

A major argument for concluding that Descartes left La Flèche in 1615 (and hence had Fr. Noël as professor of philosophy) is the testimony of François du Ban (c. 1592–1643) who claimed to have taught Descartes at La Flèche. Records show that du Ban arrived there as a first-year student in 1614, and he could not have become Descartes' "repetitor" before the academic year 1614–1615.[19] Du Ban presents an interesting instance of the shifts in religious allegiances that were not uncommon in the first half of the seventeenth century. Although a Jesuit, du Ban was converted to Protestantism in Paris around 1628 and left France for the Netherlands where he enrolled in the Faculty of Theology at Leyden in 1630. He subsequently applied for the Chair of Philosophy at the University of Utrecht that Descartes' disciple Henri Reneri (1593–1639) was awarded in 1634. (Reneri was also a convert who had come to Leyden after leaving the Roman confession.) In 1635 du Ban began teaching logic at Leyden. He was granted the title of Extraordinary Professor of Logic in 1636 and allowed to teach physics in 1638. It was through him that a younger colleague, Adriaan Heereboord, was introduced to Cartesian philosophy. Du Ban died in Leyden in May

---

[16] Letter of Descartes to Etienne Noël, 14 June 1637. A.T., I, p. 383. The original is not extant, and the addressee is merely indicated as "A Reverend Jesuit Father" by Clerselier who first published the letter.

[17] Descartes to an unknown correspondent, 12 September 1638, A.T., II, p. 377.

[18] Quoted in A.T., IV, p. 585. Noël's books are entitled *Aphorismi physici seu physicae peripateticae principia breviter ac dilucide proposita* (La Flèche, 1646), and *Sol Flamma, sive Tractatus de Sole, ut flamma est, ejusque pabulo* (Paris, 1646). See Descartes' letters to Mersenne, 7 September 1646, A.T., IV, p. 498, and to Noël, 14 December, 1646, *ibid.*, pp. 584–585.

[19] See Gustave Cohen, *Ecrivains Français en Hollande dans la première moitié du XVIIe Siècle* (Paris: Champion, 1920), pp. 335–339. Cohen does not cite his source for stating that du Ban taught Descartes, p. 335.

1643, but we do not know whether he actually renewed Descartes' acquaintance in the Netherlands.

The Young Lawyer

Descartes' eldest brother, Pierre, had studied law at the University of Poitiers, and René was expected to walk in his footsteps. He lodged with a local tailor in Poitiers, and was asked to be godfather at the christening of his landlord's child on 21 May 1616.[20] He passed his examinations for the baccalaureate in law on 9 November and those for the licentiate in law on the following day. Such haste was not uncommon at the time.[21] As was also the custom, the degrees were conferred "*in utroque jure*," namely, in both civil and ecclesiastical law. Descartes was never to refer to his sojourn in Poitiers nor to the fact that he was a qualified lawyer in the 498 letters of his that are extant. He was not eager to practice a profession for which he does not seem to have been particularly suited.

French Noblemen in Holland

We know nothing of Descartes' actual occupation for the next fourteen months except that he signed the registry as a witness at christenings on 22 October and 3 December 1617 at Chavagne en Sucé, near Nantes, where his father lived.[22] Like many young noblemen who had not yet fixed on a career, he decided to journey to Holland and enroll in the army. His choice was not an oddity. Many young Frenchmen were to be found at the University of Leyden or in the ranks of one of the two French regiments of Maurice of Nassau, who, in his own eyes as well as in those of his contemporaries, was the greatest general of his age. When a woman asked him one day who was the best captain of Europe, he is said to have answered, after a moment of hesitation, that the great Spanish general Spinola was the second.[23]

The Twelve-Year Truce (1609–1621) between Spain and the Netherlands was still in force, and the young Frenchmen did not expect to see active combat. But this did not stop them from bragging. Guez de Balzac, who became one of Descartes' friends and had studied at Leyden, found them tedious. To his brother, he wrote: "To avoid these great talkers, I would jump into a coach, take to the sea, flee to the end of the world . . . . They make me

---

[20] Charles Adam, *Descartes. Sa vie et ses oeuvres*, published as vol. XII of the Adam-Tannery edition, (Paris: Leopold Cerf, 1910), p. 39, note *c.*

[21] Descartes would also have passed his doctoral examination on 21 December 1616 according to J.-R. Armogathe and V. Carnaud, whose unpublished study is mentioned by Jean-Luc Marion, *Sur le prisme métaphysique de Descartes* (Paris: Presses Universitaires de France, 1986), p. VI, footnote.

[22] Charles Adam, *Descartes. Sa vie et ses oeuvres*, p. 35.

[23] *Ibid.*, p. 41, note *a.* Adam gives Guez de Balzac as his source for this anecdote.

sick when they have just returned from Holland or when they start to study mathematics."[24] Balzac's unlikely claim that the Netherlands made Frenchmen garrulous is perhaps less interesting than the disclosure that mathematics was a fad.

A Mathematical Challenge

Descartes joined the army at Breda, where Prince Maurice's troops were garrisoned, at the beginning of 1618.[25] He served as a volunteer, equipped himself at his own expense, paid his own orderly, and received no wages except an initial doubloon that he kept as a souvenir. Maurice of Nassau was almost always away, touring parts of the country where Arminians (the disciples of the Dutch theologian Jacob Harmensen known as Arminius) and the more orthodox Calvinists were creating disturbances. By the autumn of 1618, Descartes was beginning to feel the boredom of camp life when he had the good fortune of making the acquaintance of a man, some years his elder, who was, in his own words, to "wake him up."[26] This was Isaac Beeckman, who had recently received a doctorate in medicine from the University of Caen and was later to become the Director of a College in Dordrecht. In 1905 Cornelis de Waard found Beeckman's diary in Mittelburg, Beeckman's native town. It is a remarkably detailed account of the life of a seventeenth-century scientist, and it contains numerous references to Descartes, whose name appears for the first time under the entry for 10 November 1618.[27] According to Descartes' biographer, Adrien Baillet, their meeting occurred in the following way. Strolling through Breda,

---

[24] Guez de Balzac to his brother, 1 January 1624, quoted *ibid.*, p. 41, note *b*.

[25] Frans van Schooten the Younger states that Descartes told him that he had spent fifteen months in Breda (A.T., X, p. 162). Since we know that Descartes left Breda at the end of April 1619, this gives January 1618 for the date of his arrival in that city.

[26] Letter of Descartes to Beeckman, 23 April 1619, A.T., X, p. 162.

[27] *Ibid.*, Isaac Beeckman, *Journal*, p. 46. The passages from the diary that mention Descartes are reproduced in vol. X of the *Oeuvres*. The complete diary was edited by Cornélis de Waard: Isaac Beeckman, *Journal, 1604–1634*, 4 vols. (The Hague: Martinus Nijhoff, 1939–1945). Beeckman was born in Mittelburg on 10 December 1588 and was Descartes senior by eight years. He studied medicine at the University of Leyden but went to Caen in the summer of 1618 to take his degree. The University of Caen enjoyed no particularly high repute, but it was the closest to the port of Dieppe or Le Havre. With Cartesian celerity, he was made a bachelor and a licentiate of medicine on 18 August, and on 6 September, he defended his views on tertian fever and received his doctorate, having promised not to practice in Rouen, Rheims, or Paris. Why this pledge was required is unknown. The document released to Beeckman clearly stated that he was qualified to practice and teach medicine "the world over" (A.T., X, p. 30). It may be that Caen was not over enthusiastic about the competence of the candidates it sped through the examination process. The practice of taking one's degree in a different university was not uncommon, however. Copernicus, who studied at Padua, spent a few weeks in Bologna to receive his doctorate from the local university. It has been suggested that this was to avoid the expense of the

Descartes came across a crowd staring at a poster on which a mathematician, as was the custom, issued a challenge to solve a particular problem. The writing was in Dutch, which Descartes had not yet mastered, and he asked the person next to him whether he could tell him in Latin or French what it was all about. The man, who happened to be Beeckman, replied in Latin, explained the nature of the problem and gave Descartes his card. To Beeckman's intense surprise, an unannounced visitor the next day turned out to be the young Frenchman who was calling to say that he had worked out the answer.[28] Beeckman was, of course, delighted, and the two young men soon became fast friends. Their interest ranged over a wide field of topics from the law of falling bodies that, unknown to them, had been preoccupying Galileo in Italy, to the nature of musical consonance and the possibility of magic. As a Christmas gift for Beeckman, Descartes wrote a musical treatise in Latin, the *Compendium musicae*, which ends with a request that it be kept private. Descartes was willing to speculate on the relations between mathematical proportions and musical harmony, but he was anxious to avoid hostile criticism. The *Compendium* was only published posthumously in 1650, a few months after his death.

Beeckman did not arrive in Breda in the autumn of 1618 to open a new practice, but to help his uncle Peter slaughter pigs, November being the time for this in Holland. He had also come to find a wife, a quest that was to remain unsuccessful until a year later when he was married in Mittelburg on 20 April 1620. Shortly after meeting Descartes, he jotted down in his *Journal* the following flattering comment: "This native of Poitou knows several Jesuits and many other scholars and learned persons. Nonetheless, he says that he has never met anyone that has a method that so accurately combines physics with mathematics as the one in which I rejoice."[29]

Beeckman encouraged Descartes to spell out his views on mechanics and geometry, but after Beeckman's departure, Descartes confessed in a letter of 24 January 1619 that he had hardly done more than jot down the title of the books that Beeckman had urged him to write. His excuse was that he was busy studying painting, military architecture, and mainly Dutch. He assured Beeckman that he valued a scientific correspondence, but that it was less to him than friendship. "I am not only interested in science but in yourself," he wrote, and he ended his letter with these strong words: "Rest assured that I would rather forget the Muses than yourself. Indeed, they have bound me to you with everlasting affection."[30] On 23 April, the eve of his

---

party a graduate was expected to throw in his own institution. Such entertainment was expected to be lavish, and Copernicus' purse was not always well lined. For Beeckman's life and works, see Klaas van Berkel, *Isaac Beeckman (1588–1637) en de Mechanisering van het Wereldbeeld* (Amsterdam: Rodopi, 1983).

[28] Adrien Baillet, *Vie de Monsieur Des-Cartes*, A.T., X, p. 50.

[29] *Ibid., Journal*, p. 52.

[30] *Ibid.*, letter of Descartes to Beeckman, 24 January 1619, pp. 151, 153.

departure from Breda, Descartes proclaimed that Beeckman was "the instigator and first author of my research." Waxing dithyrambic, he even added: "You stirred a lazy man, made him recall the knowledge he had just lost, and set him on a better pursuit than the ones to which he had strayed. Should anything worthy of praise come from my work, you will have the right to claim it wholly as your own."[31]

Finding Longitude

But Descartes was not a man to whom trust came easy, and there is an early incident that reveals his reluctance to be perfectly candid even with his best friends. In April 1619, it occurred to him that there might be an easy way of determining longitude at sea. Although it had long been known how to determine the latitude of a ship by observing the elevation of a star or of the sun at noon, the determination of longitude was still an unresolved problem in the seventeenth century. It greatly exercised Descartes' contemporary, Galileo, who for several years sought to use the eclipses of the four satellites of Jupiter that he had discovered as indicators of the longitude at which they were observed, since their eclipses would not occur at the same time as they would at the place, say Florence, where the official tables were made. This method rested not only on the possibility of judging when an eclipse occurred (this is where Galileo's telescope added precision), but on excellent tables and on the availability of clocks that would keep accurate time on board a frail craft tossed by the waves.[32]

Descartes thought of using the moon. He did not have lunar eclipses in mind, but the fact that the moon rises later every day by about 50 minutes, or, in astronomical language, that it retreats in its monthly course through approximately 360° ÷ 30, or 12° per day. This means that the position of the moon with reference to the fixed stars changes appreciably in a couple of hours, even as judged by very simple instruments. Thus the moon can be used as a clock that registers short intervals of time. Once we have discovered how to map out the moon's relation to the apparent rotation of the fixed stars, the motion of the moon may be used to compare local time with time at a standard observatory. For instance, we can measure the distance of the moon from a given fixed star, compute their conjunction, and compare it with the time of conjunction at a given place. This is the method that occurred to Descartes who consigned it in veiled language in his notebook. Here is this specimen of juvenile encoding:

> If leaving Bucolia, we wish to head straight for Chemnis or any other port of Egypt, we must note carefully, before leaving, how far Pythius and

---

[31] *Ibid.*, letter of Descartes to Beeckman, 23 April 1619, pp. 162–163.

[32] See Stillman Drake, *Galileo at Work.* (Chicago: Chicago University Press, 1978), pp. 257–261, 386–387.

Pythias are apart at the entrance of the Nile. We shall then be able, in any location, to find our road by looking at Pythias and the servants of Psyche that accompany it.[33]

Leibniz, who copied this text, deciphered it as follows: "*Bucolia*, starting point; *Egypt*, globe of the earth; *entrance of the Nile*, starting point; *Pythius* and *Pythia*, Sun and Moon; *the servants of Psyche*, the fixed stars."[34]

Instead of conveying his idea to his friend Beeckman, Descartes merely informed him that he had struck upon a way of determining longitude at sea, but that it seemed so obvious that he would be surprised if it had not been discovered already.[35] Would Beeckman let him know what solutions had been offered to this problem? Beeckman's reply is lost, but it is clear from Descartes' acknowledgment of 23 April that Beeckman had thought of the same method long before. Indeed, five years earlier, Beeckman had consigned the idea to his *Journal* fully aware that the success of the method depended for its accuracy on the newly invented telescope.[36]

A Mathematical Teaser

The first passage in Beeckman's *Diary* that refers to Descartes begins,

> Yesterday, which was November 10th, the Frenchmen from Poitou tried to prove in Breda that *there is really no angle* with the following argument:
> An angle is formed by the intersection of two lines in one point, for instance *ab* and *cb* in point *b* [see figure 1]. Now if you make angle *abc* by drawing line *de*, you will have divided point *b* in two parts in such a way that one half is added to *ab* and the other to *bc*. But this goes against the definition of a point, which has no parts.[37]

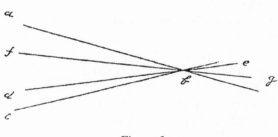

Figure 1

Hence, Descartes seems to have concluded, you cannot really divide an angle, indeed, you cannot even have an angle!

There is just a chance that this problem is the one that appeared on the poster that brought Descartes and Beeckman together. It is the kind of bizarre question that someone would cook up for a contest, and Descartes' solution is equally fanciful. Beeckman's reply was that Descartes had assumed that a point

---

[33] *Cogitationes Privatae*, A.T., X, p. 227.

[34] *Ibid.*, pp. 227–228, note *d*.

[35] *Ibid.*, letter of Descartes to Beeckman, 26 March 1619, pp. 159–160.

[36] Isaac Beeckman, *Journal*, entry made in 1614, quoted *ibid.*, p. 163, note *c*.

[37] *Ibid.*, Isaac Beeckman, *Journal*, p. 46.

has size, when it only has position. The lines *fg* and *de* divide the angle *abc*, but they do not decrease the length of lines *ab* and *cb*; they merely separate them from one another.[38]

The importance of this problem does not lie in its intrinsic merit, but in the fact that it provided Descartes with the opportunity of discussing mathematics, and soon a host of other topics, with a lively and sympathetic young scholar. Among these topics, figure prominently the acceleration of falling bodies, the pressure exerted by water, mean proportions, the nature of consonance, and the hidden powers of nature. I shall examine each in turn, beginning with the first two in the next chapter.

---

[38] *Ibid.*, p. 47.

Chapter Two

The Early Physics

The Problem of Falling Bodies

Shortly after meeting Descartes, Beeckman asked him a question about falling bodies. Descartes' solution was misunderstood by Beeckman, but in such a way that he found the right answer to the problem he had posed! This comedy of errors can be followed by combining the information available from three different sources: (a) the interpretation that Beeckman gave of Descartes' reply in his *Journal,* (b) the memorandum Descartes wrote for Beeckman, and (c) Descartes' own working notes published under the title *Cogitationes Privatae.*

Let us begin by considering the question that Beeckman actually posed.

Assuming that motion is conserved and that the space above the earth is a vacuum, Beeckman asked, "How far will a stone fall in one hour if we know how far it falls in two?[1] The question is straightforward but strikes the modern reader as quaint. The converse question, "How far will a stone fall in *two* hours if we know how far it falls in *one* hour?," seems much more natural to us.

The awkwardness we find in Beeckman's formulation and our desire to turn the question round are really the outcome of our elementary education

---

[1] Isaac Beeckman, *Journal,* A.T., X, p. 60. Beeckman's question and his interpretation of Descartes' answer are brilliantly analyzed in Alexandre Koyré, *Galilean Studies,* John Mepham, trans. (Atlantic Highlands, NJ: Humanities Press, 1978), pp. 79–94.

in classical mechanics. We no longer feel that we have to be informed about the final destination of a moving body to determine its velocity. But the natural imagination, untutored in Newtonian physics, does not view motion in this way. The ancients, and Aristotle in particular, considered motion as a *process* from an initial to a terminal point, and Beeckman still approached the problem of freely falling bodies within this traditional framework. He visualized a stone falling from the top to the bottom of a tower and supposed that the distance traversed and the time elapsed would provide the measured quantities from which the position of the stone at an earlier time could be determined.

An analogous difficulty can be seen in the way Beeckman describes his further assumption that the stone is being attracted by the earth, a postulate that was by no means generally accepted in his day.

> In the first moment, it covers as much distance as it can under the pull of the earth. In the second, it perseveres in this motion while a new motion is added by the pull such that it traverses twice the distance in this second moment. In the third moment, *the double distance perseveres (duplex spacium perseverat)* to which is added a third pull of the earth so that, in one moment, three times the first distance is traversed.[2]

The clumsiness of the underlined expression, "the double distance perseveres," could easily be eliminated if it were made to read "double the velocity is conserved," assuming that *spacium* is a *lapsus calami* for *motus*, as Jacques Sirven does in his analysis of this passage.[3] What is conserved is the speed, of course, but Beeckman did not distinguish between the qualitative notion of greater or lesser motion and the more precise, quantitative concept of velocity. There is no slip of the pen here—Beeckman "pictures" the stone's progress, and what "perseveres" for him is the ability to cover twice the distance in a given time.

We must also bear in mind that we are dealing with an idealized situation and that dropping bodies from towers (leaning or otherwise) was not common practice in the seventeenth century. What we have is a thought-experiment, and neither Beeckman nor Descartes carried out experiments to verify their theoretical results. It was Galileo who had the original idea of repeatedly rolling balls down inclined planes and teasing the correct law of free fall ($s = 1/2 \ at^2$) from the results.

Beeckman's Interpretation

Descartes rose to the challenge and provided Beeckman with a short reply that Beeckman subsequently bound with his *Journal*. But before examining the actual wording of Descartes' memorandum, let us look at the way Beeck-

---

[2] *Ibid.*, p. 58.

[3] J. Sirven, *Les années d'apprentissage de Descartes*, p. 74, note 4.

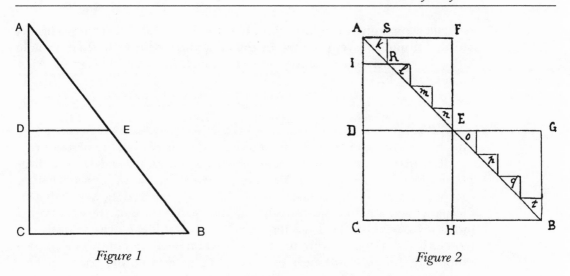

Figure 1   Figure 2

man understood Descartes' answer. Using our modern idiom, we can say that Beeckman assumed that Descartes plotted the increase of time along the vertical axis AC and the increase in speed along the horizontal axis CB (see Figure 1). This would have enabled Descartes to express the distance traversed in one hour to the distance traversed in two hours as the area of triangle ADE is to the area of triangle ABC. This is in agreement with the law of free fall as we know it since Galileo.

In the language of his day, however, here is how Beeckman summarized what he thought Descartes intended to say.[4] Let AC stand for two hours and AD (= 1/2 AC) for one hour. Assume that the distance covered in one hour is represented by the area ADEF and the distance covered in two by the area ACBGEF (see Figure 2), where we note that ACBGEF = ACB + 2 AFE (since AFE = EGB). If we divide the two hours into eight smaller intervals of time, the space traversed will be represented by smaller areas, starting with AIRS. The parts of these areas that project above the diagonal AB (the small triangles k, l, m, n, o, p, q, t) can be made as small as we please until, if the intervals are small enough, they become negligible quantities. At the limit, the area left above line AB vanishes, and all we have to consider is the area under this line, which is to say that the ratio of the space traversed in one hour to the space traversed in two hours becomes from:

$$\frac{ADE + (h + l + m + n)}{ACB + (h + l + m + n + o + p + q + t)}$$

simply,

$$\frac{ADE}{ACB.}$$

4 Isaac Beeckman, *Journal*, A.T., X, pp. 58–61.

Beeckman gives an illustration. If a stone falls 1,000 feet in two hours, and that distance is represented by the area of triangle ACB, then triangle ADE will represent the distance covered in one hour. Taking AC = 100, AD = 50, and DE = 10, we have:

$$\frac{ADE}{ACB} = \frac{1/2\,AD \times DE}{1/2\,AC \times CB} = \frac{50 \times 10}{100 \times 20} = \frac{1}{4}$$

namely, only one-fourth of the total distanced is covered in the first hour.

The proof rests on evanescent spatial quantities, ultimately on indivisible points of space, and Beeckman was uncomfortable with an analysis at variance with his atomic conception of matter. He realized, however, that an alternative explanation was possible: if the spatial minima were extended and not indivisible, the resulting progression would be arithmetical, not geometrical. But if such were the case, he would need, not only one, but two temporally different instances of free fall to determine the basic smallest spatial minimum. "This is what I had assumed," he writes, "but since the hypothesis of an indivisible point seems to enjoy more favor, I shall not say more."[5] Nonetheless, Beeckman goes on to say more and to explain how his own hypothesis would account for the ratio 1:4 that he had arrived at from his reading of Descartes' memorandum.

Assuming the simplest arithmetical progression with a common difference is one, Beeckman compares the sum of the first half of a series of numbers to the whole series. For instance, taking the first two natural numbers of the series, he obtains:

$$\frac{1}{1+2} = \frac{1}{3}\;;$$

taking the first eight:

$$\frac{1+2+3+4}{1+2+3+4+5+6+7+8} = \frac{10}{36.}$$

With sixteen numbers the ratio becomes 36:136. In other words, as the numbers in the series increase, the ratio gets closer and closer to 1:4 until it is practically indistinguishable from that ratio. Now this is what happens in the case of falling bodies, argues Beeckman, because the time intervals during which the pull of the earth is exerted are both very small in size and very large in number.

Beeckman anticipated the interpretation that Giovanni Battista Baliani and Honoré Fabri were to offer of Galileo's law of falling bodies more than 20 years later. Without denying Galileo's experimental results, Baliani and Fabri contended that a deeper analysis revealed that behind Galileo's odd-number rule there lay the simpler and correct rule of the natural numbers, 1, 2, 3, . . . for the spaces traversed in successive times. The proof runs as follows: take a distance actually traversed and divide it into ten sections

5 *Ibid.,* p. 61.

progressing in length as the natural numbers. Let the first ten sections be traversed in a given time, the next ten sections in a second equal time, and so on. The distance covered in the first time is 55, namely, the sum of the first ten spaces; the distance covered in the second time is 155, the sum of the eleventh to the twentieth space; and that in third, 255. But 55:155:255 are near to 1:3:5, and if we subdivide the distance traversed into 100 parts instead of 10, we get an even closer approximation, namely, 5050:15050:25050. Hence, Baliani concludes, the spaces actually passed in very small intervals of time can be as the natural numbers 1, 2, 3, although for the purpose of measurement (we might say at the macroscopic level), the distance will appear as 1, 3, 5 . . . .[6]

Descartes' Actual Words

If we now turn to Descartes' working notes, we find that the question raised by Beeckman was not quite the one Descartes thought he was being asked. As we know from Beeckman's diary, the question was, "How far will a stone fall in one hour if we know how far it falls in two?" Here is how the question sounded to Descartes:

> A few days ago I happened to meet a very clever man, who asked me the following question: "A stone," he said, "falls from A to B in one hour [see Figure 3]. It is attracted by the earth by the same constant force and loses none of the speed impressed upon it in the preceding attraction. What moves in a void, always moves," he stated. The question is, "In how much time will it cover that distance?"[7]

Descartes had no doubt that he had found the solution.

> I solved the question. In the right-angle isosceles triangle, the space ABC represents the motion; the inequality of space from point A to base BC represents the inequality of the motion. Hence AD is traversed in the time represented by ADE, and DB in the time represented by DEBC. Note that less space represents slower motion. AED is one third of DEBC. Therefore the stone traverses AD three times more slowly than it does DB.[8]

Descartes obviously believed that the last line provided the answer to Beeckman's question. But Beeckman had asked how *far* after half the *time*, not how *fast* during the first half of the total distance. In other words, Beeckman wanted to know the distance traversed after one hour, not the speed half-way down. This is why, when Descartes handed him not his

---

[6] See Stillman Drake, "Free Fall from Albert of Saxony to Honoré Fabri," *Stud. Hist. Phil. Science*, 8 (1975), pp. 347–366; "Impetus Theory Reappraised," *Journal of the History of Ideas*, XXXVI (1974), pp. 27–46.

[7] *Cogitationes Privatae*, A.T., X, p. 219.

[8] *Ibid.*, p. 219.

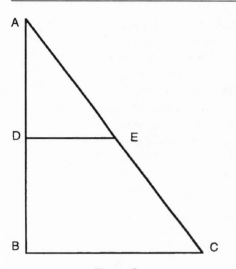

Figure 3

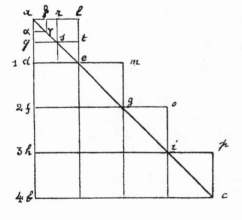

Figure 4

working notes but a memorandum, he read it with distance in mind. This memorandum was accompanied by a figure (Figure 4) and was given the following title by Beeckman, "By how much does the motion of a stone that falls towards the earth in a void increase in each moment? Descartes' Account." It began:

In the question proposed, a new force by which a heavy body falls downwards is imagined to be added at each moment. I say that this force increases as the lines *de, fg, hi,* or any other of the infinite number of transversal lines that can be imagined between them.[9]

It is tempting to summarize Descartes' approach by saying that he plotted the distance on the vertical axis and the speed on the horizontal axis. The first part of the statement (with distance represented by the vertical line *ab*) would be correct, but we cannot simply write speed for Descartes' *vis*, which is properly force. Since Newton, we know that force is proportional to acceleration, not speed, and we are familiar with the law in the form, $F = ma$. But Descartes had not travelled that far. He asserted that the hypothetical force pulling the body remained constant, but he interpreted the increase of velocity as an increment of *internal force*. In his working notes, he stated explicitly that speed is *impressed*. "*Celeritas*" (speed) and "*vis*" (force) could be equated for Descartes because he had not clearly grasped the consequences of Beeckman's principle of the conservation of motion. He still understood speed in the light of the medieval impetus theory as a force that enters into a body to give it the power to move faster. The horizontal lines *de, fg, hi, bc* may therefore be said to represent the increment of speed for Descartes, but it is a speed endowed with an intrinsic dynamic quality that has departed from the textbooks of modern physics. What the earth exerts is a force (*vis*), and the result in the body that is attracted is also a force (*vis*) that manifests itself as greater activity, enhanced power, and, empirically, heightened speed.

[9] *Ibid., Physico-Mathematica,* p. 75.

With this in mind, we can understand Descartes' argument. Let the first "minimum or point of motion" caused by the first pull of the earth be represented by the square *adel*, the second by double that amount, namely *dfgm*, the third by *fhio*, and so on. This graphic representation yields a triangle *abc* with protruding triangles *ale*, *emg*, *goi*, and *ipc*. These triangles result from the fact that the minima or points of motion were assumed to be extended, when they should have been considered as "indivisible and without parts." Better and better approximations are obtained by dividing *ad* in half (with *agsr* as the resulting first minimum of motion), then again in half (with *aαγβ* as the minimum), and so on until the parts protruding above the line are evanescent. Hence, only the area inside the triangle *abc* need be considered, and Descartes concluded that the motion of a body half-way down (from *a* to *f*) stands to its entire motion (from *a* to *b*) as the area of triangle *afg* to the area of triangle *abc*, which represent the accumulated "forces" manifesting themselves as speed. Since (by simple Euclidean geometry) the area *fbcg* is three times the area *afg*, *fb* will be traversed three times as fast.

Rightly Wrong

The reader may wish, at this point, to know how this derivation tallies with the correct law of free fall that was published for the first time by Galileo several years later and that is familiar in the form, $s = 1/2 \ at^2$. If x is the distance through which a body falls in time, t_1, on Descartes' analysis, the time, t_2, required for a body to fall through a distance of $2x$ is $4/3 \ t_1$, whereas for Galileo, this time is equal to $\sqrt{2} \ t_1$. An example will make this clear. If a body falls through 16 feet in one second, how long will it take to cover twice that distance or 32 feet? Galileo's answer is 1.4142 minute, Descartes' 1.3333 minute. Hence, bodies would fall faster on Descartes' hypothesis! But the discrepancy is only of the order of 6 percent, and it would have been difficult to discriminate between the two theories on experimental grounds. In any event, Descartes made no experiments, and he approached Beeckman's question as a purely theoretical exercise.

Beeckman read Descartes' reply to his question as though the vertical lines *ab* (the y-axis) represented time. Since the horizontal lines express the variation in speed, the correct law follows because the area $(1/2 \ vt)$ now stands for the distance traversed. For four successive intervals of time, the distances traversed increase as the areas *ade*, *dfge*, *fhig*, and *hbci*, namely as 1:3:5:7, the odd-number rule that is an equivalent formulation of the law that states that the distance covered is proportional to t^2.

For the modern reader, Beeckman's wrong (hence correct!) interpretation of Descartes is the more striking, since Descartes' assumption that the increase in speed is proportional to the square of the distance traversed makes it impossible to derive the times-squared law. The difference is clear when we tabulate the values of the parameters used by the two friends:

Beeckman		Descartes	
t	s	s	v
1	1	1	1
2	4(1+3)	2	4(1+3)
3	9(1+3+5)	3	9(1+3+5)
4	16(1+3+5+7)	4	16(1+3+5+7)

For Beeckman, s is proportional to t^2, whereas for Descartes v would appear to be proportional to s^2. If the first relation is correct, however, v is proportional to $\sqrt{s}$ not s^2! But the incompatibility of these two propositions: (1) the distance is proportional to the square of the time, and (2) the speed is proportional to the square of the distance was not obvious to anyone at the beginning of the seventeenth century. In his *Discourses on Two New Sciences* published in 1638, Galileo ruefully remarked that he had once believed that the times-squared law could be derived from the assumption that speed in fall increases as the distance from rest.[10]

Uncertain Inertia

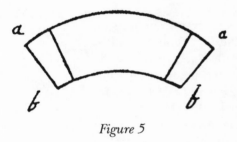

Figure 5

What hindered Descartes from applying Beeckman's fruitful insight that the motion caused by the force of attraction endures? Beeckman, as we have seen, had explicitly based his question on the principle that "what is once in motion will always continue to move in a void." This was an important step in the right direction that eventually led to Newton's First Law of Motion, which states that a body in motion will continue to move in a straight line unless some force is applied to it. But Beeckman did not realize that the motion that is conserved is necessarily rectilinear. For him, it could just as well have been circular.

The fact that a stone shot from a sling flies off in a straight line upon being released is explained by Beeckman with the aid of Figure 5 where a stone ab is twirled at the end of an extended arm rotating at right angle to the line of the shoulders. Beeckman argued that since aa, the uppermost part of the stone, revolves faster than bb (which is closer to the hand), then when aa leaves the hand, it will drag bb forward and thereby destroy the circular motion.[11] But all that this shows, according to Beeckman, is that circular motion is *difficult* to conserve. It does not prove that it is not natural. Indeed, he claims that a globe suspended from the ceiling by a string and revolving in

---

[10] Galileo Galilei, *Discourses on Two New Sciences, Opere*, vol. VIII, p. 203.

[11] *Cogitationes Privatae*, A.T., X, p. 224.

a circle would continue to move in a circle if the string were cut. In his *Journal*, Beeckman gives a fuller account of this thought-experiment and claims that the globe would be seen to move in a circle were it to fall on the unruffled surface of water in a bucket.[12]

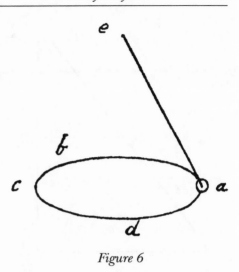

Figure 6

The physics of the situation completely escaped Beeckman. Whether it be along a vertical or a horizontal axis, circular motion is such that the greater the distance from the center of revolution, the greater the circumference, and hence the greater the speed. Whether the motive force is imparted from the center of the revolving circle (the shoulder of the rotating arm) or from a point above it, the parts of the projectile that are furthest from the center will describe a trajectory of greater radius than the parts closest to the center. The spuriousness of Beeckman's suggestion becomes apparent when we consider his own figure (Figure 6), which can easily be turned sideways to represent, no longer a sphere hanging from a ceiling, but a sling *abcd* rotated by an extended arm *ea*, a situation that is identical with the one described in Figure five.

We have no difficulty in detecting the fallacy because we know that circular motion is not inertial. A body moving in a circle requires a force emanating from the center to continue to veer it away from the straight line it would follow were no force to act upon it. With that knowledge in mind, we cannot be hoodwinked into a quest for a proof of the alleged inertial nature of circular motion. In other words, the conceptual scheme that is part and parcel of our Newtonian physics immediately flashes a red light at the suggestion that circular motion is conserved in the same way as rectilinear motion. But for the seventeenth century, the bias operated the other way round. From the Greeks onwards, the circular motion of the heavens was the prototype of perpetual motion, approximated, but never perfectly realized on earth, by such motions as that of hard balls rolling on smooth surfaces or perfect spheres rotating on frictionless axles.

According to Aristotle, the natural and eternal motion of the heavenly bodies is circular, whereas the natural and ephemeral motion of terrestrial bodies is either upwards, as with fire, or downwards, as with earth. Since Beeckman no longer believed in the theory of natural places, he did not automatically dismiss the possibility that rectilinear motion might also be preserved, but what dominated his thought was the conviction that the revolutions of the heavenly bodies were eternal.[13]

---

[12] *Ibid.*, Isaac Beeckman, *Journal*, pp. 224–225, note *b*.

[13] Beeckman was not the only one to consider the explanation of heavenly motion as the goal

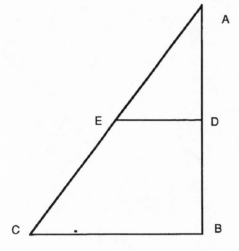

Figure 7

Inertial rectilinear motion was, in any case, mere speculation about bodies falling in a non-existent void. Beeckman knew that bodies falling in water or air reached a limiting velocity after which they continued at uniform speed. He even tried to compute when this would occur.[14]

If the area, DBCE (see Figure 7), that represents the space traversed by a falling body, is of such a size that an equivalent volume of air weighs as much as the body, then the body will cease to accelerate. Beeckman is thinking of motion through a fluid, such as water, and of the fact that the downward motion of a body ceases when the mass of an identical volume of water weights as much as the body itself. The analogy is clumsy because a body falling through air does not cease to move but merely to accelerate, but it is interesting inasmuch as we witness the ease with which Beeckman slides from a representation of *distance*, by means of extended area or *space*, to a representation of *mass*, by means of the same *space*. *Distance*, visualized as area, is conceived as surface with depth (i.e., as volume) and is assumed to have mass or weight!

Back to Descartes

At the end of the memorandum he gave Beeckman, Descartes goes on to raise the question "in a different and more difficult way," thereby indicating that it is really a matter for mathematical rather than physical investigation.[15] Assume, he says, the conservation of motion acquired in free fall, and add the further assumption that God creates a new attractive force at each moment. If a body begins to fall from point *a* at nine o'clock when God creates the first attractive force, and reaches point *b* at ten o'clock, how long did it take to cover half the distance?

Descartes' hypothesis of a force constantly increasing would give rise to a series of motions or spaces that would increase as 1, 3, 6, 10, 15, 21 . . . , a series that is known as the Pythagorean "triangular" numbers.

---

of his physics. The following entry from his *Journal*, written eleven years later, shows how happy he was to learn from a friend that Paolo Sarpi agreed with his principle, "*what is once set in motion will always move unless some impediment occurs*," and that he used it to "prove the eternity of the motion of the heavens that God originated" (*ibid.*, p. 348). The entry is dated 11 October 1629.

[14] *Ibid.*, pp. 221–222, note *c.*

[15] *Ibid.*, *Physico-Mathematica*, pp. 77–78.

Time (in seconds)	Attractive Force	Conserved Units of Motion in prior time	Sum
1	1	1	1
2	1+1=2	1	1
3	(1+1+1)=3	3	6
4	(1+1+1)+1=4	6	10
5	(1+1+1+1+)+1=5	10	15
6	(1+1+1+1+1)+1=6	15	21

The pattern of increase is as ever larger Pythagorean triangles. At the limit, when the "moments" become "instants," the motion can be represented by a triangular pyramid whose triangular horizontal sections stand for the successively larger instantaneous *minima motus*. Descartes compares the volumes of the upper and lower halves of the pyramid, which are as 1/8 and 7/8 of the total volume respectively, and assumes that they provide the ratio of the times of fall, such that the distance *ag* is traversed in 7/8th of an hour, and the remaining *gb* in 1/8th of an hour (see Figure 8).[16]

An interesting note found among Descartes' working papers, and almost certainly contemporary with his memorandum, reveals that he was still willing to entertain the notion that bodies are naturally light or naturally heavy, and that a heavier body falls faster than a light one. It is in this traditional context that he mentions, as a problem to be treated mathematically, the determination of the speed of a falling torch.[17] The rate of fall is influenced by the decrease in the torch's weight, not only because part of the material is being consumed, but more importantly because fire (which has the essential property of lightness) reduces the weight of the body in which it is found. Hence a brightly burning torch will not fall as fast as one that is smoking or, better still, fully extinguished!

Descartes was soon to rid himself of any vestige of the Aristotelian theory of natural places, but it took him longer to escape the thraldom of the impetus theory.

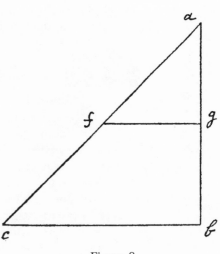

Figure 8

---

[16] *Ibid.*, p. 78, lines 9–10. The numerical values given should be inverted. The time through *ag* (the first half of the distance) cannot be smaller than the time the body falls through *gb* (the second half of the distance). Hence we read *ag* = 7/8 of an hour and *gb* = 1/8 of an hour, the converse of what is printed.

[17] *Ibid.*, *Cogitationes Privatae*, p. 221.

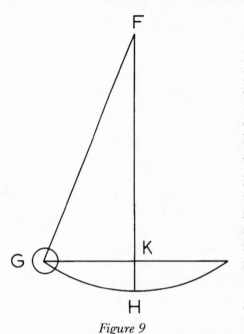

Figure 9

The Question Revisited

Descartes does not seem to have returned to the problem of falling bodies until 1629, when Mersenne wrote to enquire whether he could determine the length of a pendulum whose period was equal to half the period of a pendulum of known length. Descartes' reply clearly establishes that he stuck by his erroneous rule of 1618:

I once made the following computation: if for a string that is one foot long the bob takes one moment to go from G to H; when the string is 2 feet, it will take 4/3 of a moment; when it is 4 feet, 16/9 of a moment; when 8 feet, 64/27; when 16 feet, 256/81, which is not much more than 3 moments, and so on for the others.[18]

Descartes not only retained his earlier law of free fall; he was also confused about its application to the pendulum. He measured the fall of the bob along the length of arc GH (see Figure 9), and it was only after receiving a request for clarification from Mersenne that he corrected himself, without explicitly acknowledging his former mistake, and asserted that the distance of fall is not the arc GH but the height KH.[19]

As the following passage shows, Descartes was still operating within the medieval impetus theory:

First of all, I suppose that the motion that is once impressed on a body remains perpetually in it unless it is removed by some other cause, that is to say [here the text changes from French to Latin], that what once begins to move in a vacuum will always move at the same speed. Suppose therefore that a body located at A is impelled by its gravity *(a sua gravitate)* towards C [see Figure 10]. I say that if it were to lose its gravity at the moment it began moving, it would nonetheless continue to fall until it reached C, but it would not move faster from B to C than from A to B. But this is not the case since it has gravity which presses it downwards and at each moment adds new forces to descend. So the body covers space BC faster than AB because it retains all the impetus with which it moved through AB while constantly acquiring new impetus because of the gravity that urges it on at each successive moment.[20]

---

[18] Letter of Descartes to Mersenne, 8 October 1629, A.T., I, pp. 27–28. The lettering has been changed.

[19] *Ibid.*, letter of Descartes to Mersenne, 13 November 1629, p. 73.

[20] *Ibid.*, pp. 71–72. It is revealing that Descartes, who had begun his sentence in French, suddenly switches to Latin, the language in which the impetus theory was usually discussed. Latin provided, as it were, a groove along which thought about motion rolled only too smoothly.

Descartes is no longer relying on Beeckman's notion of attraction caused by an outside force. Gravity (namely, weight) is an intrinsic property that gives falling bodies a new impetus downwards at each instant. Acceleration is caused by these "*impeti*" and is measured by their addition. The principle of conservation of motion is affirmed, but what is conserved are the "*impeti*" or impressed forces. Descartes' diagram illustrates how the velocity increases. The first vertical line "represents the force of the speed impressed in the first moment, the second line the force impressed in the second moment, the third in the third, and so on." The triangle ACD thus represents the increase of speed from A to C, while the smaller triangle ABE stands for the increase during the first half of the fall, and the trapezoid BCDE for the increase during the second half. Since the trapezoid is three times as large as the triangle,

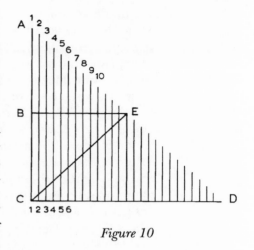

Figure 10

> it follows that the weight will traverse BC three times as fast as AB: i.e., if it falls from A to B in three moments, it will fall from B to C in one moment, namely it will cover in four moments twice the distance it covered in three moments.[21]

This, again, is not the times-squared law. According to Descartes, the distance traversed in 4 moments is double the distance traversed in 3 moments. For instance, if the latter is 9 units, the former will be 18. But, according to the times-squared rule, the distance varies as 3^2 to 4^2, namely as 9 to 16, not as 9 to 18.

We shall see in Chapter XII how Descartes subsequently dealt with the problem of freely falling bodies, but let us now return to Breda and the year 1618 when he also wrestled with the problem of weight in the context of hydrostatics. This provided him with the topic of his second memorandum.

The Memorandum on the Hydrostatic Paradox

Between 23 November and 26 December 1618, Descartes dashed off a short treatise on hydrostatics after a lively conversation with Beeckman in which he felt that he had been singularly obtuse. Descartes was later to recommend leisurely meditation, and to Princess Elizabeth he conveyed the impression that he spent most of his time observing the flight of birds and admiring wild flowers. Yet he wrote a closely reasoned essay on hydrostatics in less than a day. Why? Because his pride was wounded, and he was anxious lest his friend

[21] *Ibid.*, p. 73.

should detect the flaw in his reasoning before he had time to retract it. "I wrote this," he admitted to Beeckman, "not only because I wanted to leave you a memento of myself but because I was grieved and angered at my failure to explain—indeed to grasp—such an easy thing at the time."[22] Ten years later, we find him writing long letters to Mersenne well into the night on occasions when his vanity was at stake.

We know from Descartes' notebook, the *Cogitationes Privatae*, that the question he debated with Beeckman stemmed from Beeckman's reading of Simon Stevin, who was one of the first to realize that the pressure exerted by a fluid does not depend on the area at the bottom of the container but only on the height of the liquid.[23] This is what came to be known as the hydrostatic paradox, and the problem was to explain its cause. One of the difficulties was the lack of a clear concept of pressure, which was generally referred to as a form of "weighing." At the beginning of his essay, Descartes attempts to clarify the issue by distinguishing between the "weighing" of water on the bottom of a container, and the "weight" of water that is determined by scales.

Although water "weighing" on the bottom of a vase is not in motion, were the bottom to be removed, it would immediately begin to fall. In this sense, the pressure of the water could be considered a kind of virtual motion. This tenuous analogy suggested to Descartes that pressure might be explained in terms of virtual motion, as was often done with weights in equilibrium at the ends of the arms of a lever or a steelyard. The governing principle in the case of the lever is the equality of the product mv (mass × speed) at one end with the same product at the other. Since the speeds that are being considered are virtual velocities, the *moment* or torque of the lever (ms, namely, the product of the mass by the distance from the point of application) easily transforms itself into the *momentum* (mv) of the moving body.

A possibility of serious ambiguity is built into this model, and Descartes slips into it unawares. Since both ends of the lever move in identical times without acceleration, it is immaterial whether one uses the virtual velocities of the two weights or their virtual displacements. But velocities must be in the same proportion as their virtual displacements, and *the equivalence can hold only for the lever and analogous instances* in which a mechanical connection ensures that each body moves for the same time, and in which the motion is virtual, not accelerated. The case of free fall does not fulfill these conditions of equilibrium on a lever because the times involved are not identical and because two separate, accelerated motions take place. If there is an equality of the product of weight x distance (ms), we shall have an equality not of momentum (mv) but of kinetic energies ($1/2\ mv^2$).

---

[22] *Physico-Mathematica*, A.T., X, p. 74. The memorandum on the hydrostatic paradox is found on pp. 67–74. For his remarks to Elizabeth, see his letters of 28 June 1643 and May or June 1645 (A.T., III, p. 692, and IV, p. 220).

[23] *Cogitationes Privatae*, A.T., X, p. 228.

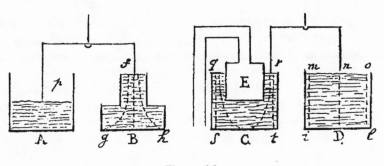

Figure 11

Bearing in mind that Descartes is relying on the model of static equilibrium of weights at the ends of a lever, we can understand why he defines "weighing" (*gravitare*) as: "The force which produces motion in the first instant, not the force which pushes it down throughout the entire motion and which can be very different." He is even more explicit in his notebook where we find: "weighing (*gravitatio*) is not taken from motion but from the inclination to descend in the last instant before motion, where there is no rate of speed."[24] Weighing is therefore virtual motion, nascent speed and, as such, prior to the actual realization of motion. It depends on the quantity of matter, but also on the initial speed that is imagined to obtain at the very outset of motion. "For instance," says Descartes, "if an atom of water were to fall twice as fast as two other atoms, it would 'weigh' as much as these two together."[25]

It is against this background that Descartes now proceeds to explain the hydrostatic paradox with the aid of a diagram (Figure 11).

Four containers A, B, C, and D have the same height, the same width at the base, and weigh the same when empty. Container B is filled to the brim with water, and the same amount is then poured into A. It follows that they have the same weight and are in equilibrium when suspended from an equal-arm balance. Vases C and D are filled to capacity.

Descartes wants to show that the same pressure is exerted on the bottom of containers B and D. His argument is worth considering, since it will reappear in a slightly modified form in his *Optics* written some 20 years later. Out of an infinite number of possible points at the bottom of the two containers, Descartes considers points *g*, *B*, *h* in B and *i*, *D*, *l* in D and argues that they are subjected "to the same force because they are pressed down by lines of water that are imagined of the same length and extend from the top to the bottom of the vase."

The immediate objection, if we glance at the diagram, is that lines *fg* and *fh* are longer than *fB* or *nD*. But Descartes is at pains to deny the literal-

[24] *Ibid.*, *Physico-Mathematica*, p. 68; *ibid.*, *Cogitationes Privatae*, p. 228.

[25] *Ibid.*, *Physico-Mathematica*, p. 68.

ness of his graphic representation: "Line *fg*," he writes, "should not be reckoned longer than *fB* or any other line."[26] Nonetheless, the clumsiness of the diagram reveals the limitation of Descartes' approach. He could not make the lines continuous without obscuring the fact that only the vertical component is relevant. The lines of pressure in container D are the same as in container B, but Descartes is faced with the problem of making this intelligible in a situation where the area at the top of container B is only roughly one-third of the area at the bottom.

Syllogistic Comfort

Descartes cast his argument in what he took to be the rigorous form of a syllogism:

> What has to be demonstrated is that point *f* alone presses the three points *g*, *B*, *h* with the same force as the three distinct points *m*, *n*, *o* press upon *i*, *D*, *l*. This is achieved by the following syllogism.
> [Major]. Heavy bodies press with the same force upon all surrounding bodies whose place they could occupy with equal ease if these bodies were expelled.
> [Minor]. Only point *f*, if it could expel the three points *g*, *B*, *h* would occupy their lower place with the same ease as the three points *m*, *n*, *o* would occupy the lower position of the three points *i*, *D*, *l* if they were to expel them.
> [Conclusion]. Therefore, point *f* alone presses upon the three points *g*, *B*, *h* with a force equal to the one with which the three discrete points *m*, *n*, *o* press the three points *i*, *D*, *l*.[27]

It is clear that Descartes knows from the outset that the pressure at the bottom of vases B and D must be the same, and that he is merely trying to construct a plausible argument out of his knowledge of statics. In a move that was to become a trade-mark of Cartesianism, he describes the major premise of his syllogism as "so clear and obvious that it can be taken as a scientific principle," where the word scientific is to be understood in the sense, still current in the first half of the seventeenth century, of genuinely epistemic, i.e., grounding true statements as opposed to merely probable assertions.

No such clarity or obviousness can be claimed for the minor premise. Nevertheless, Descartes offered a proof that he found so satisfactory that he was to use it again in his mature discussion of the transmission of light. Imagine, says Descartes, that points *g*, *B*, *h* in vase B, and points *i*, *D*, *l* in vase D are thrust open at the same moment by the weight of the water above them. When this occurs, the rate of flow in vase B can only be equal to the one in vase D if point *f* moves downward three times as fast as points *m*, *n*, *o*.

---

[26] *Ibid.*, p. 70.
[27] *Ibid.*

The reason, according to Descartes, is that the water at points *m, n, o* only has to occupy the space left vacant by the water expelled from *i, D, l,* whereas point *f* must, in the same time, fill the points *g, B, h*!

Whatever the possible merits of this bold hypothesis, it runs counter to a serious objection that Descartes recognized. Drops of water of the same size and weight fall at the same speed. How can the water at point *f* "tend to move" three times as fast as points *m, n, o?* This difficulty had initially prompted Descartes to speculate, in his conversations with Beeckman, that the water on the surface at *f* was attracted by the water lower down. In the memorandum, this idea is now condemned as "absurd, utterly wrong, and blurted out without thinking."[28] Descartes does not explain his change of heart beyond saying that we are dealing with pressure not attraction. It is easy to see, however, why the hypothesis of attraction was inadequate: the pull exerted on *f* would be the same as on points *m, n, o,* not three times greater!

Having abandoned attraction, Descartes meets the initial objection by stressing the difference between "tendency to motion" and "motion itself," or (if we allow ourselves a paraphrase) between "virtual" and "actual" velocity. A consideration of the rate of speed is only relevant *to actual motion,* says Descartes, since bodies that tend downwards have *a propensity* to reach their destination "not at this or that speed but as fast as possible." Since the water at *f* has three points through which it can flow (*g, B, h*), while the water at *m, n, o,* has only one (*i, D, l,* respectively), it follows that *f* has "a triple tendency."[29]

That Descartes sensed that there was something farfetched in his explanation seems likely. We find him emphatically denying that lines *fg, fB,* and *mi* are the actual paths of descent in the same sentence in which he claims that he traced them to make his demonstration easier! His lame excuse is that his assumptions "could only be explained in a complete treatise."[30] This reference to a larger system, already mentioned at the beginning of the memorandum, will become a frequent ploy in Descartes' writings. Repeatedly he will promise a full account of what lies behind his treatment of individual cases, but we shall have to wait for the publication of the *Principles of Philosophy* in 1644 for this promise to be fulfilled. Descartes seemed to have believed, from this early period onwards, that because a specific problem could be solved (or appeared to be solved), the general principle that rendered the solution possible lay at hand. For Descartes Lady Luck was not only fortunate but wise.

Unable to offer a convincing vindication of his own position, Descartes did the next best thing, and proceeded to attack what he took to be the consequence of a rejection of his account. If the water at point *f* did not have a triple tendency to fall downwards, then the pressure (what Descartes calls

28 *Ibid.,* p. 71.

29 *Ibid.,* p. 72.

30 *Ibid.*

gravitare or weighing) at the bottom of vase B would be less than the pressure at the bottom of vase D!

We can see what has happened. Descartes knows, and rightly so, that the pressure does not depend on the amount but on the height of the water. The explanation eludes him because of the inadequacy of the principle of the lever that he assumes to explain pressure, but this does not deter him from claiming that a rejection of his theory would automatically entail a denial of the observed facts about pressure at the bottom of containers.

Descartes experiences a further difficulty in explaining why vases C and D are in equilibrium at the ends of a balance, since there is less water in C than in D. The correct interpretation is that body E is maintained in the water with a force that is equivalent to the weight of a volume of water equal to the volume of the submerged part of E. Descartes does not see this because he is pursuing an explanation in terms of virtual velocities. Since the pressure is the same at the bottom of vases C and D, the water at point g tends towards points s and C, and the water at r tends towards C and t. By analogy with the reasoning he had offered for vase B, Descartes concludes that the water at g and r has a virtual velocity of 1½ compared to a virtual velocity of 1 at m, n, and o.

The inadequacy of Descartes' explanation becomes glaring when he compares the total weight of vases B and C. On the one hand, the pressure at the bottom may be the same, but the weights are clearly different since vase B contains less water than vase C. On the other hand, if Descartes is to reason as he did when comparing vases C and D, he would have to say that the virtual velocity at f in vase B is to the virtual velocity at g or r as 3 is to 1½, and, hence, that the vase should be in equilibrium when placed at the ends of an equal-armed balance. This had troubled Descartes when he had discussed the problem with Beeckman, but in the intervening two days he had found an explanation "that is so clear," he wrote, "that I blush when I recall that it did not occur to me a couple of days ago."[31] Vase C clearly weighs more than vase B.

One of the houses rented by Descartes in the vicinity of Utrecht.

[31] *Ibid.*, p. 74.

Whether the pressure at the bottom is identical or not is irrelevant because the pressure that is exerted on the bottom of a container is purely internal. As such, it does not contribute to the downward motion of the body. The situation, says Descartes, is analogous to pushing on the inside wall of a cabin on a ship. Push as you may, you will never move the ship by exerting pressure on its walls!

The memorandum on hydrostatics has attracted less attention than the one on free fall, and it is tempting to say that Descartes' clarifications are mere manipulations. The lines of pressure that he drew were arbitrary, and he was himself eager to deny that they should be taken literally. But what is important is the crucial distinction between actual motion and tendency to motion that will reappear in his mature works. As we shall see in the *Optics*, Descartes will claim that the instantaneous propagation of light becomes intelligible if it is understood in terms of tendency or inclination to motion.

Chapter Three

The Mathematical Breakthrough

W E HAVE SEEN that a fanciful mathematical problem was the fortuitous occasion of the meeting of Descartes and Beeckman in Breda in November 1618. We know from Beeckman's *Journal* that the new friends continued to discuss mathematics, and that he was asked by Descartes how to find a square equal to the square root of another square (e.g., $x^2 = y$, where y = side of known square and x = side of unknown square). The problem is simple, but Beeckman made heavy water of it.[1] In turn, he posed Descartes the much more arduous task of determining whether the shape assumed by a chain suspended from two nails at the same horizontal height is a conical section. This is the famous problem of the "chaînette," which was to exercise mathematicians throughout the seventeenth century. Descartes jotted the question down in his notebook, with the laconic but revealing comment, "I cannot discuss this at leisure now."[2]

What Descartes did discuss was something more important and of far greater consequence: his discovery of a method of generating mean proportionals by means of a new kind of compass. Beeckman's *Journal* is silent on this development, and it is likely that he was not in a position to offer

---

[1] *Journal de Beeckman*, A.T., X, pp. 54–56. Readers who prefer to postpone a detailed study of Descarte's mathematical procedure can turn to pages 66–67 where the main points are summarized.

[2] *Ibid., Cogitationes Privatae*, p. 223.

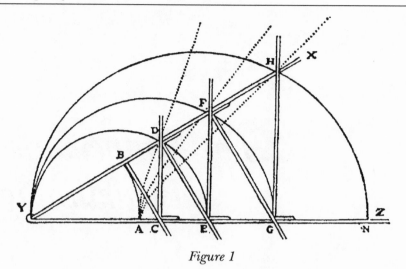

Figure 1

much beyond praise and encouragement. But, at this stage in Descartes' career, this is what he needed most!

We cannot reconstruct the genesis of Descartes' ideas to our complete satisfaction, but his notebook, the *Cogitationes Privatae*, contains several descriptions and diagrams of a compass used to produce a series of mean proportionals. I shall first describe the final version as it appeared some 20 years later in the *Geometry* and then examine its sources.[3]

The Compass

The compass XYZ (see Figure 1) encloses a series of L-shaped rulers or squares of which BC, DE, and FG are set at right angles to XY, while CD, EF, and GH are at right angles to YZ. BC is fixed to XY at B, but the rest of the rulers can slide along the base of the inner side of the branch on which they rest. As the compass is opened, BC pushes CD along YZ, and CD in turn pushes DE along YX, and so on. If pens are placed at B, D, F, and H, the motion of the compass generates a series of curves of increasing complexity starting with a circle, which is traced by B around center Y. In the *Geometry*, Descartes is mainly interested in the compass as an instrument for generating these curves, which he then proceeds to define algebraically and classify according to the degree of complexity of their algebraic equations.

By contrast, the notes of 1619 show no interest in this use of the *proportional compass*, as I shall refer to it from now on. He mentions the curves but does not attempt to describe them algebraically. What struck and interested Descartes was the fact that he had invented a machine to produce mean proportionals. This becomes obvious as soon as we note that triangles CBY, DYC, EYD, FYE, GYF, and HYG are similar and right-angled for all

[3] *Geometry*, A.T., VI, pp. 391–392 and 443–444.

openings of the compass. Hence we have the following series of continued geometrical proportions:

$$\frac{YB}{YC} = \frac{YC}{YD} = \frac{YD}{YE} = \frac{YE}{YF} = \frac{YF}{YG} = \frac{YG}{YH}$$

The discovery was momentous because mathematicians had been looking since antiquity for an easy way of producing two mean proportionals, and here was an instrument that generated not two but a whole series simply by being opened!

The Ancient Quest for Mean Proportionals

The problem of mean proportionals stemmed, according to tradition, from the dilemma that the inhabitants of the island of Delos faced when the oracle commanded them to double an altar if they wanted to be rid of the plague. Since the altar was cubical, this meant finding a cube twice the size of the original one, or "duplicating the cube," the name under which it became famous along with two other problems, the squaring of the circle (i.e., finding a square with the same area as a given circle) and the trisection of the angle. All these questions were to interest Descartes, especially the first and the last.

Hippocrates of Chios, who was active at the beginning of the fourth century B.C., is credited with the discovery that the solution lay in finding two mean proportionals between the length of the original cube and twice that length.

Let a = side of original cube, a^3 = original cube, $2a^3$ = size of unknown cube, x = first mean proportional, y = second mean proportional. Then:

$$\frac{a}{x} = \frac{x}{y} = \frac{y}{2a} ,$$

by compounding ratios, we have

$$\frac{a^3}{x^3} = \frac{a}{x} \times \frac{x}{y} \times \frac{y}{2a} ,$$

$$\frac{a^3}{x^3} = \frac{a}{2a} ,$$

$$x^3 = 2a^3$$

Needless to say, this merely shows that if we know the two mean proportionals between a and $2a$, we can duplicate the cube. It does not tell us what these values are. Hence the quest for a method of determining these two mean proportionals, and the various solutions that were proposed in antiquity. Two of the most famous were devised by Menaechmus. Given their relevance to the development of Descartes' ideas, we shall examine them later in this chapter.

Contemporary Approaches

The problem was still topical in Descartes' own day and several authors were on the hunt for simpler and more practical solutions, usually with very limited results. In 1619 alone, two works that purported to introduce notable improvements were published. The first appeared in Germany where the mathematician Molther summarized past attempts and loudly proclaimed the superiority of his own. In France, even politicians thought of lending a hand. Paul Yvon, the mayor of La Rochelle, published (in Latin and in French) a work in which he claimed to have found how to square the circle and duplicate the cube.[4]

Descartes could have known about the solutions proposed by the Ancients from more authoritative, if less colourful, sources, such as Christoph Clavius' *Geometria Practica*, where the known methods were summarized, or Commandino's edition of Pappus' *Mathematical Collections*, where they are given at the beginning of the book.[5] Descartes later studied these opening pages with care, as we shall see further on, but in the winter of 1618–1619, he was not directly concerned with the specific problem of the duplication of the cube, which he does not even mention. I believe that the actual source of Descartes' inspiration can be found in a very different kind of work.

We know that Descartes spent much of his time at the end of 1618 discussing musicology with Beeckman and that he wrote for his friend a substantial monograph, the *Compendium Musicae*, for which he later displayed considerable pride of authorship, and which we shall examine in the next chapter. A prominent question that was debated among the two friends was musical consonance and, more specifically, how to divide a string in equal half-tones. It would be surprising if Descartes had not looked for a solution among contemporary or fashionable musicologists of which there were several. In the *Compendium of Music*, however, we find only one name, that of Gioseffo Zarlino. Now Zarlino considers how to divide equal tones in music when discussing mean proportionals!

Since the octave is characterized by the ratio 1:2 and consists of twelve semitones, each separate interval can be found by taking eleven mean

---

[4] Molther, *Problema Deliacum de Cubi Duplicatione nunc tandem post infinitos praestantissimorum mathematicorum conatus expedite et geometrice solutum* (Frankfurt, 1619); Paul Yvon, *Circulum quadrandi et cubarum duplicandi modus versus a nemine hactenus mortalium cognitus* (La Rochelle, 1619), and in French, *Quadrature du cercle ensemble le double du cube* (La Rochelle, 1619). Mersenne gives a brief survey of attempts at solving the problem in his *Vérité des Sciences* (Paris, 1625). Facsimile (Stuttgart-Bad Cannstadt: Frommann Verlag, 1969), pp. 859–861.

[5] Christopher Clavius, *Geometria Practica* (Rome, 1604), pp. 297–304; *Pappi Alexandrini Mathematicae Collectiones*, Federico Commandino, ed. (Pesaro, 1588), pp. 1–7. The first and second books having been lost, the work opens with the third book.

proportionals between 1 and 2 or between 1 and 1/2. The first step is to find two mean proportionals between a string and its half. Zarlino knew that this could not be done by ruler and compass alone, but he showed how it could be achieved with an instrument invented by Eratosthenes in the third century B.C. and known as the *mesolabium*, the very word that Descartes used for his own instrument.[6]

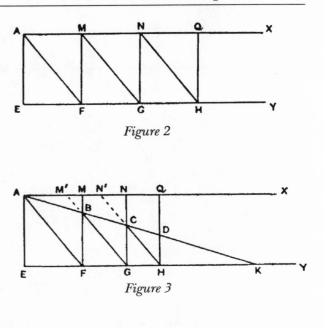

Figure 2

Figure 3

Eratosthenes' mesolabe consists of three rectangles or three right-angled triangles placed between parallel rulers that form a frame and are fitted with groves so arranged that the rectangles can slide over one another. Zarlino uses rectangles, but the proof he gives rests on the triangles that are formed by drawing the diagonals of the rectangles. For illustrative purposes, I shall also use triangles.[7]

Let the given lines between which the two mean proportionals are sought be *a* and *b*.

Arrange the instrument so that the parallel rulers AX, EY are at a distance AE = *a* from one another. In the initial position shown in Figure 2, the three triangles AMF, MNG, and NQH are side by side. In Figure 3, DH = *b* is marked off on QH. Triangle MNG is made to slide behind triangle AMF, and triangle NQH behind MNG so that NQH takes up position N'QH and MNG position M'NG. Draw a line through D intersecting MF at B, NG at C, and EY at K.

BF and CG will be the two required mean proportionals between AE (= *a*) and DH (= *b*).

[6] *Cogitationes Privatae*, A.T., X, pp. 238–239. The mesolabe is described in Zarlino's two main works, the *Istituzioni Harmoniche* (Venice, 1558, 2nd ed. 1562, 3rd ed. 1573), where the relevant passage appears on pp. 113–114, and the *Dimostrazioni Harmoniche* (Venice, 1571), pp. 163–168. Descartes was almost certainly acquainted with Zarlino's works, since he writes in his *Compendium Musicae*: "Zarlino enumerates at length all the kinds of these cadences. He also has general tables where he explains what consonances can follow a given consonance in a song. He gives reasons for all of these but many, according to me, can be deduced more plausibly from our premises" (A.T., X, pp. 133–134). There is an interesting note left by a friend of Descartes, Frans van Schooten the Elder (1581/82–1645), which reads: "Testimony of Descartes . . . Zarlino and Salinas, both Italians, wrote music free from the faults of the ancients, one in Italian, the other in Latin" (*ibid.*, p. 638).

[7] See Thomas Heath, *A History of Greek Mathematics*, 2 vols. (Oxford: Clarendon, 1921), vol. I, pp. 258–259.

Proof: Since triangle AEK, BFK, and CGK are similar, and

$$\frac{EK}{KF} = \frac{AK}{KB} = \frac{FK}{KG} \; ,$$

and

$$\frac{EK}{KF} = \frac{AE}{BF} \; , \text{ while } \frac{FK}{KG} = \frac{BF}{CG} \; ;$$

therefore,

$$\frac{AE}{BF} = \frac{BF}{CG} \; .$$

Similarly,

$$\frac{BF}{CG} = \frac{CG}{DH} \; ,$$

so that AE, BF, CG, DH are in continued proportions, and BF, CG are the required mean proportionals. Q.E.D.

Eratosthenes' mesolabe is by no means Descartes' proportional compass, but it may well have been the spark that fired his imagination and led to his remarkable discovery.

Trisecting the Angle

Having found, in principle, how to duplicate the cube, Descartes proceeded to solve yet another famous problem, the trisection of an angle.

Between 20 and 26 March 1619, Descartes had an outburst of mathematical creativity in which he saw how his proportional compass could be modified to trisect an angle. On 26 March, he apprised Beeckman by letter of his discovery but provided no explanation or diagram. The instrument, however, is described in his notebook, the *Cogitationes Privatae*.

Like the first compass to generate mean proportionals, this new instrument is remarkable for its simplicity. Four rulers, AB, AC, AD, and AE all pivot at A (see Figure 4). Points F, I, K, and L are equidistant from A (i.e., AF = AI = AK = AL), and rods FG,

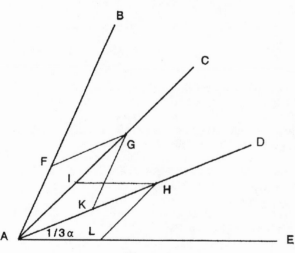

Figure 4

GK, IH, and LH, which are all equal
to AF, pivot around points F, I, K, and
L, and are so arranged that G can
slide along ruler AC, and H along
ruler AD.[8]

If a given angle α has to be trisected, the compass is opened until
angle BAE = α. Since triangles AFG,
AKG, AIH, and ALH are always equal,
it follows that their corresponding
angles FAC, GAD, and DAE are always
equal regardless of the size of angle
BAE. Hence, we only have to apply
the compass to a given angle to trisect
it.

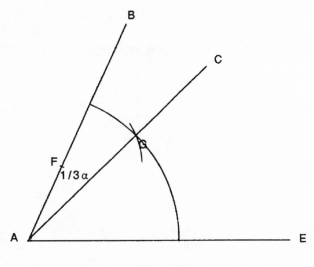

Figure 5

We can also, as Descartes adds,
trace the curve made by the point G
as the compass is opened until AE
and AB coincide with the sides of the given angle α (see Figure 5).[9] Then, if
we trace a circle of radius FG around F, the intersection of this circle and the
curve will locate the point G through which line AC is drawn, dividing the
angle in a ratio of 2:1, and hence making angle FAC = 1/3 of angle BAE.
Descartes immediately saw that the addition of one or more rulers would
allow for the mechanical division of an angle into four or more parts. He had
not only trisected the angle; he had found a way of dividing an angle into as
many equal parts as might be desired!

It is interesting to note that the power and generality of the compass
are intuited in the instrument itself. It is not derived from a mathematical
insight into a class of problems.[10]

---

[8] *Cogitationes Privatae*, A.T., X, p. 240.

[9] *Ibid.*, p. 241.

[10] In John Aubrey's *Brief Lives*, we find an anecdote about Descartes that Aubrey claimed to
have from Alexander Cowper, a portrait painter who had met Descartes in Stockholm. "He
was so eminently learned that all learned men made visits to him, and many of them would
desire him to show them ... his instruments (in those dayes mathematicall learning lay
much in the knowledge of instruments, and, as Sir H[enry] S[avile] sayd, in doeing of
tricks), he would drawe out a little drawer under his table, and show them a paire of
Compasses with one of the legges broken: and then, for his ruler, he used a sheet of paper
folded double. *"Brief Lives" Chiefly of Contemporaries, Set Down by John Aubrey, between the years
1669 and 1696*, Andrew Clark, ed., 2 vols. (Oxford: Clarendon, 1898), vol. I, p. 222. Whether
apocryphal or not, this story highlights the importance that the seventeenth century
attached to articulated instruments and the fact that seeing (or imagining) a curve being
traced out before one's own eyes carried with it the feeling that the nature of the curve was
being understood.

Solving Cubic Equations

Mechanical manipulation may have been the source of Descartes' brilliant discovery of the proportional compass and the compass to trisect angles, but he soon realized their wider implications. Immediately after mentioning to Beeckman that he could trisect the angle, he added that he had found how to solve the following three kinds of cubic equations:

$$x^3 = \pm\ ax \pm b \tag{1}$$

$$x^3 = \pm\ ax^2 \pm b \tag{2}$$

$$x^3 = \pm\ ax^2 \pm bx \pm c \tag{3}$$

Mathematicians in the seventeenth century excluded the cases where no *positive* root was obtained, i.e., cases:

$$x^3 = -\ ax - b \tag{4}$$

$$x^3 = -\ ax^2 - b \tag{5}$$

$$x^3 = -\ ax^2 - bx - c \tag{6}$$

This meant that of the sixteen possible equations for (1), (2), and (3), only thirteen remained for consideration. "I have not studied them all yet," Descartes wrote to his friend, "but I believe it will be easy to extend to other cases what I have found to hold for some." As we have already seen, by finding a method of generating two continuous mean proportionals, Descartes had provided a solution for duplicating the cube, in other words, for solving a cubic equation. When he pondered this, it flashed upon him that the solution of equations consisted in discovering proportional magnitudes and that this was just what his instrument could do. The proportional compass seemed to unlock the door to a "*completely new science . . .* to solve generally *all* questions in any genus of quantity."[11]

Descartes was buoyed by great hopes, but in his initial enthusiasm he slipped unawares into a wrong application of his compass. Since the errors of great men are always instructive, I shall examine one case where he uses the compass to solve the cubic equation, $x^3 = 7x + 14$, which is an instance of type (1), namely, $x^3 = \pm\ ax \pm b$.

First, Descartes simplifies the equation by dividing it throughout by 7, thereby obtaining:

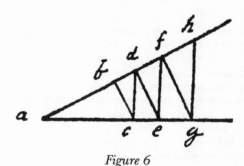

Figure 6

$$\tfrac{1}{7}\,x^3 = x + 2.$$

[11] Letter to Isaac Beeckman, 26 March 1619, A.T., X. pp. 156–157, emphasis added.

He then proceeds to solve the equation $x^3 = x + 2$, erroneously assuming that all that has to be done when the value of x^3 is found is to multiply it by 7!

Let $ab = 1$, $ac = \text{x}$. Then, since

$$\frac{ab}{ac} = \frac{ac}{ad} = \frac{ad}{ae} = \frac{ae}{af} = \frac{af}{ag} = \frac{ag}{ah} ,$$

we have,

$$\frac{1}{x} = \frac{x}{x^2} = \frac{x^2}{x^3} = \frac{x^3}{x^4} = \frac{x^4}{x^5} = \frac{x^5}{x^6} ,$$

but,

$$ce = ae - ac = x^3 - x,$$

hence,

$$x^3 = x + ce.$$

If we make $ce = 2$ by opening or closing the compass *hag*, then $x^3 = (ac)^3$ (since we let $ac = x$), and the value of ac can be read directly off the compass (see Figure 6).[12]

It would seem therefore that Descartes realized that the equation $x^3 = x + 2$ could be solved on his compass, and that he took this equation as a paradigm for the general demonstration of equations of the form $x^3 = ax + b$. Since $x^3 = 7 \, x + 14$ could be reduced to $1/7 x^3 = x + 2$, he rushed headlong, dismissed the coefficient of x^3, and assumed that it could be reinstated by a simple multiplication after solving the equation $x^3 = x + 2$. There are two other instances in the *Cogitationes Privatae* where he makes the same mistake in his haste to show his new insight at work.[13]

Descartes also failed to notice that his compass was of no help for equations in which a negative term appears on the right side. If we look at Figure 6, we see that x^3 is constructed from $ac + ce$, and that ac and ce must be positive values.

These failings should not blind us to the magnitude of Descartes' discovery of a practical method of solving cubic equations. His instruments, when correctly applied, traced out the curves that embodied the simple geometrical ratios that the equations contained. In this way, cubic equations were translated into concrete spatial relationships, and the door was opened for the geometrization of algebra.

[12] *Ibid.*, *Cogitationes Privatae*, pp. 234–235.

[13] *Ibid.*, pp. 236–237.

A Completely New Science

A grand design was beginning to mature in Descartes' mind, and he clearly saw it as an alternative to the scheme of representatives of the Hermetic-Cabalist tradition, such as Raymond Lull. Having indicated what he hoped to achieve in his treatment of cubic equations, he proceeded to disclose his "incredibly ambitious" program to his friend:

> And, to tell you frankly what I have in mind, I do not wish to propound an *Ars Brevis* like Lull, but *a completely new science*, to solve generally all questions that can be put forward in any genus of quantity, continuous as well as discrete. But each according to its nature. For, as in arithmetic, some questions can be solved by rational numbers, some only by surds, whereas others can be imagined but not solved, so I hope to demonstrate that, in continuous quantity, some problems can be solved with straight or circular lines, while others can only be solved with curved lines that arise from one single motion and can be traced by the new compasses that I consider no less certain and geometrical than the ordinary ones with which circles are drawn. Finally, other problems can only be solved by curved lines generated by different motions that are not subordinated to each other and that are certainly only imaginary: such a curve is the well-known quadratrix. I do not think that anything can be imagined that cannot be solved at least by these lines, but I hope to demonstrate which questions can be solved and in what way, *so that scarcely anything will remain to be discovered in geometry*. The work required is virtually infinite and cannot be done by one person alone. It is *an incredibly ambitious task*, but with the light that I have seen shining through the gloom and confusion of this science, I believe that the darkness, however dense, can be dispelled.[14]

I have quoted this manifesto at length because it remained at the forefront of Descartes' concerns and reappeared as the famous programmatic pronouncement at the beginning of Book II of the *Geometry*. Note that Descartes does not propose, as has often been assumed, to "algebrize" geometry, but rather to solve problems on the analogy with the procedure used in arithmetic. At this state in his development, what is uppermost in his mind is not the analogy between geometry and algebra, but the analogy between geometry ("continuous quantity") and arithmetic ("discrete quantity"). Descartes explicitly draws a comparison between three kinds of arithmetical questions that he characterizes as: (a) soluble by rational numbers, (b) soluble by surds, and (c) imaginable but insoluble, and three kinds of geometrical problems: (a) soluble by straight lines and circles, (b) soluble by curved lines arising from one continuous motion, and (c) soluble only by curved lines arising from two or more unsubordinated motions. In both instances, Descartes appears to consider that the three kinds of problems cover all the cases that can arise in arithmetic or algebra. We can see why this

---

[14] *Ibid.*, letter to Isaac Beeckman, 26 March 1619, pp. 156–158, emphasis added.

is the case if we briefly examine the mathematical background that Descartes takes for granted and against which his own work must be assessed.[15]

The Case for Construction

In the classical mathematical works of Euclid, Archimedes, and Apollonius that provided the conceptual framework for mathematical investigation at the beginning of the seventeenth century, there are two kinds of mathematical propositions, namely, theorems and problems. Theorems have to be proved, problems to be *constructed*, and their construction has to be shown to possess the required properties. Euclid in his *Elements* uses only construction by means of circles and straight lines, and his "ruler and compass" approach was often considered normative. Circles and straight lines may have been privileged in this way simply because they are easier to trace than other curves, such as the parabola or the hyperbola. Proclus, in his Commentary on the First Book of Euclid's *Elements*, argues that straight lines and circles are fundamental because all other curves, for instance, the spiral, are in fact a combination or mixture of straight and circular motion. Pappus, in his *Mathematical Collections*, enshrined the threefold division of geometrical problems as: (a) *plane*, if they can be constructed by straight lines and circles; (b) *solid*, if conic sections are required; and (c) *linear* (or "line-like"), if more complicated curves are necessary.

It is important to bear in mind that Descartes will always see the solution of geometrical problems primarily in terms of construction, and not, as we would assume, in terms of a satisfactory algebraic solution. Even in the *Geometry* that he published eighteen years later, he never systematically uses an equation to represent a curve. In several cases, he treats the curves without giving their equations, while in others he provides the equations almost casually during the argument. Descartes saw the equation of a curve as a tool, not as a means of definition or representation.

But I am anticipating. In the letter of 26 March 1619, which we are considering, Descartes does not mention the instrumentality of equations. His thought is dominated by the proportional compass that he has recently discovered, and which, he claims, "is no less certain and geometrical" than the ordinary compass used to draw circles. This new instrument does not have to be physically applied; it is enough to be able to visualize it and use it as a computing device. In other words, pen and paper are all that is required, since the nature of a curve is revealed in its tracing, a viewpoint echoed in such phrases of the *Geometry* as "ways of tracing and conceiving curved lines" or "to know and trace the line."[16]

The compass remained a privileged instrument of intelligibility for

---

[15] See the excellent discussion in A.G. Molland, "Shifting the Foundations: Descartes' Transformation of Ancient Geometry," in *Historia Mathematica* 3 (1976), pp. 21–49.

[16] *Geometry*, A.T., VI, p. 392, lines 15–16; p. 380, lines 11–12.

Descartes, even when he realized later on that the classification of curves was less straightforward than he had assumed. In Book II of the *Geometry*, he appeals to his famous canon of clarity and distinction to validate his process. Referring to lines AD, AF, AH traced out by the compass (see Figure 1), he writes:

> I see no reason why the description of this curve [AD] cannot be conceived as *clearly and distinctly* as that of the circle, or at least as that of conic sections; or why the second [AF], the third [AH], or any other curve cannot be as well conceived as the first.[17]

Or again, at the beginning of Book III where the compass is reintroduced as a means of finding several mean proportionals, he states:

> I do not believe that there is an easier way of finding any number of mean proportionals, nor one whose demonstration is clearer *(plus évidente)* than the one which employs the curves described by the instrument XYZ.[18]

If we turn to the second kind of geometrical problems that Descartes mentions in his letter of 26 March 1619, we find them characterized as those that can be solved "with curved lines that arise from one single motion" or, as he adds a few lines later, "with motions that are subordinated to one another." By looking at Figure 1 above, we can see that one continuous, counter-clockwise motion of ruler XY will produce a series of related motions in rulers DC, ED, FE, GF, and HG.

Independent Motions

The third class of problems consists of those that can only be solved, which is to say constructed, with the aid of two independent motions. The example that Descartes gives is the quadratrix, a curve that Pappus had described as follows: Suppose that ABCD is a square, and BED a quadrant of a circle with center A (see Figure 7). Let BC move uniformly from BC to AD, while remaining parallel to BC. In the *same time*, the radius AE revolves uniformly from AB to AD. AE and BC arrive at AD, where they coincide at the same moment. At any previous instant during the motion, the moving line and the moving radius will by their intersection determine a point, such as F or L. The locus of these points is the quadratrix.

The quadratrix is traced, therefore, by the intersection of a horizontal line moving uniformly downward, so that its motion is completed at the same time as the uniform rotation of the radius through a quadrant of the circle. But the motion, i.e., velocity, of line BC cannot be adjusted to the velocity of radius AE unless we know the ratio of the radius of the circle to one-quarter of the circumference. Since the relation of the circumference to the radius is $2\pi r$, and π cannot be expressed as a whole number or a whole fraction of a

[17] *Ibid.*, p. 392, emphasis added.
[18] *Ibid.*, pp. 442–443.

number, the exact ratio of the speed of BC or AE cannot be determined (namely, π cannot be represented in a short, precise form like a recurring decimal. All we can do is give better and better approximations, for instance, 3.1416 when 3 1/7 is too rough for our purposes).

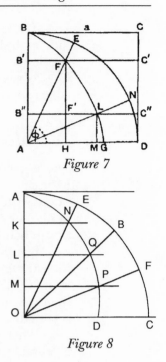

Figure 7

The subject was hotly debated in Descartes' own day, and Clavius, in his *Commentary on Euclid*, argued that the following pointwise construction was satisfactory. With an ordinary compass, bisect the arc AC into 2, 4, 8, 16, parts (see Figure 8), and with a ruler divide radius OA into the same number of parts.

Then draw radii, such as OB, OE, and OF to the points of division on arc AC, and draw the horizontals from the corresponding points K, L, M to radius OA. Their points of intersection, such as N, Q, P, are on the quadratrix. In this way points on the quadratrix, lying arbitrarily close to each other, can be geometrically constructed. If we go on bisecting angle POD, then its half toward OC, and so on, we can approximate to the position of D as nearly as we please. But this process is equivalent to approximating to π. It does not yield a more exact or precise result and would not have impressed Descartes.[19]

Figure 8

In 1619, Descartes' proportional compass was not only a means of tracing curves but a criterion of their geometrical acceptability. In 1637, in the *Geometry*, he will still object to what he considers a misleading distinction made by the "ancients" between geometrical and mechanical lines, as though the latter were defined in a different way because they can only be traced out by instruments. He points out that the ruler and compass used to trace out straight lines and circles are also instruments, and that they are not more accurate than his proportional compass. Geometrical, says Descartes, is what is "precise and exact." It follows that

> one must no more exclude the more compounded lines than the more simple, provided that one can imagine them to be described by one continuous movement or by several which follow one another, and of which the later are entirely determined by those which come before.

This statement does not differ from the one Descartes made in his letter of 26 March 1619, and it is again followed by the exclusion of the quadratrix and the spiral "because one imagines them described by two separate movements which have no ratio between them that can be measured exactly."[20] The conchoid, however, is considered geometrical. This is interesting in view of the fact that Descartes rejects the pointwise construction of the quadratrix endorsed by Clavius. We shall return to this below.

[19] Christopher Clavius, *Commentarium in Euclidis Elementa* (Rome, 1589), Appendix to Book VI, quoted in Luder Gäbe, *Descartes Selbstkritik* (Hamburg: Meiner, 1972), p. 170, n. 5.

[20] *Geometry*, A.T., VI, pp. 389–390.

The enthusiasm that Descartes experienced in 1619 was never to leave him entirely. The series of interdependent motions of his compass, all regulated and determined by the motion of the first, may well have given him "occasion to imagine that all things than can fall under human knowledge follow one another in the same way."[21]

A Note on Notation

The notation that Descartes used in 1619 is borrowed from Clavius. The basic signs are & for our =, ϑ = radical or x, and z = square or x^2. Where we would write $x^2 = ax + b$, Clavius wrote in his *Algebra*, z & ϑ + N, and Descartes in his letter of 26 March 1619, $1z$ & O ϑ + ON, where the addition of a coefficient before ϑ and N is of little value, since it stands for numbers that can vary. It is clear from this notation that Descartes was not yet acquainted with the writings of Viète and Ramus or those of their disciples. By the time he wrote the *Rules for the Direction of the Mind* around 1628, Descartes had considerably improved his notation. &, for our =, was replaced by ∞ which he retained in the *Geometry*.

What was at stake was the translation of a geometrical problem into algebraic terms in order to construct the solution. The definitive method is not arrived at before the *Geometry* where Descartes' actual practice can be summarized in terms that are familiar to any modern high school student. The known and the unknown line segments are identified by letters, with the first letters of the alphabet, a, b, c, ... , indicating the known, and the last letters, x, y, z, the unknown. The data and their relations are expressed in equations, and as many equations are to be found as there are unknowns. The unknowns are then successively eliminated until we are left with one equation involving one unknown only. The problem is then to solve this equation, find the one unknown, and from its value derive the values of the other unknowns.

This procedure was not perfectly clear to Descartes in 1619, but even if it had been, the equation would not always have been enough for his geometrical purposes. For instance, if we apply this method to the problem of finding two mean proportionals, x and y, between two given lengths, a and b, we easily arrive at the equation $x^3 = a^2b$, which can be solved algebraically to give $x = \sqrt[3]{a^2b}$. But this solution is not sufficient for a geometrical problem because it does not tell us how the length of $x = \sqrt[3]{a^2b}$ should be geometrically constructed. Descartes could only know this with the aid of his compass.

The Representation of Curves

But how did Descartes come to represent curves by equations in the first place? We do not have his account of the evolution of his ideas on this point,

---

[21] *Ibid.*, *Discourse on Method*, Second Part, A.T., VI, p. 19.

but one crucial step was surely the discovery that expressions such as "square" for x^2 or "cube" for x^3 do not necessarily represent a given shape. He tells us in his *Rules for the Direction of the Mind* that he was "deceived for a long time by these names."[22] Equally crucial was the close analogy that he saw between continuous and discrete quantity or, as we would put it, between operations on line segments and operations on numbers. In particular, by the assumption of an arbitrarily chosen unit, Descartes was able to interpret the multiplication of two straight lines as giving rise to a third straight line rather than a rectangle. This was one of the features of the "general algebra" that he was anxious to show Beeckman when they met again in the autumn of 1628. This step was of fundamental importance in making easier the representation of curves in algebraic terms.

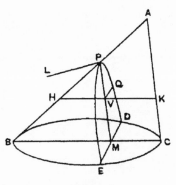

Figure 9

The ancients defined curves, and in particular conic sections, by their specific properties, but these were not couched in algebraic equations. The simplest case is the parabola. Suppose PM is a diameter with P on the parabola, and PL (called *latus rectum*) is taken such that PL : PA = $(BC)^2$: BA × AC (see Figure 9). By using similar triangles, we can show that for any ordinate QV to the diameter PM, the following relation obtains:

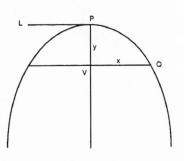

Figure 10

$$(QV)^2 = PL \times PV$$

Any curve with such a property is a parabola. If we draw the parabola in a plane, we immediately see how easy it is to read coordinate geometry back into ancient works (see Figure 10).

Let $\qquad\qquad$ PL = a (the known quantity of the *latus rectum*)

$\qquad\qquad\qquad$ PV = y

$\qquad\qquad\qquad$ QV = x.

Since $\qquad\qquad\qquad (QV)^2 = PL \times PV,$

hence $\qquad\qquad\qquad x^2 = ay,$

which is the equation of the parabola in what we now call Cartesian coordinates.

We can then find the value of x required to solve, i.e., construct the parabola, by using Descartes' compass.

Since

$$\frac{AB}{AC} = \frac{AC}{AD} \, ,$$

[22] *Rules for the Direction of the Mind*, Rule 16, A.T., X, p. 456.

if we let   AB = *a* (the *latus rectum*),

                   AC = *y*

                   AD = *x*

we have,

$$\frac{a}{y} = \frac{y}{x}$$

$$y^2 = ax.$$

Descartes' interest in mean proportionals probably led him to realize that they could be expressed as equations. Namely, if *x* and *y* are two mean proportionals between straight lines *a* and *b*, that is:

if

$$\frac{a}{x} = \frac{x}{y} = \frac{y}{b},$$

then

$$x^2 = ay; \quad y^2 = bx, \quad \text{and} \quad xy = ab.$$

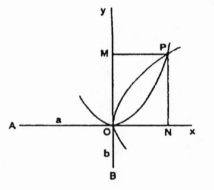

Figure 11

The modern reader, acquainted with "Cartesian coordinates," will immediately recognize the first two pairs ($x^2 = ay$ and $y^2 = bx$) as the equations of parabolas, while $xy = ab$ is the equation of a hyperbola, more specifically a rectangular hyperbola. Things were less obvious for the ancients who had a more cumbersome terminology and a less lucid frame of reference. Nonetheless, Menaechmus was able to work out two solutions to the problem of mean proportionals: the first rests on the intersection of a parabola ($x^2 = ay$) with the hyperbola ($xy = ab$), the second on the intersection of two parabolas.

The second solution, which I shall give here, could have inspired Descartes.[23]

Let the two given lines between which two mean proportionals (*y*, *x*) are to be found the AO be OB where AO > OB. Let AO = *b* and OB = *a* (see Figure 11).

[23] See Heath, *A History of Greek Mathematics*, vol. I, pp. 254–255. Descartes' interest in the problem of mean proportionals may have led him to inquire into the methods that had hitherto been proposed. Pappus does not mention the two elegant solutions by the Greek mathematicians Menaechmus but they are described by Eutocius, the Byzantine mathematician whose commentary on the first four books of Apollonius' *Conics* was published by Federico Commandino in Bologna in 1566.

Place AO perpendicular to OB. Let ON = x and OM = y.

Suppose the problem solved, and the mean proportionals to be OM and ON measured along OB and AO produced.

Complete rectangle OMPN.

Since

$$\frac{AO}{OM} = \frac{OM}{ON} = \frac{ON}{OB} \, ,$$

we have:

$$OB \times OM = (ON)^2 = (PM)^2 \text{ (or } x^2 = ay),$$

so that P lies on a parabola with O as vertex, OM as axis, and OB as *latus rectum*.

In the same way, we can show:

$$AO \times ON = (OM)^2 = (PN)^2 \text{ (or } y^2 = bx),$$

so that P lies on a parabola with O as vertex, OM as axis, and AO as *latus rectum*.

The solution, therefore, lies in constructing two parabolas with the given characteristics. The point of intersection, P, gives the solution, for we then have the value $x =$ PM and $y =$ PN for the series

$$\frac{AO}{PN} = \frac{PN}{PM} = \frac{PM}{OB}$$

A New Method

At a date that is impossible to determine with certainty, but that could be as early as 1620, Descartes made another momentous breakthrough. He realized that two mean proportionals could be found not only with his compass but with the aid of a parabola and a circle, hence with conic sections alone. He mentioned his discovery to his friends in Paris when he sojourned there in 1625–1628, but he withheld the proof. The first mention of it in print occurred ten years later in two overlapping books that Marin Mersenne published in 1636, the *Harmonicarum Instrumentorum Libri IV* in Latin and the *Harmonie Universelle* in French.

In both works the context is musical theory, and Descartes' method is said to be relevant to the division of the scale into tones and semitones. This confirms our hypothesis that he originally thought of mean proportionals in relation to musical consonance. The Latin version adds that the method will prove useful to bell-founders; the French that it will be found practical by organ-makers.

Descartes' silence about his proof, declares Mersenne, is but an instance of his excessive modesty:

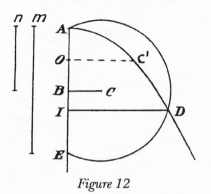

Figure 12

I want to add here a geometrical way of finding mean proportionals that depends on one parabola only. It was discovered by one of the best minds alive, a man whose modesty is so great that he does not wish to be identified.[24]

The method, as it is quoted in Latin in the *Harmonicorum Instrumentorum Libri IV*, was probably formulated by Descartes himself. It has the interest of not being as perspicuous as Descartes could easily have made it, and it reads as follows (see Figure 12):

Describe part DA of a parabola whose vertex A is removed from the focus O by one quarter of the given lines, for instance, line *m*. Take, on the axis of the parabola, BA = 1/2 *m*, and from B draw BC = 1/2 *n* at right angles to the axis. Then with C as centre draw a circle of radius CA cutting the parabola at D, and draw DI perpendicular to the axis. DI will be the greater of the mean proportionals, IA the lesser. The demonstration with many other things is awaited from the inventor.[25]

Descartes was anxious lest his Parisian acquaintances, Mersenne, Roberval, and Mydorge among others, find the procedure too simple, and he obscured the fact that *n* is the *latus rectum* by referring to AO as equal to 1/4 *m* instead of 1/2 *n*, which it is (*viz.*, 1/4 *m* = 1/2 *n*). This, however, was immediately apparent to Roberval and Mydorge, who pointed out that the construction is much easier to grasp if the *latus rectum* AB is clearly identified as *n*, and if AB is made equal to 1/2 *n* and BC equal to 1/2 *m*. For then OC' lies on the parabola. Here is Roberval's construction, which Mersenne rightly commends as "the simplest discovered thus far":[26]

Let *m*, *n* be the two given lengths between which two mean proportionals are to be found (see Figure 13).

Draw AE = *m*, and EH = *n* perpendicular to AE.

Divide AE in half at B, and erect BC = 1/2 EH perpendicular to AB.

From C as center trace a circle with radius AC, which will pass through H and E because AC = CH = CE.

[24] Marin Mersenne, *Harmonie Universelle*, 3 vols. (Paris, 1636). Facsimile (Paris: C.N.R.S., 1975), vol. III, Book VI, p. 407, quoted A.T., X, pp. 652–653.

[25] Marin Mersenne, *Harmonicorum Instrumentorum Libri IV* (Paris, 1636), liber tertius, Prop. II, pp. 146–147, quoted in Marin Mersenne, *Correspondance*, C. de Waard, A. Beaulieu, *et alii*, eds., 17 vols. (Paris: C.N.R.S., 1933–1988), vol. I, pp. 256–257.

[26] Marin Mersenne, *Harmonie Universelle*, A.T., X, p. 653. Roberval's proof follows, pp. 655–657.

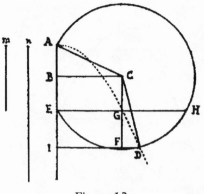

Figure 13

With AE as axis and A as vertex, draw the parabola AGD with AE as *latus rectum*, and cutting the circle at G and D.

Draw DI perpendicular to line AE prolonged.

DI and AI will be the two mean proportionals.

The proof consists in showing that

$$\frac{AE}{DI} = \frac{DI}{AI} = \frac{AI}{EH}$$

This can be done by elementary Euclidean geometry. Roberval used Proposition VII of the second book of Euclid. Mydorge used similar triangles, a method that Descartes preferred and which he later told Princess Elizabeth lay at the core of his geometrical procedure.[27]

Mean proportionals must have become topical again in Paris in 1632, since we find Mersenne forwarding to Descartes in Holland a demonstration that in all likelihood is the one by Roberval. Descartes affected to be unimpressed and reminded Mersenne that he had never found the demonstration difficult, and that Mydorge had grasped it upon seeing the construction. It would have been better, he added, to show them the method for trisecting an angle "that I gave you at the same time as the other, if my memory serves me right. It is somewhat less easy, and M. Mydorge admitted to me that he had been unable to find the proof."[28] Descartes must be refer-

---

[27] As much as possible, "when seeking the solution of a geometrical question, I make the lines that I use parallel or perpendicular, and I do not use any other theorems beyond the one that states that the sides of similar triangles are similar, and the one that says that the square on the hypotenuse is equal to the sum of the squares on the two other sides" (letter to Princess Elizabeth, November 1643, A.T., IV, p. 38).

[28] Letter of Descartes to Mersenne, June 1632, A.T., I, p. 256. In an earlier letter to Mersenne, written in October or November 1630, Descartes says that he had shown the construction to Claude Hardy and Claude Mydorge, and that Mydorge had no trouble finding the proof

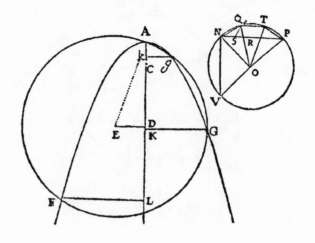

Figure 14

ring to the figure in Book III of the *Geometry* (see Figure 14) where we find a demonstration of the trisection of an angle, which is now called "*easy to see with the aid of calculation* (*ainsi qu'il est aisé a voir par le calcul*)."[29] The ease here seems largely a matter of familiarity acquired over the years!

The Universal Secret

Having discovered that two mean proportionals could be found by using a parabola and a circle, and that his method was embodied in a cubic equation, Descartes began to consider whether all cubic and quartic equations could not be solved in a similar way. The first indication of his success is found in a note that Beeckman inserted in his diary sometime after Descartes visited him in Dordrecht in October 1628. The solution is full-fledged and does not differ from the one that Descartes later gave in his *Geometry* where he shows how to reduce any third or fourth-degree equation to the forms:[30]

$$x^3 = \pm\ apx \pm a^2q$$
$$x^4 = \pm\ apx^2 \pm a^2q \pm r$$

(*ibid.*, p. 175). This demonstration was sent by Descartes to Beeckman who inserted it in his *Journal* around 1 February 1629 (Isaac Beeckman, *Journal*, C. de Waard, ed., 4 vols. (The Hague: Martinus Nijhoff, 1939–1953), vol. IV, pp. 136–138. It is also published in full in Marin Mersenne, *Correspondance*, vol. I, pp. 269–272, but with the last part omitted in A.T., X, pp. 342–344.

[29] *Geometry*, A.T., VI, p. 471.

[30] *Journal de Beeckman*, A.T., X, pp. 344–346; *Geometry*, A.T., VI, pp. 464–466.

Problems whose constructions are sought by means of these kinds of equations are termed "solid" by Descartes. They can all be solved (i.e., constructed) by means of a circle and a parabola. Descartes gives four illustrative cases for instances where a = 1.

$$x^4 = px^2 - qx + r \tag{1}$$

$$x^4 = -px^2 - qx + r \tag{2}$$

$$x^4 = px^2 - qx - r \tag{3}$$

$$x^3 = a^2q \tag{4}$$

Case (4) corresponds to Descartes' earlier problem of inserting two mean proportionals between two given lines, for if *a* and *q* are the given lines, then

$$\frac{a}{x} = \frac{x}{y} = \frac{y}{q} \, ,$$

and hence

$$x^2 = ay, \text{ and } y^2 = xq$$

so that

$$x^4 = a^2y^2 = a^2xq.$$

Therefore,

$$x^3 = a^2q.$$

I give here Descartes' demonstration of the validity of his procedure for case (1), namely, when $x^4 = px^2 - qx + r$.

Let parabola FAG be traced with axis ACDK, and let AC = 1/2 *a*, where *a* = *latus rectum* (see Figure 15).

Cut off CD = 1/2 *p* on this axis.

Draw DE = 1/2 *q* perpendicular to the axis.

On AE cut off AR = *r*, and on AE prolonged, take AS = *a*.

Describe a circle with RS as diameter.

Draw AH perpendicular to RS meeting the circle at H.

Trace a circle with centre E and radius EH.

Draw MK = ED. Join EM.

The positive root of the equation is GK, the negative FL.

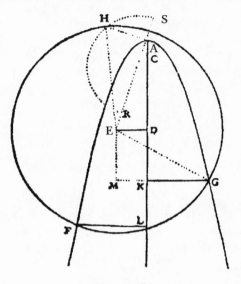

Figure 15

Proof:

Let GK = x, AK = y, and a = *latus rectum* = 1.

Since $x^2 = ay$,

therefore, $x^2 = y$. Now

DK = AK − AD

$\quad = x^2 - (AC + CD)$

$\quad = x^2 - (1/2 + 1/2\, p)$

$\quad = x^2 - 1/2\, p - 1/2.$

$(DK)^2 = (EM)^2 = x^4 - px^2 - x^2 + 1/4\, p^2 + 1/2\, p + 1/4.$

DE = KM = $1/2\, q$.

$(GM)^2 = (GK + MK)^2$

$\quad\quad = x^2 + qx + 1/2\, q^2.$

$(EG)^2 = (EM)^2 + (GM)^2$

$\quad\quad = x^4 - px^2 + qx + 1/4\, q^2 + 1/2\, p^2 + 1/2\, p + 1/4.$

$(EA)^2 = (AD)^2 + (ED)^2$

$\quad\quad = (1/2\, p + 1/2)^2 + 1/4\, q^2.$

Since $(AH)^2 = AR \times AS$ (from Euclid, Bk VI, Prop. 13),

and AR = r, AS = 1,

therefore, $(AH)^2 = r$.

Now $(EH)^2 = (EA)^2 + (AH)^2$

$$= 1/4\ q^2 + 1/2\ p^2 + 1/2\ p + 1/4 + r.$$

Equating $(EH)^2 = (EG)^2$, we obtain

$$x^4 = px^2 - qx + r.$$

When Descartes communicated his discovery to Beeckman in 1628 he was conscious of a towering achievement, and he described it in terms that leave no doubt about his feeling of having achieved a major mathematical breakthrough. He referred to it as "*the universal secret* to solve by geometrical lines all equations of the third or fourth degree."[31] After jotting down the construction that Descartes gave him, Beeckman once again recorded the importance that Descartes attached to it:

Mr. Descartes considers this invention so highly that he declares that he has never made a greater one or, for that matter, that no one has ever made one that is greater.[32]

Eight years later, in the *Geometry*, Descartes recorded his success, but in a much more subdued tone of voice:

Now when we are sure that the proposed problem is solid, whether the equation through which we seek its solution is of the fourth or only of the third degree, its roots can always be found by one of the three conic sections or even by some part of one of them, however small, using nothing but straight lines and circles. But I shall content myself with giving here a general rule for finding them all by means of a parabola, since this is, in some respects, the most simple.[33]

This is a far cry from the triumphal proclamation to Beeckman that he had discovered "the universal secret" to solve cubics and equations. The reason is that Descartes had come to see that other conic sections would do just as well, and that for certain problems they are actually simpler and more practical.

The relativization of his discovery should not make us forget the exceptional, indeed, unique, significance that Descartes originally ascribed to it. It may well have been the brilliant insight that Descartes made on the anniversary of his famous dream of 1619, and that he recorded in his *Notebook*: "11 March 1620, I have begun to understand the foundation of a marvellous invention."[34]

[31] *Journal de Beeckman*, A.T., X, p. 344.

[32] *Ibid.*, p. 346.

[33] *Geometry*, A.T., VI, p. 464.

[34] *Olympica*, A.T., X, p. 179.

The Classification of Curves

The discovery that a parabola and a circle were sufficient not only to find mean proportionals, but to solve cubics and quartics played a role in the development of Descartes' ideas on the classification of curves.[35]

In 1619, Descartes' distinction between geometrical and non-geometrical curves was not based on their equations, but on the ease with which they were "instrumentally" constructed with one continuous motion of his compass. As we have seen, Descartes maintained that the curves traced out by his compass were clearly and distinctly (*nettement et distinctement*) conceived, but it must soon have become clear to him that the equations of these curves are complex.

If we turn to the diagram of Descartes' compass (Figure 1), and let YA = YB = a, YC = x, CD = y, YD = z, we easily find the equations of the curve traced by D when the compass is being opened.

Triangles YBC and YCB are right-angled, hence similar:

Therefore,
$$\frac{YD}{YC} = \frac{YC}{YB} \text{ , namely, } \frac{z}{x} = \frac{x}{a}$$

Hence
$$z = \frac{x^2}{a}$$

But in triangle YCD:
$$(YD)^2 = (YC)^2 + (CD)^2,$$
$$z^2 = x^2 + y^2$$

Hence $z = \dfrac{x^2}{a}$), the equation of curve AD is:

$$x^4 = a^2 (x^2 + y^2)$$

Likewise, while the compass is being opened, point F traces out curve AF, and point H, curve AH. By comparing similar triangles, we find just as easily that the equation of curve AF is $x^8 = a^2 (x^2 + y^2)^3$, and of curve AH, $x^{12} = a^2 (x^2 + y^2)^5$. It is clear, however, that the simplicity of the "mechanical" construction is not mirrored in the degrees of the equation.

---

[35] See the excellent articles of H.J.M. Bos, "On the Representation of Curves in Descartes' Géométrie," *Archive for History of Exact Sciences* 24 (1981), pp. 295–338, and "Arguments on Motivation in the Rise and Decline of a Mathematical Theory; the Construction of Equation, 1637–ca. 1750," *Archive for the History of Exact Sciences* 30 (1984), pp. 331–380. See also Jules Vuillemin, *Mathématique et metaphysique chez Descartes* (Paris: P.U.F., 1960), pp. 77–98; G.-G. Granger, *Essai d'une philosophie du style* (Paris: Armand Colin, 1968), pp. 43–70; and Jean Dhombres, *Nombre, mesure et continu. Epistémologie et histoire* (Paris: Fernand Nathan, 1978), pp. 134–147.

This may not have troubled Descartes initially because he did not see an equation as a sufficient representation of a curve. In 1619, his only criterion for the acceptability of curves in geometry was that they be traceable by one continuous motion or two subordinated and regulated motions. But, as we have just seen, the curves thus produced can be algebraically very complex. Descartes addressed this problem in Book III of the *Geometry* where he stipulated that we should choose the simplest curve to "construct the problem at hand." The subsequent development reveals a certain embarrassment:

> By the simplest curves, we should understand not only those that are most easy to describe or the ones that make the construction or the demonstration of the proposed problem easier, but mainly those that are of the simplest kind that can be used to determine the quantity that is sought.[36]

Simple, then, means the lowest possible degree, and Descartes proceeds to apply this criterion to his compass as a generator of curves. On the one hand, he maintains that "there is no way of finding mean proportionals that is easier or whose demonstration is more evident." On the other hand, since mean proportionals can be found with conic sections whose equations are simpler than those of curves AD, AF, or AH, Descartes admits that "it would be a geometrical error to use them."[37] This is as clear as Descartes came to recognizing the *incompatibility* between his *instrumental* and his *algebraic* criteria for the classification of curves as geometrical. If the simplicity of the equation is to guide us in the choice of our method of solving a problem, then we might as well keep our compasses permanently shut! This is not stated by Descartes, of course, and he was not merely averting his eyes from an unpleasant conclusion. Although the properties of a curve may be expressed in its equation, Descartes did not think this was enough, as he intimates in the following passage from the *Geometry*:

> If one knows the relation of all the points of a curved line to all those of a straight line in the way that I have explained [i.e., when the equation is known], it is easy to find their relation to all other given points and lines, and hence, to find the diameters, axes, centres and other lines or points to which each curved line has some special, or more simple, relation than to others, and so to imagine various ways of describing them and choosing the easiest ones.[38]

We see from this quotation that although equations incorporate information about the properties of curves, they do not provide a *sufficient representation* of their geometrical reality. We still have to "imagine various means of describing the curve and choosing the easiest ones."

Algebraic equations will remain for Descartes primarily a tool for the construction of geometrical problems and their classification. In most cases,

[36] *Geometry*, A.T., VI, p. 443.

[37] *Ibid.*, pp. 443–444.

[38] *Ibid.*, pp. 412–413.

Descartes got through his calculation without even writing down the equation of the curve explicitly. Even the equations of the curves AD, AF, and AH traced out by his compass are not given in the *Geometry*.

If each and every point of a curve is not relatable to a rectilinear coordinate through a finite number of algebraic operations, the curve is not admissible in geometry. This much Descartes recognized, but he never took the next step of actually *defining* geometrical curves as those which admit of algebraic equations, since he was mainly concerned with the way the curves are actually traced. The next generation of mathematicians was satisfied with the equations and did not concern itself with actually performing the construction of the curves, a step that would have surprised Descartes.

The Problem of Pappus

In 1631, Descartes was asked about a celebrated problem in Pappus by the Dutch mathematician Jakob Golius. Descartes' original answer is lost, but we know from his letter of 5 April 1632 to Mersenne that he spent six weeks on it.[39] The problem is central to the *Geometry*, and Descartes claimed that its solution was one of the proofs that his method was superior to those of his rivals.[40] An examination of the problem will further enhance our understanding of Descartes' mathematics.

The problem is as follows. There are given n straight lines. From a point c, lines are drawn making given angles with the given lines. If $n = 3$, the ratio of the product of two of the lines from c to the square of the third is given. If n is even and greater than two, the ratio of the product of $n/2$ of the lines from c to the product of the other $n/2$ lines is given. If n is odd and greater than three, the ratio of the product of $(n+1)/2$ of the lines to the product of the other $(n-1)/2$ lines together with a given line is given. It is required to find the locus of c.

In Book I of the *Geometry*, Descartes carries out the solution for the case where $n = 4$, namely, where four straight lines AB, AD, EF and GH are given.[41] To apply his algebraic analysis, he takes AB (see Figure 16) as the reference line and denotes it by x; CB is the line drawn from a possible position of c falling on AB at a given angle and is denoted by y. Implicit in this

[39] Letter of Descartes to Mersenne, 5 April 1632, A.T., I, p. 244. Leibniz says that he was told by Claude Hardy in Paris (where Leibniz sojourned between 1672 and 1676) that Golius (Jakob Gool, 1596–1667) asked Descartes about Pappus' problem ("Remarques sur l'abrégé de la vie de Mons. des Cartes," in G.W. Leibniz, *Die Philosophischen Schriften*, C.J. Gerhardt, ed., 7 vols. (Berlin, 1875–1890). Reprint (Hildesheim: Olms, 1978), vol. IV, p. 136). On the problem of Pappus, see H.J.M. Bos, "On the Representation of Curves in Descartes' *Géométrie*," pp. 298–303, 332–338.

[40] Letter of Descartes to Mersenne, end of December 1637, A.T., I, p. 478.

[41] *Geometry*, A.T., VI, pp. 377–387; 396–411. Descartes quotes the problem (pp. 377–379) in Latin from the edition by Federico Commandino, *Pappi Alexandrini Mathematicae Collectiones* (Pesaro, 1588), pp. 164 verso–165 verso.

procedure is the basic strategy of analytical geometry, except that the *x*- and
y-coordinates are not at right angles.
Throughout the *Geometry*, Descartes
varies his axial system to fit the problem; nowhere do our standard Cartesian coordinates appear.

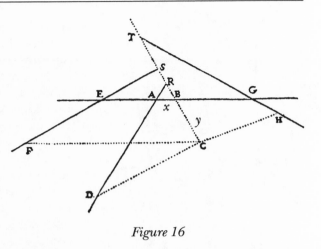

Having designated these two
lines as *x* and *y* (see Figure 16),
Descartes then shows how the lengths
of the other lines from *c* to the given
lines at the given angles can be expressed in terms of *x* and *y*. Multiply-
ing these expressions produces an
equation whose degree depends on

Figure 16

the number of lines (in the case of four lines, the equation is of the second
degree). Descartes considered this equation as representing the curve that is
the locus of *c*.[42]

But the production of the equation did not solve Pappus' problem. The
curve still had to be found, namely, constructed. Descartes' method was to
choose an arbitrary value for *y* (in our diagram the length of BC), and then
construct geometrically the corresponding value for *x*. By repeating this
process, taking other values for *y*, he found as many points as he wished on
the locus. This *pointwise construction* is not a *construction by continuous motion*.
The process only yields a *finite* number of *arbitrarily* determined points. Since
Descartes had laid down in March 1619 that continuous motion was necessary for the production of a geometrically acceptable curve, he obviously
faced a problem. This does not mean that he faced it squarely.

In the first book of the *Geometry* he deals with it by preterition. That is,
he does not say that his pointwise construction can be considered as a
construction of the locus of a curve. At the beginning of Book II, for the
cases where three or four lines are involved (as in Figure 16), Descartes
indicates how the position of vertices, axes, *latus rectum*, and *latus transversum*
could be found. In the notation with which we are familiar (*i.e.*, when the
vertex of the conic section is taken as the origin and the *x*-axis is along the
diameter), we have the formulas $y^2 = ax$ (parabola); $y^2 = ax - a/b\, x^2$ (ellipse);
and $y^2 = ax + a/b\, x^2$ (hyperbola). This provides a representation of the curve
by identifying it as a conic section (e.g., ellipse, hyperbola) and giving its
parameters. Here Descartes turned to good use his knowledge of Apollonius'
treatment of conic sections. In the higher cases, involving five lines and
more, there was no Apollonius to turn to, and he was left to his own devices.

Descartes made no attempt at a general treatment but focussed on two

---

[42] Actually two equations of the given degree are required, but Descartes recognized only one
because of inadequacies in his technique of dealing with changes of sign. See A.G. Molland,
"Shifting the Foundations: Descartes' Transformation of Ancient Geometry," p. 39.

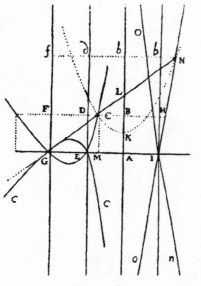

Figure 17

special cases of the five-line locus (see Figure 17). In these, four of the given lines are taken as parallel with equal intervals between them. The fifth line is perpendicular, and all the given angles are right angles. In the first case, Descartes showed that the locus was a parabola (later known as a "Cartesian parabola") that he had introduced earlier in Book II as the curve described by a combined motion of a ruler and a parabola. For the second case, which is formulated in an obscure way, he gave a property of the locus from which at best a pointwise construction can be derived. He does not say how the locus could be traced by one continuous motion but merely states: "I have not undertaken to say everything, and having explained how to find an infinity of points through which the lines pass, I believe I have said enough about the way of describing them."[43]

Pointwise Constructions

Descartes must, therefore, make room for pointwise constructions, and he attempts to do so in the next section entitled, "What curved lines, described by finding many of their points, can be accepted in geometry?"

As we have seen above, Descartes excluded pointwise constructions of the quadratrix and the Archimedean spiral. He now explains the difference between these unacceptable constructions and those he recognizes:

> It should be noted that there is a great difference between this way of finding several points in order to trace a curved line, and the one that is used for the spiral and similar curves. For in the latter, we do not find indiscriminately *(indifféremment)* all the points of the line that is sought, but only those that can be determined by a simpler process than the one required for the composition of the curve.[44]

In other words, curves such as the quadratrix could only be constructed from special points. In the case of Clavius' construction described above, these are the points that we find upon reiterated bisection. The curves that Descartes accepts as geometrical admit a pointwise construction in which every point on them can, in principle, be constructed. We can see what Descartes had in mind if we consider the conchoid, which he explicitly mentions, and whose pointwise construction struck him as being essentially different from the one for Clavius' quadratrix.[45]

[43] *Geometry*, A.T., VI, pp. 411.

[44] *Ibid.*

[45] *Ibid.*, pp. 423–424.

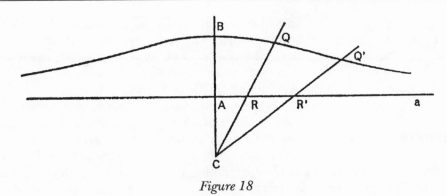

Figure 18

The fundamental property of this curve is that if any radius vector be drawn from C to the curve, as CQ, the length intercepted on the radius vector between the curve and the straight line AB is constant. (In Figure 18, this means that RQ = R'Q'.) A possible pointwise construction is the following: choose *any* point R on straight line AB, and draw CR extending beyond to Q whence RQ is the given constant. Choose "indifferently" *any* other point R' and repeat the same operation making R'Q' = RQ. This operation can, in principle, be reiterated an infinite number of times, thereby allowing to find all the points on the curve. This was enough, in Descartes' mind, to establish a correspondence between "indifferent" pointwise construction and tracing by continuous motion:

> And because this way of tracing a curved line by taking many of its points at random *(indifféremment)* is only applicable to curves that can also be described by a regular and continuous motion, we should not exclude it entirely from geometry.[46]

In the absence of proof, this is merely a bold conjecture trying to pass muster as a firm assertion.

The importance of pointwise constructions is made even clearer when Descartes proceeds to illustrate the relevance of his mathematics to optics. The *ovals* that he introduces have the property of converging light rays on a given point and are of genuine interest in physical optics, but Descartes gives no indication how they could be constructed by one "continuous and regular motion."

Here is a summary of the description of the first oval (see Figure 19).[47] Two lines intersect at any given angle at A. The ratio of AF to AG is given. On the other line cut off AR = AG. The oval is constructed as follows: take an arbitrary point K on AG. Draw a circle with center F and radius FK. Draw KL perpendicular to AR (this makes AL/AK = AF/AG because triangles ALK

---

[46] *Ibid.*, p. 412.

[47] *Ibid.*, pp. 424–425. See the lucid exposition in H.J.M. Bos, "On the Representation of Curves in Descartes' Geometrie," pp. 318–319.

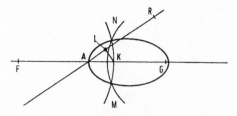

Figure 19

and ARG are similar). Draw a circle with center G and radius RL. The two points M and N of the two circles lie on the oval. By repeating the construction from other points K on AG, many points of the oval can arbitrarily be found.

Having broadened the geometrically acceptable methods of tracing a curve from the continuous and regular motion of the arms of a compass to pointwise constructions, Descartes adds, in Book II of the *Geometry*, a third way of representing curves, namely, with the aid of strings. Descartes explicitly refers to his *Optics*, where he describes the methods used by gardeners to give their flower beds the shape of an ellipse or an hyperbola.[48]

In Figure 20, the two ends of a string, BHI, are tied together and placed around stakes H and I that have been driven into the ground. The string is stretched by a tracing pin B that is moved around H and I, the string being kept taut. The result is an ellipse with foci A and B.

To make a hyperbola, the pegs are driven in at H and I (see Figure 21).[49] A ruler, AX, pivots at I; a string slightly shorter than AX is fixed at H and at point X on the ruler. The string is stretched by a tracing pin B, which is kept pressed against the ruler. When the ruler is turned around I with B kept fixed to the ruler and HB stretched, B describes an arm of a hyperbola with foci I and H.

In the *Optics*, Descartes had introduced his description of the gardener's construction of the ellipse by saying that although it was "very rough and not very accurate," nonetheless, "it rendered its nature more comprehensible than either the section of a cone or a cylinder" (i.e., the customary explanation).[50] We witness here the tension in Descartes' mind between the *greater clarity* of an instrumental tracing and the traditionally more highly regarded sectioning of the cone.

Geometrical and Non-Geometrical

When he wrote the *Optics* around 1632, Descartes did not recognize string constructions as genuinely geometrical representations of curves. By the time he wrote the *Geometry* four years later, he had come to regard some string construction as akin to constructions made with instruments like his compass. But Descartes maintained his basic objection to procedures that introduced what he took to be the essentially unknowable ratio between straight and curved lines:

---

[48] *Ibid.*, *Optics* [*La Dioptrique*], p. 166.

[49] *Ibid.*, p. 176.

[50] *Ibid.*, p. 166.

For although we cannot accept as geometrical lines that are like strings (that is, that are sometimes straight and sometimes curved) because the ratio between straight and curved lines is unknown, and, I believe, unknowable, so that we cannot conclude anything exact and certain from it. However, since in these constructions we use strings only to determine straight lines whose lengths are known exactly, there is no reason for rejecting them.[51]

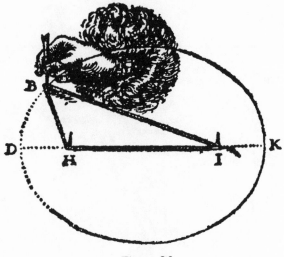

Figure 20

The absence of a strictly measurable ratio is the essential consideration for Descartes. This is why the separation between geometrical and non-geometrical curves rests ultimately on his belief that proportions between curved and straight lines cannot be found exactly. This view was deeply embedded in contemporary mathematical practice, and goes back to Aristotle under whose banner Descartes unwittingly enlisted himself.[52]

Descartes' belief that the exact mathematical relationship between straight and curved lines is, in principle, unknowable, explains why the first rectification of algebraic curves (i.e., geometrical curves for Descartes) in the late 1650s appeared so profoundly revolutionary. The frontiers of the knowable were literally pushed back![53]

What may have encouraged Descartes to give his formal blessing to the string constructions that he had used as mere illustrations in the *Optics* was the fact that they could be used in lieu of pointwise constructions to represent his ovals. He avails himself of this possibility a few pages later in the *Geometry*.[54]

Here is a summary of the string construction of the oval whose pointwise construction we have already considered (see Figure 22). FE is a ruler pivoted at F. A string is attached to E and pressed along EC, then slung over peg K and returned to C from whence it is brought to peg G and

[51] *Ibid., Geometry*, p. 412.

[52] Aristotle, *Physics*, Book VII, Chapter 4, 248[a]10–[b]12. See Thomas Heath, *Mathematics in Aristotle* (Oxford: Clarendon Press, 1949), pp. 140–142.

[53] Rectifications of algebraic curves were discovered independently by Fermat, Neil, and van Heuraet. See M.E. Baron, *The Origins of the Infinitesimal Calculus* (Oxford: Pergamon Press, 1969), pp. 223–228. Leibniz pointed out that Descartes had a tendency to take his limitations for those of mankind (G.W. Leibniz, *Die Philosophischen Schriften*, vol. IV, pp. 278, 286, 347).

[54] *Geometry*, A.T., VI, pp. 427–428.

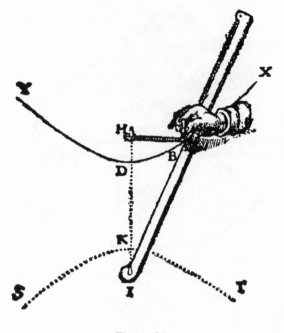

Figure 21

fastened. The string is kept taut along E–C–K–C–G, and as the ruler revolves around F, the tracing pin C draws the oval.

Conclusion

We have seen how Descartes was launched on his reform of geometry by the discovery that his compass enabled him to find mean proportionals and to trace out curves of increasing complexity.

Since the parts of Descartes' proportional compass slid along straight lines, and the top ruler when opened described a circle, it could be considered a generalization of the ruler and compass, the instruments that Euclid used in his *Elements*. The solution of a problem in geometry was generally considered to lie in its construction, and Descartes initially thought of classifying curves according to the ease with which they were traceable. This is how he came to define geometrical curves as those described by one continuous motion or series of interdependent motions, such as those of the rulers of his compass, all regulated and determined by the motion of the first.

Shortly after outlining his program to Beeckman in the Spring of 1619, Descartes began considering the possibility of finding mean proportionals through the intersection of conics, and he found that the intersection of a circle and a parabola solved all equations of the third and fourth degree. At a date that is unknown but is probably later than 1628 (since he did not mention it when he met Beeckman again in the autumn of that year), Descartes extended his research to equations of the fifth and sixth degree and succeeded in solving the conic sections, which later became known as the "Cartesian parabola." These results led Descartes to consider the degree of equation of the curve, rather than the simplicity of the process of tracing the curve with an instrument, as the criterion of simplicity of geometrical curves. But he did not give up his first criterion, and in the *Geometry* we find him appealing to both, although he recognized that the classification of problems according to their ease of constructability did not coincide with the classification of the corresponding equations as to their degree.

This is interesting in view of the fact that Descartes found himself relying even more heavily on algebra when he tackled the problem of Pappus or used pointwise constructions. Why then did he not simply define geometrical curves as those that have algebraic equations? The answer lies in his traditional conception of geometry as the *construction* of a problem, and his belief that only when the intersection of curves was traced out by one continuous motion, and thereby rendered visible to the physical eye or to the imagination, could we have a *clear* and *distinct* conception of the geometrical solution. He could not have renounced the criterion of tracing by continuous motion without leaving the

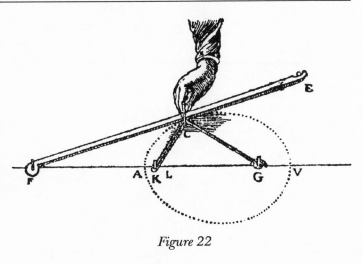

Figure 22

status of a given algebraic equation unclear. Whereas later mathematicians would consider the constructed curves merely as loci, and thus defined by an equation, Descartes always paid strict attention to the way the curve was actually traced out. Even though a considerable part of the *Geometry* is devoted to algebraic techniques (such as reduction of equations, removal of terms from an equation, change of negative roots into positive ones, etc.), Descartes never *defined* as geometrical those curves that admit of algebraic equations.

Descartes was convinced that the problem of Pappus and other problems that he had solved with the aid of algebraic equations could, in principle, be solved by continuous motion. This is why he consistently excluded the possibility of considering as geometrical pointwise or string constructions that lacked "precision" because of the incommensurability of straight and curved lines. Descartes was the victim of overconfidence in the first case, and of pessimism in the second. If he asserted too much when he claimed that his pointwise construction was susceptible of a construction by continuous motion, he underestimated the human mind when he described the rectification of curves as impossible.

These weaknesses should not blind us to the magnitude of Descartes' achievement. Of the three famous problems of antiquity, the duplication of the cube, the trisection of an angle, and the squaring of a circle, he solved the first two with methods of the highest ingenuity, characterized by ease of application for anyone able to open and close a compass. He simplified algebraic notation and set geometry on a new course by his discovery that algebraic equations were useful not only in classifying geometrical curves, but in actually devising the simplest possible construction. He set the coordinates for which he is justly remembered, and it was his new world of relations that seventeenth-century mathematicians entered with pride.

Chapter Four

The Quest for Musical Harmony

DESCARTES HAD A MUSICAL BACKGROUND and had almost certainly studied music at the College of La Flèche, since he was able, less than six weeks after meeting Beeckman, to write the *Compendium Musicae*, a 40-page essay that he presented to his friend as a New Year's present. Music was part of a gentleman's training and had a long-recognized place in the *quadrivium* along with arithmetic, geometry, and astronomy. Two works by the Italian musicologist, Gioseffo Zarlino (1517–1590), the *Istitutioni Harmoniche* and the *Dimostrationi Harmoniche*, were extremely influential, and, as we have already noted, Descartes explicitly refers to Zarlino in his *Compendium*. This does not necessarily mean that he had actually read Zarlino's works, since he may have been recalling views aired in a course that he attended at La Flèche. He states that he has forgotten much (*"multa oblivione . . . omitto:*), and, specifically, that he cannot remember how the sharps work. The rules he had deduced, he says, "escaped his memory during his travels."[1] In other

---

[1] *Compendium Musicae*, A.T. X, pp. 140, 133. Zarlino wrote in Italian, which does not seem to have posed a problem for Descartes. Italian was spoken at the Court where Marie de Medici was Queen Regent from the death of her husband Henri IV in 1610 until the accession of her son Louis XIII in 1617. Descartes later read and commented Machiavelli's *Prince* at the request of Princess Elizabeth in 1647 (letter of Descartes to Elizabeth, September 1646, A.T., IV, p. 486). His comments are in French, and there was a French translation of Machiavelli by Guillaume Coppel (Paris, 1553), and a Latin one published in Basel in 1560 and reprinted in 1566, 1580, and 1589, but Descartes may have read the original Italian. A

words, Descartes speaks like a normal 22-year-old for whom the lectures he attended as an undergraduate seem light-years away.

The Problem of Consonance

Interest in music in the seventeenth century stemmed from a theoretical as well as a practical concern. The theoretical side was a direct consequence of Humanism and the desire to revive the music of antiquity, which was assumed to have a powerful ethical and emotional force. For instance, Galileo's father, Vincenzo Galilei, was convinced that modern music was much inferior to the ancient, and he saw his task as a musician to be mainly the restoration of the simplicity and close union of music and accompanying text.[2]

This was not at the forefront of the concerns of Beeckman and his young friend. What loomed large in their eyes was the practical problem of consonance that had its roots in the remotest antiquity. According to tradition, Pythagoras was the first to discover that musical consonances result from the division of a string in simple mathematical ratios. If a string is divided into two equal parts, and one plucks first the half and then the whole string, one hears the consonance *octave*; if the string is divided at 2/3 of its length, and one plucks first the 2/3 part and then the whole string, one hears the consonance *fifth*; if the string is divided at the fourths of its length, and one plucks first the 3/4 part and then the whole string, one hears the consonance *fourth*. These consonances—the octave (1/8), the fifth (2/3), and the fourth (3/4), plus the unison (1/1)—were the basis of the division of the scale. The difference of the fifth and the fourth (e.g., C–G minus C–F = 2/3 ÷ 3/4 = 8/9) provided the value for the whole tone (C–D, D–E, F–G, G–A, A–B), while the size of the two smaller steps or diatonic semitones (E–F, B–C', where C' is an octave higher than C) was calculated by considering that

---

more conclusive argument for his knowledge of Italian is his ability to read Galileo's *Dialogi sopra i due massimi sistemi* and his *Discorsi e dimostrazioni matematiche intorno a due nuove scienze*, which were published in 1632 and 1636 respectively. We cannot rule out that Descartes learned Italian when he sojourned in Italy for about a year in 1624–1625, but evidence for direct acquaintance with Zarlino's text before 1618 is provided in the following passage from the *Compendium Musicae*: "Zarlino enumerates at length all the kinds of cadences. He also has a general table in which he explains what consonances can follow a given consonance in a song. He gives reasons for all of these but many, according to me, can be deduced more plausibly from our premises" (A.T., X, pp. 133–134). Beeckman, whose knowledge of Italian was poor, found Zarlino hard going (*Journal*, entry for 11 July 1620, *ibid.*, p. 134, note *a*). For a critical edition of the *Compendium Musicae*, see René Descartes, *Compendium Musicae*, Frédéric de Buzon, ed. (Paris: Presses Universitaires de France, 1987).

[2] See H.F. Cohen, *Quantifying Music. The Science of Music at the First Stage of the Scientific Revolution, 1580–1650.* (Dordrecht: Reidel, 1984), pp. 78–85. I am much indebted to this excellent study of the relations between music and science at the time of Descartes.

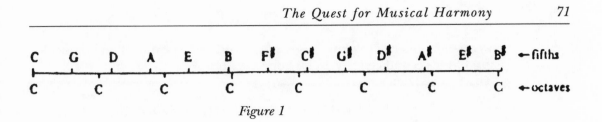

Figure 1

C–F is equal to both a pure fourth (3/4) and the product of the difference between C–D, D–E, and EF, namely,

$$C - F = \frac{3}{4} = \frac{8}{9} \times \frac{8}{9} \times \text{semitone},$$

hence semitone = 243/256.

So for the Pythagorean scale we have:

C 8/9 D 8/9 E 243/256 F 8/9 G 8/9 A 8/9 B 243/256 C'.

The Pythagorean scale presents two problems. The first concerns the *thirds* and the *sixths*, which are considered dissonances (for instance, the major third (C–E), which consists of two tones, is $(8/9)^2 = 64/81$, which makes for a harsh sound). The second concerns the incompatibility of the pure consonances, and results because derivations of the Pythagorean scales are incompatible. For instance, if we start with C and add fifths and octaves, we shall never end on the same C again (see Figure 1).

The reason is clear: $(1/2)^7 \neq (2/3)^{12}$ because the powers of different prime numbers can never be equal. B# and C differ by a slight amount (roughly 73/74) that is called the *Pythagorean comma*.

These problems were minor ones until the thirteenth century when two radically new developments precipitated a crisis: the invention of polyphony and the introduction of the thirds and sixths as consonances. The major third that figures prominently in fifteenth-century compositions was not the dissonant Pythagorean third, but the pure major third 4/5. The difference between the pure and the Pythagorean third is 64/81 ÷ 4/5 = 80/81, a small interval that is called the *syntonic comma*.

The introduction of the consonant thirds: major third (4/5), e.g., C–E; minor third (5/6), e.g., A–C'; and sixths: major sixth (5/6), e.g., C–A; minor sixth (5/8), e.g., E–C', presented a problem both for consonance and for the division of the octave.

Zarlino's Scale

Gioseffo Zarlino was the one who clearly defined the problem and found a solution by reverting to the division known as the "diatonic syntonon" that

was mentioned by Ptolemy, the great Alexandrian astronomer and musicologist of the second century, in his book *On Music*.[3]
This is the scale:

C 8/9 D 9/10 E 15/16 F 8/9 G 9/10 A 8/9 B 15/16 C'.

On this scale, the octave C–C' is pure (i.e., $8/9 \times 9/10 \times 15/16 \times 8/9 \times 9/10 \times 8/9 \times 15/16 = 1/2$). The fifth C–G and the major third C–E are also pure. But given the incompatibility of pure consonances, this could not hold for the entire scale: D–A falls short of the pure fifth by a small value ($9/10 \times 15/16 \times 8/9 \times 9/10 = 27/40$); likewise, D–F falls short of the pure minor third ($9/10 \times 15/16 = 27/32$). It follows that if we insist on taking all consonances as pure, we can no longer maintain the original pitch. This can be seen from an example taken from Christiaan Huygens (see Figure 2.)[4]

Figure 2

If the singer takes all intervals as pure, he will end on a C sharpened by one syntonic comma, since $(2/3 : 3/4) \times (2/3 : 3/4) : 4/5 = 80/81$. What the singer has to do in practice is the dilemma that theoreticians tried to solve. But while the debate raged on between men, such as Gioseffo Zarlino and Vincenzo Galilei, instruments still had to be played and tuned, bearing in mind that keyboard instruments cannot be tuned while they are being played. In practice, concessions were made to the purity of one or other of the consonances; in other words, various "temperaments" were devised on the empirical ground that the human ear is willing to tolerate slight deviations from the absolute purity of consonance.

Beeckman's Views

When Descartes met Beeckman in the autumn of 1618, he was acquainted with the general terms of the problem, having either read Zarlino or having heard lectures given by a Jesuit who used Zarlino as the source of his teaching. Beeckman had been thinking about the production of sound for several years, and he believed that it could be explained in mechanical and corpuscularian terms. The vibrating string, he argued, slices the surrounding air into spherical corpuscles that are physically projected and strike the ear where they are perceived as sound. As early as 1614, Beeckman had a

---

[3] Gioseffo Zarlino, *Istitutioni Harmoniche* (Venice, 1573), pp. 139–143.

[4] Quoted in H.F. Cohen, *Quantifying Music*, p. 40. The reference is to Christiaan Huygens, *Oeuvres Complètes*, 22 vols. (The Hague: M. Nijhof, 1888–1950), vol. 20, p. 77.

mathematical proof for the inverse proportionality between the length of a string and its frequency, and, by the time he met Descartes, he had persuaded himself that pitch corresponds to frequency, and loudness to the amount of air struck (what we interpret as amplitude).

Neither Beeckman nor Descartes excelled in vocal or instrumental music. Beeckman candidly acknowledged that he had been the worst pupil of his singing master and that he did not always notice discords.[5] Descartes was never able to sing up the scale or judge whether this was done correctly.[6] He admitted to Huygens that he was "almost [tone] deaf," and to Mersenne that he could not distinguish a fifth from an octave.[7] These musical shortcomings, which we might consider disastrous for anyone wishing to speak authoritatively on consonance, do not appear to have hindered the two friends from laying down rules with the assurance and peremptoriness of youth.

The Compendium Musicae

Descartes tells his reader at the beginning of the *Compendium Musicae* that he wishes to study sound in order to have a better insight into the way music can move us. But the analysis of music as an affective language plays virtually no role in what follows. Descartes assumes that it can easily be inferred from his examination of the two basic properties that enable sound to move us, namely, duration and pitch. What he means is that a simple mathematical analysis of consonance will tell us all we have to know about the production of sound and, by the same token, about the nature of music.

Musical pleasure results from a deep-seated conformity between the mind and intervals that rest on the ratios of the first few integers. Descartes does not attempt to solve the mystery of consonance, which for him is but an instance of the fact that any pleasing object is perceived as simple. Arithmetical series are simpler than geometrical ones; hence they are preferable. Their numbers increase by an even amount, so "the senses do not have to strain so much to distinctly perceive the items in it."[8] Descartes proceeds to translate the musical ratios into line segments to make them visible to the eye and hence intuitively clear.

The ratio of the lines in the arithmetical progression 2, 3, 4 "is very easily distinguished by our eyes,"[9] whereas the ratio of lines in the geometrical progression 2, $\sqrt{8}$, 4 is less clear because *ab* and *bc* (on the last line) are

[5] Isaac Beeckman, *Journal*, vol. III, p. 221.

[6] Letter of Descartes to J.A. Bannius, written in 1640, A.T., III, pp. 829–830; letter to Constantin Huygens, 30 November 1646, *ibid.*, p. 788.

[7] Letter of Descartes to Constantin Huygens, A.T., II, p. 699, line 103; letter to Mersenne, 15 April 1630, A.T., I, p. 142, line 26.

[8] *Compendium Musicae*, A.T., X, p. 91.

[9] *Ibid.*, p. 92.

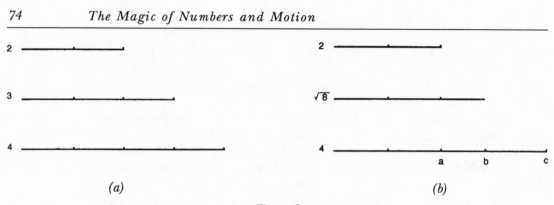

(a)   *(b)*

Figure 3

incommensurable (see Figure 3). Since simple ratios are the key to aesthetic pleasure, Descartes assumes that auditory simplicity will be mirrored in visual simplicity, thereby subordinating mathematical ratios to the visual perception of line segments.

Generating Consonance

This reliance on simple mathematical operations performed on lines led Descartes to an original and brilliant derivation of the consonances.[10] The process consists in a continued bisection of a string AB (see Figure 4) first at C, thereby generating the octave (1/2) AC–AB, then at D, halfway between C and B, with the resulting segments AC and AD "properly generating" the fifth (2/3), while segments AD and AB "accidentally" yield the fourth (4/3), DB. Why Descartes should call DB "a mere residue," and hence the fourth an "accidental consonance," seems arbitrary, and is probably only a convenient, if unpersuasive, device to place the third, which he considers "the most gracious and pleasing to the ear," above the fourth even at the level of bisection.[11] One more bisection, at E, "directly" generates the major third (4/5) AC–AE, "and by accident all remaining consonances."[12]

But Descartes himself is not entirely convinced of the satisfactoriness of his distinction between "proper" and "accidental" consonances, and he offers an experimental confirmation "lest someone should think that what I have just said is a fiction":

> I know from experience that when the string of a lute or some other string instrument is plucked, only the strings that are higher by a fifth or a third resound.[13]

[10] *Ibid.*, pp. 96–105.

[11] *Ibid.*, p. 105. The problem of the fourth (*diatesseron*: 3/4) is that it is less consonant than the third (4/5) or the sixth (3/5), although the theory of simplicity would seem to require that the smaller the number of parts, the greater the consonance.

[12] *Ibid.*, p. 102.

[13] *Ibid.*, p. 103.

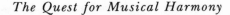
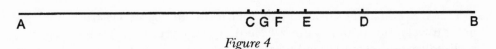

Figure 4

Descartes was familiar with the phenomenon of sympathetic resonance, and he felt that there must be an underlying connection between resonance and consonance. He assumed that consonances that resound are more "proper" or "direct" than those that do not, and since consonances are generated from line segments, some segments must be "proper" while others are merely "accidental."

But why stop the bisection at E? The only reason we are given is that a further division at F would generate the major tone (8/9) AC–AF, and the minor tone (9/10) AF–AE, both of which are dissonances. We halt, therefore, on experimental grounds alone. There is no intrinsic reason why bisection should suddenly lose its ability to produce pleasant sounds.

Having arbitrarily discarded further bisection, Descartes tacitly returns to Zarlino's scale a few pages later and gives the numerical ratio 15/16 for the major semitone and the minor semitone that *should result* from a further division of CF at G (namely AC–AG and AG–AF).[14] If he had *actually bisected* CF at G, however, he would have obtained different values, namely, AC/AG = 16/17, and AG/AF = 17/18. This deviation from 15/16 was never noted by Descartes because he did not bother to proceed with the bisection. It was detected by Beeckman, however, but only later in 1628 when he carried the bisection further than Descartes had ventured and discovered the limitations of thoroughgoing quantification.[15]

High and Low Notes

From the principle, "sound is to sound as string is to string,"[16] Descartes inferred that since a shorter string is contained (as a segment) in a longer string, so the higher notes are contained in the lower ones. This is why the lower note is "more important" and "more powerful."[17] As a confirmation, Descartes adds, as if it were an ascertained fact, that greater force must be exerted to sound a high note than a low one.

This erroneous belief is already in Aristotle. It probably rests on the experience that a string has to be shortened as one moves up the scale, and that this requires the application of a little force.[18] Descartes also subscribed

---

[14] *Ibid.*, p. 118, where Descartes has the ratio 405/432 (= 15/16) for the major semitone in the first diagram, and the ratio 360/384 (= 15/16) for the minor semitone in the second diagram.

[15] Isaac Beeckman, *Journal*, A.T., X, p. 348.

[16] *Compendium Musicae, ibid.*, p. 97.

[17] *Ibid.*, pp. 124, 97.

[18] *Ibid.*, p. 115. See Aristotle, *Problems*, Bk XIX, § 37, 920ᵇ16–20.

to a second, equally false, belief (this time found in Plato's *Timaeus*) that high notes travel faster than low ones.[19] Neither Plato nor Descartes seem to have realized that this would entail that when we listen to an orchestra the higher notes of the flute would reach our ears before the lower notes of the trombone, or that in a recital the part sung by a soprano would be heard before the one sung by the bass.[20]

The Note and Its Octave

Descartes also observed that every musical note contains its octave, a phenomenon that had already been mentioned by Aristotle, but Descartes appears to have been the first to use it to explain the poor quality of the fourth.

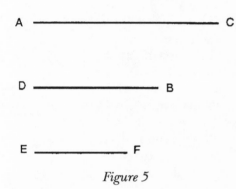

Figure 5

Let the segment AC be the length of the octave, DB that of the fifth, and EF the length of a note an octave higher (see Figure 5). Sounding AC will make EF resound, thereby producing a note an octave higher. Now this higher note is a fourth counting from the note sounded by DB. Hence, says Descartes, we see that the fourth "is almost the shadow of the fifth,"[21] a reflection of the greatest and most pleasing consonance. Unfortunately, as Pirro has pointed out, the argument is as deceptive as it is simple. It takes into consideration only the upper partial of the higher note of the interval and blissfully neglects the lower partial.[22]

The Scale Revised

Descartes was aware that on Zarlino's scale all consonances are pure, except for the minor third D–F and the fifth D–A, both of which are false by one syntonic comma (80/81). This meant that the purity of the consonance could not be maintained throughout. Descartes' solution was to give D two slightly different values, D, and D*, one syntonic comma below the first, a process that came to be known as "mobilization." This had the advantage of restricting the change of pitch in the course of a piece to one particular note. Thus consonances were kept pure, and the pitch was stabilized by mobilizing one of the notes. As we know from his *Journal,* Beeckman had considered this

19 *Compendium Musicae,* A.T., X, p. 136. See Plato, *Timaeus,* 80[a-b].

20 André Pirro says that Descartes writes "like someone who has never heard music" (André Pirro, *Descartes et la musique.* (Paris: Fischbacher, 1907), p. 72). This book is still the fullest treatment of Descartes' musical interests. For an excellent short survey, see H.F. Cohen, *Quantifying Music,* pp. 161–177.

21 *Compendium Musicae,* A.T., X, p. 108.

22 André Pirro, *Descartes et la musique,* pp. 37–38.

solution before Descartes but had rejected it as unsatisfactory, since it meant that the singer never returned to the same note.[23]

Descartes remained committed to the ideal of pure consonance, and 25 years later, in a letter to Andreas Colvius, we find him proposing a solution to the tuning problem for keyboard instruments based on the same strategy, mobilizing the D, the C, and all the five accidentals. The result was a division of the octave not into twelve, but into nineteen intervals, which maintained mathematical precision, at the price of increased complexity for the players.[24]

Beeckman's Influence on Descartes

At least two passages in the *Compendium Musicae* were inspired by comments that Beeckman made or that Descartes saw in Beeckman's *Journal*.[25] The first concerns the number of notes. The traditional scale, *ut, re, mi, fa, sol, la*, comprised only six notes instead of the seven with which we are familiar. The *si* or *B* was introduced in the sixteenth century and rapidly became popular because it made solmization easier.

Since the *si* came with no mathematical warrant, and since Descartes could not appreciate its practical advantages, he dismissed it as superfluous, even harmful.[26] Beeckman, who was also unable to sing in tune, carried simplicity a step further and reduced the number of notes from six to four, claiming that *fa, sol, la, mi* were enough to express the differences between the notes.[27] Descartes had Beeckman in mind when he repudiated this reform as excessive, since it would make the transition from low to high notes too abrupt.[28]

The second passage where Beeckman's influence is clearly marked is the section on sympathetic resonance, which Descartes discusses in terms of the coincidence of line segments in order to show that resonance at the major seventeenth is stronger than at the major third (4/5), adding, as though it were an afterthought:

> This could be conceived in the same way if someone were to say that sound strikes the air with many strokes, and the faster, the higher the sound.[29]

---

[23] *Compendium Musicae*, A.T., X, pp. 125–127; Isaac Beeckman, *Journal*, vol. I, pp. 56–57, quoted in H.F. Cohen, *Quantifying Music*, p. 152. In the *Cogitationes Privatae*, written at roughly the same time as the *Compendium Musicae*, Descartes describes "a musical instrument made with mathematical precision," where D is rendered "mobile," i.e., mobilized (A.T., X, p. 227).

[24] Letter of Descartes to Colvius, 6 July 1643, A.T., IV, pp. 678–683. See also pp. 722–725.

[25] Beeckman showed his *Journal* to only three persons: Descartes in 1618–1619, Mersenne in 1630, and his pupil Hortensius (*Journal*, vol. III, p. 354).

[26] *Compendium Musicae*, A.T., X, p. 121.

[27] Isaac Beeckman, *Journal*, vol. I, pp. 50–51 (entry made between April 1614 and January 1615), and 89–90 (entry made between 6 February and 23 December 1616).

[28] *Compendium Musicae*, A.T., X, p. 224.

[29] *Ibid.*, p. 110.

The source of this comment is clear from an entry in Beeckman's *Journal* dated 2 January 1619 where he notes that Descartes must have been pleased with his views "on the strokes of sound," since he inserted them in his *Compendium Musicae*.[30] A passage in Descartes' *Cogitationes Privatae* confirms that Beeckman's analysis of sound was new to him:

> The same person [i.e., Isaac Beeckman] suspects that the strings of a lute move more rapidly the higher the pitch, so that the higher octave makes two motions while the lower makes one.[31]

Before meeting Descartes, Beeckman had discovered an elegant geometrical proof of the inverse proportionality of string length and frequency. He communicated it in 1629 to Mersenne who published it in his *Harmonie Universelle* in 1636. Beeckman's proof is that when the lengths of the strings stand in the ratio 1:2 (and hence produce the octave), they vibrate in frequencies that are as 2:1 (see Figure 6).

String AC, together with its half, CD, gives an octave. If D is stretched to B, F is stretched to E. When the string is released, points B and E move back to D and F at the same speed. But BD = 2EF. Hence E moves at the same speed but passes through F twice in the time that B passes through D once. In other words, half the string vibrates twice as fast as the whole string. We consider this merely a proof that pitch is determined by the frequency of the vibration, but Beeckman was convinced that he had provided much more, indeed, that he had found the geometrical proof or reason of the *sweetness of the consonance*.[32]

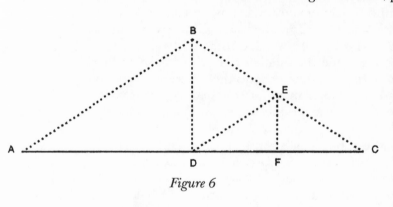

Figure 6

There is no mention of Beeckman's elegant geometrical proof in the *Compendium Musicae*, and it may well have been communicated to Descartes only in 1619 after he had written his musical treatise.

[30] Isaac Beeckman, *Journal, ibid.*, pp. 61–62.

[31] *Cogitationes Privatae*, A.T., X, p. 224.

[32] Isaac Beeckman, *Journal*, vol. I, pp. 54–55. See Beeckman's letter to Mersenne, June 1629, in Marin Mersenne, *Correspondance*, vol. II, p. 232 and notes, pp. 234–236. The letter is also published in *Journal*, vol. IV, pp. 145–148. I use the figure on p. 146. The proof was published by Mersenne in his *Harmonie Universelle* (Paris, 1636). Facsimile (Paris: C.N.R.S., 1925), vol. I, pp. 157–158.

Music through the Years

Descartes was to return to the problem of musical consonance over the years, usually at the prodding of friends, such as Constantin Huygens and Mersenne, for whom music was a reflection of the divine harmony that pervades the world.

When Descartes returned to Holland in the autumn of 1628, he went to Middelburg to call on Beeckman who had left his native town some nine years earlier. Descartes was surprised to learn that Beeckman now resided in Dordrecht where he was Rector of the Latin School. We know from Beeckman's *Journal* that Descartes called on him on 8 October and showed himself eager to renew an acquaintance that he had made no attempt to keep up for ten years. Now that Descartes was considering settling down in the Netherlands to garner the fruits of his travels and meditations, he found it convenient to call on the man to whom he paid the fulsome homage of not having found anyone in his extensive journeys throughout Europe "with whom it gave him more pleasure to discuss or from whom he could expect more help in furthering his studies."[23] Desirous, no doubt, of impressing his friend, Descartes declared that he "had nothing more to wish for in arithmetics and geometry: namely, that he had, in the last nine years, made as much progress in these subjects as the human mind was capable of making."[34] He informed Beeckman of the outcome of Mersenne's experiments on the relation between the pitch, the tension, and the thickness of a string, a result that Descartes himself used in his *Rules for the Direction of the Mind* around this time.[35]

Bruised Susceptibilities

By an interesting coincidence, the Protestant theologian, André Rivet, recommended to Mersenne in 1629 that Beeckman be added to his list of correspondents. In his reply to Rivet, Mersenne enclosed a sheet of queries that were to be shown to Beeckman. One question was about the sweetness of consonances, and Beeckman, who was under the impression that Descartes had returned to Paris, assumed that it stemmed from him. Why not ask Descartes himself? he told Rivet, who forwarded the suggestion to Mersenne but did not mention Descartes by name. He merely referred to a well-known "gentleman." This puzzled Mersenne and led to the first of a series of misunderstandings:

> Concerning the problem I proposed to Mr. Becman [sic], I have no
> recollection that the gentleman you mention was able to satisfy me. I do

---

[33] Isaac Beeckman, *Journal*, A.T., X, p. 332.

[34] *Ibid.*, p. 331.

[35] *Ibid.*, p. 337; *Rules for the Direction of the Mind*, Rule 13, *ibid.*, p. 431.

not even know who he is, unless it be Mr. de Cartes [sic], who is the brightest man I have ever met.[36]

In March 1629, Beeckman wrote himself to Mersenne and confirmed that he had had Descartes in mind:

He is the person to whom, as I said, I communicated ten years ago what I had written on the causes of the sweetness of consonances, and who, I assumed, had been the occasion of your question. He was here a while ago and (being fond of travel) has returned to you.[37]

This innocuous and entirely truthful comment was to fill Descartes with indignation when it was communicated to him by Mersenne in the autumn of 1629. Mersenne's letter is lost, but Descartes' reply is extant:

You have obliged me very much by warning me of the ingratitude of my friend. I believe that he was dazzled by the honour of receiving a letter from you, and assumed that you would think even more highly of him if he wrote that he had been my master ten years ago. But he is quite mistaken, for what glory can there by in having taught a man who knows very little and openly confesses it, as I do? I shall not write to him since you do not wish me to do so, but I could put him to shame, especially if I had the whole letter.[38]

Whether Mersenne complied with the request to see Beeckman's letter in full is not known, but if he sent a copy, it is hard to see why Descartes was not mollified. Nonetheless, in November 1629, he contacted Beeckman and asked that the *Compendium Musicae* (his *gift* of 1619) be returned.[39]

Mersenne's Mediation

Mersenne must have been unhappy at the trouble he had unwittingly caused, and we have an interesting example of the kind friar's attempt to achieve a reconciliation in a letter that he wrote to Descartes at the end of 1629 or early in 1630. The letter is lost, but we have a good idea of its content, since Descartes replied to its twelve queries point by point. The last three refer to Beeckman and are preceded by an entirely different and apparently irrelevant question that Descartes answers as follows:

As for your question, How the Christian virtues agree with the natural ones, I have nothing to say except that just as a crooked stick is made

---

[36] Letter of Mersenne to Rivet, 28 February 1629, Marin Mersenne, *Correspondance*, vol. II, p. 205.

[37] *Ibid.*, letter of Beeckman to Mersenne, mid-March 1629, p. 218.

[38] Letter of Descartes to Mersenne, 8 October 1629, A.T., I, p. 24.

[39] *Ibid.*, letter of Descartes to Mersenne, 18 December 1629, p. 100: "I got the original of the small treatise back a month ago."

straight, not merely by removing the curve, but by bending it the other way, likewise, since our nature is too prone to vengeance, God commands us not only to forgive our enemies but to do good to them.[40]

The friar's innocent stratagem was entirely lost on Descartes, who does not seem to have noticed the proximity of this question on Christian charity (for which the Minim priest needed no instruction from a layman) to the next one about Beeckman. This concerned the authorship of a passage on consonance in a letter that Beeckman had written to Mersenne on 1 October 1629. Descartes repudiated the suggestion that it might stem from himself: the style was surely not his own, indeed it was not even intelligible![41]

Mersenne quoted two other passages from Beeckman's letter, one on the vibration of a bell, the other on the breaking point of a monochord. Again, Descartes affected to find them unintelligible. This is particularly unfortunate because Descartes and Beeckman both had part of the answer to the question: Why does the string of a monochord snap at the ends when it is tightened too much? Beeckman, on the one hand, noted that the increased tension is more easily shared by the parts in the middle than by those at the ends of the string, and he conjectured that the tension at the ends must be double that at the middle because the string at the end can only be stretched on one side. Descartes, on the other hand, noted that when the peg is turned slowly, the tension is evenly distributed.[42] Descartes and Beeckman missed a golden opportunity for fruitful cooperation.

Beeckman's Corpuscular Theory of Sound

In this same letter to Descartes, Mersenne raised another question that came directly out of his correspondence with Beeckman, but without stating his source. It concerned the corpuscular theory of sound, and Descartes was not likely to be in the dark about its provenance. Beeckman, like Gassendi, with whom he had friendly conversations in 1629, was an atomist for whom all qualities were explainable in terms of small particles of different size moving at varying speeds. Before meeting Descartes, he had, in 1616, applied the theory to the production of sound, which he claimed resulted from the slicing of air into spherical globules by the vibrating strings or the vocal chords. The faster a string vibrates, the finer the globules of air that are cut. Hence the size of the globules is inversely proportional to the pitch. Since the number of globules is greater for higher notes, Beeckman also concluded that loudness is a function of the quantity of globules.

---

[40] *Ibid.*, letter of Descartes to Mersenne, January 1630, p. 110.

[41] Letter of Beeckman to Mersenne, 1 October 1629, in Marin Mersenne, *Correspondance*, vol. II, pp. 277–278; letter of Descartes to Mersenne, January 1630, A.T., I, p. 110.

[42] Compare to following passages in the letters quoted in the previous footnote, Mersenne, *Correspondance*, vol. II, p. 280, and A.T., I, p. 112.

The globules travel to the ear where they are perceived as sound. The distinctive feature of Beeckman's theory is summarized in a passage of his letter of 1 October 1629 to Mersenne: "The cause of the sound that is heard is the very same air that was in the mouth of the speaker." For "the very same air," the Latin has "*idem numero aer*," which can be translated by "exactly the same air," or "quantitatively the same air."[43] The second makes Beeckman's theory less outlandish, but H.F. Cohen has shown that Beeckman meant the first. The air globules that leave the string or the vocal chords are identical with the ones that strike the eardrum![44]

Descartes contemptuously rejected this view as "ridiculous," but Beeckman's theory should be seen against the background of seventeenth-century physics. The alternative to the corpuscular theory of sound was the wave theory, which was defended, for instance, by Francis Bacon in his *Sylva Sylvarum*.[45] Beeckman clearly grasped how waves were formed in the sea by a succession of condensations and rarefactions that he compared to a vibrating string.[46] If he did not apply this analogy to the production of sound, it was because, at the time, the wave theory was wedded to a different illustration, namely, that of ripples spreading out from the spot where a stone has been dropped in a pool. This comparison, according to Beeckman, was untenable, for if sound were really like a wave of air, not only would we experience sound the way we feel a breeze, but the slightest breeze would be perceived as sound! Furthermore, we know that sounds can travel in opposite directions without clashing, whereas air currents interfere with one another.[47]

Beeckman's strictures only hold if the wave analogy entails that ripples physically move from the center to the circumference. The analogy, of course, requires no such physical transportation of water from the center of the disturbance to the periphery. A wave can easily be made to travel along a rope that only moves up and down, and although the water in the sea appears to be travelling towards the shore, in fact it is not. If all the water were going ashore, it would pile up there into a sort of permanent wave, whereas nothing of the kind is seen. The astonishing thing is that Beeckman understood perfectly well that the wave analogy did not require the propaga-

[43] Letter of Beeckman to Mersenne, 1 October 1629, in Marin Mersenne, *Correspondance*, vol. II, p. 282.

[44] H.F. Cohen, *Quantifying Music*, p. 275, note 22.

[45] Francis Bacon, *Sylva Sylvarum: or a Natural History*, Century III, 287 in Francis Bacon, *Works*, J. Spedding, R.L. Leslie, *et alii*, eds., 14 vols. (London 1857–1874). Facsimile (Stuttgart-Bad Cannstatt, Frommann, 1963), vol. II, pp. 435–436.

[46] Isaac Beeckman, *Journal*, vol. II, pp. 37–38. The passage is translated in H.F. Cohen, *Quantifying Music*, p. 121.

[47] Isaac Beeckman, *Journal*, vol. I, p. 92. Also quoted in Marin Mersenne, *Correspondance*, vol. II, pp. 293–294, and partly translated in H.F. Cohen, *Quantifying Music*, p. 122, where the reader will also find a helpful commentary.

tion of air itself, but only the regular succession of pulses of compressed air.[48] He was unable to build on his own insight.

Mersenne in Holland

In the summer of 1630 (having shed his religious habit at the borders as Dutch law required), Mersenne visited several of his friends in the Netherlands. He spent a few days with Beeckman at Dordrecht, and during his stay was shown Beeckman's *Journal*, the first person to be granted this privilege since Descartes more than ten years earlier. From the *Journal*, Mersenne got an impression of the relations between Descartes and Beeckman that was considerably at variance with the one that had been conveyed by Descartes. Nonetheless, he counselled forbearance to Beeckman, who wrote to Descartes shortly after Mersenne's departure. He received no acknowledgment until his co-rector, Abraham van Elderen, called on Descartes on a trip to Leyden or Amsterdam, and elicited the following reply:

> I asked you to return my *Music* [i.e., the *Compendium Musicae*] last year, not because I needed it but because I heard that you talked about the content as though I had it from you. I did not wish to write immediately lest I should appear to doubt a friend's loyalty merely upon the report of a third party. But since many other things have confirmed that you prefer empty boasting to friendship and truth, I want you to know that if you really taught someone something it is odious to say so. It is more odious if it is not true, and utterly odious if, in fact, it is the other way round.[49]

Descartes could not deny that he had once written to Beeckman that he had learned much and expected still more from him. He now claimed that these were nothing but French-style civilities that only a cad could have taken at face value. If he ever learned anything from Beeckman, it was in the way he was in the habit of learning "from ants and worms."[50]

In his answer, Beeckman must have reminded Descartes of the subjects they had discussed and identified Mersenne as the person who had, however unwittingly, incensed Descartes. In the only remaining fragment of his letter, he says that Mersenne spent several days reading his *Journal* and

> saw in it many things that he had thought were yours and (from the dates that were indicated) rightly began to doubt who was their author. I dis-

---

[48] Isaac Beeckman, *Journal*, vol. II, pp. 37–38, translated in H.F. Cohen, *Quantifying Music*, pp. 121–122.

[49] Letter of Descartes to Beeckman, September or October 1630, A.T., I, pp. 155–156.

[50] *Ibid.*, p. 156. In his next letter, dated 17 October 1630, Descartes stated, as an elementary principle, "If you know something, it is entirely your own even if you learned it from someone else" (p. 159).

closed, perhaps more freely than was pleasant for you or him, how things really stood.[51]

Descartes wrote in reply a violent and abusive letter of some 3,000 words in which he claimed that he could not make up his mind whether Beeckman was "demented" or just "a boor." The only cure for such a person, he stated, would be to have him follow Descartes' own modest behavior:

> I am ashamed to cite myself as an example, but you compare yourself so often to me that it seems necessary. Have you ever heard me boast that I taught anyone anything? Have I ever claimed to be, I do not say better, but as good as anyone else?[52]

As we have seen, Descartes had borrowed from Beeckman the explanation of consonance by the coincidence of "strokes." He now chose to consider Beeckman's theory a trivial reformulation of an old idea about which only a pedant would dream of gloating:

> First, as to those *strokes*, if you had taught your pupils something a little loftier than the alphabet, you would have found in Aristotle the very thing you claim as your own (namely, that sound originates from repeated strokes of chords or other bodies on the air). And you complain that I do not praise you for discovering it! Aristotle is the thief! Bring him to court, have him restore your idea to you! And what did I do? Writing on music, when I was explaining something that did not depend on a detailed knowledge of sound, I added that it could be conceived either way, whether sound struck the ear with many strokes, or whether, etc. Did I steal what I did not take? Or should I have praised what I did not say was true? Or was I bound to ascribe to you what all, except yourself, have learned from Aristotle? Would they not have been right in laughing at my ignorance?[53]

Descartes is being nasty and pedantic. Sound was discussed since antiquity, but only in the broadest terms, in the light of two different conceptions about the nature of its transmission. The first was connected with atomism and assumed that the human voice or a musical instrument emitted small particles that flew through the air and turned into audible sound upon reaching the listener's ear. The second, which Aristotle espoused, conceived of sound as the result of the air being struck by the vocal chords or the strings of a musical instrument. If Beeckman's theory stood in any tradition, it was clearly in the first, not the second! But neither the atomists nor Aristotle had suggested that consonance resulted from the frequent coincidence of pulses. This was unquestionably Beeckman's achievement, and Descartes was being petty when he tried to belittle it.

---

[51] Quoted by Descartes in a letter to Mersenne, 4 November 1630, *ibid.*, p. 130.

[52] *Ibid.*, letter of Descartes to Beeckman, 17 October 1630, p. 165. The letter runs for eleven pages (pp. 157–167).

[53] *Ibid.*, pp. 162–163.

Descartes ends his letter by claiming that he associated with Beeckman in 1618 because he was the only person who spoke Latin in the town in which he was garrisoned. This extraordinary document, as H.F. Cohen puts it,

> is really a classic example of psychological projection, for clearly the obsession with 'praise' and 'being taught' is Descartes' own, not Beeckman's. Descartes' professed humility, which so inadequately tries to hide the colossal vanity of the man who is convinced of having discovered the true principles leading to certain knowledge, is in total contrast to Beeckman's sober self-esteem and great willingness to give everyone his due.[54]

Beeckman was indeed scrupulous to a fault. Not only did he acknowledge those from whom he learned something in books or conversation, but he felt bound to cite his sources even if they were children or analphabets he had met incidentally.[55] By contrast, Descartes seldom mentioned his sources and gave the impression that although he might occasionally pick up a fact here or there, he was never indebted to anyone for its correct interpretation.

Descartes continued to seethe with indigination for several days after despatching his letter to Beeckman. Some two weeks later, he declared to Mersenne that if he ever wrote on ethics he could not find a better example than Beeckman's letters to "show how ridiculous the silly boasting of a pedant really is."[56] But Descartes' moral sensitivity did not extend to his own personal conduct, and he had no qualms about lying outright when he denied that Mersenne had informed him of his correspondence with Beeckman.[57]

Beeckman was a man of infinite patience, and the kind of person who will excuse anything in the interest of peace. In October 1631, he called on Descartes who was recovering from an illness. Three years later he spent part of a weekend with him in Amsterdam. Beeckman arrived as the bearer of Galileo's *Dialogue on the Two Chief World Systems*, which had appeared in 1632, but which Descartes had not yet seen, and upon which he commented in a letter to Mersenne written on the day Beeckman returned to Dort.[58] They had a leisurely discussion on the speed of light, and since Descartes failed to convince Beeckman of its instantaneous transmission, he spelled out his argument at length in a letter of 22 August 1634. But despite having mended

---

[54] H.F. Cohen, *Quantifying Music*, p. 196.

[55] Isaac Beeckman, *Journal*, vol. III, p. 67.

[56] Letter of Descartes to Mersenne, written between 21 October and 4 November 1630, A.T., I, p. 172.

[57] *Ibid.*, letter of Descartes to Beeckman quoted in Descartes' letter to Mersenne, 4 November 1630, pp. 171–172.

[58] *Ibid.*, letter of Descartes to Mersenne, 14 August 1634, pp. 303–306. The 14th of August fell on a Monday that year.

his fences, Descartes remained the injured party and took pleasure in reminding Mersenne of Beeckman's falsehood.[59]

Beeckman passed away unexpectedly on 20 May 1637, and Descartes was informed of the news by Colvius to whom he replied in a tone that he believed becoming to a Stoic philosopher:

> Passing through this city [Leyden] upon my return from a trip that took more than six weeks, I found the letter that you took the trouble of writing, and by which I learned the sad news of Mr. Beeckman's death. I am sorry, and I know that as one of his best friends you will be saddened. But, Sir, you know much better than I that the time that we live in this world is so short compared to eternity that we should not worry if we are taken a few years earlier or a few years later. Since Mr. Beeckman was extremely philosophical, I have no doubt that he accepted long ago what has come to pass. I hope that God enlightened him so that he died in his grace.[60]

The last sentence, with its veiled implication that Beeckman may not have died in a state of moral rectitude, is particularly distressing.

A year later, on 11 October 1638, it was Galileo's turn to be accused of plagiarism, and Beeckman was again singled out for contumely:

> I never met Galileo nor had any correspondence with him, hence I cannot have borrowed anything from him. Furthermore, I find nothing to envy in his books, and hardly anything that I would like to call my own. The best is what he has on music, and those who know me will more readily believe that he got it from me rather than I from him, since I wrote almost the same thing 19 years ago, at a time when I had not yet been in Italy, and I had given my essay to Mr. Beeckman who, as you know, showed it off and wrote about it as though it were his own.[61]

Galilean Coincidence Theory

The passage to which Descartes alludes is the discussion on music at the end of the First Day of Galileo's *Discourses on Two New Sciences* in which consonance is explained along the lines suggested by Beeckman to Descartes in 1618.

> Agreeable consonances are pairs of tones which strike the ear with a certain regularity; this regularity consists in the fact that the pulses delivered by the two tones, in the same interval of time, shall be commensurable in number, so as not to keep the ear drum in perpetual torment,

---

[59] On 25 May 1637, Descartes wrote to Mersenne that Beeckman was one of those persons "who try to acquire a reputation under false pretence" (*ibid.*, p. 375).

[60] *Ibid.*, letter of Descartes to Colvius, 14 June 1637, pp. 379–380.

[61] Letter of Descartes to Mersenne, 11 October 1638, A.T., II, pp. 388–389.

bending in two different directions in order to yield to the ever-discordant impulses.[62]

Having followed the vicissitudes of the Descartes-Beeckman relationship to its bitter end, we are not likely to be impressed by the suggestion that Galileo was a plagiarist. Descartes and Galileo arrived independently at similar formulations of the coincidence theory, but Descartes developed his version after writing his *Compendium Musicae* and only after it had been suggested to him by Beeckman. In 1629, however, after Descartes broke with Beeckman, we find him describing his current ideas as though he had already had them in 1618. The text is worth quoting extensively:

> It is certain that the return of two strings that produce the twelfth and are in the ratio 1:3 must meet at the same point twice as often as those that give the fifth and are in the ratio 2:3. I recovered last month the original of a small treatise where I explain this and of which you saw an excerpt. It was in Mr. Beeckman's hands for eleven years and, if this is time enough for prescription, he has the right to call it his own. Now consonance is explained as follows:
>
> Let strings A and B be in the ratio 3:1 and strings A and C in the ratio 3:2 [see Figure 7].
>
> Let A take one moment to come or go, so that B will take one third of a moment and C two thirds. If A and B are set in motion at the same time, A will make one oscillation while B makes three. It follows that when A begins its second oscillation, B will begin its fourth, and when A begins its third, B will begin its seventh. In this way they will begin their cycle together at intervals of one moment. Now if A and C are set in motion together, A will have completed one oscillation when C is already half way through its second. Hence C will not be able to start again with A at the second moment of time, but only at the third (for when A makes two oscillations, C makes exactly three). Therefore they will only begin together at intervals of two moments, whereas strings A and B start together at each moment, and this makes the sounds blend better and produce a sweeter harmony.[63]

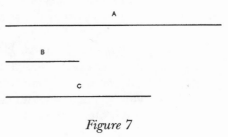

Figure 7

This is a lucid exposition of the coincidence theory and is similar to the one that Galileo published in 1638 in the *Discourses*. But it represents a *novel* development since the *Compendium Musicae* in which Descartes had argued that the twelfth was sweeter than the fourth on purely *numerical* grounds, namely, because the ratio 3:1 is simpler than 3:2. It is only here, in this letter, that we first find him developing the idea mentioned to him by Beeckman

[62] *Discourses on Two New Sciences*, First Day, in Galileo Galilei, *Opere*, vol. VIII, p. 147.

[63] Letter of Descartes to Mersenne, 18 December 1629, A.T., I, pp. 100–101.

that the sweetness of consonances depends on how often the strokes produced by sounding bodies coincide at regular intervals. Descartes is reading this theory back into the *Compendium of Music* in an attempt to deny Beeckman's originality.

The theory is clear and allows one to infer with mathematical rigor what consonances will be more pleasing. But Descartes makes no attempt to give his theory the predictive power that it appears to possess. He goes on instead to tackle the problem of the bad quality of the fourth (4/3), and the fact that the minor sixth (5/8) is consonant, while the simpler ratio (5/7) is not.

Pragmatic Sanctions

In the *Compendium Musicae*, Descartes had explained the poor quality of the fourth by appealing to the upper partial, namely, the fact that every musical note contains its higher octave. He now extends the same idea to the minor sixth (5/8), arguing that a string of eight units of length is accompanied by the resonance of half its length, so that we also hear 5/4 when we sound 5/8. The real difficulty arose with the interval 1/7, which Descartes had dismissed in the *Compendium Musicae* because it could not be generated by the first three bisections of the string. It is generated by a fourth bisection that also generates other ratios that are clearly dissonances, such as the tone 8/9.

As we have seen above, bisection had been halted by Descartes on pragmatic grounds. He gives a similar justification for not accepting the interval 1/7. "The reason," he writes to Mersenne, "is clear because after this one we would have to accept many others that exceed the capacity of our ear."[64] The coincidence theory serves to explain "perfection" or "sweetness," but it offers no reliable guide to pleasantness or agreeableness:

> All that calculation does is reveal what consonances are the simplest or, if you prefer, the sweetest and most perfect, not the most agreeable. If you read my letter carefully you will see that I did not say that that made a more pleasing consonance, for the unison would then be the most pleasing of all. In order to determine what is most pleasing, we must consider the hearer's capacity, and this, like taste, varies from person to person. Some will prefer to hear a single melody, others music sung in parts, etc., just as someone will prefer what is sweet while someone else prefers what is a little bitter or acid.[65]

When Mersenne pressed him on this point, he repeated in even stronger terms that the mathematical theory of consonance cannot provide a criterium of aesthetic quality:

---

[64] *Ibid.*, letter of Descartes to Mersenne, January 1630, pp. 108–109.

[65] *Ibid.*, p. 108.

You embarrass me as much by asking me by how much one consonance is more pleasing than another, as you would were you to ask by how much I prefer fruit to fish.[66]

But is it not strange that a clearly formulated mathematical theory with a detailed mechanism of strokes and percussion should be of such limited value? Why should this be the case? Mersenne kept hounding Descartes, who agreed to explain his position once again in October 1631:

Concerning the sweetness of consonances, two things should be distinguished: namely, what makes them simpler and more accordant, and what makes them more pleasing to the ear. Now, what makes them more pleasing depends on the places where they are employed.[67]

This means that there can be no solution to the age-old problem of consonance. The analysis of musical intervals in terms of simultaneous pulses at mathematically determined intervals does not exhaust the musical reality. In other words, acoustical analysis does not capture aesthetic pleasure.

The two reasons that Descartes gives for this cleavage between simple frequency ratios and the experience of consonance are the variety of personal taste and the problem of context. Let us consider them in turn.

The first reason is hardly valid coming from a man who always insisted that truth was not a matter for a plebiscite. We may not always be in the right mood for music, but then neither are we always in the right mood for doing mathematics or pursuing abstract philosophical thought. To say that not everyone agrees on how to judge consonances is at best a half truth, since virtually no one disagrees about the order of consonances when listened in isolation. If two strings are sounded and the various tones are produced, the classification arrived at by persons with a modicum of musical sensitivity will almost invariably be the familiar one: the octave (1/2), the fifth (2/3), the major third (4/5), the minor third (5/6), the major sixth (3/5), the minor sixth (5/8), and the fourth (3/4). But this order is not the one that follows from the simple ratios generated on the coincidence theory, where we have: the octave (1/2), the fifth (2/3), the fourth (3/4), the major sixth (3/5), the major third (4/5), the minor third (5/6), and the minor sixth (5/8). Thus music would seem to reveal that numbers exert only a partial rule over the world of sound.

The second reason that Descartes adduces is more interesting. It is the difference brought about by the musical context. Even if a satisfactory mathematical and physical account of the pleasure of consonance could be given, it would be as different from actual music as statics is from dynamics. The pleasure of music is not achieved by placing consonances one after another, but by combining them in a rich and diversified pattern. Descartes sensed

---

[66] *Ibid.*, letter of Descartes to Mersenne, 4 March 1630, p. 126.

[67] *Ibid.*, letter of Descartes to Mersenne, October 1631, p. 223.

this and backed off from any claim that his mathematical physics could explain aesthetic pleasure. As we have seen, he does this in a decided and abrupt way. Since the coincidence theory does not provide the *full* explanation, it would seem that it provides no explanation at all. We have here an instance of the all-or-nothing attitude that will characterize Descartes' scientific style. In the *Rules for the Direction of the Mind*, he will make this clear: science is certain, or it is not science. Science does not deal in probabilities and has no truck with the merely plausible.

The problem is that Descartes also believed that clarity and rigor lead to certainty, and he made no attempt to deny that the coincidence theory possessed these characteristics. The theory is restricted because Descartes' musical experience is sufficiently broad and deep to rebel at the imposition of an ordering of consonances exclusively on the grounds of simple ratios. We have here a striking instance of *feeling* prevailing over mathematical rigor.

Descartes as Musical Critic

Although Descartes no longer hoped after 1629 to explain the pleasure of music, he continued to enjoy musical performances and to be consulted as a critic and arbiter of taste. In 1640, one of his Dutch friends, the Catholic priest John Albert Ban (1597–1644), entered a musical competition in which he set to music a short poem that had already been set to music by Antoine Boësset, the greatest French composer of the day. Ban had made his own Descartes' division of the octave into eighteen unequal steps, and he claimed to compose music by following rigorous scientific rules. It was normal that he should turn to Descartes as to an ally, but Descartes again allowed his ear to take precedence over not only mathematics but friendship. He explained to Mersenne that although he approved of rules in music, Ban was a mere schoolboy compared to Boësset. In a longer and more tactfully worded letter to Ban himself, Descartes explained why Boësset's air is superior in a way that has earned high praise from modern musicologists.[68]

Overtones

If we turn from music to the physics of sound, we find that Descartes clearly saw that sound was "nothing but a certain trembling of the air that titillates our ear."[69] He was less lucky in his interpretation of overtones. As we have seen, he knew (as Aristotle had already observed) that in some undefined

---

[68] Letter of Descartes to Mersenne, December 1640, A.T., III, p. 225; to Ban, 1640, *ibid.*, pp. 829–834. See D.P. Walker, "Mersenne's Musical Competition of 1640 and Jean Albert Ban," *Studies in Musical Science in Late Renaissance.* (London: Warburg Institute, 1978), pp. 81–110, especially pp. 101–105.

[69] Letter of Descartes to Mersenne, October 1631, A.T., I, pp. 223–224.

way any given note contains its octave. Mersenne went beyond this vague observation and discovered that any tone produced by a string, a pipe, a bell, or a human voice

Figure 8

consists of the mixture of a fundamental tone with several higher-pitched but weaker partial tones. Apart from the fundamental, Mersenne clearly distinguished four upper partial tones, at frequencies defined by the first few integers. The overtones (see Figure 8) are the octave (1/2), the twelfth (1/3), the fifteenth (1/4) and the seventeenth (1/5).[70]

Mersenne was at a loss to explain where the overtones came from, and in the summer of 1633, he turned to Descartes for advice. Descartes replied that he had observed that a string occasionally gives out two sounds, and he suggested that this resulted from a second vibration caused by some unevenness in the thickness of the string. In the course of the regular stroke from 1 to 6 that gives the fundamental note (see Figure 9), the varying thickness is the cause that the string

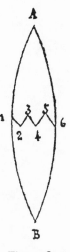

Figure 9

> having reached 2, returns to 3, then goes on to 4, and from there to 5, and finally to 6. This is what produces a higher note by one twelfth. If this second vibration is double the first, we shall have an octave, if it is four times the first, the fifteenth, and if five times the first, the major seventeenth.[71]

Mersenne was baffled by this weird explanation. He repeated his question in the autumn of 1633, and once more in the spring of 1634. In both instances, Descartes gave the same answer over again.[72] Here mathematics clearly had the upper hand, and Descartes does not seem to have worried how a physical string, however uneven, could follow such a strange path.

Mathematics and Music: A Case of Dissonance?

As we have seen above, in the section entitled *Pragmatic Sanctions*, Descartes admitted, when pressed by Mersenne, that no mathematical theory could determine what consonances would be most pleasing. This was a grudging admission, and he never drew the implications for the scheme he devised, as early as 1618, for increasing the number of notes from seven to nineteen. This innovation greatly increased the complexity of musical instruments and offered no appreciable advantage beyond perfect mathematical ratios be-

---

70 See H.F. Cohen, *Quantifying Music*, pp. 102–103.

71 Letter of Descartes to Mersenne, 22 July 1633, A.T., I, pp. 267–268.

72 *Ibid.*, letters of Descartes to Mersenne, end of November 1633, p. 272, and 15 May 1634, pp. 296–297.

tween the intervals of successive notes. When musicians objected to these perfect consonances on the grounds that the difference between the half-tones could not be discriminated, Descartes replied that they were actuated by a spirit of contradiction or were "hard of hearing."[73] In another letter to Mersenne, he supported his case with an appeal to architecture: to complain that the difference between certain intervals cannot be detected by the ear "is just like saying that the proportions that architects determine for columns are useless, since the columns would look just as nice if they were off by a fraction or so."[74]

When not compelled to ask why a specific musical composition was agreeable, Descartes allowed himself to be guided by the theoretically clear but experimentally unsound principle that "sound is to sound as chord is to chord." In the light of this assumption, whereby the length of the chord directly determines the value of the sound, music became a mere matter of working out mathematical ratios. As late as 1643, Descartes instructed Colvius in his system "of constructing a perfect musical instrument" without even mentioning the attendant practical difficulties.[75] Theory spoke with a loud voice and stilled the quiet demur of experience.

Music played an important role in the development of Descartes' ideas, but another facet of his early training must not be forgotten: his interest in the fashionable reform movement that went under the name of Rosicrucianism. To study this aspect of his career, we shall return in the next chapter to the young Descartes of 1619, and his first separation from his friend Beeckman.

[73] *Ibid.*, letter of Descartes to Mersenne, 15 May 1634, p. 295.

[74] *Ibid.*, letter of Descartes to Mersenne, April 1634, p. 286.

[75] Letter of Descartes to Colvius, 6 July 1643, A.T., IV, pp. 678–680. See above, pp. 76–77.

Chapter Five

Descartes and
the Rosicrucian
Enlightenment

The Wandering Soldier-Scholar: 1619–1622

Descartes was left alone in Breda when Beeckman returned to Middelburg early in January 1619. He missed his friend and wrote to say that he would visit him at the beginning of Lent.[1] Ash Wednesday fell on 14 February that year, but it was only a month later that Descartes went to Middelburg and found that Beeckman was not there. Back in Breda, he informed Beeckman that the small vessel, in which he had returned from the island of Walcheren, had been caught in a storm, and that he had been pleased to discover that he was neither seasick nor afraid. He now felt bolder and more eager to undertake the journey to the south of Germany that he had been contemplating.

Descartes had originally considered taking the direct route along the Rhine, but since the Defenestration of Prague on 23 November 1618, and the outbreak of the Thirty Year War, the roads had been rendered unsafe by troop movements. Now confident of his seafaring abilities, Descartes resolved to take the longer maritime journey to Copenhagen, Gdansk, and then proceed through Poland and Hungary to Austria and Bohemia.[2] Descartes boarded a ship for Amsterdam on 29 April 1619 and eventually joined the troops of the Duke of Bavaria, one of the leaders of the Catholic party in the war. He attended part of the coronation ceremonies of the Emperor

---

[1] Letter of Descartes to Beeckman, 24 January 1619, A.T., X, p. 152.
[2] *Ibid.*, letter of Descartes to Beeckman, 26 March 1619, pp. 158–159.

Ferdinand II in Frankfurt that lasted from 20 July to 9 September 1619.[3] He was then quartered in a small town of Bavaria where he had his famous dreams on the night of 10–11 November 1619.[4]

Descartes visited the mathematician Johann Faulhaber in Ulm in 1620, but his movements are not well known until the end of 1621, when he returned to Denmark and thence to Holland. Having landed at Emden in East Friesland, Descartes arranged to be conveyed the short distance to West Friesland on a small private craft. He was accompanied by a manservant with whom he spoke French, and the sailors took him for a rich merchant who knew no Dutch. Within his hearing they openly plotted to relieve him of his money and toss him overboard. No sooner had they formulated their plan than Descartes sprang to his feet, drew his sword, and told them in their own language that he would kill them if they tried any tricks. The would-be pirates were immediately reduced to docility.

Descartes seems to have been as surprised as his assailants. In his account of the incident, he marvels as much at his boldness as at their cowardice! Like the crossing of the turbulent straits between the island of Walcheren and the Dutch coast, this second victory at sea raised his self-esteem. "It was on this occasion," writes Baillet, "that he discovered what impression daring can make on a craven soul, I mean a daring that goes so much beyond what is actually feasible that it would, under other circumstances, be simply ridiculous."[5] Descartes' subsequent intellectual swaggering may have some of its roots in his adventures at sea.

A Gentleman of Independent Means

Descartes returned to France in March 1622, but having heard that Paris was not yet free from the plague that had broken out two years earlier, he went directly to his father's home in Rennes. His brother Pierre and his sister Jeanne had already received their share of their mother's inheritance, and René was placed in possession of his third. This was a substantial fortune, comprising three farms, a large tract of arable land, and a house in the city of Poitiers. He sold these properties, and later invested the proceeds in a bank in Amsterdam from which he received an annual interest of two thousand livres. After his father's death in 1641, he inherited two more farms and a

---

[3] The contenders to the throne of Bohemia were the Protestant Frederick V, Elector of the Palatinate, and the Catholic Ferdinand of Austria, first cousin of the Emperor Mathias. The Elector Palatine was defeated at the battle of the White Mountain on 8 November 1620. He retired to the Netherlands where he died in exile in 1632. He had married Elizabeth Stuart, the daughter of James I and the sister of Charles I. They had thirteen children among whom was the Princess Elizabeth who became Descartes' correspondent and friend.

[4] *Olympica*, A.T., X, pp. 179–188, which I discuss later in this chapter, pp. 115–118.

[5] Adrien Baillet, *Vie de Monsieur Des-Cartes*, vol. I, p. 103, *ibid.*, p. 190. Baillet refers to an autobiographical fragment that was entitled *Experimenta* and is now lost (*ibid.*, pp. 189–190).

house in Châtelleraut. Descartes' considerable income was estimated by his first biographer, Pierre Borel, at six to seven thousand livres *per annum*.[6]

A Brother of the Rosy Cross?

After visiting his relatives in the west of France, Descartes went to Paris at the end of February 1623. In Paris he made or renewed the acquaintance of Marin Mersenne, whose cell was the seat of an informal society of natural philosophers, and he met Claude Mydorge (1585–1647), a gifted mathematician who was interested in optics. The discovery that Descartes had just returned from Germany created a stir, and Descartes found himself suspected of being a member of the Brotherhood of the Rosy Cross, a secret organization that was rumored to have descended on Paris.

Rosicrucians were believed to lie in ambush everywhere, and the presses groaned with descriptions of their dreadful plans. In 1623 alone, Parisians were offered three full-fledged accounts based on hearsay evidence: (1) the *Effroyables Pactions faites entre le Diable et les prétendus Invisibles* [*Horrible Pacts Between the Devil and the Alleged Invisibles*], an anonymous pamphlet that denounced the Rosicrucians as in league with Satan; (2) Gabriel Naudé's more temperate *Instruction à la France sur la vérité de l'histoire des Frères de la Rose-Croix* [*France Informed on the Truth of the History of the Brothers of the Rosy-Cross*]; and (3) François Garasse's fierce and ponderous (it ran to 1,100 pages) *La doctrine curieuse des beaux esprits de ce temps, ou prétendus tels contenant plusieurs maximes pernicieuses à l'Estat, à la Religion, et aux bonnes moeurs* [*The Curious Doctrine of the Alleged Finer Minds of our Time, with Several of their Maxims which are Fatal to the State, Religion and Morality*].

According to Naudé, Parisians awoke one morning to find the following placard at various crossroads:

> We, the delegates of the Main College of the Brothers of the Rosy Cross, are making a visible and invisible visit to this city by the Grace of the Almighty toward whom the hearts of the just are turned. We teach without books or signs all the languages of the countries where we wish to be in order to draw our fellow-men from deadly error.[7]

As Baillet puts it:

> The fact that they were said to have arrived in Paris at the same time as M. Descartes might have had unpleasant consequences if he had concealed himself or lived in solitude, as he had usually done in his travels. But he confounded those who wished to use this coincidence to slander him, by making himself visible to all the world, and particularly to his friends, who

---

[6] *Ibid.*, pp. 116–117, vol. II, pp. 459–461 (Borel's estimate is quoted on p. 459.)

[7] Gabriel Naudé, *Instruction à la France sur la vérité de l'histoire des Frères de la Rose-Croix* (Paris, 1623), p. 27.

needed no other argument that he was not one of the Brotherhood or the Invisibles.[8]

If all the disproof that was needed was "to make himself visible," then Descartes had an easy time of it! In any event, he was indeed lucky, since the Jesuit François Garasse believed the Rosicrucians deserved "the rack or the noose."[9]

The Elusive Brotherhood

Who were these dreadful Rosicrucians, and can Descartes be said to have been in contact with them, or have had any sympathy for their movement? The problem in answering this question lies, quite simply, in the fact that the Rosicrucians never existed. All we find are sympathisers of all, or some, of the ideals proclaimed in the so-called Rosicrucian tracts that appeared between 1614 and 1619, namely, between Descartes' eighteenth and twenty-fourth birthdays, a period in life when the mind is still open to bold ideas and grandiose schemes. These tracts include the *Fama Fraternitatis* (1614), the *Confessio* (1615), the *Chemical Wedding of Christian Rosencreutz* (1616), and the *Raptus Philosophicus* (1619) to mention but a few.[10] The *Fama* and the *Confessio*, which also appeared in several modern languages, were easy to read because they were short (together they run to about 20 pages of printed text), and attractive because they attacked the Establishment. Short shrift is made of the acknowledged authorities: the Pope in religion, Aristotle in philosophy, and Galen in medicine.

The hero of these tracts is a mysterious Rosencreutz who, according to the *Confessio*, was born in 1378 and lived for 106 years. He travelled in the East where he learned the "Magia and the Cabala," and entered into "the harmony of the whole world." He returned to Europe to found a society for

---

[8] Adrien Baillet, *Vie de Monsieur Des-Cartes*, vol. I, p. 108.

[9] For good measure, Garasse compares the Rosicrucians to Luther who was "a perfect atheist." François Garasse, *La doctrine curieuse des beaux esprits de ce temps* (Paris: Sébastien Chappelet, 1623). Facsimile in 2 vols., but with continuous pagination (Westmead, Farnborough: Cregg International Publishers, 1971), vol. I, pp. 91–92, 214.

[10] The *Fama* and the *Confessio* are conveniently reprinted in the English translation given by Thomas Vaughan in 1652 as an appendix to Frances A. Yates, *The Rosicrucian Enlightenment* (London: Paladin, 1975), pp. 279–306. Lenglet de Fresnoy lists 43 works concerning the Rosicrucians published between 1613 and 1619, all in Germany. In 1619–1620, fifteen more appeared. The first French works date from 1623–1624 (*Histoire de la philosophie hermétique* (Paris, 1742), vol. III, pp. 279–287, numbers 651–705). On the relation of these tracts to the Paracelsian movement, see Allen G. Debus, *The Chemical Philosophy*, 2 vols. (New York: Science History Publications, 1977), vol. I, pp. 211ff. For the climate in Italy, see Cesare Vasoli, *Profezia e Ragione* (Naples: Morano, 1974). The *Fama* and the *Confessio* were widely read throughout the seventeenth century, and Isaac Newton annotated Vaughan's English translation. See Frank E. Manuel, *The Religion of Isaac Newton* (Oxford: Clarendon Press, 1974), p. 46, note 28, and Betty Jo Teeter Dobbs, *The Foundations of Newton's Alchemy* (Cambridge: Cambridge University Press, 1975), pp. 53–62.

the reformation of universal knowledge at a time that brought forth such men as Theophrastus (Paracelsus), who was "well-grounded in the aforesaid harmonia," although he was not a member of the Fraternity.[11] The author of the *Fama* recounts the history of the fictitious Order culminating with the recent discovery of the entrance to the vault in which Brother Rosencreutz was buried in Germany. This is seen as a symbol heralding the dawn of a new age: "For like as our door was after so many years wonderfully discovered, also there shall be opened a door to Europe (when the great wall is removed) which already doth begin to appear, and with great desire is expected of many."[12] The *Fama* ends by exhorting its readers "to declare their mind . . . in print."[13] Several did and were contacted by others who had also read the Rosicrucian manifestos, but there is no recorded instance of anyone ever meeting a member of the alleged Fraternity.

Adrien Baillet tells us that Descartes heard of the Brothers of the Rosy Cross in Germany from occasional visitors during the winter of 1619–1620. Baillet's account is particularly instructive because he had access to Descartes' manuscript notes that have since been lost:

> It was in conversations with them that he heard of a Brotherhood of scholars [scavants] established in Germany some time ago under the name of the *Brothers of the Rosy-Cross*. They were greatly praised, and Descartes was told that they knew everything and promised a new wisdom, the true science that had not yet been discovered. Upon hearing these remarkable things, and knowing the stir that the new Society was making in the whole of Germany, Descartes was shaken. He, who openly professed his general contempt of scholars because he had never met a real one, now accused himself of having been rash. He began to hope he could emulate them and his desire was strengthened by the fact that this news about the Brotherhood reached him at a time when he was in the greatest perplexity concerning the way that he should follow in his quest for truth. He felt that he could not remain indifferent to them.[14]

As was to be expected, Descartes was unsuccessful in his attempt to contact the Fraternity, "and he almost decided that the whole thing was a hoax."[15]

Baillet gives as his source an early Latin essay by Descartes that bore the title *De Studio Bonae Mentis* [*On Having the Right Mind*] that is no longer extant. It would seem to have been the draft of a general work on the same theme as the *Rules for the Direction of the Mind* that he wrote ten years later. It discussed the longing for knowledge, the disposition of mind required, and

---

[11] *Fama Fraternitatis*, in F.A. Yates, *The Rosicrucian Enlightenment*, pp. 284, 286.

[12] *Ibid.*, pp. 290–291.

[13] *Ibid.*, p. 296.

[14] Adrien Baillet, *Vie de Monsieur Des-Cartes*, vol. I, p. 87, cited in A.T., X, p. 193.

[15] *Ibid.*, p. 90, in A.T., X, p. 196.

the proper method to follow. He wrote it for someone that he called Musaeus, who, writes Baillet, was later variously identified as Beeckman, Mydorge, or Mersenne.[16] Since at the time Descartes was not acquainted with Mydorge and had, as yet, no personal ties with Mersenne, the first identification is the only plausible one. Indeed, Descartes had promised Beeckman that he would write his works on mechanics and geometry as soon as he had some leisure.[17] His winter quarters were suitable, and it was while he was pondering "the way that he should follow in his quest for truth" that he heard about the Rosicrucians and their ambitious program of reforming the whole of knowledge.

A Completely New Science

Descartes' interest in the Rosicrucians will not appear completely sudden if we recollect that as early as 29 March 1619 he had written to Beeckman to contrast his "completely new science" with that of the mnemonist and hermeticist Raymond Lull.[18] A month later, he had reported a long conversation on the technique of Lull with an old man who claimed that he could hold forth on any topic for an hour, and then start again on a different subject and go on for up to 20 hours. Although Descartes thought the man "somewhat garrulous," he did not dismiss the claim as preposterous, but asked Beeckman to look up, in his personal copy of Cornelius Agrippa's *Commentary on Raymond Lull's "Ars Brevis,"* whether there was anything really ingenious in Lull's proposals.[19]

Later in his mature *Discourse on Method,* Descartes was to give no inkling of his early curiosity about mnemonics. The "art of Lully" is summarily dismissed as serving merely "to speak without judgment of things that one does not understand."[20] But the Lullian influence was probably more perva-

---

[16] *Ibid.*, vol. II, p. 406, in A.T., X, p. 191.

[17] Letter of Descartes to Beeckman, 23 April 1619, A.T., X, p. 162. In his letter to Descartes of 6 May 1619, Beeckman reminded him of this promise, (*ibid.*, p. 168). In a passage in the *Cogitationes Privatae*, we read: "I shall definitely finish my treatise by Easter and if I can find a publisher I shall have it printed as I promise today, 23 September 1620" (*ibid.*, p. 218, note *b*). Baillet, referring to the same passage, gives the date as "23 February 1620" (*ibid.*, p. 187).

[18] *Ibid.*, letter of Descartes to Beeckman, 26 March 1619, p. 156. See above, Chapter three, pp. 188–200. Raymond Lull (1235?–1316) wrote the *Ars brevis* at the beginning of the fourteenth century. It was printed in 1481 and frequently reissued thereafter. His most important follower in the sixteenth century was Cornelius Agrippa (1486–1535) whose *De Occulta Philosophia* appeared in 1531.

[19] *Ibid.*, letter of Descartes to Beeckman, 29 April 1619, p. 165, and Beeckman's reply, 6 May 1619, *ibid.*, pp. 167–169. On Lullism as on art of memory, see Frances A. Yates, *The Art of Memory*, (London: Routledge and Kegan Paul, 1966), pp. 173–198. One of Lull's basic devices consisted of a set of concentric circles, marked with letter notations standing for concepts. These circles were revolved to obtain combinations of concepts.

[20] *Discourse of Method*, Part II, A.T., VI, p. 17.

sive than Descartes realized or wished to acknowledge. The second of the four famous rules of method in the *Discourse on Method* reads "to divide each of the difficulties I examine into as many parts as possible," and the fourth "to make enumerations so complete, and reviews so comprehensive, that I could be sure of leaving nothing out."[21] It is interesting to compare these rules with the entry that Beeckman made in his *Journal* after rereading Cornelius Agrippa's *Commentary on Raymond Lull* at Descartes' request. Lull's aim in the *Ars Brevis*, he says, is "to provide a brief summary of everything, namely, he divides everything in such a way that there is nothing that cannot be reduced to some part of a division."[22]

There is one instance in which Descartes gave a brilliant display of what the art of dividing and ordering can do. This is when he debated with the alchemist Chandoux in the presence of Cardinal Bérulle and the Papal Nuncio, Cardinal Bagni, in Paris in 1628. Descartes dazzled his audience by producing a dozen plausible refutations of an obviously true statement, followed by a dozen plausible proofs of an equally false proposition.[23]

A further indication of Descartes' interest in mnemonics is a long note in the *Cogitationes Privatae* or *Private Thoughts* that he wrote between 1619 and 1621. It concerns the *Art of Memory* of a popular German writer, Lambert Schenkel:

> On reading through Schenkel's profitable trifles (in the book *De arte Memoria*), I thought of an easy way of making myself master of all I discovered through the imagination, namely through *the reduction of things to their causes*. Since all can be reduced to one it is obviously not necessary to remember all the sciences. When one understands the causes, all vanished images can easily be found again in the brain through the impression of the cause. This is the true art of memory and it is plainly contrary to his (Schenkel's) nebulous notions. Not that his art is without effect, but it occupies the whole space with *too many things* and *not in the right order. The right order is that the images should be formed in dependence on one another.* He (Schenkel) omits this which is the key to the whole mystery.
>
> I have thought of *another way; that out of unconnected images* should be composed *new images common to them all*, or that the one image should be made which should have reference not only to the one nearest to it but to them all—so that the fifth should refer to the first through a spear thrown on the ground, the middle one through a ladder on which they descend,

---

[21] *Ibid.*, pp. 18–19.

[22] Letter of Beeckman to Descartes, 6 May 1619, A.T., X, p. 168.

[23] Adrien Baillet, *Vie de Monsieur Des-Cartes*, vol. I, p. 162. Descartes makes claims for his method that have the hallmark of Lullian propaganda, as when he writes in his *Rules for the Direction of the Mind*: "By 'a method' I mean reliable rules which are easy to apply, and such that if one follows them exactly, one will never take what is false to be true or fruitlessly expend one's mental efforts, but will gradually and constantly increase one's knowledge till one arrives at a true understanding of everything within one's power" (A.T., X, pp. 371–372).

the second one through an arrow shot at it, and similarly the third should be *connected in some way* either *real or fictitious*.[24]

If we found an echo of Lullian ideas in Descartes' second and fourth rules on method, the third rule will be seen to bear some affinity with the passage I have just quoted:

> The third was to direct my thinking in an *orderly way*, by beginning with objects that were simplest and easiest to understand, in order to climb, little by little, gradually, to the knowledge of the most complex, *by supposing some order even among those objects that do not naturally precede each other*.[25]

The Ideal of Simplicity

If Descartes had already read some of the Rosicrucian manifestos, he would have known that they also recommended a universal science based on clear and straightforward language. The *Confessio*, for instance, voices this concern in moral terms:

> We must earnestly admonish you, that you put away, if not all, yet most books written by false Alchemists, who do think it but a jest, or a pastime, when they either misuse the Holy Trinity by applying it to vain things, or deceive the people with most strange figures, and dark sentences and speeches, and cozen the simple of their money; as there are nowadays too many such books set forth, which the Enemy of man's welfare doth daily, and will to the end, mingle among the good seed, thereby to make the Truth more difficult to be believed, which in herself is simple, easy, and naked.[26]

The *Raptus Philosophicus* of 1619 makes this point in its very title: *Raptus philosophicus, das ist Philosophische Offenbarungen ganz Simpel und Einfaltig gestellet, und an die Hochlöbliche und berühmte Fraternitet R.C. unterthänig geschrieben.* [*Philosophical Rapture, namely, Philosophical Revelations Very Simply and Clearly Presented, and Humbly Dedicated to the Praiseworthy and Famous Brotherhood of the Rosy Cross*].

The Rosicrucian manifestos affirm the fundamental harmony of all branches of knowledge, and ask that the true face of science be unveiled. We find analogous sentiments in Descartes' *Cogitationes Privatae*:

---

[24] *Cogitationes Privatae*, A.T., X, p. 230, translated by Frances A. Yates in *The Art of Memory*, pp. 373–374. The emphasis is mine. Yates adds that Descartes' "new idea of organizing memory on causes sounds curiously like a rationalisation of occult memory" (p. 374), and Paolo Rossi remarks that Descartes not only accepts Schenkel's terminology but also his way of raising the problem (Paolo Rossi, *Clavis Universalis* (Milan: Riccardo Ricciardi, 1960), pp. 154–155). On Schenkel, see Yates, *The Art of Memory*, pp. 299–302.

[25] *Discourse on Method*, Part II, A.T., VI, pp. 18–19, emphasis mine.

[26] Yates, *The Rosicrucian Enlightenment*, p. 305.

The sciences are now masked, but when the masks are lifted, they will be seen in their beauty. Upon inspecting the chain of the sciences, it will not appear more difficult to remember them than a series of numbers.[27]

This is why the Rosicrucians did not profess a new but a restored knowledge. "Our philosophy also," we read in the *Fama*, "is not a new invention, but [is] as Adam after his fall hath received it, and as Moses and Solomon used it."[28]

"Something Divine . . . "

We must put an end to the obfuscation of truth by pedantry and conceit. But there is more still. We must recognize a higher and purer source of knowledge than mere reason. Here is how Descartes puts it in the *Cogitationes Privatae*:

> It may seem surprising to find weighty judgments in the writings of poets rather than in those of philosophers. The reason is that the poets were driven to write by enthusiasm and the force of imagination. We have within us the sparks of knowledge, as in a flint [the Latin has "*sunt in nobis semina scientiae, ut in silice,*" literally, "we have within us the seeds of science, as in a flint"]; philosophers extract them through reason, but poets force them out through sharp blows of the imagination, so that they shine more brightly.[29]

Descartes was never to lose the conviction that poetry is above philosophy, although he never publicized it in the works he published in his own lifetime. In his posthumous *Rules for the Direction of the Mind*, written around 1629, he made the same point in speaking of the necessity of a general scientific method:

> the great minds of the past were to some extent aware of it, guided as they were by nature alone. For the human mind has something divine, in which the first seeds of useful ideas are sown. Even if neglected and stifled by unproductive studies, these seeds often bear fruit of their own accord.[30]

---

[27] *Cogitationes Privatae*, A.T., X, p. 215.

[28] Yates, *The Rosicrucian Enlightenment*, p. 295.

[29] *Cogitationes Privatae*, A.T., X, p. 217.

[30] *Ibid.*, p. 373. A few pages later, Descartes reiterates his conviction "that certain primary seeds of truth naturally implanted in human minds thrived vigorously in that unsophisticated and innocent age—seeds which have been stifled in us through our constantly reading and hearing all sorts of error," (*ibid.*, p. 376). In the *Discourse on Method*, Descartes states that he derived the general principles or first causes of everything "only from certain seeds of truth which are naturally in our souls" (*ibid.*, VI, p. 64). On the sources of the notion of "seeds of truth," see Henri Gouhier, *Les premières pensées de Descartes* (Paris: Vrin, 1968), pp. 93–94.

When discussing a proposal for a universal language in a letter to Mersenne, Descartes assumes that the primitive language had no irregularity (i.e., it was simple and regular in its flexional system and syntactical relations). Irregularities and exceptions can only come "from the corruption wrought by usage."[31] This is why Descartes is sympathetic to the search for an underlying universal language that would express the true nature of things. "I believe," he writes, "that this language is possible and that we can find the science upon which it rests. By its means, peasants would be better judges of the truth than philosophers at the present time."[32] Note how conveniently peasants will be spared the tedious task of reading what philosophers have written. The obsolescence of our departments of philosophy awaits the discovery of a universal language!

Descartes' account of the "revelation" that came to him on the night of 10–11 November begins with the words: "10 November 1619, when I was full of enthusiasm and had found the foundation of the admirable science." He did not, therefore, claim to have made his fundamental discovery "through reason" like the philosophers, but "full of enthusiasm" like the poets.[33]

The Search for Like-Minded Mathematicians

We know that Descartes was not successful in his quest for the elusive and, indeed, illusory Brothers of the Rosy Cross, but he met in Ulm in 1619 or 1620 another mathematician who was making the same attempt. This is Johann Faulhaber (1580–1635), who was converted to hermeticism by the Rosicrucians' tracts around 1613 and lived thereafter in the hope of meeting a member of the Brotherhood. In a letter written in January 1618, he wrote: "I spare no efforts to become better informed about the estimable Society of

[31] Letter of Descartes to Mersenne, 20 November 1629, A.T., I, p. 77. In a letter written in praise of his friend Guez de Balzac, Descartes explicitly stated his belief in an *ancient wisdom* that was corrupted by the passage of time: "In early and primitive times, before quarrels arose in the world, speech gladly followed the emotions of a candid soul and a certain divine force of eloquence was found in the best minds. This divine force, which flowed from a rich understanding and zeal for truth, led our forefathers out of the wild, gave them laws and established cities. It had the power to persuade and to rule" (*ibid.*, letter to an unknown correspondent, written between January and March 1628, p. 7). Descartes' views evolved on this question, since we find him writing to Mersenne in 1640 that *our words*, "which were invented at the beginning, have been, and go on, being corrected and softened by usage which achieves more in such cases than the best understanding," *ibid.*, letter to Mersenne, 4 March 1640, p. 126.

[32] *Ibid.*, p. 81. On the history of such attempts see Rossi, *Clavis Universalis*; James Knowlson, *Universal Language Schemes in England and France 1600–1800* (Toronto: University of Toronto Press, 1975); Mary M. Slaughter, *Universal Languages and Scientific Taxonomy in the Seventeenth Century* (Cambridge: Cambridge University Press, 1982).

[33] *Olympica*, A.T., X, p. 179. To Isaac Beeckman Descartes described the music of the ancients as "more powerful than ours" because they were actuated by "the sheer force of imagination" uncorrupted by theory (letter to Beeckman, 28 December 1629, A.T., I, pp. 101–102).

the Rosy Cross, but I believe it is not yet God's will that I be deemed worthy to known them."[34]

Faulhaber and Descartes

According to Daniel Lipstorp, Descartes called on Faulhaber in Ulm and, when he was asked whether he knew some geometry, he replied in such a peremptory tone of voice that Faulhaber almost burst out laughing at what he took to be an empty boast. But when Descartes showed he could answer Faulhaber's questions, he was invited to his home where he presumably saw the mathematician's "collection of instruments, models and other new inventions that would fill a room in a museum."[35] No document survives in which Descartes mentions Faulhaber by name, but we find the following autobiographical note in his *Cogitationes Privatae*:

> I saw a useful instrument for transferring all kinds of drawings. It consists of a stand with a two-legged compass. Another to trace out any kind of clock; this I could do myself. A third to measure angles of solid bodies. A fourth made of silver to measure flat surfaces and pictures. Another beautiful instrument to transfer drawings. Another tied to the leg of a speaker to measure time. Another to guide artillery missiles at night.—Peter Roth *Arithmetica Philosophica*—Benjamin Bramer.[36]

[34] Cited in Lüder Gäbe, *Descartes' Selbstkritik. Untersuchungen zur Philosophie des jungen Descartes* (Hamburg: Felix Meiner, 1972), p. 141, n. 10. Gäbe gives as his source Albert Weyermann, *Nachrichten von Gelehrten . . . aus Ulm* (Ulm, 1798), pp. 206–210. Prior to 1613, namely, before the beginning of the Rosicrucian craze, Faulhaber wrote mathematical treatises with forbidding but philosophically unproblematic titles, such as *Arithmeticus cubicossicus hortus* (Tubingen, 1604), *Usus de novo invento instrumenti alicuius Belgae* (Augsburg, 1610), *Novae geometriae & opticae inventiones, aliquot peculiarium instrumentorum* (Frankfurt, 1610), *Speculum mathematicum polytechnicum novum, tribus visionibus illustre* (Ulm, 1612). After 1613, we find the following publications: *Ansa inauditae novae & admirandae artis, quam Spiritus Dei aliquot propheticis & Biblicis numeris ad ultima usque tempora obsignare & occultare voluit* (Nuremberg, 1613), *Caelestes arcana magia, sive cabalisticus, novus, artificiosus & admirandus computus de Gog & Magog* (Nuremberg, 1613), and *Mysterium arithmeticum sive cabalistica et philosophica inventio, nova admiranda et ardua, qua numeri ratione et methodo computantur. . . . Cum illuminatissimis laudatissimisque Frat. R.C. Famae viris humiliter et syncere dicata* (Ulm, 1615). The last is one of the earliest works dedicated to the Rosicrucians. On Faulhaber, see A.G. Kästner, *Geschichte der Mathematik*, 4 vols. (Göttingen, 1796). Facsimile (Hildesheim: Georg Olms, 1970), vol. 3, pp. 29–35, 111–152. Pierre Costabel has shown that Descartes could have been inspired by Faulhaber's method of the gnomon when he wrote, sometime between 1620 and 1628, his highly original essay on polyedra (Descartes, *Exercices pour les éléments des solides. De solidorum elementa*, Pierre Costabel, ed. (Paris: Vrin, 1987), pp. 52–56, 89–90).

[35] This is stated by the editor of Faulhaber's *Fama Siderea Nova* (Ulm, 1618), quoted in Lüder Gäbe, *Descartes' Selbstkritik*, p. 16. Daniel Lipstorp's account of the meeting between Descartes and Faulhaber in his *Specimina Philosophiae Cartesianae* (Leyden, 1653) is cited in A.T., X, pp. 252–253. For a critical assessment, see Jean-Luc Marion, *Sur la théologie blanche de Descartes* (Paris: Presses Universitaires de France, 1981), pp. 196–200.

[36] *Cogitationes Privatae*, A.T., X, pp. 241–242.

The probability that this description refers to Faulhaber's private collection is heightened by the reference at the end to two mathematicians who belonged to his circle of acquaintances.[37]

Like many Cabalists, Faulhaber believed that the interpretation of number symbolism was relevant to trigonometry and astronomy. Descartes may have had him in mind when he spoke of the triangle as a "hieroglyph of the Divinity" in his early notebook.[38]

As was the wont of mathematicians, including such eminent figures as Tycho Brahe and Johann Kepler, Faulhaber published an annual calendar of astrological forecasts. For 1618 he computed that the longitude of Mars and the latitude of the Moon would both be 3° 33', and it struck him that their sum (in a cabalistic sense) is 333 + 333 = 666. The result could not fail to impress readers in a country where Luther had virtually made every verse of the Bible a household word. Indeed, we read in *Revelation*, Chapter 13, verse 18: "This calls for wisdom. If anyone has insight, let him calculate the number of the beast, for it is man's number. His number is 666." On the strength of this discovery, Faulhaber predicted that a comet would appear on 1 September 1618. Although slightly late, the heavens did not forsake him. Indeed, he received a threefold confirmation: a first comet was sighted in mid-October, a second in mid-November, and a third, much more conspicuous, at the end of the month. Faulhaber regarded himself as having scored one of the greatest astrological triumphs of all time!

The Feud over the Comets

The appearance of comets in 1618 gave rise to a veritable flood of books including works by Galileo and Kepler.[39] In Ulm itself, the rector of the gymnasium, the humanist Johann Baptist Hebenstreit, denounced the validity of Faulhaber's system of prognostications in a pamphlet entitled *A Philosophical Query Concerning the Comets*. In his haste to rush in print before the comet disappeared altogether (the third was last seen in January 1619),

---

[37] According to Lipstorp, Faulhaber asked Descartes questions out of his *Cubische Cossiger Lustgarten von allerhandt schönen Algebraisten Exempeln* (Nuremberg, 1604), and then went on to ask him more difficult questions that had been raised by Peter Roth. The book in which Roth offered solutions to Faulhaber's problems and added some of his own is the *Arithmetica philosophica* (Nuremberg, 1607) mentioned by Descartes. Benjamin Bramer (1588–1649/50) developed ideas that he had in common with Faulhaber (see A.T., X, p. 242, note *b* for the title of two of his relevant works).

[38] *Excerpta Mathematica*, A.T., X, p. 297, line 6; *Cogitationes Privatae, ibid.*, p. 229, lines 12–13.

[39] See Chapter 4, "The Challenge of the Comets," in William R. Shea, *Galileo's Intellectual Revolution* (New York: Science History Publications, 1977), pp. 75–108. In his *Principia Mathematica* published in 1687, Newton showed how the orbit of the comets could be explained by the attraction of the sun, but he continued in his private writings to speculate on the meaning of 666 in *Revelation*, Chapter 13, verse 18. See, e.g., "Fragments for a Treatise on Revelation," in Frank E. Manuel, *The Religion of Isaac Newton*, p. 116.

Hebenstreit confused the planet Mars with the bright star Arcturus.[40] When this was pointed out to him, he sought to vindicate himself by attacking what he assumed was Faulhaber's school of thought, and he published a second and more strongly worded pamphlet, *De Cabala Log-arithmo-geometro-mantica*, in 1619. Writing to Kepler on 6 October 1619, Hebenstreit explicitly calls his opponents members of "the Brotherhood of the Rosy Cross," and compares them to "a church intent on divining the last things."[41]

The quarrel between Faulhaber and Hebenstreit spread to their partisans, and anonymous tracts appeared in support of either side. Hebenstreit posed as a disciple of Kepler, who eventually joined the fray with a 30-page pamphlet entitled *Childish Canons, namely, a Chronology from Adam to the Current Year A.D. 1620*, which he signed Kleopas Herennius (an anagram of Johann Kepler), and which Hebenstreit sped through the press in Ulm in 1620.[42]

A French Bystander

We have two indications that Descartes may have become involved in this debate, at least as an interested bystander, and was probably courted by Hebenstreit who spoke French. The first occurs in a tract published in 1619 by Simbert Wehe, a friend of Hebenstreit, who was much given to punning and refers to a scholar whom he calls CASTRA, CASTRAE. This could be Descartes whose name was often spelt "des Cartes."[43] A more interesting, but no less controversial indication, is a passage in a letter dated 1 February 1620 in which Hebenstreit asks Kepler whether he received a letter entrusted to

> a certain Cartelius, a man of genuine learning and singular urbanity. I do not wish to burden my friends with ungrateful and shameless vagrants, but Cartelius seems of a different sort and really worthy of your help.[44]

The editor of Kepler's collected works, Max Caspar, suggests that Cartelius is a slip of the pen for Cartesius. Descartes could have brought a letter to Kepler in Linz, but the matter remains highly conjectural.

---

[40] This was reported to Kepler with withering scorn by Wilhelm Schickhard in a letter of 27 December 1618 (Kepler, *Gesammelte Werke*, Max Caspar, Franz Hammer, *et alii*, eds., 20 vols. to date. (Munich: C.H. Beck, 1938–), vol. 17, p. 310. The original title of Hebenstreit's book is *Cometen Fragstuck aus der reinen Philosophie* (Ulm, 1618).

[41] Letter of Hebenstreit to Kepler, 6 October 1619, Kepler, *Gesammelte Werke*, vol. 17, p. 404. Hebenstreit published a third pamphlet, *De principiis enuntiationum Dissertatio Prior*, in 1619. This also attacks the genuineness of Faulhaber's vaticination.

[42] Johann Kepler, *Kanones Pueriles, id est Chronologia von Adam biss auff diss jetz lauffende Jahr Christi 1620* (Ulm, 1620), in *Gesammelte Werke*, vol. 5, pp. 373–394.

[43] Simbert Wehe, *Postulatum Aequitatis Plenissimum* (Ulm, 1619), p. 36, quoted in Lüder Gäbe, *Descartes' Selbstkritik*, p. 16.

[44] Letter of Hebenstreit to Kepler, 1 February 1620, Kepler, *Gesammelte Werke*, vol. 17, p. 416.

Attracting Attention

Descartes may have considered that the best way of attracting the attention of the Rosicrucians was to dedicate a book to them. In his *Cogitationes Privatae* we find the following title:

> *The Mathematical Treasure Trove of Polybius, Citizen of the World.* This work lays down the true means of solving all the difficulties in the science of mathematics, and demonstrates that the human intellect can achieve nothing further on these questions. The work is aimed at certain people who promise to show us miraculous discoveries in all the sciences, its purpose being to chide them for their sluggishness and to expose the emptiness of their boasts. A further aim is to lighten the agonizing toil of those who struggle night and day with the Gordian knots of this science, and who squander their intellectual resources to no avail. The work is offered afresh to learned men throughout the world and especially to the distinguished B.R.C. (Brothers of the Rosy Cross) in Germany.[45]

To date, no one has been able to trace this book. Henri Gouhier surmises that it is the title of a projected work in which Descartes would appear on the "theatre of the world . . . wearing a mask." As a resolute defender of Descartes' "rationality," Gouhier interprets the dedication to the Rosicrucians as ironical.[46] But we need not share Gouhier's qualms about admitting that Descartes was interested in the Rosicrucian movement, for what intelligent 20-year old misses the opportunity of jumping on an exciting bandwagon that trundles through campus? Descartes may have wished to gain the respect of the elusive Rosicrucians by displaying his recent advances in mathematics. He does not seem to have been reluctant, for instance, to speak of the Cabala of the Germans in a mathematical note of uncertain date but surely prior to 1629. Having explained some trigonometrical relationships, he concludes:

> From these we can deduce an infinite number of theorems, and easily explain the arithmetical progressions that include the bases or the sides of all triangles of this nature, thereby imitating the Cabala of the Germans.[47]

This may involve a reference to one of Faulhaber's books, the *Mysterium arithmeticum sive cabalistica et philosophica inventio qua numeri ratione et methodo computantur*, which is dedicated, like the *Thesaurus mathematicus* of Polybius

---

[45] *Cogitationes Privatae*, A.T., X, p. 214.

[46] Henri Gouhier, *Les premières pensées de Descartes* (Paris: Vrin, 1958), p. 110. I find no irony in the following remark with which we are already acquainted: "The sciences are at present masked, but if the masks were taken off, they would be revealed in all their beauty. If we could see how the sciences are linked together, we would find them no harder to retain in our minds than the series of numbers." (*Cogitationes Privatae*, A.T., X, p. 215).

[47] *Excerpta Mathematica*, A.T., X, p. 297.

the Cosmopolitan, to the Rosicrucians. This would explain the words "of-fered afresh" in the last sentence of the extended title I have quoted above.

The Hermeticist or the Mathematician?

It is tempting at this stage in our narrative to exclaim, "But Descartes was interested in Faulhaber, the mathematician, not Faulhaber, the Hermeticist!" But was this distinction, so obvious to us, equally clear in the sixteenth and seventeenth centuries? That this was not the case is brought home if we consider two distinguished editors of Euclid, John Dee in England and François de Foix de Candalle in France. Dee wrote a lengthy preface to the first English translation of Euclid, but he lavished much more time on the *Monas Hieroglyphica*, a lengthy treatise on a mystical sign composed out of the characters of the seven planets. Candalle translated Euclid into French, but also the Pimander of Hermes Trismegistus. The great French librarian Gabriel Naudé provides additional evidence. When he lists Rosicrucians in 1623, he gives not only the names of Dee and Candalle, but also those of Oxford mathematicians, such as John Hentisbury and Richard Swineshead.[48]

The Science of Miracles

Mathematicians were often considered magicians because of the wonders they worked. John Dee complains of being falsely accused of being a "conjurer" because of his mathematical skill and his ability to produce mechanical marvels.[49] Descartes, like Dee, was very interested in mechanical devices and optical illusions. He read Giambattista della Porta's *Magia Naturalis* and jotted down in his *Cogitationes Privatae* how mirrors could be used to make "chariots and tongues of fire" as well as other shapes appear in the air.[50]

---

[48] Gabriel Naudé, *Instruction á la France sur la vérité de l'histoire des Frères de la Rose-Croix*, p. 31.

[49] *The Elements of the Geometrie of the Most Ancient Philosopher Euclide of Megara, Faithfully (now first) translated into the English toung, by H. Billingsley, Citizen of London . . . With a Very Fruitful Preface Made by M.J. Dee* (London, 1570), quoted in Francis A. Yates, *The Theatre of the World* (Chicago: Chicago University Press, 1969), p. 31. Dee's *Preface* is available in a facsimile edition with a useful introduction by Allen G. Debus, *The Mathematical Preface to the Elements of the Geometrie of Euclid of Megara (1570)* (New York: Science History Publications, 1975).

[50] *Cogitationes Privatae*, A.T., X, pp. 215–216. See John Baptista Porta, *Natural Magick* (anon. translation) (London: Thomas Young and Samuel Speed, 1658). Facsimile (New York: Basic Books, 1957). Book XVII, chapters 2, 4, 5, 6, 7, and 10 discuss this kind of optical trick. The first edition of the *Magia Naturalis sive de miraculis rerum naturalium* in four books appeared in Naples in 1558 and was reprinted at least thirteen times between 1560 and 1588, not counting the numerous reprints of the Italian, French, and German versions. The second edition in twenty books was published in Naples in 1589, and was frequently reprinted, as well as translated into Italian, French, German, and English. See Luisa Muraro, *Giambattista della Porta mago e scienziato* (Milan: Feltrinelli, 1978), and Geneviève Rodis-Lewis, "Machineries et perspectives curieuses dans leurs rapports avec le

When Beeckman and Descartes met again in the Netherlands, Beeckman mentioned to Descartes that Cornelius Agrippa claimed that letters could be inscribed on the face of the moon, and that in this way a message could be transmitted to persons at some distant point on the earth provided the sky was clear. Descartes immediately replied that della Porta thought this could be achieved with lenses.[51]

Celestial Conversations

Descartes and Beeckman believed that the magnifying power of the new spyglasses could be greatly enhanced. Indulging in early science fiction, they speculated that if we could make telescopes powerful enough to observe the inhabitants of the moon and found them as well equipped as we are, we might ask them to signal to us what is going on in the southern hemisphere.[52]

To the French lens-maker, Jean Ferrier, whom he wanted to hire as his assistant, Descartes wrote on 13 November 1629, "I venture to hope that, with your aid, we will see whether there are living beings on the moon."[53] In the *Optics* that he published in 1637, Descartes reaffirmed his conviction that if the skill of the workers did not fail him he would be able "to see on celestial bodies objects as particular and as small as those we commonly see on earth."[54]

Descartes also hoped that Ferrier would help him develop "what I call the science of miracles because it teaches how to use air and light in such a way that we can perform all the illusions that magicians are said to make with the help of demons."[55] The *Meteors*, published with the *Discourse on Method*

---

cartésianisme," *XVIIe Siècle*, no. 32 (1956), pp. 461–474. Compare the following passages: (1) *Cogitationes Privatae*, A.T., X, 209, and *Natural Magick*, Book XX, Chapter 9, p. 408 on making bystanders appear colored; (2) *Cogitationes Privatae*, A.T., X, p. 244 and *Natural Magick*, Book XVI, Chapter 2, p. 341 on making invisible ink readable by heating the paper; (3) *Cogitationes Privatae*, A.T., X, p. 244 and *Natural Magick*, Book IV, Chapter 5, p. 332 on fishing with a submerged candle; (4) *Cogitationes Privatae*, A.T., X, p. 232 and *Natural Magick*, Book XX, Chapter 10, p. 409 on a mechanical dove.

[51] Isaac Beeckman, *Journal*, A.T., X, p. 347. This entry was made around 1 February 1629. After musing on the possible applications of parabolic mirrors that "burn at an infinite distance," della Porta concludes: "I have observed, that we may use this Artifice in great and wonderful things, and chiefly for inscribing letters on a full Moon" (*Natural Magick*, Book XVII, Chapter 17, p. 376). Agrippa speaks of raising letters and reading them on the disk of the moon "as was done by Pythagoras," but he does not claim he knows how to do it (Henricus Cornelius Agrippa of Nettesheim, *De Occulta Philosophia*, Book I, Chapter 6, cited in A.T., X, p. 347, from the *Opera Omnia*, Lyons, 1600, vol. I, p. 347).

[52] Isaac Beeckman, *Journal*, A.T., X, p. 347. In the same year, Mersenne expressed to Galileo the hope that the new telescope would reveal whether there are living beings on the moon (letter of 1 February 1629, in *Correspondance du Père Marin Mersenne*, vol. II, pp. 175–176).

[53] Letter of Descartes to Ferrier, 13 November 1619, A.T., I, p. 61.

[54] *Optics*, Ninth Discourse, A.T., VI, p. 206.

[55] Letter of Descartes to an unknown correspondent, probably written in September 1629, A.T., I, p. 21.

and the *Optics* in 1637, bears witness to Descartes' abiding fascination with this "science of miracles." He tells, for instance, of a way of using his newly acquired knowledge of the formation of rainbows "to make signs appear in the sky that could cause great wonder in those who are ignorant of the cause."[56]

The Rule of the Brotherhood of the Rosy-Cross

If the first reason why Parisians suspected Descartes of being a Rosicrucian was his recent sojourn in Germany, a second may be found in the Rule of the Brotherhood as it was set out in the *Fama Fraternitatis*, which comprised six short articles whereby the members were enjoined: 1) to cure the sick free of charge; 2) to wear no special habit but follow the custom of the country in which they happened to be; 3) to meet once a year; 4) to find a worthy person to succeed them; 5) to use C.R. as their seal; and 6) to maintain the Fraternity secret for 100 years.

I shall indicate briefly how, in the heated Parisian climate of 1623, these rules could have been seen as fitting Descartes' behavior.

Prolonging Life

Although he was not a licensed physician, Descartes followed the first rule. He gave free medical advice to his friends, usually with the request that they tell no one.[57] In 1629 Descartes turned seriously to the study of medicine, which he hoped to "base on infallible demonstrations,"[58] and, when he wrote the *Discourse on Method* in 1637, he expressed the greatest hope in the future of medicine: "If it is possible to find some means of making men in general wiser and more skillful than they have been up till now, I believe we must look for it in medicine."[59] In 1645 he wrote to the Marquis of Newcastle: "The preservation of health has been *at all times* the *main goal* of my studies."[60]

Descartes was convinced that life could be prolonged, and he confided to Constantin Huygens that he hoped to live more than 100 years (the

---

[56] *Meteors*, Eighth Discourse, A.T., VI, p. 343.

[57] Descartes gave medical advice to Mersenne for their mutual friend Claude Clerselier, but requested that it be imparted to those who attended him "without their knowing in any way that it comes from me" (letter to Mersenne of 23 November 1646, A.T., IV, p. 566). In the same year, he gave advice to an acquaintance who suffered from nose-bleeding with the same proviso (*ibid.*, p. 698).

[58] Letter to Descartes to Mersenne, January 1630, A.T., I, p. 106; see also his letter to Mersenne of 18 December 1629 (*ibid.*, p. 102). See Richard B. Carter, *Descartes' Medical Philosophy* (Baltimore: Johns Hopkins University Press, 1983).

[59] *Discourse on Method*, A.T., VI, p. 62.

[60] Letter of Descartes to the Marquis of Newcastle, October 1645, A.T., IV, p. 329, emphasis mine.

Rosicrucians generally aimed at 120) and that he was writing a medical treatise to that end.[61] The testimony of Claude Picot, the French translator of the *Principles of Philosophy*, is particularly striking in this respect. He spent three months with Descartes in Holland in 1647, and when he returned to France,

> he resolutely gave up high living, to which he had not hitherto been opposed, and adopted M. Descartes' diet in the belief that it was the only way of ensuring the success of the secret method that he claimed that our Philosopher had found to make men live *four or five hundred years.*[62]

According to Baillet, Picot was so convinced of the efficacy of Descartes' regimen that he was ready to swear:

> that barring an unusual and violent cause (such as the one that put his machine out of order in Sweden) he would have lived five hundred years, having discovered the art of living for several centuries.[63]

According to Des Maizeaux, Kenelm Digby visited Descartes in the Netherlands around this time and urged him to devote his efforts to finding means of prolonging life. To which Descartes replied "that he had thought about the matter, and that although he could not promise to render man immortal he was certain that he could render his life as long as that of the Patriarchs."[64] Since, with the exception of Enoch who departed from the earth at 365 years of age, the ages of the Patriarchs vary from 777 (Lamech) to 969 (Methuselah), Descartes may be said to have had high expectations! These were not fulfilled and, by the spring of 1648, when he was interviewed by Frans Burman, he had given up the hope of reaching such a ripe old age. "How life was so vastly extended before the Flood is something that is beyond philosophy," he said to the young man. But he had not abandoned his conviction that life could be extended and added: "We must not doubt that human life could be extended if we knew the proper art."[65] When Descartes died in Stockholm at the age of 53, the *Gazette* of Antwerp scoffed at his alleged claims of longevity. "A fool, who said he could live as long as he wished,

---

[61] Letter of Descartes to Constantin Huygens, 4 December 1637, A.T., I, p. 649. In his letter to Descartes of 25 January 1642, Huygens refers to Descartes' treatise on "Extending Life" which he assumes is nearing completion (A.T., III, p. 779).

[62] Adrien Baillet, *Vie de Monsieur Des-Cartes*, vol. II, p. 448. Descartes favoured a light diet with plenty of vegetables and fruits. He also believed that wearing a wig was particularly good for the health, and he recommended it to Picot as a way of avoiding colds and headaches (*ibid.*, p. 446).

[63] *Ibid.*, pp. 452–453.

[64] Des Maizeaux, "La vie de monsieur de Saint-Evremond," in *Oeuvres de Saint-Evremond* (Amsterdam, 1726), cited in A.T., XI, p. 671. The text is dated 15 November 1706.

[65] *Conversation with Burman*, A.T., V, p. 178.

has died in Sweden."[66] Discreet as he may have tried to be, Descartes had acquired, like the disciples of Robert Fludd, the reputation of being a "long-liver."

The second Rosicrucian rule enjoined the brothers to dress and live like everyone else, and Descartes was careful to do just this. He was anxious not to appear singular in his dress or his person.[67] When he heard of Galileo's condemnation in 1633, he wrote to Mersenne that he had decided not to publish his cosmological treatise *Le Monde*, in keeping with his motto, "*bene vixit, bene qui latuit* (he who lives in obscurity lives happily)".[68]

The third and fourth rules enjoined the brothers to meet once a year and find a successor. The fifth rule declared that R.C. should be the only seal or mark of the Brotherhood. This has given rise to much speculation, especially when conjoined with the following passage from the *Fama Fraternitatis*:

> After a time there will be a general reformation, both of divine and human things . . . in the meantime some few, who shall give their names, may join together, thereby to make a happy and wished for beginning of our *Philosophical Canons*, prescribed to us by our brother R.C..[69]

R.C., of course, are the initials of Renatus Cartesius. But as Etienne Gilson sensibly remarked, "If René Descartes had been called Pierre Gassendi, the argument from the seal would be singularly stronger."[70]

A Very Private Scholar

The sixth and final rule that prescribes secrecy about the Brotherhood is not particularly helpful, since we can hardly use silence about the society as evidence of membership. Nevertheless, there is a curious text in Descartes' early notebook that has never been elucidated:

---

[66] Cited in Christiaan Huygens' letter to his brother Constantin, 12 April 1650, A.T., X, p. 630. The prolongation of life was discussed by several authors since Roger Bacon in the thirteenth century. Bacon referred to Scripture to prove the possibility of living almost 1,000 years, and like Descartes, he emphasized a sane and moderate diet. For a short survey of Bacon's views, see the chapter "De retardatione accidentium senectutis, et de prolongatione vitae humane," in his *Epistola de secretis operibus artis et naturae et de nullitate magiae*, in Roger Bacon, *Opera quaedam hactenus inedita* (J.S. Brewer, ed. (London: Longman, 1859), vol. I, pp. 538–542).

[67] "He especially avoided dressing like a philosopher" (Adrien Baillet, *Vie de Monsieur Descartes*, vol. II, p. 447).

[68] Letter of Descartes to Mersenne, April 1634, A.T., I, p. 286.

[69] Yates, *The Rosicrucian Enlightenment*, p. 294.

[70] Etienne Gilson, *Etudes sur le rôle de la pensée médiévale dans la formation du système cartésien* (Paris: Vrin, 1967), p. 278.

Actors, taught not to let any embarrassment show on their faces, put on a mask. I will do the same. So far, I have been a spectator in this theatre which is the world, but I am now about to mount the stage, and I come forward masked.[71]

Descartes was to remain a very retiring person all his life. When he visited Paris, he usually stayed at the house of Nicolas Le Vasseur, Seigneur d'Etioles, a friend of his father, but in 1628 he sought lodgings elsewhere to avoid importunate visitors and "make himself visible to only a very small number of friends."[72]

Later, in the Netherlands, he became notorious for his love of privacy. The physician Vopiscus-Fortunatus Plempius states that around 1629 Descartes lived in the Kalverstraat in Amsterdam "unknown to anyone (*Nulli notus*)."[73] Here is what a fellow Frenchman has to say about him when he came to Leyden to supervise the printing of the *Discourse on Method* in 1637:

He has been in town since they began printing his book, but he hides and only shows himself very rarely. In this country, he always lives in some small and remote town. Some say that this is how he got the name d'Escartes [namely the Man-who-lives-apart] for he used to be called something else.[74]

The Quest for Sympathies

If Descartes' Parisian friends had had access to his *Compendium Musicae*, they might have been strengthened in their suspicion that he was not opposed to explanations couched in terms of occult forces, as when he avers that

the human voice is pleasant because it agrees with our dispositions. What makes the voice of a friend more agreeable than that of an enemy is probably the sympathy or antipathy that we experience. For the same reason, a drum covered with the skin of a lamb ceases to vibrate and becomes silent when, as we are told, its sound sets up a resonance in another drum covered with the skin of a wolf.[75]

The source of this story could again be della Porta who gives two versions of it:

The Wolf is hurtful and odious to sheep after he is dead: for if you can cover a drum with a wolf's skin, the sound of it will make the sheep

---

[71] *Cogitationes Privatae*, A.T., X, p. 213.

[72] Adrien Baillet, *Vie de Monsieur Des-Cartes*, vol. I, p. 153.

[73] V.P. Plempius, *Fundamenta Medicinae*, 3rd edition (Louvain, 1654), cited in A.T., I, p. 401.

[74] Letter of Claude de Saumaise to M. de Puy, 4 April 1637, cited in A.T., X, pp. 555–556. When Descartes first came to Holland in 1618, he called himself du Perron (e.g., A.T., X, pp. 56, 153, 160, 161, 164, 166).

[75] *Compendium Musicae*, A.T., X, p. 90.

afraid . . . if you hang several skins one against the other . . . the Wolf's skin eats up the Lamb's skin.[76]

There is Antipathy between Sheep and Wolves, as I said often, and it remains in all their parts; so that an Instrument strung with Sheep strings, mingled with strings made of a Wolf's guts, will make no music, but jar, and make all discords."[77]

There is always, of course, the possibility of a mechanical explanation of such phenomena, as Descartes urged in 1644 in the Fourth Part of his *Principles of Philosophy*.[78] But in 1619, we may wonder whether he would not have been sympathetic to explanations of the kind della Porta offers for "infected mirrors." Della Porta informs us in Book I of the *Magia Naturalis* that a harlot possesses a "virtue" such that "if someone often looks at himself in her mirror, or puts on her clothes, he will become as insolent and lewd as she is."[79] Seven books later, having kept us on epistemological, if not moral, tenterhooks, he offers the following explanation:

> The polished mirror fears the look of an immoral woman, as Aristotle says, for her look soils it and reduces its splendour. This is because the vapour of her blood coalesces on the surface of the mirror.[80]

I hasten to add that we do not find this explanation in Descartes' own writings: nonetheless, in a fragment dated 1631, we read:

> Spirits are exhaled through the eyes as can be seen in menstruating women whose eyes are said to emit vapours. The whole body of a woman is

---

[76] Della Porta, *Natural Magick*, Book I, Chapter 14, pp. 19–20.

[77] *Ibid.*, Book XX, Chapter 7, p. 403. Della Porta ascribes this view to Pythagoras. The earliest source that I have come across is Fracastoro's book on *Sympathy and Antipathy* of 1550 in which he writes, "striking a drum made of the skin of a wolf will, they say, shatter drums made of the skin of lambs" (H. Fracastoro, *De Sympathia et Antipathia Rerum* (Lyons, 1550), p. 22). There are many variants on this theme. For instance, Burton applies it to Jan Zizka, the fifteenth-century national hero of Bohemia: "The great captain Zisca would have a drum made of his skin when he was dead because he thought the very noise of it would put his enemies to flight" (Robert Burton, *The Anatomy of Melancholy*, first published in 1621. Everyman's Library reprints the 6th edition of 1651, 3 vols. (London: Dent, 1932), vol. I, p. 38).

[78] After stating that he has explained all the properties of magnets and fire by "the shape, size, position and motion of particles of matter," Descartes adds: "And anyone who considers all this will readily be convinced that there are no powers in stones and plants that are so mysterious, and no marvels attributed to sympathetic and antipathetic influences, that are so astonishing, that they cannot be explained in this way" (*Principles of Philosophy*, Part IV, article 187, A.T., VIII–1, pp. 314–315). The French version of Picot adds the following marvels—not mentioned in the original Latin version—said to result from the motion of parts of the first element: (1) "making the wounds of a dead man bleed when the murderer draws near, (2) exciting the imagination of those who are asleep (or even awake) and giving them ideas that warn them of what is happening far away" (A.T., IX–2, p. 309).

[79] Della Porta, *Natural Magick*, Book I, Chapter 13, p. 19. I have modernized the translation.

[80] *Ibid.*, Book VIII, Chapter 14, p. 230. I have modernized the translation.

full of vapours when she has her days. The heavier humour is purged through the vagina, the subtler higher up, namely, through the eyes.[81]

In his early notebook, we find this cryptic sentence about women and science:

Science is like a woman: if she stays faithful to her husband she is respected; if she becomes common property she grows to be despised.[82]

We also know that about this time Descartes read Campanella's *De sensu rerum et magia libri quatuor, pars mirabilis occultae philosophiae, ubi demonstratur mundum esse Dei vivam Statuam beneque cognoscentem* (Frankfurt, 1620), which he described, some fifteen years later, as having left no impression on him except one of superficiality.[83] By then, however, Descartes was years away from the intellectual atmosphere of his youth and quite unwilling to let his memory challenge the role he had learned to play on the theatre of the world. This is not to say that his escape was complete.

Dutch Echoes

The rumor that he was a Rosicrucian followed Descartes to the Netherlands where it appeared in print for the first time in a lampoon entitled *Admiranda Methodus Novae Philosophiae Renati Descartes* published in Utrecht in 1643. The book is anonymous but is probably the work of Martin Schook who wrote the Preface.[84] In his satirical *Nouveaux mémoires pour servir à l'histoire du cartésianisme* published at the end of the seventeenth century, Daniel Huet describes Descartes as the perfect Rosicrucian. "I renounced marriage," he has him say, "I led a wandering life, I sought obscurity and isolation, I abandoned the study of geometry and of the other sciences to apply myself exclusively to philosophy, medicine, chemistry, the cabala and other secret sciences."[85]

Huet writing in 1692 is not a reliable source of information about the working of Descartes' mind more than half a century earlier, but it proves

---

[81] A.T., XI, p. 602. The passage in Aristotle that is the source of the remarks of both Della Porta and Descartes occurs in *On Dreams* II, 459 b 28–31: "If a woman looks into a highly polished mirror during the menstrual period, the surface of the mirror becomes clouded with a blood-red colour" (Aristotle, *On the Soul. Parva Naturalia. On Breath*, W.S. Kett, trans., Loeb Classical Library (London: Heinemann, 1975), p. 357.

[82] *Cogitationes Privatae*, A.T., X, p. 214.

[83] Letter of Descartes to Constantin Huygens, March 1638, A.T., II, p. 48.

[84] The author says that he does not believe the imputation because Descartes is too vain to accept the rule of silence of the Brotherhood (A.T., VIII–2, p. 142, note b).

[85] Pierre-Daniel Huet, *Nouveaux mémoires pour servir à l'histoire du cartésianisme* par M.G. de l'A. (initials of Gilles de l'Aunay, the pseudonym used by Huet) (Paris, 1692), p. 42, cited in Henri Gouhier, *Les premières pensées de Descartes*, p. 128.

that the charge of being a Rosicrucian, levelled in 1623, stuck. Nicolas Poisson, in his *Commentaire ou Remarques sur la Méthode de René Descartes*, published in 1670, goes out of his way to vindicate Descartes of this accusation. His main argument, arrived at with all the advantages of hindsight, is quite simply that Descartes "was too sophisticated to be a friend of these visionaries who rest all their arguments on empirical evidence rather than on reasoning."[86]

Descartes' Dreams

The interesting question, of course, is whether this lengthy discussion of the Rosicrucian atmosphere (or craze) can shed light on Descartes' intellectual outlook. I believe that it can help us understand the famous autobiographical passage in the *Discourse on Method* where Descartes tells us how he discovered his new method:

> At the time I was in Germany, where I had been called by the wars that are not yet ended there. While I was returning to the army from the coronation of the Emperor, the onset of winter detained me in quarters where, finding no conversation to divert me and fortunately having no cares of passions to trouble me, I stayed all day shut up alone in a stove-heated room, where I was completely free to commune with my own thoughts.[87]

The exact location of Descartes' winter quarters is not known, but Daniel Lipstorp, writing in 1653, three years after Descartes' death, suggests a village near Ulm, where the mathematician Faulhaber lived.[88]

"Finding no conversation to divert me and fortunately having no cares of passions to trouble me . . . I was completely free to commune with my own thoughts." How detached and serenely philosophical all this sounds! The mature Descartes would have us believe that he arrived at his insight in the posture a sculptor would choose to represent "the thinker." It is, in fact, a posture. In 1619, Descartes described the change in his life in a language far removed from the cool and calm prose of the *Discourse on Method*. It is couched in the language of dreams and, although the twelve-page manu-

---

[86] A.T., X, p. 197, note a.

[87] *Discourse on Method*, Part II, A.T., VI, p. 11.

[88] Daniel Lipstorp, *Specimina Philosophiae Cartesianae* (Leiden: Elzevier, 1653), pp. 78–79, cited A.T., X, p. 252. Adrien Baillet, in his two volume *Vie de Monsieur Des-Cartes*, published in 1691, does not identify Descartes' winter retreat in 1619, but has him sojourn in Ulm from the end of June to the beginning of September (vol. I, p. 96). In the abridged version that he published a year later, he states without further explanation that Descartes took up his winter quarters in the Duchy of Neuburg in October 1619 (*Abrégé de la vie de M. Descartes* (Paris, 1692), p. 39. The book is reprinted in the Collection "Les Grandeurs" (n.p.: La Table Ronde, 1946), where the relevant passage occurs on p. 33). Neuburg is not near Ulm but is situated on the Danube in Northern Bavaria a few kilometers to the west of Ingolstadt.

script in which he wrote out a detailed account of his visionary experience has vanished, it was seen by Leibniz during his visit to Paris in 1675–1676, and it was translated by Baillet in the first volume of his biography.[89]

Descartes records that on the night of 10–11 November 1619 he had, in rapid succession, not one but three dreams "which he imagined could only come from on high." In the first dream, he was frightened by ghosts and buffeted by a strong wind that kept him from going where he wanted to go. The imagery is vivid and would have meant more to a seventeenth-century hermeticist than it does to us. He felt, for instance, a weakness on the right side, a whirlwind made him spin three or four times on his left foot, others walked straight while he wavered, and so forth. Descartes woke up in a fright, confessed his sins to the Almighty, and fell asleep again. The second dream ended with a piercing noise like a clap of thunder. On opening his eyes,

> he perceived a large number of fiery sparks all around him in the room. *This had often happened* to him at other times; *it was nothing extraordinary for him* to wake in the middle of the night and find his eyes sparkling to such a degree as to give him glimpses of the objects nearest to him.[90]

Quite a feat, even for a philosopher!

The third dream, which followed fast upon the second, was peaceful by contrast. He saw a book that he took for a dictionary, and a collection of poems, which he opened at random. He fell on a poem by Ausonius that began "Quod vitae sectabor iter?" At that moment an unknown person handed him another poem which began with "*Est & Non.*" It then occurred to Descartes, in the midst of this dream, to ask himself whether he was dreaming. He not only concluded that he was dreaming but started to

---

[89] Adrien Baillet, *Vie de Monsieur Des-Cartes*, vol. I, pp. 81–86, in A.T., X, pp. 181–188. This passage is translated in Norman Kemp Smith, *New Studies in the Philosophy of Descartes* (London, Macmillan, 1952), pp. 33–39. Descartes gave the Latin manuscript the title *Olympica.* It is not clear why, but the word belongs to the hermetic and Paracelsian tradition. Among popular emblems in Descartes' day, Olympian meant, "*Soli in Deo Securitas* (Only in God Is There Security)," as we find in Henrico de Soto, *Emblemas Moralizadas* (Madrid, 1599), p. 26 *b* (quoted in Arthur Henkel and Albrecht Schöne, *Emblemata. Handbuch zur Sinnbildung des 16. und 17. Jahrhunderts* (Stuttgart: Metzler), 1976, p. 60). At the College of La Flèche, students made and interpreted emblems on feast days. See Camille de Rochemonteix, *Un Collège des Jésuites aux XVIIᵉ et XVIIIᵉ Siècles. Le Collège Henri IV de la Flèche*, 4 vols. (Le Mans: Leguicheux, 1889), vol. I, pp. 146–150. The text began with the famous words, "*X Novembris 1619, cum plenus forem Enthousiasmo, et mirabilis scientiae fundamenta reperirem* (10 November 1619, as I was filled with enthusiasm and had found the foundations of a marvellous science)." Baillet mentions a note in the margin written in the same hand with a different ink, "*XI Novembris 1620, coepi intelligere fundamentum Inventi mirabilis*" (A.T., X, p. 179; see also the inventory of Descartes' papers, *ibid.*, p. 7).

[90] A.T., X, p. 182, emphasis mine, N. Kemp Smith, trans., p. 35. In the *Optics*, Descartes states that light streams out of the eyes of cats, and he implies that this is also the case for men who rise above the ordinary . . . (A.T., VI, p. 86.). Was he thinking of exceptional people like himself? According to Sextus Empiricus, the Emperor Tiberius could see in the dark (*Outline of Pyrrhonism*, Book I, Chapter 14, p. 84, R.G. Bury, trans., Loeb Classical Library (London: Heinemann, 1976), vol. I, p. 51).

interpret the dream while still asleep. When he awoke, "he continued the interpretation of the dream on the same lines."

Note the continuity between the sleeping and the waking state. He judged the dictionary to be the "sciences gathered together," the collection of poems, "the union of philosophy and wisdom," and the poets assembled in the collection, the "revelation and inspiration, by which he hoped to see himself favoured." The *"Est & Non"* of the poem he interpreted as "the Yes and No of Pythagoras," meaning truth and error in human knowledge and the secular sciences. The clap of thunder that he heard in the second dream he took to be "the signal of the Spirit of truth descending to take possession of him." Lest this new Pentecost be greeted like the first one with jeers ("They are filled with new wine," *Acts* 2, 13), Descartes, like Peter before him, affirms that he was not drunk, having "passed the evening and the whole day in a condition of complete sobriety," and, for that matter, not having touched wine for three months![91]

Descartes' dream was an intensely personal experience, but he may also have welcomed it as a literary device that allowed the use of symbols that would appear incongruous if the narrator were in the waking state. Every educated person in the seventeenth century was familiar with the Dream of Scipio and knew from both biblical and classical sources that God communicates with men in dreams. As a poetico-philosophical device, it was common in the sixteenth century. But what about the seventeenth century, and, to return to our topic, what about the Rosicrucian treatises? I have already mentioned the *Raptus philosophicus* published in German in 1619. This is the account of the dream of a young man at the crossroads. He wonders what path to take and—one readily guesses—chooses the straight and narrow. After several dangerous incidents, he meets a young woman who asks him: "Where are you going? What Spirit brings you here?" and shows him a book "that contained all that is in earth and in heaven but not ordered methodically." A young man, dressed in white, then reveals to him that this woman "is Nature . . . at the present time unknown to scientists and philosophers."[92]

Henri Gouhier acknowledges the resemblances between this work and Descartes' dream, but he dismisses them as *"une influence purement*

---

[91] *Ibid.*, pp. 182–186.

[92] Rodophilus Staurophorus, *Raptus Philosophicus*, quoted in P. Arnold, *La Rose-Croix et ses rapports avec la Franc-Maçonnerie* (Paris: G.-P. Maisonneuve et Larose, 1970), pp. 160–161. On the importance of dreams, see André Chastel, *Marsile Ficin et l'art* (Geneva: Droz, 1954), pp. 147–148, and notes on p. 154; Jean-Marie Wagner, "Esquisse du cadre divinatoire des songes de Descartes," *Baroque*, 6 (1973), pp. 81–95. In Cicero's widely read *De Divinatione*, Quintus, Cicero's interlocutor, remarks: "The Stoic view of divination smacked too much of superstition. I was more impressed by the arguments of the Peripatetics and Dicaearchus, among the Ancients, and of our contemporary Cratippus. According to them there is within the human soul some sort of power—'oracular' I might call it—by which the future is foreseen when the soul is inspired by a divine frenzy, or when it is released by sleep and is free to move at will" (Cicero, *De Senectute, De Amicitia, De Divinatione*, W.A. Falconer, trans. (London: Heinemann, 1923, p. 483).

ornamentale."[93] In the light of Descartes' subsequent intellectual development this sounds plausible, but I cannot help wondering whether Gouhier is not making too little of what may have been a brief, but not necessarily a superficial, phase in his life. Baillet tells us that Descartes explicitly states that he had been *expecting* some significant dreams for several days:

> He adds that the Genius that produced the enthusiasm with which his brain had been inflamed for several days had predicted these dreams to him before he went to bed, and that the human mind had no share in them.[94]

Descartes concluded that the third dream "signified the future and that its sole purpose was to indicate what would happen to him in the rest of his life."[95] Although he changed residence repeatedly between 1619 and 1650, he never parted with the manuscript of his dreams, and there is no reason to believe that it did not play in his life a role analogous to the famous *Memorial* of the night of 23 November 1654 that Pascal sewed into the lining of his waistcoat and kept close to his heart to his dying day.

Our acquaintance with the vast Renaissance literature on dreams is too slight to allow us to see Descartes' account against a background that was so familiar in his day as not to be considered worth mentioning. Francesco Trevisani has drawn attention to Cardano's symbolic interpretations of dreams, but there are scores of such works to be explored.[96] A famous contemporary of Descartes, J.B. Van Helmont, gives 1610 as the date of his own enlightenment:

> In the years 1610 after a long weariness of contemplation, that I might acquire some gradual knowledge of my own minde, since I was then of opinion, that self-cognition was the Complement of wisdom, fallen by chance into a calm sleep, and wrapt beyond the limits of reason, I seemed to be in a Hall sufficiently obscure. On my left hand was a table, and on it a faire large Vial, wherein was a small quantity of Liquor: and a voice from that liquor spake unto me: "Wilt thou Honour and Riches?"[97]

The Inner Voice

Descartes went on to become the father of modern rationalism, but he never wavered in his belief in the role of inspiration. To Princess Elizabeth with

---

[93] Henri Gouhier, *Les premières pensées de Descartes*, p. 140.

[94] A.T., X, p. 186, N. Kemp Smith, trans., p. 38.

[95] *Ibid.*, p. 185, p. 37.

[96] Francesco Trevisani, "Symbolisme et interprétation chez Descartes et Cardan," *Rivista Critica di Storia della Filosofia*, XXX (1975), pp. 27–47.

[97] J.P. Van Helmont, *Ternary of Paradoxes*, Walter Charleton, trans. (London, J. Flesher, 1650), p. 123.

whom he entertained a free and easy correspondence, he expressed himself clearly on the subject. After mentioning that a happy frame of mind makes things appear brighter, he pursues:

I am even bold enough to believe that inner joy has a secret force to make Fortune more favourable. I would not write this to people with weak minds lest they should be led to superstition, but, in the case of your Highness, I rather fear that she will laugh at my credulity. But *I have a very large number of experiences*, as well as the authority of Socrates, to confirm my opinion. I have often noticed that what I undertake gladly and without inner repugnance generally goes well even in games of chance where Fortune alone holds the sway.[98]

Note that Descartes not only believed in his inner voice, but claimed that he had "a very large number of experiences" (in French "*une infinité d'expériences*") that confirmed its reliability.

The young Descartes' interest in hermeticism helps us understand why he attached such deep significance to his threefold dream. I believe it also casts light on his ready and willing enthusiasm for a cosmic scheme that would embrace the stars. Descartes was to become more cautious as he grew older, but as late as 1632, when he was 36 years old, he could still write to Mersenne as someone who is about to fulfil the abiding dream of the astrologers:

In the last two or three months, I have penetrated deeply into the heavens and having satisfied myself about its nature and that of the celestial bodies that we see, as well as many other things that I would not even have dared to hope a few years ago, I have become so bold that I now dare to seek the cause of the position of each star. Even if they appear to be strewn haphazardly in the heavens, I do not doubt that there is a regular, fixed and natural order among them. Knowledge of this order is the key and the foundation of the highest and most perfect science that man can have about natural things. The more so, since, by its means, we could know *a priori* all the varied forms and essences of terrestrial bodies, whereas, without it, we have to rest content with guessing them *a posteriori* and by their effects.[99]

After stating that the observation of comets and a historical catalogue of the position of heavenly bodies would be of assistance, Descartes reverts, but this time with a tremor in his voice, to his grandiose project:

I think it is a science that surpasses human understanding, but I have so little wisdom that I cannot help myself from dreaming about it, even though I believe it would only be a waste of time.[100]

[98] Letter of Descartes to Princess Elizabeth, November 1646, A.T., IV, p. 529.

[99] Letter of Descartes to Mersenne, 10 May 1632, A.T., I, pp. 250–251.

[100] *Ibid.*, p. 252. Note how Descartes cannot stop himself from dreaming ("*je ne sçaurois m'empêcher d'y resver*"). In Rule 8 of the *Rules for the Direction of the Mind*, he states that there is

The grand scientific scheme, the great instauration that Descartes nurtured, was something that he shared with the authors of several Rosicrucian tracts. His answer was novel, but the goal and the quest were less so. The mechanical philosophy had to fit, however uneasily, into a framework of other things that Descartes, like most of his contemporaries, believed he understood and about which he spoke but little.

Descartes is not to be identified with every book he perused. He was attracted by the moral purpose of the Rosicrucians, but he did not find the ultimate truth in their writings. Nonetheless, his willingness to look everywhere for the keys to the world of nature should not be overlooked, and it should prepare us to read the mechanical philosopher in a broader and more resonant context. The eschatological and millenarian side of the Rosicrucian movement appealed to something in Descartes, and it certainly contributed to his feeling that he had a mission and was destined to usher in the great day of genuine knowledge.

---

no point in casting horoscopes unless we know whether human reason can determine something about the influence of the stars (A.T., X, p. 398); in Rule 5, astrologers are condemned, not for their aim, but for neglecting to study the exact nature and motions of the heavenly bodies (*ibid.*, p. 380). It is not always clear, at the beginning of the seventeenth century, whether astrology itself is being criticized, or the uncritical way with which it is applied. Descartes' professor of mathematics at La Flèche, the Jesuit Jean François (1582–1668), attacked astrology in his *Traité des influences célestes* (Rouen, 1660), but he was not without his fair share of superstition. He claims, for instance, that no one dies a natural death on the coast of Dieppe except when the tide is going out, and in Guyana when the tide is coming in (quoted in Etienne Gilson's commentary on the *Discours de la méthode.* (Paris: 1925), p. 120).

Chapter Six

The Search for Method and Rules for Direction

Skies Italian

After his threefold dream in 1619, Descartes pledged himself to a life of research, called upon God "to guide him in his search of truth," and invoked the help of the Blessed Virgin Mary. He vowed to make a pilgrimage to the Sanctuary of Our Lady of Loretto in Italy, and planned to leave "in a few days."[1] This trip was postponed for unknown reasons and was only undertaken four years later, in the autumn of 1623. The immediate cause of Descartes' departure were family matters. M. Sain, the husband of his godmother and Senior Commissariat Officer for the French Army in the Alps, had just died, and Descartes was sent off to settle his affairs and see whether he might not succeed him in his post.

According to Baillet, Descartes was present at the annual feast of the marriage of Venice with the Adriatic on Ascension Day, which fell on 16 May 1624. Descartes fulfilled his vow to go to Loreto and then went on to Rome, where he arrived at the end of November. He may have met Pierre de Bérulle (1575–1629), the founder of the Oratory and future cardinal, who was in Rome in the autumn of that year, and who was later to influence Descartes' life.

The great event of that year was the official opening of the Great

---

[1] *Olympica*, A.T., X, p. 186.

Jubilee of 1625 on Christmas Eve 1624.[2] Descartes may also have witnessed an even more sensational event a few days earlier. On 21 December, on the market-place of the Campo del Fiore (where Giordano Bruno had been burnt at the stake in 1600), the effigy, the books, and the mortal remains of Marcantonio de Dominis were consigned to the flames. De Dominis had published a book on optics in 1611 in which he explained the rainbow, but his notoriety stemmed from his unusual ecclesiastical career. A former Jesuit who had become Archbishop of Spalato, he left Italy in 1616 to join the Church of England. James I made him Dean of Windsor, and gave him precedence over all church dignitaries except the archbishops of Canterbury and York. De Dominis wrote several tracts against the papacy, but by 1622 he had fallen out with Protestantism and returned to Rome where he was made welcome by his kinsman, Pope Gregory XV. The pope died in 1623, and although de Dominis had repudiated his anti-papal writings, proceedings against him were revived, and he was incarcerated in the Castel San Angelo in April 1624. He died on 8 September before the end of his trial, but the Church would not be defrauded of a chance to display its renewed doctrinal rigor. This is why on 21 December, in front of the church of the Minerva (where Galileo was made to recant nine years later, on 22 June 1633), a formal sentence of death against de Dominis was read before a huge crowd including several cardinals. His body was then handed over to the secular arm for the auto-da-fe. The event was widely reported in the international press and given full coverage in the French weekly, the *Mercure François*.[3]

A Career in France

Descartes returned to France in the Spring of 1625. He had now entered his thirtieth year, and it was becoming time for him to settle down. His maternal grandfather, René Brocard, had been Lieutenant-General (civic administrator) of Poitiers, and Descartes was offered the same high office in Châtellerault. He feared that his father, who was on a business trip in Paris, might consider him too old to begin the practice of law, and he wrote to suggest that he could be articled to a lawyer at the Châtelet in Paris until he had acquired enough legal knowledge.[4] We do not have his father's reply, but we can assume that it was down to earth and practical if we can trust his subsequent disparagement of a life of scholarly leisure. After the publication of his son's first book, the *Discourse on Method*, he is alleged to have said: "Only one of my children has given me displeasure. How can I have given birth to a son silly enough to have himself bound in calf!"[5]

[2] Adrien Baillet, *Vie de Monsieur Des-Cartes*, vol. I, pp. 118–122.

[3] *Mercure François*, vol. XI, pp. 134–151. An extended passage is quoted in Charles Adam, *Descartes. Sa Vie et ses Oeuvres*, p. 65, n. *a*.

[4] Adrien Baillet, *Vie de Monsieur Des-Cartes*, vol. I, p. 129.

[5] S. Ropartz, *La famille de Descartes en Bretagne (1586–1762)*, 1876, p. 100, cited in Charles Adam *Descartes. Sa Vie et ses Oeuvres*, pp. 433–444, note.

Offices were sold under the Ancient Regime in France, and Descartes was asked for 50,000 livres for the post in Châtellerault. He declined on the grounds that he only had 30,000, although a friend offered to raise the difference.[6]

Descartes' family and friends were also anxious to see him married. The young lady they had in mind later became Madame du Rosay, who confided to Fr. Poisson that Descartes "had whispered no more gallant word than that he found no beauty comparable to that of truth." Always fastidious, Descartes is reputed to have said to a group of friends, who were discussing matrimony, that as far as he was concerned, "a beautiful woman, a good book and an accomplished preacher were among the most difficult things to find in this world." Madame du Rosay also claimed that Descartes fought a duel in her honor and, having disarmed his rival, spared his life "for her sake."[7] As far as we know, this was Descartes' only brush with matrimony.[8]

Parisian Interlude

Apart from occasional trips to the northwest of France, Descartes spent the period 1626–1628 in Paris where he renewed the acquaintance of Mersenne and Mydorge and met a number of distinguished scientists, scholars, theologians, and literary figures, including the mathematicians Claude Hardy (c. 1605–1678) and Florimond de Beaune (1601–1652), the engineer Etienne de Villebressieu (fl. 1626–1653), the artisan Jean Ferrier, the astronomer Jean-Baptiste Morin (1583–1656), the philosopher Jean Silhon (1596–1667, who published in 1626 a book entitled *Two Truths: the First on God and His Providence, the Second on the Immortality of the Soul*, the themes of Descartes' *Meditations* of 1641), the priest of the Oratory Guillaume Gibieuf (1591–1650), and especially Pierre de Bérulle whom he may have already met in Rome.

---

[6] Adrien Baillet, *Vie de Monsieur Des-Cartes*, vol. I, p. 129.

[7] *Ibid.*, vol. II, p. 501. Descartes was interested in the theoretical as well as the practical side of duelling, and he wrote around this time a treatise on the *Art of Fencing* that was subsequently lost. In a letter to Mersenne on 22 December 1630, he refers to a book by Gérard Thibaut where mathematics and hermeticism are combined to disclose the secrets of wielding the sword on foot or on horseback, *Académie de l'épée où se démontrent par règles mathématiques sur le fondement d'un cercle mystérieux la théorie et la pratique des vrais et jusqu'à présent inconnus secrets du maniement des armes à pied et à cheval* (Leiden: Elzevier, 1630) (A.T., I, p. 195, see also X, pp. 535–538).

[8] In his treatise, *On the Passions of the Soul*, dedicated to a spinster, Princess Elizabeth, Descartes expresses himself like a hardened bachelor: "When a husband weeps over the death of a wife which (as is sometimes the case) he does not wish to see revived, it may well be that he is moved by the atmosphere of the funeral and the removal of a person whose conversation was familiar to him. Some shreds of pity or love may stir his imagination and bring tears to his eyes, even though, at the bottom of his heart, he experiences a secret joy" (A.T., XI, p. 441).

The Literary Gent

Descartes was interested in literature and struck up a friendship with the trendy literary critic Jean-Louis Guez de Balzac (1595–1654). But the most colorful and controversial literary figure of the period was the poet Théophile de Viau (1590–1626) whose clamorous trial on the charge of writing scurrilous and irreligious verse was held in Paris from 11 July 1623 to 1 September 1625, roughly the time that Descartes was in Italy. Théophile had powerful protectors, including the Duc de Montmorency, lord of the impregnable castle at Chantilly, and he absented himself from the first part of his trial, which ended with the burning of his effigy in Paris on 19 August 1623. He was captured at the border when he tried to slip out of France, and imprisoned at the Conciergerie in Paris in September 1623. He now had to attend his trial, which ended on 1 September 1625 with a sentence of banishment. It is an indication of the unruly state of politics in this period that Théophile was able to remain in France after his condemnation, travel to the island of Ré on the west coast, and then to Chantilly before returning to Paris where he died on 25 September 1626, at the early age of 36. On the following day, he was buried in great pomp with no fewer than eighteen priests in attendance.[9]

We do not know whether Descartes met Théophile, but he greatly admired his work, and more than 20 years later, he could quote from memory one of Théophile's quatrains in a letter to Chanut.[10] In the entire *corpus* of Descartes' writings, this is the only quotation from a contemporary poet.

In the light of our discussion of the Rosicrucian craze in Paris in 1623, it is symptomatic that François Garasse should have described his violent diatribe against the "invisible Rosicrucians" as his *Anti-Théophile*. Garasse lumped together reformers, hermeticists, heretics, and free-thinkers in an ominous category called "*beaux esprits*." He took pleasure in recalling the execution in Toulouse of Lucilio Vanini, "the Prince of Atheists," on 9 February 1619, "a poor butterfly that came from the bottom of Italy to roast on the fire of Languedoc." He also recalled Jean Fontanier, executed for the crime of atheism in Paris in 1621, and admonished writers of like mind: "Can you pass the Place de Grève [where executions were held] without trembling and without remembering that there is still room for you, and enough wood to reduce you to ashes?"[11]

---

[9] Frédéric Lachèvre, *Le procès du poète Théophile de Viau*, 2 vols. (Paris: Honoré Champion, 1909), vol. I, p. 576. Rumors of poisoning were, of course, rampant.

[10] Letter of Descartes to Pierre Chanut, 1 February 1647, A.T., X, p. 617.

[11] François Garasse, *La doctrine des beaux esprits de ce temps* (Paris: Sébastien Chappelet, 1623). Facsimile in 2 vols. but with continuous pagination (Westmead, Farnborough: Cregg International Publishers, 1971), p. 702. On Vanini, see pp. 144–147, on Fontanier, pp. 147–154. Garasse's book was finished printing on 18 August 1623, on the eve of the public burning of the portrait of Théophile. A copy of an anonymous pamphlet, *Les Enfans de la Croix Rouge*, had been found in Théophile's lodgings, and he was interrogated on two occasions on the

Garasse estimated that atheists made up 0.1% of the population of Paris.[12] Sensing that this was not dramatic enough, Mersenne, in some copies of his *Questiones in Genesim* published in 1623, suggested that they might number as many as 50,000. Since the population of the French capital was around 400,000 at the time, the Minim friar can hardly have intended his "statistics" to be taken literally. The inflated number tells us something, however, about the atmosphere that reigned in Paris.

Aristotle Denounced

During the trial of Théophile, the alchemist Jean Bitault, the iatrochemist Etienne de Claves, and the philosopher Antoine Villon offered to publicly defend fourteen anti-Aristotelian theses, including that matter is composed of atoms and that substantial forms are unnecessary. Copies of the theses were printed, and the meeting was advertised for Saturday, 24 August and Sunday, 25 August, the national feast of St. Louis. One of the largest halls in Paris, the Palais de la Reine Marguerite, had been rented for the occasion, but the police had not expected 1,000 people to show up. The chief magistrate grew alarmed at the size of the audience and had the hall cleared before the session began. At the request of the Sorbonne, the Parlement of Paris ordered the theses shredded on 4 September 1624, and the three authors banished from Paris with strict injunction not to teach philosophy publicly or privately in the kingdom of France. Etienne de Claves was made to witness the destruction of the seized copies of the theses, but Villon and Bitault escaped before the trial.[13]

Clitophon or Gersan

The proprietor of the hall where the three radicals were to have refuted Aristotle was François de Soucy, sieur de Gersan, an influential hermeticist

---

book. Each time he pleaded ignorance (Frédéric Lachèvre, *Le procès du poète Théophile de Viau*, vol. I, p. 444–445, 453, 500–501).

[12] *Ibid.*, p. 783.

[13] Charles Adam, *Descartes. Sa Vie et ses Oeuvres*, pp. 85–87; Frédéric Lachèvre, *Le procès du poète Théophile de Viau*, vol. I, p. 564, note 1, where he quotes the *Mercure François*. See also Mersenne, *Correspondance*, vol. I, pp. 167–168. The trial had a curious sequel inasmuch as Antoine Villon had described himself in the manifesto as "*miles philosophus*," the expression that Jean de Beaugrand later contemptuously applied to Descartes (Paul Tannery, *La correspondance de Descartes* (Paris: Gauthier-Villars, 1893), p. 44). It merely means the "soldier-philosopher" but may well have been used as a way of associating Descartes' name with Villon, who had been banished for daring to attack traditional philosophy. That this is not a fanciful speculation can be seen from a passage in a letter of the physician Christophe Villiers to Mersenne on 24 November 1640: "I do not think that M. des Cartes can do without forms. I heard, when I was at the College des Grassins some 24 years ago [Villiers means in *1624*], that the *miles philosophus* along with some chemists wanted to remove them" (A.T., III, p. 137).

and soon to become a friend of Descartes. We know of their acquaintance from a letter that Balzac wrote to Descartes, who had left for the west of France, on 30 March 1628.

> By the way, Sir, please remember THE HISTORY OF YOUR MIND. It is awaited by all your friends, and you promised it to me before Father Clitophon, who is known in the vernacular as M. de Gersan. He will be delighted to read about your sundry adventures in the middle and highest region of the air, your feats against the giants of the Schools, the path you followed, and the progress you have made in discovering the truth about nature.[14]

It is interesting that Descartes, usually so reserved, should have promised an autobiographical account of his intellectual development (the *History of His Mind*), not to a philosopher or a mathematician, but to a man of letters, and an alchemist who shared his belief in the possibility of prolonging life.[15] The reference to "the middle and highest region of the air" has nothing to do with space travel, but refers to Descartes' novel results in optics and the tricks that he worked with lenses.

The tone of the letter reminds us that good science could still be good fun, and Balzac ends with a witty celebration of the superior quality of dairy products from northwest France.

> I almost forgot to tell you that your butter triumphed over the one of the Marquise. To my taste, it is not less scented than the marmalade from Portugal that arrived by the same courier. I believe you feed your cows marjoram and violets. I even wonder whether sugar canes do not grow in your fens and serve to fatten those outstanding dairy cows![16]

O Beata Solitudo

Baillet describes Descartes' life-style as modest but proper for his station. He dressed in green, then the fashionable color, and he went about with a feather in his cap and a sword at his side, the two distinctive signs of a

---

[14] Letter of Guez de Balzac to Descartes, 30 March 1628, A.T., I, pp. 570–571. This was a covering letter for three essays that Balzac dedicated to Descartes as a thank-offering for a Latin apology that Descartes had written in defence of Balzac's views on eloquence. Descartes praised the purity and naturalness of Balzac's style, but not without avoiding a certain preciosity himself, as when he claimed that Balzac's "graces" were as different from vulgar ornament as "the artless blush of a fair maiden is unlike the flaming fard of prurient old ladies" (A.T., I, pp. 8–9).

[15] Gersan made his views known in the *Sommaire de la médecine chymique* (Paris, 1632), and *Le grand or potable des anciens philosophes* (Paris, 1653).

[16] Letter of Balzac to Descartes, 30 March 1628, A.T., I, p. 571. The identity of the marquise remains a mystery.

gentleman.[17] When he returned to Paris in 1625, he was for a while a guest at the house of Nicolas Le Vasseur, sieur d'Etioles, the district tax officer and a friend of his father. In June 1626, Descartes settled in the rue du Four but, having given his address to Mersenne and Mydorge, he soon discovered that they had passed it on and that he was swamped with callers. He then moved back to Le Vasseur's home, but the flow of visitors did not abate.

One morning, without saying a word to his host, Descartes left the house and took up lodgings with his manservant in a part of the city where he was unknown. Le Vasseur was greatly concerned and strove without success to discover his whereabouts until one morning, some five or six weeks later, he chanced to meet Descartes' servant in the street. He immediately asked where Descartes lived and whether he could find him at home. The servant replied that his master was in bed when he left to go shopping, and that he expected to find him, as usual, still in bed upon his return. Le Vasseur and the servant arrived at Descartes' apartment shortly after eleven. They let themselves in quietly and instead of knocking at Descartes' bedroom-door, Le Vasseur peeped through the key-hole. The curtains were still drawn, and next to the bed was a night-table with pen and paper. Descartes would occasionally stir, lay hold of the writing implements, scribble a few words, and lie down again. Le Vasseur watched this performance for a while before knocking. When Descartes recognized his father's friend, he put on the best countenance he could muster and invited him to stay for lunch. In the afternoon, he accompanied Le Vasseur back to his home and presented his apologies to Madame Le Vasseur.[18]

This incident convinced Descartes that he could only find peace and quiet outside Paris. He decided to spend the winter of 1627–1628 in Brittany, but he soon discovered that his relatives were too close, and after a few months he began thinking of removing himself even further.[19] He would gladly have returned to Italy, but he found the climate too hot in summer and the streets too little patrolled at night.[20] The weather in the Netherlands may not be the best, but the streets were safe, and he could go about his business without anyone caring who he was or what he was doing. As he put it in the *Discourse on Method*, he chose the Netherlands because:

> the armies maintained in this country seem to serve only to make the enjoyment of peace all the more secure. Among a great throng of busy

---

[17] Adrien Baillet, *Vie de Monsieur Des-Cartes*, vol. I, pp. 130–131.

[18] *Ibid.*, pp. 153–154.

[19] "Before I came to this country to find solitude, I spent a winter in the countryside in France" (letter of Descartes, probably to Pollot around 1648, A.T., V, p. 556). In January 1628, Descartes was in Brittany where he attended the christening of a nephew (A.T., I, p. 6). In his letter of 30 March 1628, Balzac clearly assumes that Descartes was still in that part of France (A.T., I, p. 570).

[20] Letter of Descartes to Balzac, 5 May 1630, A.T., I, p. 204. Letter to Mersenne, 13 November 1639, A.T., II, pp. 623–624.

people who are more interested in their own affairs than curious about those of others, I have been able to lead a life as solitary and withdrawn as if I were in the most remote desert, while lacking none of the comforts found in the most populous cities.[21]

This, of course, is how things turned out. In 1628 the future was not so clear, and Descartes made a trip to the Netherlands to see whether the country was still suitable for a scholar who valued his comfort and, above all, his privacy. As we already know, he went to Middelburg fully expecting to find Beeckman there, although his friend had left his home town as early as 1619. This would seem to indicate that Descartes was not looking for Beeckman as much as he was anxious to secure information about a suitable place to work in peace and seclusion.

Descartes found Beeckman in Dordrecht on 8 October 1628, as we know from an entry in Beeckman's diary. Descartes conveyed the impression that he looked forward to returning to the Netherlands, "in order", wrote Beeckman,

> that we may complete together what rests to be done in the sciences. Having travelled through France, Germany and Italy, he said that he had not found anyone with whom he could talk as freely or from whom he could expect as much help in pursuing his studies.[22]

The work to be done was in the nature of a mopping up operation, since Descartes proclaimed that over the last nine years he had made in arithmetic and geometry "as much progress as can be achieved by mortal man." He also apprised Beeckman of his research in other areas and explicitly mentioned that he had: (1) a universal scientific method, (2) a "general" algebra, (3) a new way of finding mean proportionals, (4) a general solution of all cubics and quartics, and (5) the correct law of refraction. He added that he continued to be interested in musical consonance, and to think about possible inhabitants on the Moon.[23] He had not written anything as yet but, having entered his thirty-third year, it was time to set himself to the task. Beeckman was suitably impressed. "Of all the mathematicians and geometers that I have read or spoken to," he wrote, "there is none that I prefer to him."[24]

God Will Bless Your Work

What other parts of the Netherlands (if any) Descartes may have visited at that time is unknown, but Baillet has him journey to the west of France to see the siege of La Rochelle, which was not only a major military operation

---

[21] *Discourse on Method*, Third Part, A.T., VI, p. 31.

[22] Beeckman, *Journal*, A.T., X, p. 332.

[23] *Ibid.*, pp. 331–348.

[24] *Ibid.*, p. 332.

against the last stronghold of French Protestantism, but an attraction that drew huge crowds. On 11 November 1628, the feast of St. Martin, Descartes was back in Paris, and a few days later he was invited to attend a lecture by the alchemist de Chandoux at the palace of the Papal Nuncio, Guidi di Bagno, whom the French called Bagné.[25] Pierre de Bérulle, recently elevated to the cardinalate, was present, and when he noticed that Descartes did not seem impressed with the lecturer's arguments, he asked him whether he would like to say a few words. Descartes accepted and, after praising the rhetorical gifts of the speaker, marvelled at the willingness of the audience to be swayed by merely plausible reasons. He then gave a virtuoso demonstration that any true statement could be challenged by a dozen likely arguments, and ended by claiming that genuine science must rest on unassaillable foundations.

Bérulle was struck by the sheer brilliance of Descartes' performance and asked him to call on him. Descartes complied and gave Bérulle an account of his philosophical outlook in which he stressed

> the usefulness that would result for the public at large if his method were applied to medecine in order to restore and preserve health, and to mechanics, to make work lighter and easier.[26]

Bérulle was an intellectual who believed in the influence of ideas and a devout priest for whom the relief of man's estate was to be warmly encouraged. He praised Descartes' intentions and "laid upon his conscience" the duty of not allowing his great intellectual gifts to go to waste. "God," said Bérulle, "cannot fail to bless your work."[27] This encouragement from one of the highest prelates in France confirmed Descartes in his resolve to retire to the Netherlands and fulfill the mission that he had received on the fateful night of 10–11 November 1619.

The Rules for the Direction of the Mind

We have seen that Descartes was able to give Bérulle an outline of his philosophy and that he informed Beeckman when he met him on 8 October 1628 that he now had a general method. In all likelihood he was referring to the work he had drafted during the winter of 1627–1628, an extended essay entitled *Rules for the Direction of the Mind* that was only published posthu-

---

[25] Adrien Baillet, *Vie de Monsieur Des-Cartes*, vol. I, p. 160. We have no information on Chandoux beyond Bérulle's statement that he was an alchemist who believed that fortune had favored him with the discovery of the transmutation of metals. The civil authorities and the public assayers were not so easily convinced, and he was executed in Paris for putting his gold into circulation, i.e., for falsification of currency, in 1631 (*ibid.*, pp. 230–231).

[26] *Ibid.*, p. 165. Baillet gives as his source the manuscript of a memoir by Claude Clerselier (*ibid.*, pp. 165–166). He also quotes a letter of Descartes to Villebressieu (*ibid.*, p. 163, cited A.T., I, p. 213).

[27] *Ibid.*

mously.[28] I shall outline the main trust of this work before considering in greater detail Descartes' ideal of simplicity and his intuitionistic model of knowledge.

The Path of Knowledge

As we have seen in our analysis of Descartes' contribution to mathematics in Chapter Three, his genius lay in his ability to see the universal applicability of a solution that had been devised to meet a specific problem. The act of generalization is indeed the crucial insight that unlocks the door of learning. It is the mental operation of lifting the universal out of the particular that struck Aristotle as the act of knowledge *par excellence*, the characteristic of genuine intellectual activity. As such it can only be acknowledged; it resists analysis, even adequate description.

The young Descartes was more sanguine. He felt that the road leading to insight (*intuitus*) could be smoothed and he hoped to achieve this task with the aid of explicit rules. He tells us at the end of Rule 12 of the *Rules for the Direction of the Mind* that the work was originally intended to consist of three parts comprising twelve rules each covering: (a) simple propositions, (b) satisfactorily posed questions, and (c) unsatisfactorily posed questions.[29]

This division would seem to have been an afterthought, and to have occurred to Descartes only when he turned from simple propositions, which he believed he had treated exhaustively, to the art of formulating questions that admit of reliable answers. It is ironical that the patron of order and method should have gone about his work without a clear plan of where he was going, but we must remember that he was forging a new way and not following a beaten path. The strategy that looked promising at the end of Rule 12 soon proved unsatisfactory, however, and the work was abandoned less than half way through the second section.

The first section of the *Rules for the Direction of the Mind* aims at preparing our minds to grasp (*intueri*) simple propositions clearly and distinctly, and Descartes believed that he had achieved his goal as much as is humanly possible. Genuine knowledge, Descartes argued, can only be based on indubitable truths that are so luminous that we cannot help *seeing* (in Descartes'

---

[28] *Regulae ad directionem ingenii*, first published in Amsterdam in 1701 is reproduced in A.T., X, pp. 359–469. A French translation with extended notes by the translator Jean-Luc Marion, and mathematical notes by Pierre Costabel has been published under the title *Règles utiles et claires pour la direction de l'esprit et la recherche de la vérité* (The Hague: Martinus Nijhoff, 1977). L.J. Beck, *The Method of Descartes. A Study of the* Regulae (Oxford: Clarendon, 1952) is still essential reading. The best English translation is in *The Philosophical Writings of Descartes*, J. Cottingham, R. Stoothoff and D. Murdoch, trans., 2 vols. (Cambridge: Cambridge University Press, 1985), vol. I, pp. 9–76. This edition has the advantage of giving the corresponding pages in A.T.

[29] *Rules for the Direction of the Mind*, Rule 12, A.T., X, pp. 428–429.

terminology, *intuiting*) them. But to see, we have to be looking in the right direction (hence the title of the work), and this means following a method. To see through the thicket of confused notions, hearsay evidence, and traditional saws, we have to reduce the complex to the simple and to show how propositions are linked in a continuous deductive sequence. When we come to a point that we cannot grasp clearly, we should stop and review the entire process. We should exercise ourselves in the art of clearly grasping simple natures or genuine essences by examining matters that are simple, indeed, trivial, and asking ourselves wherein lies their simplicity. To this end we should go over solutions found by others and focus on the *order* in which things must be placed for the correct solution to emerge. We should practice seeing the whole deductive sequence at one go, embracing the premises and the conclusions in one comprehensive sweep. We should also use all the help we can get from our sense, our imagination, and our memory.

Descartes could not claim to make men more intelligent, but he believed he could teach them to use their native intellect to best advantage. This was his boast. When he wrote his *Discourse on Method* some ten years later, he had come to realize that his rules could be reduced to the four canons of evidence, division, order, and exhaustion with which we are familiar: (1) nothing is to be assented to unless evidently known to be true; (2) every subject-matter is to be divided into the smallest possible parts, and each dealt with separately; (3) each part is to be considered in the right order, the simplest first; and (4) no part is to be omitted in reviewing the whole.[30]

From the twelve rules governing the quest for genuine insight, Descartes went on to explain how we should proceed to solve questions whose meaning is clear even if the solution eludes us. We should, he tells us, remove every superfluous notion, and aim at simplicity and order. In other words, we are to handle questions in the same spirit in which we deal with simple natures or basic propositions. Descartes saw no difficulty in transferring these abstract rules to real matter (in his terminology "real extension"), but he recommends the use of our imagination, properly speaking, of our pictorial phantasy. We are to visualize shapes and figures, although information that is not immediately relevant to a question at hand should be stored in abstract symbols.

The Grammar of Science

The practical rules that Descartes gives are essentially those that he will later recommend at the beginning of his *Geometry*: (1) give a symbol to known

---

[30] Descartes, *Discourse on Method*, Second Part, A.T., VI, pp. 18–19. For an excellent account of Descartes' mature views in the light of recent developments in the philosophy of science, see Desmond M. Clarke, *Descartes' Philosophy of Science* (Manchester: Manchester University Press, 1982). There is an illuminating chapter on Descartes in Gerd Buchdahl, *Metaphysics and the Philosophy of Science* (Oxford: Basel Blackwell, 1969).

quantities (lower case *a, b, c*) as well as unknown ones (upper case A, B, C—replaced by the last letters of the alphabet, *x, y, z* in the *Geometry*); (2) determine their mutual relations neglecting the difference between known and unknown quantities; (3) use the four basic operations of addition, subtraction, multiplication, and division; (4) find two equations containing the unknown; and (5) simplify when possible.

Descartes considers mathematics as a propaedeutic to philosophy, and transfers to mathematics what his Jesuit masters said of Latin and Greek, the classical languages that were believed to instil the ability of ordering one's thoughts clearly and marshalling them effectively. They spoke of Latin grammar as the embodiment of logic; Descartes, surely with more justification, considered mathematics a paradigm of clear, distinct, and cogent reasoning.

Mathematics is not the end-all of philosophy; strictly speaking, it is not even the *means* to philosophizing. It is essentially an exercise, just as Latin was. Latin syntax was not studied to apply it uncritically to English sentences but in the hope of mastering the underlying structure of rational discourse. This was the belief that motivated the insistence on classical languages in the curriculum that was normative in European schools between 1600 and 1900. This myth of the superiority of Latin over English or French was replaced by another myth, that of the superiority of mathematics over other forms of reasoning. "If I learn my Latin well," said the Humanist, "I shall acquire a method of reasoning that will serve me everywhere." "If I become proficient in mathematics," says Descartes, "I shall have mastered the technique of clear insight and rigorous deduction that will unlock all the doors of knowledge."

The Ideal of Simplicity

Descartes embarked upon his quest for true and indubitable knowledge by observing that arithmetic and geometry are more certain than other disciplines because (a) their object is pure and simple, and (b) their deductions are clear and rigorous. Any general method or *mathesis universalis* must incorporate these two features. At the more personal level, Descartes was motivated by his success in mathematics and the ease with which he could solve problems. In an interesting autobiographical aside in Rule 10, Descartes tells us that whenever he saw a book, advertised as offering a new solution to a problem, he would try to work out the answer before turning the pages. "I took great care," he writes, "not to deprive myself of this innocent pleasure through a hasty reading of the book." Success was so frequent that he came to realize that he was not making his way to the truth "as others usually do by way of aimless and blind enquiries, and more by luck than by skill, but by following certain rules."[31] The problem was to spell those rules out.

[31] Descartes, *Rules for the Direction of the Mind*, Rule 10, A.T., X, p. 403.

Once in a Lifetime . . .

"At least once in our life," writes Descartes, "we ought to examine what is the nature and scope of human knowledge." This does not appear to him "an arduous or even a difficult task,"[32] provided we start from simple instances and ask ourselves what makes them readily intelligible. Here is the illustration that he offers in Rules 6 and 11.

If we note that 6 is twice 3, and ask what is twice 6, we find that it is 12. If we double 12, we obtain 24, and if we double that again, we obtain 48. We can then easily see that the ratio between 3 and 6 is the same as between 6 and 12, or 12 and 24, and so on, and hence that the numbers 3, 6, 12, 24, 48 are continued proportionals. This may "seem almost childish," says Descartes, but if we ponder this example, we shall know in what order proportions or relations are to be investigated, and that this "embraces the whole of the science of pure mathematics."[33]

The illustration is meant to cast light on the notions of simplicity and ease. It is no more difficult to find the double of 12 than it is to find the double of 6. Indeed, when we have found a certain ratio between any two numbers, we can find innumerable other numbers that have the same ratio. We can also note that if two numbers, such as 3 and 6, are given, it is easy to find a third in continued proportion, that is, 12. But if we are given the two extremes 3 and 12, it is not so simple to find the mean proportional, 6. Why? Because, in this case, when we are looking for the mean proportional, we have to attend simultaneously to the two extremes and the ratio between them (the problem is to find an x such that $3/x = x/12$, which Descartes expresses as a division of 3 by x, and x by 12). The difficulty is increased when the extremes are 3 and 24, and we have to determine the intermediate proportionals, namely, 6 and 12, since the number of factors to which we must attend have increased. If the extremes are 3 and 48, we might expect the difficulty to be even greater, but it is actually less because the task can be simplified. All we have to do in this case is to seek the mean proportional between 3 and 48, that is, 12, next the mean proportional between 3 and 12, that is, 6, and, finally, the mean proportional between 12 and 48, that is, 24. What looked harder turns out to be easier once we go about it the right way.[34]

I have given this example at length because Descartes seems to consider it particularly important, but it is clear that if we are to understand what he means by simplicity, we must examine more closely what he takes to be the simplicity of the act of cognition as well as the simplicity of the object of knowledge.

---

[32] *Rules for the Direction of the Mind*, Rule 8, p. 398.

[33] *Rules for the Direction of the Mind*, Rule 6, pp. 384–385.

[34] *Ibid.*, pp. 385–387. See also Rule 11, pp. 409–410.

Intuition or Plain Seeing

Descartes speaks of intuition or deduction as two ways of knowing, but since deduction is merely a concatenation of intuitions, intuition is obviously basic.

The word "*intuitus*" is not original to Descartes, but he disowns historical antecedents and claims to return to the original Latin meaning of "vision" (hence *sight* at the level of sensation; *insight* at the level of intellection). In the intellectual sphere, intuition or insight is neither the deliverance of our senses nor the mirror of our imagination, but the proper activity of the mind, the application of the "natural light" that Descartes uses elsewhere as a synonym of intuition:[35]

> By *intuition*, I do not mean the fluctuating testimony of the senses or the deceptive judgment of the imagination that puts things together wrongly, but the conception of a clear and attentive mind which is so easy and distinct that it leaves no room for doubt. Alternatively, and this comes to the same thing, intuition is the indubitable conception of a clear and attentive mind which proceeds solely from the light of pure reason.[36]

For Descartes, therefore, to know is to see. This is the fundamental and guiding analogy of his philosophy of knowledge. In Rule 9, he says explicitly, "we learn how to use our mental intuition by comparison with our eyes," and he suggests that we strengthen our ability of examining simple natures just as goldsmiths sharpen their eyesight by focusing on minute objects.[37]

Simple Natures

The proper objects of the act of intuition are simple natures of which there are three kinds. The first are "purely intellectual," and examples are knowing, doubting, ignoring, and willing. The second are "purely material" and are only to be found in physical bodies, such as figure, extension, and motion. The third are common to both spiritual and material things and include such concepts as existence, unity, duration, as well as relations of the type "if two things are identical with a third, they are identical with one

---

[35] Descartes' letter to Mersenne, 16 October 1639, A.T., II, p. 599. In Rule 1, Descartes enjoins us "to think only of increasing the natural light of our reason" (A.T., X, p. 361).

[36] Descartes, *Rules for the Direction of the Mind*, Rule 3, A.T., X, p. 368. In Rule 13, Descartes writes: "there can be no falsity in the mere intuition of things, be they simple or conjoined" (p. 432). We could think of a resemblance with the Thomistic doctrine of the *simplex apprehensio*, the vision of the *quidditas* of things, that precedes the act of judgment. In the *Summa Theologiae*, I, qu. 85, a. 6 *in corpore*, Thomas Aquinas writes that the intellect "cannot be deceived *per se* in regard to the essence of a thing, though it may be deceived *per accidens* in relating essences, *componendo et dividendo*." The source is Aristotle, *On the Soul*, Book III, ch. 6, 430b 27–30.

[37] *Rules for the Direction of the Mind*, Rule 9, p. 401. See also *Optics*, A.T., VI, p. 164.

another," or privations and negations such as nothing, instant, and rest.[38] According to Descartes, "these simple natures are all self-evident and never contain any falsity." Error can only occur in putting them together. It follows that we cannot be ignorant of these simple natures although we can believe we are![39]

The list of simple natures provided by Descartes seems, at first blush, to be a very mixed bag. How was it compiled? Simple natures are not determined or classified in the light of ontological considerations as is the case for Aristotle's *genera* and *species*. In Rule 6, Descartes makes this plain. Indeed, he calls it "the main secret of my method":

> all things can be arranged in a series, not in so far as they can be referred to some ontological category (such as the categories into which philosophers divide things), but in so far as some things can be known on the basis of others.[40]

The example that Descartes uses in Rule 12 is that of an extended body. From the point of view of the object, it is one, single, and simple, but from the point of view of our understanding, it is complex and made up of "body," "extension," and "shape." These cannot exist in isolation, yet they must be thought of as separate before we can judge that they are joined in the same object:

> That is why, since we are concerned here with things only in so far as they are perceived by the intellect, we term simple only those things which we know so clearly and distinctly that they cannot be divided by the mind into others which are more distinctly known. Shape, extension and motion, etc. are of this sort; all the rest we conceive to be in a sense composed out of these.[41]

---

[38] *Rules for the Direction of the Mind*, Rule 12, pp. 419–420. In Rule 6, Descartes had divided things into "absolute" and "relative," *ibid.*, pp. 381–382.

[39] *Ibid.*, Rule 12, p. 420. The import of this statement is somewhat mitigated by what Descartes writes in Rule 6: "there are very few pure and simple natures that we can intuit straight off and *per se*" (*ibid.*, p. 381).

[40] *Rules for the Direction of the Mind*, Rule 6, p. 381.

[41] *Rules for the Direction of the Mind*, Rule 12, p. 418. We can perhaps clarify Descartes' position by contrasting it with Bacon's discussion of simple natures in his *Novum Organum*, Book II, Aphorism V, where he writes: "The rule or axiom for the transformation of bodies is of two kinds. The first regards the body as an aggregate or a combination of simple natures (*Primum intuetur corpus ut turmam sive conjugationem naturarum simplicium*)." Bacon then lists for gold: yellow, heavy, of a certain weight, malleable, ductile, not volatile, fluid at high temperatures, and so on. He proceeds: "This kind of axiom, therefore, deduces the thing from the forms of simple natures (*Itaque hujusmodi axioma rem deducit ex Formis naturarum simplicium*). For he who knows the forms of yellow, weight, ductility, fixity, fluidity, solution, and so on, and the methods for superinducing them, and their gradations and modes, will make it his care to have them joined together in some body, whence may follow the transformation of that body into gold" (Francis Bacon, *Novum Organum* in *Works*, J. Spedding, R.L. Ellis, and D.D. Heath, eds., 14 vols. (London, 1857–1874). Reprint

Note that things are considered "only in so far as they are perceived by the intellect." The perspective is entirely epistemological. The basis of the ordering of "natures" is their logical dependence in a deductive series. "Simple natures" are not *genera* that contain composite natures. As L.J. Beck puts it,

> Descartes is thinking in terms of mathematical classification where such considerations have no meaning: the "straight-line" is not more general than the "triangle," the "angle" is not more particular than the "straight-line." The relationship between the triangle, straight-line, and angle is not to be expressed in terms of genus and specific difference . . . . The rejection of the Aristotelian and Scholastic method of classification, essentially based on a graduated hierarchy of concepts, involves also the rejection of all subsumptive deduction and its first principle *dictum de omni, dictum de nullo*—in a word, the rejection of syllogistic reasoning.[42]

Simple natures cannot be broken down into more easily intelligible parts and are, by definition, self-evident. The problem is to combine them. "The whole of human knowledge," writes Descartes, "consists in this alone: to clearly see how these simple natures come together to compose other things."[43]

Continuous Thinking

Since Descartes recognizes only intuition and deduction as the intellectual means of acquiring knowledge, the combining or mixing of simple natures must be a form of deduction. In Rule 3, deduction is defined as a movement along a chain of reasoning in which each link is intuitively known, and in which the connection of the links is apprehended "in a continuous and uninterrupted act of thought."[44] It differs from intuition inasmuch as it is not instantaneous but is deployed in time and depends on memory. It is striking that throughout the *Rules for the Direction of the Mind*, Descartes is less concerned with describing the deductive process in detail than with liberating it from the uncertainties of memory and converting it into intuition. We are urged to acquire greater and greater celerity in passing through the links of a

---

(Stuttgart-Bad Canstatt: Frommann, 1962), vol. IV, p. 122). Descartes' "simple natures" are clearly on a different plane. His target is not the "form" of the individual thing but the "idea."

[42] L.J. Beck, *The Method of Descartes. A Study of the Regulae* (Oxford: Clarendon Press, 1952), pp. 80–81.

[43] Descartes, *Rules for the Direction of the Mind*, Rule 12, p. 427. Or, again, in the same rule: "we need take no great pains to discover these simple natures, because they are self-evident enough. What requires effort is distinguishing one from another, and intuiting each separately with a steadfast mental gaze" (p. 425).

[44] *Rules for the Direction of the Mind*, Rule 3, p. 369.

demonstration until we can see them in one single comprehensive flash of insight.

The Machinery of Deduction

In Descartes' view, we do not manipulate concepts according to formal laws, we link simple natures intuitively perceived. Can this procedure be specified, or is it a vague appeal to exercise care and attention? At the beginning of Rule 14, Descartes states that we cannot arrive, by sheer deduction, at a new kind of entity. All we can discover are combinations of simple natures intuitively known. It would be impossible, for instance, to make a man, blind from birth, perceive the true nature of colors by mere force of argument because the idea of color is derived from the senses. But if a man had seen the primary colors (Descartes probably means red, blue, and yellow), he might be able to construct for himself, "by a kind of deduction," images of the secondary colors that are blends of the primary ones. The least that can be said is that the illustration is not intuitively obvious. It did not convince even Descartes, who wrote in the margin, "This is not completely true, but I did not have a better example."[45]

Starting from the intuition of simple, self-evident natures, Descartes would have us compare them with other things whose nature they share in some respect or other. The procedure is epitomized in the inference: "All A is B, all B is C, therefore all A is C." Although this is a typical syllogism, Descartes insists that it has nothing to do with the formal aspect of Scholastic logic. What he has in mind is a procedure inspired from mathematics, in which comparing an unknown quantity, x, with a known quantity, y, consists in determining their mutual relations and expressing them in equations, i.e., putting x in an equation with y. This will be unambiguously stated in the *Geometry*; in the *Rules for the Direction of the Mind*, Descartes is still groping for a satisfactory way of expressing his insight.

Descartes is clear, however, that we must turn to "the images depicted in our imagination" to understand "magnitude in general" abstracted from particular objects.[46] This brings us to a consideration of his physiology of perception.

Seeing Is Believing

In Rule 12, Descartes offers an account of perception that is purely passive, "occurring," he says, "in the same way in which wax takes on an impression for a seal." And lest we should dismiss this as a mere comparison, he insists:

> It should not be thought that I have a mere analogy in mind here: we must think of the external shape of the sentient body as being really changed by

[45] *Rules for the Direction of the Mind*, Rule 14, p. 438.

[46] *Ibid.*, pp. 440–441.

the object in exactly the same way as the shape of the surface of wax is altered by a seal.[47]

The shape received by the senses is instantly relayed to the "common" or internal sense that coordinates the incoming impressions. In turn, the common sense impresses the figure upon the imagination or "phantasy," which Descartes defines as "a genuine part of the body, large enough for its various parts to take on many distinct figures and retain them for a long time."[48] This is the psycho-physiological basis on which he rests his appeal to the imagination as "of all places, the one in which all the various differences in ratios are clearly displayed."[49]

Bearing in mind that genuine knowledge for Descartes is the result of *insight* (or intuition) into a *simple nature*, the procedure is as follows: Our aim is to study the relations or proportions of magnitude in general, so as to be able to express them in the form of equations. But magnitude in general is a form of extension, and extension is not only simple nature but real body. This is why magnitude is properly known in the intuitive inspection of corporeal extension in our imagination. Descartes goes as far as saying that an extended body that cannot be imagined cannot be genuinely conceived.[50]

If someone were to argue that all extended bodies could be destroyed and extension *as such* survive, he would only have to turn to the idea of extension in his imagination to be convinced of his error. "Henceforth," adds Descartes in a gesture that embraces all the community of future scholars, "we shall not undertake anything without the aid of the imagination."[51] The reason is that the corporeal pattern impressed on the imagination is our warrant for the intuitive truth of the fundamental operation of comparing magnitudes. Indeed, the richness of the pattern in the imagination exceeds the limited or abstract viewpoint on which the intellect focuses:

> even if the intellect attends solely and precisely to what the word signifies, the imagination nonetheless ought to form a real idea of the thing, so that the intellect, when required, can be directed towards the other features of the thing which are not conveyed by the term in question.[52]

---

[47] *Rules for the Direction of the Mind*, Rule 12, p. 412.

[48] *Ibid.*, p. 414.

[49] *Rules for the Direction of the Mind*, Rule 14, p. 441.

[50] "We generally do not recognize philosophical entities of the sort that are not genuinely imaginable" (Rule 14, *ibid.*, p. 442). Compare the following entry in Beeckman's *Journal* for 1629: "I do not admit anything in philosophy but what can be represented as a sensible object in the imagination (*nihil enim in philosophia admitto quam quod imaginationi velut sensibile representatur*)." Beeckman, *Journal,* vol. IV, p. 162.

[51] *Ibid.*, p. 443. We should in our investigations: (a) select those dimensions "which will be of the greatest assistance to our imagination" (Rule 14, p. 449), and (b) bear in mind that we cannot attend to more than one or two of them as depicted in our imagination" (*ibid.*, and again, Rule 16, p. 454).

[52] *Ibid.*, Rule 14, p. 445. See also Rule 16, p. 454.

For instance, we can understand that a triangle is a combination of simple natures, such as shape, extension, the number three, and line, but if we examine the two-dimensional figure that is intuited in the imagination, we can be led to see other features (Descartes calls them "natures") that are implicitly contained, such as that the sum of the angles is equal to two right angles.[53] What is essential is that the analysis of the triangle never leaves the ontologically certified ground of the corporeal extension in the imagination.

But what is this extension? Descartes' answer is: "whatever has length, breadth and depth," a notion that needs "no further elucidation, for there is nothing more easily perceived by our imagination."[54] The touchstone of the idea of extension is clearly and directly intuitable corporeal reality. But Descartes does not, as yet, equate extension with matter as such, a step that he will take a couple of years later in *The World*.

The Model at Work

The problem, of course, is how well this works. Let us examine four instances in which the model is applied: (a) the basic operations of addition, subtraction, multiplication and division; (b) the explanation of sound; (c) the investigation of magnetism; and (d) the status of secondary qualities and the nature of color.

The Basic Mathematical Operations

The quest for simplicity and intuitive clarity pushes Descartes into trying to represent the basic mathematical operations (addition, subtraction, multiplication, and division) by means of lines and rectangular surfaces. Addition and subtraction present obvious cases of the laying off of line segments to generate sums or differences. In Rule 18, Descartes shows how the multiplication of two magnitudes, a and b, presented as straight lines, can be accomplished by fitting them together at a right angle to form a rectangle. If the rectangle ab so produced has to be multiplied by a third magnitude, c, then we consider ab as a line and fit it to c to form another rectangle abc. Similarly in divisions where the divisor is given, we take the magnitude to be divided as the rectangle, the divisor as one side, and the quotient as the other.

The assumption is that any power of any quantity can be represented by a straight line or a rectangular surface. As Descartes summarizes it:

> It is therefore important to explain here how every rectangle can be transformed into a line, and conversely how a line or even a rectangle can be transformed into another rectangle, one side of which is specified.[55]

---

[53] *Rules for the Direction of the Mind*, Rule 12, p. 422.

[54] *Rules for the Direction of the Mind*, Rule 14, p. 442.

[55] *Rules for the Direction of the Mind*, Rule 18, p. 468.

The point is that Descartes is not merely envisaging the geometrical representation of quantities, he is arguing that the operations of mathematics are clearly imagined or perceived. The abstract notation $a \times b = ab$ is the *record* of the manipulation of bodies, either in the physical world with rods and sticks, or in the imagination, which is also an extended surface. Figure 1 shows the graphic illustration of Rule 18:

Given a and b

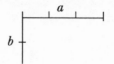

we fit one line at right angles to the other, thus:

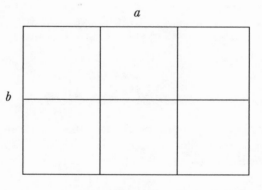

to make the rectangle:

Figure 1

We can do all this without leaving the playground of the imagination. There is one case, however, where the playground is too narrow. This is the extraction of roots, what Descartes calls "a division in which the divisor is not given."[56]

Roots and Their Problems

The extraction of roots is to be construed, says Descartes, as one of finding a mean proportional x between 1 and a ($1/x = x/x$, hence $a = \pm a$), and the way to do this "will be disclosed in its proper place," a promise that remained unfulfilled, since the text of the *Rules for the Direction of the Mind* breaks off a couple of pages later.

[56] *Ibid.*, p. 467.

The interpretation of root extraction as the discovery of mean proportionals is not really amenable to imaginative representation. It is, of course, perfectly feasible with the aid of Descartes' proportional compass. We can say (using Figure 1 of Chapter Three, page 36 above) that when YB = 1, the mean proportional, YC, is equal to √YD (because YB/YC = YC/YD), but this is far from being intuitive in pictorial or imaginative terms. This difficulty may well be the reason why the *Rules* effectively come to an end with Rule 18.

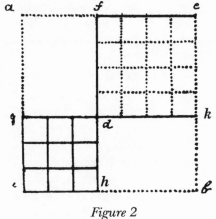

Figure 2

Descartes was surely aware of the tensions he had unwittingly set up. We can call on the witness of Isaac Beeckman who entered in his *Journal*, shortly after Descartes' visit on 8 October, a summary of what his friend told him about his method of equations by manipulating line segments and surfaces. The example he records is Descartes' handling of the equation $x^2 = 6x + 7$ with the aid of a diagram illustrating the appropriate manipulations (see Figure 2).[57]

Let x^2 be represented by square *acbe*, from which $6x$ is to be removed.

Divide $6x$ by 2, obtaining $3x$.

Mark out 3 units (*af*) on *ae*, and 3 units (*gc*) on *ac*. Therefore *achf* = *gcbk* and each "contains" $3x$.

Subtract $6x$ from square *acbe* by imagining *achf* and *gcbk* to be removed.

But this means that we have taken square *gchd* twice and, in fact, subtracted $6x - 9$ from *ab*. Therefore, we must consider the remaining square *fdke* to consist not of 7 units but of $7 + 9 = 16$ units. Thus the root of square *fdke* = 4, and adding *af* = 3, we obtain 7 as the side of square *acbe*.

Since $x^2 - 6x - 7 = (x - 7)(x + 1)$, the roots of the equation are not only 7 but also –1, which cannot be represented in this way. This illustrates the difficulties that Descartes ran into in his attempt to provide an intuitive-imaginative justification of mathematics. He was able to represent graphically the steps involved in finding the root of $x^2 = 6x + 7$ because of two features that are present in some but not in all equations, namely, a perfect square and one real positive root.

Negative and imaginary roots, and mathematical operations such as the extraction of higher roots could not be embodied in straight lines and rectangles. Descartes was conscious of this, and he discussed the problem with Beeckman who noted:

[57] Beeckman, *Journal*, A.T., X, pp. 334–335.

Irrational numbers, which cannot be explained otherwise, he explains by a parabola. He also calls some roots "true," some "implicit," that is less than zero, and some "imaginary," that is altogether inexplicable.[58]

The technique involving a parabola to find two mean proportionals was one of Descartes' recent triumphs, and Beeckman copied it out in his *Journal* a few pages later. It was applied to equations of the third and fourth degree. On the extraction of roots, however, Descartes need not have invoked the parabola, since the continued geometrical proportions that were mechanically produced by his compass was all that was required. But since he had told Beeckman that he went about solving equations by manipulating lines and surfaces, he could not very well use a mechanical device, and he did not mention his compass.

The Nature of Sound

The second case where the imagination is assumed to be the touchstone of genuine knowledge is the investigation of sound. Assume that three strings, A, B, and C give out an identical sound when B is twice as thick as A, but of equal length, and is tensioned by a weight twice as heavy, while C, as thick as A and twice as long, is tensioned by a weight four times as great.[59]

This is an interesting case, since sound (like weight and speed) is not a geometrical or arithmetical property like line or number. In Rule 14, Descartes declares such intensive magnitudes to be on the same methodological footing as length, width, and breadth.[60] Physical dimensions are the object of scientific discourse inasmuch as they are *ordered, measured*, and *registered in the imagination* under the categories of figure and extension.

The way Descartes sets up the problem of sound, the data are readily available to visual intuition, since his dimensions are length, cross-section, and weight. The first two are easily pictured or imagined, and the notion of weight can be reduced to the image of superimposed blocks of a standard size or, following Descartes' suggestion in Rule 9, to the intuition (here clearly visual inspection) of the motion of weights at the end of a balance of unequal arms.[61]

This approach is satisfactory as long as questions that go beyond the mere correlation of length, cross-section, and weight are not raised. But such questions are always lurking in the background, and Descartes was surely aware of them. For instance, we could ask: what is the nature and the role of the medium through which sound travels? Or, how do we explain the cohesion of the vibrating parts? Quantifiable answers may be forthcoming,

---

[58] *Ibid.*, p. 335.

[59] Descartes, *Rules for the Direction of the Mind*, Rule 13, A.T., X, p. 431.

[60] *Ibid.*, Rule 14, p. 447.

[61] *Ibid.*, Rule 9, p. 403 where the Latin for "I shall look at a pair of scales" is "*intuebor librum.*"

but it is not immediately obvious that they can be intuited in the corporeal patterns impressed on the brain.

The Pull of the Magnet

The problem begins to surface with the loadstone, a popular topic of research, since the publication of Gilbert's *De Magnete* in 1600, and one that occupied such pioneers of the Scientific Revolution as Galileo and Kepler. In Rule 13, Descartes asks, "What can we infer about the nature of the magnet from the experiments Gilbert claims to have made, be they true or false?"[62] Note that Descartes is not thinking of verifying the alleged experimental data but of seeing what can be *inferred* from them. He clearly assumes that this can be done by combining "simple natures" that are intuited in the imagination.

In Rule 12, Descartes had been even more explicit:

> Someone who thinks that nothing in the magnet can be known which does not consist of certain self-evident, simple natures, cannot be in doubt about how he should proceed. First he carefully gathers together all the available *observations* concerning the stone in question; then he tries to *deduce* from this what sort of mixture of simple natures is necessary for producing all the effects which the magnet is found to have. Once he has discovered this mixture, he is in a position to make the bold claim that he has grasped the true nature of the magnet, so far as it is humanly possible to discover it on the basis of given *observations*.[63]

Descartes does not pursue this analysis, which is indeed a "bold claim." In the case of geometrical shapes, such as a triangle, the lines are observable. In the case of sound, the tone and the consonances can be heard and correlated with visual dimensions, such as lengths and thickness. But what specific observable properties of the magnet can be correlated with lines or simple geometrical shapes? No answer is given. All we are told is that "ideas of all things can be formed by means of figures alone."[64]

Descartes could perhaps have pointed out that the magnet is amenable to his mode of treatment because it is a source of motion, and motion is a self-evident simple nature. But what combination of simple natures in the loadstone produces the magnetic effect of motion? Adding two lines at right-angle and joining their ends with a third will produce a triangle; doubling the length, the thickness or the weight of a string will alter the tone. But what, in Descartes' panoply of simple natures, can give rise to magnetic

---

[62] *Rules for the Direction of the Mind*, Rule 13, p. 431.

[63] *Ibid.*, Rule 12, p. 427. Emphasis mine. The Latin word that is rendered by "observations" is *experimenta*, which covers the semantic range of both *experiment* and *experience*. The ambiguity survives in the French "expérience."

[64] *Ibid.*, Rule 14, p. 450.

attraction or repulsion? Here we find no materially extended pattern in the imagination that can be directly intuited.

What Descartes needs are entities that operate below the threshold of visible magnitude and are not open to intuitive inspection, although they can be mentally constructed on the analogy of objects visible to the naked eye. Descartes took this step in his *Principles of Philosophy* of 1644. The magnifying glass and the microscope, he says, can reveal smaller and smaller entities, but these are always characterized by extension, shape, and motion just like macroscopic objects.[65] In the *Rules for the Direction of the Mind*, however, Descartes does not adopt this strategy. He merely states a methodological principle that appears to justify the operation of mathematics as the manipulation of visible or imagined magnitudes. This offers little comfort when dealing with "forces" emanating from a magnet. Even if they could be quantified, they could not be translated into straightforwardly intuitable lines or shapes.

Secondary Qualities and the Problem of Colors

Descartes does show some uneasiness about what later came to be known as the problem of secondary qualities, namely, those that are not simple natures like extension, figure, and motion, but result from the action of simple natures on our senses. In the corpuscularian tradition, they are explained by atoms whose diverse configurations and speed give rise to sensations of colors, scents, sounds, and tastes. The reduction of secondary qualities to primary qualities was seen by Galileo, for example, as an essential element in the destruction of a Scholastic epistemology that saw forms, potencies, and qualities where there was nothing but matter in motion.

Atomism is surprisingly absent from the *Rules for the Direction of the Mind*. Descartes is putting all his money, neither on substance like the Aristotelians, nor on atoms like Democritus, but on extension perceived in the "phantasy." Invisible corpuscles cannot be imagined, hence they are of no epistemic interest. But if all that can be known is matter extended in space, how do we account for the perception of qualities, such as color *qua* color or sound *qua* sound? The direct intuition of bodies does not seem enough to explain why we admire a great painting or a beautiful sunset, or why we listen to music.

This is the challenge that Descartes faces. Guided by the analogy of a seal leaving its imprint on wax, he attempts an account of the perception of colors based on the same kind of mechanical action. Our external senses are altered by the objects they perceive "in exactly the same way as the shape of the surface of the wax is altered by a seal."[66] Descartes insists that this is the case, not only when we feel that something is extended, hard, or rough, but

---

[65] Descartes, *Principles of Philosophy*, Part Four, art. 203, A.T., VIII–1, pp. 325–326. For Descartes' explanation of magnetism, see below, chapter 12, pp. 302–305.

[66] Descartes, *Rules for the Direction of the Mind*, Rule 12, A.T., X, p. 412.

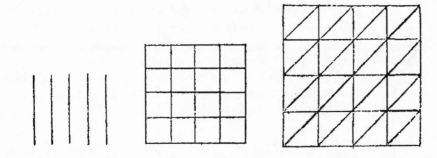

Figure 3

also when we feel that it is hot or cold, precisely the example that Galileo used in his *Assayer* to prove that atoms are responsible for our sensations.[67] Descartes does not explain what it could mean for cold to be impressed like a seal on wax, but rushes to extend his theory to light: "thus, in the eye, the first opaque membrane receives the shape impressed upon it by multi-colored light."[68] The reception is purely passive and hence completely faith-ful.

But what is the specific relation of color to extension? Although we cannot perceive color without also perceiving shape, Descartes cannot very well claim that we perceive color *qua* color as a corporeal pattern. In Rule 12, he suggests that

> we simply make an abstraction, setting aside every feature of colour apart from its possessing the character of shape, and conceive of the difference between white, blue, red, etc. as being like the difference between the following figures or similar ones.[69] [See Figure 3].

Descartes claims that this can be done for all our sensations. In Rule 14, he reaffirms that "the imagination, along with the ideas existing in it, is nothing but a real body with real extension and shape." This is his warrant for reaffirming the reduction of color and sound to extension:

> One thing can of course be said to be more or less white than another, one sound more or less sharp than another, and so on; but we cannot deter-mine exactly whether the greater exceeds the lesser by a ratio of 2 to 1 or 3 to 1 unless we have recourse to a certain analogy with the extension of a body that has shape.[70]

---

[67] See William R. Shea, *Galileo's Intellectual Revolution*, 2nd edition (New York: Science History Publications, 1972), pp. 100–106.

[68] Descartes, *Rules for the Direction of the Mind*, Rule 12, A.T., X, p. 412.

[69] *Ibid.*, p. 413.

[70] *Rules for the Direction of the Mind*, Rule 14, p. 441.

Descartes' successful correlation of sound with the length, thickness, and weight of a string helps us understand what he is aiming at. But colors are much more difficult to quantify in this manner, and Descartes himself confesses that "an infinite number of shapes" can be added to those of Figure 3.[71] What shapes are relevant, and how are they to be chosen? These questions were to exercise Descartes, and in his *Optics*, he will offer an entirely different solution based on a corpuscularian hypothesis.

The Rules That Failed

Descartes' avowed goal is certainty and the need to avoid "the fluctuating testimony of the senses." He thought he could do this by founding his *mathesis universalis* upon the clear and distinct intuitions of corporeal patterns impressed by material objects on our imagination. These extended shapes were to be our safeguard against ascribing to numbers "marvellous properties and illusory qualities."[72] But this empiricism of the senses and the imagination is not without its tensions, since Descartes maintains that it is the mind, the *cognitive force* (*vis cognoscens*), that applies itself to the shapes projected on the extended screen of our imagination. How this is achieved is not explained, and we probably have here the reason of the tentativeness with which he introduced his hypothesis of corporeal patterns and simple natures. "Of course," he says in Rule 12, "you are not obliged to believe that things are as I suggest." A few pages later, he compares his assumption to "the imaginary circles which astronomers use to describe the phenomena they study," but adds reassuringly, "this matters little, provided we can, with their aid, distinguish what might be true or false."[73] There could be no more perfect epistemological limbo. The mind can act on the imagination, but it can also be moved by it.[74]

But even if intuition were infallible, can the same be said of our imagination? To take Descartes' example, a man who has jaundice judges that something is yellow when it is not. Hence there are instances when colors cannot be simply intuited in the imagination. Reason must be allowed its say. The ambiguity is clearly revealed in Rule 12 where Descartes affirms: (a) that we cannot go wrong if we carefully attend to what is really in our imagination, and (b) that we can only go wrong unless our reason confirms that our imagination is in good working order. The wise man, he says,

---

[71] *Ibid.*, Rule 12, p. 413.

[72] *Rules for the Direction of the Mind*, Rule 14, pp. 445–446. On the problems that Descartes experienced in articulating a "universal mathematics," see John A. Schuster's persuasive essay, "Descartes' Mathesis Universalis: 1619–28" in Stephen Gaukroger (ed.), *Descartes: Philosophy, Mathematics and Physics* (Brighton: The Harvester Press, 1980), pp. 41–46.

[73] *Rules for the Direction of the Mind*, Rule 12, pp. 412, 417.

[74] *Ibid.*, p. 416. On the "uncertain" metaphysics of the *Rules for the Direction of the Mind*, see Jean-Luc Marion, *Sur l'ontologie grise de Descartes* (Paris: Vrin, 1975).

will judge that whatever comes to him from his imagination really is depicted in it. He will never assert that it passes, complete and unaltered, from the external world to his senses, and from his senses to the corporeal imagination, unless he already has some other grounds for claiming to know this.[75]

Hence the epistemic foundation in the spatial extension of the imagination is itself in need of further buttressing. Indeed, as we have already intimated, it floundered in both mathematics and physics. In mathematics the extraction of square roots and the representation of negative or imaginary roots were obviously beyond the manipulative possibilities of simple geometrical lines and figures that could be clearly imagined. In physics the nature of the magnet and the concept of force could not be captured in bidimensional macroscopic patterns, and colors could only be arbitrarily correlated with shapes.

Physiological realism would simply not do, and in the first sentence of *The World*, which Descartes wrote a couple of years later, he repudiated the notion that the nature of external objects is disclosed in the way they impress their shape upon our senses. "*The first point,*" says Descartes,

> that I want to draw to your attention is that there may be a difference between the sensation we have of light (i.e., the idea of light which is formed in our imagination by the mediation of our eyes) and what it is in the objects that produces this sensation within us (i.e., what it is in a flame or the sun that we call by the name 'light'). For although everyone is commonly convinced that the ideas we have in our mind are wholly similar to the objects from which they proceed, nevertheless *I cannot see any reason* which assures us that this is so.[76]

What Descartes meant, and should have written, is that he could *no longer* see any reason why this should be the case.

---

[75] *Ibid.*, p. 423.

[76] Descartes, *The World*, A.T., XI, p. 3.

Chapter Seven

The Optical Triumph (1625–1628)

THE LAW OF REFRACTION is one of the simplest and most basic laws of optics, but it escaped everyone before Descartes. It can be stated as follows: when a ray of light passes from one medium to another, the sine of the angle of incidence bears a constant ratio to the sine of the angle of refraction. That ratio (= sin i/sin r) is called the refractive index from one medium to another, for instance, in the case of a ray passing from air to water, it is 4/3. This is why it is also known as the sine law.

Descartes discovered this law before returning to the Netherlands in the autumn of 1628, probably during his stay in Paris between 1625 and 1628, but the fact that he never provided an autobiographical account of the path he followed led, after his death, to doubts being raised about the originality of his discovery.

Wilibrod Snell, the professor of mathematics at Leyden from 1615 to his death in 1623, determined the law of refraction under a somewhat different form (where the refractive index is expressed as the ratio cosec r/cosec i), but he never published it. His manuscript was later seen by Isaac Vossius and Christiaan Huygens who rashly concluded that Descartes had derived his ideas from Snell. It is generally agreed that this cannot have been the case, since Descartes had formulated the law of refraction before 1628, the earliest date when he could have been apprised of the different route Snell had followed.[1] Moreover when Descartes informed Snell's successor,

---

[1] Isaac Vossius was the first to level the charge of plagiarism in is *De lucis natura et proprietate*

Jakob Gool, of his sine law in February 1632, Gool never suggested that Snell had arrived at a similar result but behaved as though Descartes' law were entirely new to him.

Parisian Optics

When Descartes returned to Paris in the summer of 1625 after spending more than a year touring Italy, he found that his French acquaintances had been galvanised by Mersenne into pursuing intensive research in optics. In his encyclopaedic *Quaestiones in Genesim* published in 1623, and in *La Vérité des Sciences*, which appeared two years later, Mersenne had summarized the state of the art in the three branches of optics as they were then known: *optics* proper, the study of the rectilinear propagation of light; *catoptrics*, the study of reflection in mirrors; and *dioptrics* (which Mersenne also calls *mesoptics*, *anaclastic* or *diaclastic*), the study of refraction.[2] The last was thrust to the fore, and Claude Mydorge among others attempted to determine the lens-section that gives a true point-focus with parallel light. Mydorge was a gifted mathematician, but he was also a keen experimenter and, according to Adrien Baillet in his *Vie de Monsieur Des-Cartes*, he spent the lavish sum of 100,000 *écus* on the design and execution of optical instruments.[3] Interest in the matter extended beyond the capital, as we can see from a passage in a letter than an engineer, Robert Cornier, wrote to Mersenne on 18 August 1625:

> I do not know of any other means of making parabolic mirrors beyond those with which you are acquainted, especially since you have the paper of Mr. Mydorge who knows all that can be known on the matter. I can only tell you that Mr. Le Vasseur says that he has found an absolutely certain way *by the sines*. But I cannot say more since I do not yet know how he goes about it.[4]

(Amsterdam, 1662), p. 26, and was echoed by Leibniz in his *Discours de métaphysique*, art. 22, in Gottfried Wilhelm Leibniz, *Die philosophischen Schriften*, C.J. Gerhardt, ed., 7 vols, (Berlin, 1879–1890), facsimile (Darmstadt: Olms, 1978), vol. IV, p. 448. See D.J. Korteweg, "Descartes et les manuscrits de Snellius d'après quelques documents nouveaux," *Revue de métaphysique et de morale* 4 (1896), pp. 489–501. Unfortunately, Snell's manuscript was subsequently lost. See Cornelis de Waard, "Le manuscrit perdu de Snellius sur la réfraction," *Janus* 39 (1935), pp. 51–73. Excellent modern studies of Descartes' optics are: A.I. Sabra, *Theory of Light from Descartes to Newton* (London: Oldbourne, 1967), and A. Mark Smith, "Descartes' Theory of Light and Refraction: A Discourse on Method," *Transactions of the American Philosophical Society*, vol. 77, part 3 (1987), pp. 1–92. See also John A. Schuster's scholarly and suggestive *Descartes and the Scientific Revolution 1618–1644* (unpublished Ph.D. dissertation, Princeton University, 1977).

[2] Marin Mersenne, *La vérité des sciences* (Paris, 1625), pp. 229–230.

[3] Baillet, *Vie de Monsieur Des-Cartes*, vol. II, p. 326.

[4] Mersenne, *Correspondance*, vol. I, pp. 260–261.

Pierre Costabel has recently suggested that Le Vasseur, "whom Descartes will later admit to have known well," could have provided the suggestion that was to prove so fruitful in the hands of Descartes.[5] Unfortunately, this is a case of mistaken identity: the Le Vasseur Descartes knew and at whose house he was a welcome (if not always courteous) guest was the Seigneur d'Etioles who resided in Paris and was a friend of Descartes' father, whereas the person mentioned in the letter is Guillaume Le Vasseur, who lived in Rouen, and made a name for himself as an instrument-maker.[6]

Mersenne kept Cornier informed about developments in Paris, and it is in Cornier's letter of acknowledgment of 16 March 1626 that we find the first mention of Descartes as having provided "the reason of refractions," and the first reference to the craftsman Jean Ferrier whom Descartes was soon to employ.[7] Ferrier had made instruments for Jacques Aleaume, a Parisian scholar, whose books and instruments were sold at his death in 1627. It would appear that Mydorge purchased all or part of this legacy and that around this time he began to employ his artisan. Ferrier also received employment from Jean-Baptiste Morin, the professor of mathematics at the Collège de France. In all likelihood, Ferrier was introduced to Descartes through Mydorge or Mersenne in 1626 or 1627. He was to prove invaluable in putting Descartes' ideas into execution.

The Anaclastic

The main problem that interested Parisian scientists was the determination of the anaclastic, or the line on which parallel rays will intersect at a single point after going through a refracting medium. This requires the knowledge of the curvature that a lens must have to bring all parallel rays to a single focal point. In turn, this is only possible if the law of refraction is known, and it is because Descartes had such a law that he was able to solve the problem. In a letter to Constantin Huygens, written in 1635, Descartes gave an account of how "eight or nine years" earlier his craftsman Ferrier succeeded in grinding a lens that brought all the incident parallel rays to focus at a distance of eight inches:

> But let me tell you with what care we cut the glass. First, I had three small identical triangles made. Each had a 90° and a 30° angle so that one side was twice the other. The first was made of rock-crystal, the second of Venetian glass or crystalline, and the third of common glass. A copper

[5] René Descartes, *Règles utiles et claires pour la direction de l'esprit et la recherche de la vérité*, Jean-Luc Marion, trans., with mathematical notes by Pierre Costabel (The Hague, Martinus Nijhoff, 1977), p. 317.

[6] On Nicolas Le Vasseur, Seigneur d'Etioles, see Baillet, *Vie de Monsieur Des-Cartes*, vol. I, pp. 130–131, 136, 152–154. On Guillaume Le Vasseur, see Mersenne, *Correspondance*, vol. I, pp. 242–243.

[7] Mersenne, *Correspondance*, vol. I, pp. 418, 420.

ruler with two pinnules was constructed and the triangles placed on them to measure the refractions, as I explain in the *Optics*. This is how I found that refraction is much greater in rock-crystal than in glass of less purity, but I do not remember what the actual sizes were.

You may have heard of M. Mydorge whose skill at drawing geometrical figures is beyond compare. He took a compass with points of steel as fine as needles, and he traced out the hyperbola related to refraction through Venetian glass on a large copper plate that had been highly polished. He then cut out this hyperbola and filed it carefully along the edge traced by the compass. An instrument maker named Ferrier used this pattern to grind a mould of copper on a turning-lathe and give it the curvature corresponding to the shape that the lens was to receive. In order not to damage the model by applying it repeatedly to the mould, he cut out cardboard pieces on the copper plate and used these as templates instead. When the mould was ready, he fastened the lens to the lathe, put some sandstone between the mould and the lenses, and ground the lens by pressing it against the mould. But when he went on to grind a concave lens in the same way, it turned out to be impossible because the lens was less worn in the middle than at the circumference since the motion of the lathe is slower at the centre.[8]

From this account it is clear that Descartes depended on the draughtsmanship of Mydorge and the craftsmanship of Ferrier to illustrate experimentally the law of sines, but he does not tell Huygens how he arrived at it. He merely describes how the glass was ground and the outcome: a very good hyperbolic convex lens could be constructed, but a concave one proved to be beyond the available technical means.

Measuring Refraction

If we now turn to Discourse X of the *Optics*, written roughly at the same time as the letter to Huygens which I have just quoted, we find Descartes' account of the method he used to determine the refractive index, what he calls "the proportion used to measure the refractions" of a given piece of glass or crystal.[9] Descartes uses a plane board EFI (see Figure 1). EA and FL are two uprights with a small opening at A and L such that a beam of light AL is parallel to the base EFI. A right-angled prism whose angle PRQ is more acute than angle RPQ is placed as shown. The ray AL strikes the face QR perpendicularly, and is not refracted but is

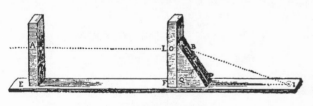

Figure 1

[8] Letter of Descartes to Constantin Huygens, 11 December 1635, A.T., I, pp. 598–600.

[9] Descartes, *Optics* [*Dioptrique*], A.T., VI, p. 211.

deviated upon emerging at B and goes to I. The points B, P, I are now transferred to a sheet of paper (see Figure 2).

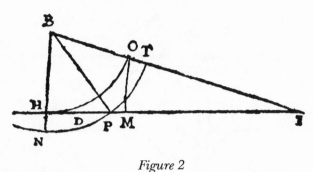

Figure 2

With center B and radius BP, trace an arc cutting BI at T, and make arc PN equal to arc PT. Join B and N. The straight line thus produced cuts IP produced in H. With center B and radius BH, draw arc HO cutting BI in O, whence "we will have the ratio between the lines HI and OI as the common measure of all refractions that can be caused by the difference between the air and the glass that is being examined."[10]

Note that Descartes *does not mention* that OI is the *sine of the angle of incidence* and that HI is the *sine of the angle of refraction*. Hence he offers no proof either! Rather he immediately goes on to state that if we take, on HI, MI = OI, and HD = DM, we shall have D for the vertex, and H and I for the foci of the hyperbolic lense that we wish to make.

I believe that the procedure described in the *Dioptrics* is the one Descartes originally used. This is confirmed by his letter to Ferrier of 13 November 1629 in which he refers to the same device but proceeds directly to a determination of the vertex and foci of the hyperbolic lenses. The construction is as follows (see Figure 3).[11] The ray ID is refracted at D and proceeds to A. Draw a line DC meeting the plane board EA at C so that angle CDF = angle ADF. Make CK = CD and AL = AD. Bisect KL at B.

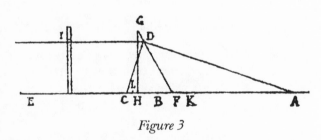

Figure 3

Without mentioning the sine of the angles of incidence or refraction, Descartes then gives Ferrier a simple way of tracing a hyperbola with a compass using points A, B, C as reference points (see Figure 4).[12] Take points N and O on line AC such that BN = BO, and from A as center trace arc TOV. Now from C as center and with CN as radius, draw arc VNT intersecting arc TOV at V and T. Repeat the same operation with slightly greater arcs XQY and YPX. The hyperbola will lie along the points of intersection of the arcs, and will have B as vertex.

Here again there is no mention of the sines of incidence or refraction, and no proof. Presumably, this was not necessary for Ferrier who only wanted

---

10 *Ibid.*, p. 213.

11 Letter of Descartes to Ferrier, 13 November 1629, A.T., I, p. 63.

12 *Ibid.* The same procedure is recommended in the *Optics*, A.T., VI, p. 215.

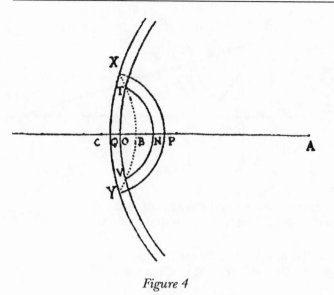

Figure 4

practical guidance in grinding lenses. But can we reconstruct the path that led Descartes to his discovery?

"My First Teacher in Optics"

One thing is clear: when Descartes called on Beeckman on 8 October 1628, he informed him that he had determined the angle of refraction with the device we have just been examining, and two diagrams in Beeckman's *Journal* are an important indication of how he conveyed his results to his friend (see Figure 5). Under the figure, Beeckman wrote: "Having determined the amount of refraction for one angle, he deduced the values for the others according to the sines: 'as *ab* is to *hg*', he said, 'so is *cd* to *if*.'"[13] (Figure 5b).

Nowhere does Descartes indicate where he might have got the idea of measuring refraction in precisely this way, but there is a sentence in his letter to Mersenne of 31 March 1638 that is revealing because it is one of the rare places where Descartes admits that he has learned something from someone else. He writes: "Kepler was my first teacher in optics."[14]

Since Descartes vigorously denies that he borrowed the elliptical and hyperbolic lenses that he uses in his *Optics* from Kepler, what can he have learnt from him?[15] I believe that the answer is to be sought at the beginning of Kepler's influential *Dioptrice* where we find a diagram (Figure 6)[16] that is

[13] Beeckman, *Journal*, A.T., X, p. 336.

[14] Letter of Descartes to Mersenne, 31 March 1638, A.T., II, p. 86.

[15] "The person who accuses me of having borrowed from Kepler the ellipses and the hyperbolas of my *Optics* is either ignorant or malicious" (*ibid.*, pp. 85–86).

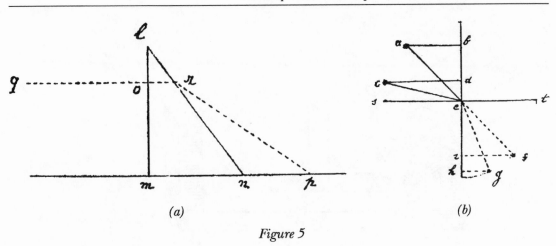

Figure 5

very similar to the one that Descartes gave Beeckman (Figure 5a). Kepler uses the arrangement illustrated to measure refraction much as Descartes does in his letter to Ferrier (see Figure 3) and in his *Optics* (see Figures 1 and 2). This is still a long way from the sine law, but I believe that the diagram marks the starting point of Descartes' quest *for a constant ratio* that eventually led him to a pair of lines that could be directly correlated to the sines of the angles of incidence and refraction.

The Law Disguised

Whatever the route Descartes followed, he was anxious to conceal his discovery. Although he corresponded regularly with Mersenne from 1629 onwards, he only disclosed his sine law in a letter of June 1632: "As to my way of measuring the refraction of light, I compare the sines of the angle of incidence and the angle of refraction, but I would be happy if this were not made known as yet."[17] Earlier, in a letter dated 25 November 1630, he stated that he did not fear that others would precede him in print "unless they draw it from the letters that I sent Ferrier."[18]

---

[16] Kepler, *Dioptrice*, in *Gesammelte Werke*, M. Caspar, F. Hammer, *et* alii, eds., 20 vols. to date (Munich: C.H. Beck, 1938–), vol. IV, p. 355. The work first appeared in 1611. Note that it bears the same title, albeit in Latin, as the one Descartes gave his own book, which in French is *La Dioptrique*.

[17] Letter of Descartes to Mersenne, June 1632, A.T., I, p. 255. Four years later, Mersenne divulged the law in his *Harmonie Universelle* and called upon Descartes (whom he did not mention by name) to explain it: "Since one of the most brilliant minds of this century has discovered the true ratio between incident and refracted rays, I want to mention it here so that, when it is confirmed by experiments, all scientists may join in asking him to provide a full explanation" (Marin Mersenne, *Harmonie Universelle*, 3 vols. (Paris, 1636), facsimile (Paris: C.N.R.S., 1975), vol. I, p. 65). Mersenne adds that the law of sines will be demonstrated in Descartes' forthcoming *Optics*, which appeared in 1637.

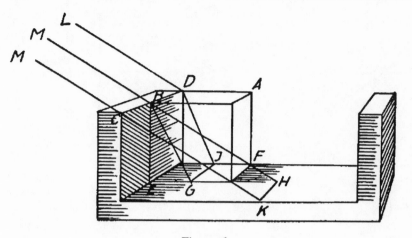

Figure 6

As we have seen, Descartes did not communicate to Ferrier the law of refraction but only a practical way of measuring refraction. What could a careful and astute reader have found in these letters that would have given him a clue to the law itself? I believe we can see what Descartes had in mind if we examine Figure 2 above. This is taken from the *Optics*, but it is merely a variant of Figure 3 that Descartes sent Ferrier on 13 November 1629,[19] and I shall use it to indicate how Descartes might have proceeded in his discovery of the law.

When considering how ray AB (see Figure 7) enters the prism and emerges along BI, it would have been natural for Descartes to measure the angle of incidence and the angle of refraction at point B. To do this he simply had to add CE, the normal at B, namely, the straight line that is perpendicular to the side of the prism BP. He could then have seen that HI is sin r (the sine of the angle of refraction), and OI sin i (the sine of the angle of incidence) by some such route as the following:

Join HO.

Since BH = BO, HO is parallel to the normal CE.

Now the incident ray AB is parallel to the plane HI.

Hence angle of incidence ABC = angle OHB, and angle of refraction EBI = angle BOH.

Hence, angle HOI = 180° − r.

---

[18] Letter of Descartes to Mersenne, 25 November 1630, A.T., I, p. 180.

[19] In Figure 2, arcs PN and PT are equal by construction, hence angle PBH = angle PBI, just as in Figure 3, the corresponding angles FDC and FDA are equal. I am following here a suggestion of Pierre Costabel who develops the argument using Figure 3 from Descartes' letter of 13 November 1629. See Pierre Costabel, *Démarches originales de Descartes savant* (Paris: Vrin, 1982), pp. 68–70.

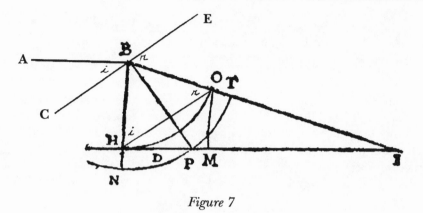

Figure 7

Now Descartes knew that in any triangle, the ratio of the sines of two interior angles is equal to the ratio of the sides opposite them.

Hence in triangle OHI,

$$\frac{\sin \text{HOI}}{\sin \text{OHI}} = \frac{\text{HI}}{\text{OI}} \text{ , namely}$$

$$\frac{\sin 180° - r}{\sin i} = \frac{\text{HI}}{\text{OI}}$$

but sin 180° − r = sin r, therefore

$$\frac{\sin i}{\sin r} = \frac{\text{HI}}{\text{OI}}$$

If Descartes followed this simple route, he stumbled, as it were, on the fact that the constant ratio of refraction (the refractive index) for a given material is the ratio of the sine of incidence to the sine of refraction. The derivation is purely geometrical and makes no appeal to higher physical laws.

Applying the Law to Lenses

Once Descartes had found the sine law, the next step was to use it to construct lenses that would bring all incoming parallel rays to a focus, thereby yielding the anaclastic. Focuses made him think of ellipses and hyperbolas, which clearly have two. When he visited Beeckman in October 1629, he showed him how an elliptical lens would bring all incoming parallel rays to a focus if it were constructed such that (see Figure 8):[20]

---

[20] In Figure 8, I have added the letters O and P to the diagram in Beeckman's *Journal*, A.T., X, p. 339.

$$\frac{\sin i}{\sin r} = \frac{\text{length of the major axis, OP}}{\text{distance between the focuses, } ab}$$

For a parallel ray, *hc*, refracted at *c* to focus *a*, the demonstration is as follows:

Join *cb*, and drop *ef* perpendicular to *ac*, and *cd* perpendicular to *ab*. Angle *acb* is bisected by line *ce*, which is prolonged to *i*. Descartes knows from his study of geometry that this line *ice* cuts the tangent at *c* and is therefore the normal used to determine the angle of incidence *ich* and the angle of refraction *ace*.[21]

Because *hc* is parallel to *ab*, angle of incidence *ich* = angle *ceb*. Therefore,

$$\sin i = cd/ce, \text{ and } \sin r = ef/ce.$$

Hence,

$$\frac{\sin i}{\sin r} = \frac{cd}{ef}$$

The next step is to prove that

$$\frac{cd}{ef} = \frac{\text{OP}}{ab} \text{ by using similar triangles.}$$

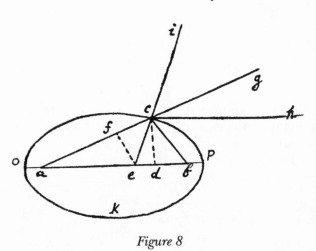

Figure 8

The proof, which is simple, is not given in Beeckman's *Journal* but is provided in Discourse VIII of Descartes' *Optics*.[22]

We know that Descartes had used a hyperbolic lens to achieve the same result when he worked with Mydorge and Ferrier in Paris. According to Beeckman, after Descartes gave him the demonstration for the ellipse, he added that the same could be shown for the hyperbola, but that he could not remember the proof on the spur of the moment. Beeckman, whose mathematical gifts were modest, was nonetheless able to work it out on his own when Descartes had left, and he was congratulated by Descartes on his return.[23] As we have seen in Chapter Four, Descartes later poured scorn on Beeckman's skills and, in his incendiary letter of 17 October 1630, he claimed that Beeckman's proof "could not

21 Descartes states this explicitly in *Optics*, Discourse VIII, A.T., VI, p. 168.

22 *Ibid.*, pp. 168–171.

23 Beeckman, *Journal*, A.T., X, p. 341.

escape anyone" who knew the sine law and the demonstration Descartes had provided for the ellipse.[24]

Despite Descartes' snide remarks, Beeckman's demonstration, which we shall now consider, provides evidence for our hypothesis that Descartes discovered the sine law by looking for

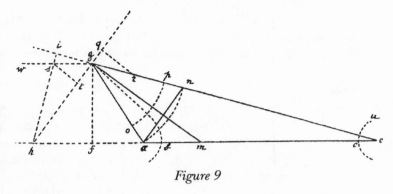

Figure 9

some constant ratio between properties of the incident and the refracted rays, and that he stumbled on lines that could be directly correlated with the sines of the angles of incidence and refraction.

The diagram in Beeckman's *Journal* (see Figure 9) is similar to the one in Figure 7 above. Ray *wg* is refracted at *g* towards *e* the focus of the second arm of the hyperbola, and the crucial steps, after bisecting angle *age*, involve tracing the normal *hgq*, and the line *an* parallel to it. With simple geometrical means and by using similar triangles, Beeckman demonstrates that

$$\frac{\sin i}{\sin r} = \frac{st}{qr} = \frac{bc}{ae} \text{ , where}$$

bc = distance between the vertices, and
ae = distance between the two foci.[25]

The Logic of Justification

We may describe Descartes' discovery of the sine law as a stroke of luck, provided we bear in mind that Fortune smiles only on the fair and the prepared. But now that he had stumbled on the correct ratio, Descartes had to justify it in physical terms, and just as he had found in Kepler the suggestion he needed for devising an instrument to measure refraction, so he turned to Kepler again for an explanation of the phenomenon.

Kepler, in his first major work on optics, the *Ad Vitellionem Paralipomena* (*Introduction to Witelo*), explicitly toyed with the idea that the lever provides the key to our understanding of refraction,[26] and Descartes made the same attempt. Here is how Beeckman summarizes Descartes' argument for the case of refraction from air to water (see Figure 10):

[24] Letter of Descartes to Beeckman, 17 October 1630, A.T., I, p. 163.

[25] Beeckman, *Journal*, A.T., X, pp. 341–342.

[26] Kepler, *Ad Vitellionem Paralipomena quibus Astronomiae Pars Optica Traditur*, in *Gesammelte Werke*, vol. II, p. 28. For Kepler, see Catherine Chevalley's excellent translation and commentary, *Johann Kepler: Les fondements de l'optique moderne: Paralipomènes à Vitellion (1604)* (Paris: Vrin, 1980).

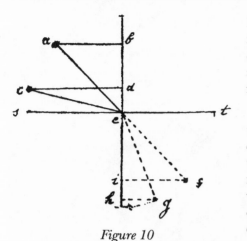

Figure 10

He assumes that there is water below *st* and that the rays are *aeg* and *cef*. These seem to undergo the same change as the equal arms of a balance at whose ends are appended weights such that the one in the water is lighter and raises the arm.[27]

The statical analogy is in keeping with a tradition that was operative throughout the seventeenth century, but it is not clear how Descartes intended to extend it. For one thing, the arms *eg* and *ef* are not raised, as would be the case for a weight buoyed up by water, but lowered, since Descartes is considering refraction from a lighter to a denser medium.

The appeal to the lever or balance was later abandoned by Descartes. It is absent from the *Optics* and his subsequent works, but I believe that it is a good indication of the procedure he followed during his Parisian years. This is confirmed by a well-known passage from Rule 8 of the *Rules for the Direction of the Mind*, written around 1627–1628, and to which we now turn.

The Right Order

Descartes considers in Rule 8 what order to follow in science and when to desist from further enquiry. The first example he gives is precisely the determination of the anaclastic. How can we find the line on which parallel rays, after going through a refracting medium, will intersect at a single point? Descartes contrasts the approach of the *pure mathematician*, who is only interested in finding ratios or proportions, with that of the *natural philosopher*, who wants to understand nature.[28]

The pure mathematician "will easily see," says Descartes, that the determination of the anaclastic "depends on the ratio of the angles of refraction to the angles of incidence."[29] In other words, it was clear to each and sundry mathematician in Paris that what had to be found was a constant ratio between some property of the angle of incidence and some other, or possibly the same, property of the angle of refraction. As we have already indicated, Descartes was looking from the outset for some such relationship. When he saw (see Figure 7 above) that HI/HO was a constant ratio for rays refracted through a given medium, he immediately looked to see whether HI and OI

---

[27] Beeckman, *Journal*, A.T., X, p. 336.

[28] The terminology is my own. Descartes speaks of "someone who only studied mathematics" (A.T., X, p. 393), and of "someone who studies not only mathematics...but the truth about any question that may arise" (*ibid.*, p. 394).

[29] *Ibid.*, *Rules for the Direction of the Mind*, Rule 8, pp. 393–394.

had something to do with the angles of incidence and refraction, and found that they were indeed sin *i* and sin *r*.

But the bare fact that HI/OI = sin *i*/sin *r* does not provide an explanation of the force or power at play. Hence the need to broaden the investigative basis. The puzzling thing is that Descartes does not say this in Rule 8. He does not even state the law, but merely declares that it can only be found by going beyond purely mathematical considerations and taking the following steps: first, noting that the ratio between the angle of incidence and the angle of refraction depends on the changes in the size of the angles caused by different refracting media; second, realizing that these changes depend on the way light penetrates the transparent medium; third, grasping that knowledge of the process of penetration presupposes knowledge of the action of light; fourth, seeing that knowledge of the action of light presupposes, in turn, knowledge of a natural power. This is the last and absolute term in the series. Once this has been "clearly perceived through mental intuition," the mathematical physicist can retrace his steps in an orderly fashion. "But if *at the second step*," writes Descartes (and here comes the passage that I believe to be the fruit of his own experience with the anaclastic),

> he is unable to discern at once what the nature of light's action is, in accordance with Rule Seven he will enumerate all the other natural powers, in the hope that a knowledge of some other natural power will help him understand this one, if only by way of analogy—but more of this later. Having done that, he will investigate the way in which the ray passes through the whole transparent body. Thus he will follow up the remaining points in due order, until he arrives at the anaclastic itself. Even though the anaclastic has been the object of much fruitless research in the past, I can see nothing to prevent anyone who uses our method correctly from gaining a clear knowledge of it.[30]

Descartes' extended description of the way the anaclastic should be investigated is perplexing in a number of ways. First, and most strikingly, the explanation of the anaclastic is not provided, and we are left to believe that the solution can only be the outcome of the philosophical route that Descartes describes. Yet by the time he wrote the *Rules for the Direction of the Mind*, he had already arrived at the sine law, and he had applied it successfully to the problem of the anaclastic. Second, Descartes is anxious to stress that the pure mathematician is at loss how to proceed. He cannot rely "on what he hears from philosophers or on what he gets from experience," nor is he allowed to postulate a ratio that he suspects is right but cannot prove to be the correct one.[31] This is bizarre because it would seem to rule out the possibility of using mathematical models. Third, Descartes is not advocating

[30] *Ibid.*, p. 395.
[31] *Ibid.*, p. 394.

making experiments but is appealing to some unspecified concept of what the action of light is in itself or by analogy with a natural power.

It is clear, however, that Descartes did not consider the fact that he had stumbled on the sine law a sufficient warrant for calling it scientific. As we have seen in Chapter Six, the *Rules for the Direction of the Mind* was his first attempt at formulating a scientific method that would yield apodictic results because it rested on the intuitive grasp of simple natures. His appeal to a "natural power" must be seen in this light. Although Descartes does not define it or explicitly equate it with a "simple nature," it is clear that a natural power is a proper object of intuition, to be grasped as he puts it "*per intuitum mentis.*"[32]

In Rule 9, Descartes illustrates what he means by intuition with the following example. If I wish to know, he says, whether a "natural power" can be transmitted instantaneously, I should not turn to magnetic force, the influence of stars, or the speed of light and ask whether their action is instantaneous, since this is an even more difficult question. "Instead," he says, "I shall consider the local motion of bodies, for no other kind of motion is more obvious to the senses." Although a stone cannot pass from one place to another in an instant because it is a body, the "power" that moves it can.

> For instance, if I move one end of a stick, however long it may be, I can easily conceive that the power which moves that part of the stick necessarily moves every other part of it instantaneously, because it is the bare power that is communicated and not the power as it exists in some body, say a stone which carries it along.[33]

As we have seen (in Figure 10), Descartes originally used the lever to explain the sine law to Beeckman. In Rule 9 of the *Rules for the Direction of the Mind*, he describes the lever or balance as a prime example of a natural power:

> In the same way, if I want to know how one and the same simple cause can give rise simultaneously to opposite effects, I shall not have recourse to the drugs of the physicians, which drive out some humours and keep others in, nor shall I prattle about the moon warming things by its light and cooling them by means of some occult quality. Rather, I shall look at a balance [the Latin has *intuebor librum*] where a single weight raises one arm and lowers the other at one and the same instant.[34]

Instantaneous motion appeared obvious to Descartes. Just as the tip of a pen cannot move without the upper part moving,[35] so one side of a lever cannot descend without the other rising. What escaped Descartes was the

---

[32] *Ibid.*, p. 395.

[33] *Ibid.*, p. 402.

[34] *Ibid.*, pp. 402–403.

[35] *Ibid.*, Rule 12, p. 414.

fact that no body is completely rigid. All substances are more or less stiff, and no motion is transmitted instantaneously.

The lever as a model of natural power proved unsatisfactory and was discarded, but Descartes was to replace it by other analogies in the *Optics*: a blind man's stick, the pressure of a liquid in a vat, and the impact of a tennis racquet. As we shall see in Chapter Ten, Descartes believed that these instances did not jeopardize his explanation in terms of instantaneous change.

Chapter Eight

Metaphysical Meditations

The Haven of the Netherlands

At the beginning of 1629, Descartes returned to the Netherlands, which he was to make his home for the next 20 years. Although he had called on Beeckman in Dordrecht in October 1628, and had expressed the hope of seeing him more frequently, Descartes did not settle in his neighborhood but in Franeker in the Province of Friesland, some 150 kilometers to the east. He took lodgings "in a small castle, separated from the two by a moat, where mass was said in safety."[1] Although officially forbidden, the Roman Catholic cult was tolerated in the Netherlands, and Descartes always lived in places where he could practice his religion without hindrance. The castle in Franeker was owned by Catholic nobles, the Sjaerdema, and later in Endegeest, he rented a castle from the Catholic family of van Foreest.

On 16 April 1629 (old style, i.e., 26 April in the Gregorian calendar), Descartes registered at the University of Franeker. He was entered as a "philosopher" instead of the more usual "student of philosophy," perhaps on account of his age, since he was already 33 years old. But register he must! Students who failed to enroll were summoned before the rector and told that they must comply with the regulations or be banned from the lecture halls.[2]

[1] Letter of Descartes to Mersenne, 18 March 1630, A.T., I, p. 129.

[2] Charles Adam, *Vie et Oeuvres de Descartes* (Paris: Léopold Cerf, 1910), pp. 123–124, note *b.*

Descartes may have wished to attend the occasional lecture, but his main aim in retiring to the more distant parts of the Netherlands was to draft the extended metaphysical essay that Cardinal de Bérulle had encouraged him to write. Apart from an ancillary interest in the practical applications of his law of refraction, Descartes spent his first nine months in the Netherlands on this project, and he was only drawn back to physics and optics in the summer of 1629, when friends urged him to explain the nature of the parhelia or mock suns that had been observed in Rome earlier that year.

The Tree of Knowledge

The genesis of Descartes' ideas is not always easy to trace, but one thing is certain. He saw himself as moving from metaphysics to physics, and in the Preface to his *Principles of Philosophy*, he later embodied his conviction in the analogy of a tree:

> whose roots are metaphysics, whose trunk is physics, and whose branches, which come out from the trunk, are all the other sciences. These can be reduced to three principal ones, namely medicine, mechanics and ethics.[3]

Descartes' deeper motivations were essentially religious, but we should bear in mind that he was not an evangelical Christian but a Roman Catholic with a strong sense of the primacy of the intellect when approaching the riddle of the universe. The mission that Cardinal de Bérulle had bestowed on him was one that he embraced wholeheartedly. Before leaving Paris, he had even asked Fr. Guillaume Gibieuf, a colleague of the Cardinal and the Head of the Community of priests of the Oratory, to go over his work when it was ready. On 18 July 1629, Descartes informed Gibieuf that he was "beginning the small treatise," by which he meant that he was in the process of setting it down in writing.[4] By the summer of 1629 therefore, Descartes had reached his main conclusions and was putting pen to paper. As we know, his work was interrupted, but we have his own account of the nature of his work in a letter that he wrote to Mersenne on 15 April 1630:

> I believe that all those to whom God has given the use of reason are bound to use it mainly to know Him and to know themselves. This is where I endeavoured to begin my own research, and I can say that I would have been unable to find the foundations of physics had I not sought after them in this way.[5]

A few months later he again confided to Mersenne that he hoped to:

> complete a small treatise on metaphysics which I began when I was in Friesland and whose main point was to prove *the existence of God and of our*

[3] *Principles of Philosophy*, Preface to the French edition, A.T., IX–2, p. 14.

[4] Letter of Descartes to Gibieuf, 18 July 1629, A.T., I, p. 17.

[5] *Ibid.*, letter of Descartes to Mersenne, 15 April 1630, p. 144.

souls when they are separated from the body, from which their immortality follows.[6]

Descartes had no doubt of his success and he claimed that he had found "a way of demonstrating metaphysical truths that is plainer [*plus évidente*] than geometrical demonstrations."[7] This early treatise is clearly a first draft of the *Meditations* that Descartes published in 1641, after having given the general line of argument in the Fourth Part of the *Discourse on Method* four years earlier.[8]

Testing the Foundations

We can assume that Descartes began his inquiry by pursuing the goal he had set out in Rule 8 of his *Rules for the Direction of the Mind*:

> the most useful inquiry we can make at this stage is to ask: What is human knowledge and what is its scope? . . . This is a task which everyone with the slightest love of truth ought to undertake at least once in his life.[9]

If the world is to be rebuilt, let us first see what instruments are available. In epistemological terms, this means what concepts are basic and reliable. But how can we be certain that any of our conceptual tools are reliable? Like Shakespeare, who was a few years his senior, Descartes was willing to entertain the idea that life is but a dream. But whereas this was a convenient literary device for Shakespeare, it became a central philosophical problem for Descartes, who was prepared to take seriously the possibility that our objective ideas are as flimsy as the notions that people our dreams. He asked, in all earnestness: how can we be sure that what we see, feel, hear or smell is not merely a figment of our imagination? What decisive test, if any, can be applied? Descartes believed that there is only one method possible: radical and universal doubt. Question everything (even the fact that you are doubting), do this systematically, and see what emerges unscathed. The result is well known and is enshrined in the lapidary phrase, "I think, therefore I am." Were the Devil himself to play havoc with my most

---

[6] *Ibid.*, letter of Descartes to Mersenne, 25 November 1630, p. 182.

[7] *Ibid.*, letter of Descartes to Mersenne, 15 April 1630, p. 144.

[8] The essential continuity between the treatise and the *Meditations* is confirmed by Descartes' insistence that the manuscript of his *Meditations* be shown to Gibieuf (see his letters to Mersenne of 30 September, 11 November and 31 December 1640, A.T., III, pp. 184, 239–240, 276–277), and his letter of 11 November 1640 to Gibieuf where he declares: "it is the cause of God that I undertook to defend" (*ibid.*, pp. 237–238). Gibieuf promoted the book in Paris (see Descartes' letter to Mersenne, 23 June 1641, *ibid.*, p. 388). According to Geneviève Rodis-Lewis, the kernel of the early treatise became the First, Third, and Fifth Meditations (see Geneviève Rodis-Lewis, "Hypothèse sur l'élaboration progressive des *Méditations* de Descartes," *Archives de Philosophie* 50 (1987), pp. 109–123).

[9] *Rules for the Direction of the Mind*, A.T., X, pp. 397–398.

commonsensical ideas and my most obvious perceptions, the fact would remain that some thinking subject is undergoing some kind of psychic experience. I can doubt the world away, but I cannot doubt myself out of existence. The "thinking I" is the rock bottom upon which an unassailable philosophy can be erected.

Cogito, ergo sum (I think, therefore I am) thus became "the first principle of the philosophy" Descartes was seeking.[10] That thinking can be conceived without the body seemed so obvious to him that he immediately proceeded to infer that the self (or the soul, as Descartes called it following the traditional terminology) is "a substance whose whole essence or nature is simply to think, and which does not require any place, or depend on any material thing, is order to exist."[11] Descartes did not shrink from the consequence that since the constitutive property of the self is thinking, the mind—even of newborn babes—is always busy with ideas.[12]

The Source of Certainty

The next step is to ask why the existence of the thinking self is clearly indubitable. What is the hallmark of this compelling evidence? Merely the fact, answers Descartes, "that I see very clearly that in order to think it is necessary to exist." From which he takes "as a general rule that the things we conceive very clearly and very distinctly are all true."[13]

We know from the *Rules for the Direction of the Mind* that Descartes' initial paradigm of clarity was not this introspective insight into the nature of the self but mathematical demonstrations. But in his effort to remove even the faintest possibility of error, Descartes was driven to recognize that even geometry can be the prey of logical fallacy. Hence the ideal insight (the "intuition" of the *Rules for the Direction of the Mind*) is no longer illustrated by mathematics but by the intuitive grasp of the self as a thinking subject.

If the idea of the self, clearly and distinctly apprehended, is self-authenticating, it is Descartes' contention that the idea of God, clearly and distinctly apprehended, yields the same result. The reason is that the concept of God has the unique feature of including its existence. In other words, existence is an integral part of the notion of God, and to truly know God is to know that he truly exists.[14] This proof, which is known as the ontological

---

[10] *Discourse on Method*, Fourth Part, A.T., VI, p. 32.

[11] *Ibid.*, p. 33.

[12] Letter of Descartes to an unknown correspondent, August 1641, A.T., III, pp. 423–424; Conversation with Burman, 16 April 1648, A.T., V, p. 149; letter to Arnauld, 4 June 1648, *ibid.*, p. 193; *Meditations*, Fifth Set of Replies, A.T., VII, pp. 356–357.

[13] *Discourse on Method*, Fourth Part, A.T., VI, p. 33.

[14] *Ibid.*, pp. 33–36; *Meditations*, Meditations Three and Five, A.T., VIII, pp. 34–52, 63–71. See Martial Guéroult, *Descartes' Philosophy Interpreted According to the Order of Reasons*, Roger Ariew, trans., 2 vols. (Minneapolis: University of Minnesota Press, 1984), vol. I, pp. 103–202, and by the same author, *Nouvelles réflexions sur la preuve ontologique de Descartes* (Paris: Vrin, 1955).

argument, had been discussed at great length, and with even greater incon-clusiveness, since it was first put forward by St. Anselm of Canterbury in the twelfth century. We are not interested here in its formal validity but in what it tells us about the role of the idea of God in Descartes' natural philosophy, and the way it illustrates Descartes reliance on innate ideas.

Innate Ideas and Universal Language

As we have seen in Chapter Five, Descartes acknowledged, from the outset of his philosophical career, "seeds of truth" as part of our native endowment.[15] Although he never provided a detailed account of the role of innate ideas, they are as important as they are ubiquitous. Human communication de-pends on their being accessible to everyone. This can be seen in Descartes' discussion of a proposal for a universal language that Mersenne sent him in 1629. Nothing more is known about this document, but from Descartes' reply, we gather that the project called for a very regular language in which the inflexions would be indicated by regular prefixes or suffixes. Descartes dismissed it as trivial, but this tells us little, since he was in the habit of calling any project submitted by someone else easy if he could do it or silly if it was beyond him. He welcomed, however, the idea of a universal language and pointed out that it presupposed

> the ordering of all the ideas that can enter the human mind on the analogy of the natural order that exists between numbers. Just as we can learn in a day how to name and write down in a foreign language all the numbers to infinity (which make up an infinity of different words), we could do the same for all the words required to express whatever falls under the apprehension of the human mind.

For someone with "the true philosophy," it should not take more than five or six days "to enumerate all the thoughts of men," before proceeding to determine and explain "the simple ideas" out of which they arise. "For such a language," Descartes adds, "is possible and we can find the science on which it depends. By its means, peasants could be better judges of the truth than philosophers at the present time."[16] It would seem therefore that for Des-cartes language is a gigantic Lego set. Once we have the basic building blocks, we can erect any structure we wish. Or to use a terminology that is closer to Descartes' own, we can say that in order to have a genuine science, we must: (a) analyze complex ideas into their simpler elements, and (b) recognize that these simple elements are not the outcome of sensory input or logical construction but are *implanted* in our minds by God himself. Since God is

---

[15] See above, Chapter Five, p. 000.

[16] Letter of Descartes to Mersenne, 20 November 1629, A.T., I, pp. 80–82. See above, Chapter Five, p. 102, note 31. Descartes' hopes are echoed in Leibniz's proposal for an alphabet of human thoughts (G.W. Leibniz, *Die Philosophischen Schriften*, C.J. Gerhardt, ed., 7 vols. (Ber-lin, 1879–1890), Facsimile (Darmstadt: Olms, 1978), vol. IV, pp. 64–65).

infallible, our science will enjoy the same property provided we faithfully describe only what our ideas clearly and distinctly represent. Our physics is thus grounded in God himself.

Eternal Truth and Radical Contingency

The dependence of our ideas on God is stressed by Descartes in his correspondence with Mersenne in 1630. When Mersenne asked whether Descartes would discuss the universal validity and permanent truth of mathematics in his *Physics*, he received the following reply:

> I shall not omit in my *Physics* to touch upon several metaphysical questions and particularly this one: that mathematical truths, which you call eternal, have been laid down by God and depend entirely on Him no less than the rest of His creatures.

This is an important point because the certainty of mathematics had not escaped unblemished from the radical doubt to which it had been subjected. It was essential that it should be reinstated, but in such a way that the power and freedom of God remained unchallenged. For Descartes nothing outside God is immutable and eternal. If mathematical propositions are universally valid, it is because God freely wills them to be so. Usually so careful not to have his opinions bruited abroad, Descartes is anxious to have this tenet of his philosophy clamored from the rooftops. "Please do not hesitate," he continues in the same letter to Mersenne,

> to affirm and proclaim everywhere that it is God who laid down these laws in nature just as a king lays down laws in his kingdom. There is not a single one that we cannot understand if we will but consider it. They are all *innate to our minds*, just as a king might stamp his laws on the hearts of his subjects if he had the power to do so.[17]

This doctrine is illuminating but also embarrassing, since it makes not only the laws of physics but all our ideas radically contingent although Descartes wants, from the vantage point of his epistemology, to claim that we find within ourselves ideas that have "their own true and immutable na-

---

[17] Letter of Descartes to Mersenne, 15 April 1630, A.T., I, p. 145. See also the letters to Mersenne of 6 and 27 May 1630, *ibid.*, pp. 149–150, 151–154. Descartes does not shirk the inference that an atheist cannot have genuine science: "I do not deny that an atheist can clearly know that the three angles of a triangle are equal to two right ones, but I claim that this knowledge is not true science, because knowledge that can be rendered doubtful should not be called science" (*Meditations*, Second Set of Replies, A.T., VII, p. 141). Descartes' doctrine of eternal truths has been extensively discussed. I have found the following particularly helpful: Margaret J. Osler, "Eternal Truths and the Laws of Nature: the Theological Foundations of Descartes' Philosophy of Nature," *Journal of the History of Ideas* 46 (1985), pp. 349–362, and Amos Funkenstein, *Theology and the Scientific Imagination from the Middle Ages to the Seventeenth Century* (Princeton: Princeton University Press, 1986), pp. 179–192.

tures," and from which we can make absolutely certain inferences.[18] In other words, there is a radical and unsolved tension in Descartes' thought between his claim that God is absolutely free and his assertion that some of our notions are immutable.

How far Descartes was willing to go in answering his critics can be seen in the illustrations that he used to drive home the radical contingency of our conceptual apparatus. To Mersenne and his friends, who had raised objections to his *Meditations*, Descartes replied that the sum of the interior angles of a triangle is equal to two right angles *merely* because God wills the triangle to have this property.[19] After the publication of the *Meditations*, but this time to Antoine Arnauld, he declared that he "would never dare to assert that God cannot make a mountain without a valley or that one and two are not three."[20] These statements are crucial because of the radical contingency they ascribe to mathematical propositions. This would seem to play havoc with Descartes' *a priori* demonstration of the existence of God and the thinking I, the two truths he claimed to have established beyond the shadow of a doubt. Let us consider each in turn.

God and the Self

In the Fifth Meditation, whose argument I date at least as far back as 1629, Descartes claims that certain ideas have a *givenness* about them that transcends the mind that conceives them:

> When, for example, I imagine a triangle, even if perhaps no such figure exists, or has ever existed, anywhere outside my thought, there is still a determinate nature, or essence, or form of the triangle that is immutable and eternal. This was not invented by me and does not depend on my mind.

and a couple of pages later, we read:

> But when I ponder this more carefully, it is quite evident that existence can no more be separated from the essence of God than that the sum of the three angles of a triangle is equal to two right angles can be separated from the essence of a triangle, or the idea of a mountain be separated from the idea of a valley. So it is not less incongruous to think of God (that is, a supremely perfect being) as lacking existence (that is, lacking a perfection) than to think of a mountain without a valley.[21]

In this way the insight that links God's essence with its existence is given the same epistemological status as the two mathematical propositions that

---

[18] *Discourse on Method*, Sixth Part, A.T., VI, p. 64.

[19] *Meditations*, Sixth Set of Replies, A.T., VII, p. 432. See also Descartes' letter to Mesland, 2 May 1644, A.T., IV, p. 118.

[20] Letter of Descartes to Antoine Arnauld, 29 July 1648, A.T., V, p. 224.

[21] *Meditations*, A.T., VII, pp. 64, 66.

Descartes undermined in his replies to Mersenne and Arnauld! How cogent can such an insight really be? The argument for the immediate disclosure of the self is similarly weakened by an appeal to the very numerical example that the letter to Arnauld recognised as true only because it was contingently willed by God. In the Third Meditation, we find a passionate declaration where the truth of $2 + 3 = 5$ is again invoked to illustrate the indubitability of the intuited self.

> Let who can deceive me, do so. He can never bring it about that I am nothing, so long as I think I am something, or make it true at some future time that I have never existed if it is now true that I exist, or that two and three make more or less than five, or anything of this kind in which I see a manifest contradiction.[22]

Spontaneous Conviction

The problem of the certainty of our ideas did not escape Descartes' readers. When they demurred, his initial reaction was to express annoyance with those who were "still stuck fast in the doubts" he had voiced at the beginning of the *Meditations*. Nonetheless, he condescended in the Second Set of Replies to state "the *basis* on which all human certainty rests." This remarkable passage has not always received the attention it deserves, and I shall quote it at length.

> As soon as we think that we correctly perceive something, we are spontaneously convinced that it is true. Now if this conviction is so firm that we can never have any reason for doubting, then there are no further questions to ask: we have everything that we can reasonably want. What is it to us if someone imagines that what we are firmly convinced to be true appears false to God or an angel, *so that it is, absolutely speaking, false? Why should this absolute falsity bother us*, since we neither believe it nor have even the slightest suspicion of it? For we suppose a conviction so firm that it cannot be destroyed, and such a conviction is clearly the same as the most perfect certainty.

A page later, Descartes repeats that we should simply ignore such radical criticism:

> It is no real objection to imagine that such truths might appear false to God or an angel, because the clarity of our perception does not allow us to listen to someone who makes up this kind of story.[23]

---

[22] *Ibid.*, p. 36.

[23] *Ibid.*, pp. 144–145, emphasis added. Writing to Mesland on 2 May 1644, Descartes makes the same recommendation: "we should not try to understand this because it is beyond our nature" (A.T., IV, p. 118).

But the point is precisely that such an objection can be raised by someone practicing the radical doubt that Descartes recommends! Descartes must retreat to one of two positions: fideism or an appeal to the moral character of God. An instance of the first strategy is found in his Sixth Set of Replies to the objections raised against his *Meditations* where we are simply enjoined to believe what we cannot fathom: "There is no need to ask how God could have brought it about from all eternity that it was not true that two times four make eight, and so on, for I admit that this is unintelligible to us."[24]

Moral Perfection

The second strategy, which is generally considered more satisfactory, is founded on God's moral character. The argument goes as follows: metaphysically speaking, we cannot rule out that God has given us a nature that errs about the most obvious things, but since perfection is of the essence of God, and truthfulness is a perfection, then God cannot be said to deceive his creatures, which would be the case if we systematically erred in making judgments that appear obvious.[25] But even if we grant that moral perfection is indeed part of the idea of God, we are still left with the mathematical analogies ($2 + 2 = 4$, $2 + 1 = 3$, and "the sum of the interior angles of a triangle is equal to 180°") whose certainty was exploded, thereby destroying our "absolute" faith in the intuitively grasped identification of essence and existence upon which the proof of the existence of God rests. If God is the necessary warrant of the objectivity of our intuitions, how can we be certain that any of our intuitions are valid prior to knowing God?

We have to appeal to God, since our dreams are as vivid as the experiences we undergo in the waking state. In the preview of the *Meditations* that he gave in his *Discourse on Method*, Descartes explicitly grounded the Rule of Clarity and Distinction in the Supreme Being:

> What I took just now as a rule, namely that what we conceive very clearly and very distinctly is true, is assured only because God is or exists, and is a perfect being, and that everything we have comes from him.[26]

Likewise, Descartes rests the whole of his science on this God-given ability to reach valid knowledge. In the Third Part of the *Principles of Philosophy*, the official textbook of Cartesian science, we read that when mathematical inferences from clear and distinct principles agree with the phenomena,

> we would seem to be offering an insult to God, if we suspected that the cause of things, discovered by us in this way, was false, as though God made

---

[24] *Meditations*, Sixth Set of Replies, A.T., VII, p. 436.

[25] *Discourse on Method*, Fourth Part, A.T., VI, pp. 38–39.

[26] *Ibid.*, p. 38.

us so imperfect that we go wrong when we use our reason in the proper way.[27]

In the very last article of the *Principles of Philosophy*, we are reminded once again that absolute certainty

is based on a metaphysical foundation, namely that God is supremely good and in no way a deceiver, and hence that the faculty he gave us for distinguishing truth from falsehood cannot lead us into error, so long as we use it properly and perceive something distinctly.[28]

In the Second Set of Replies quoted above, Descartes was willing to entertain the possibility that our epistemology can never be matched by the ontology it would seem to require. We can be absolutely certain, epistemologically speaking, even if what we believe is, strictly or ontologically speaking, completely wrong! In the passage from the *Principles of Philosophy* that we have just quoted, however, Descartes appeals to God's goodness to buttress his claim that the basic laws of nature are either intrinsically self-evident or entirely derivable by logical reasoning from self-evident premises. That this was the deepest of his convictions is clear from a letter to Henry More written in 1649:

No explanation satisfies me in physics unless it possesses the necessity that you call necessary or contradictory—excepting what can only be known through experience such as that there is only one sun or one moon around the earth, and similar cases.[29]

God-Created Certainties

There is no way of denying that Descartes never entirely came to terms with the sceptical and fideistic turns of his mind, but if we try to capture the main drift of his argument, it would seem to lie along the following lines: God, having freely chosen one kind of mathematics and one kind of matter, implanted corresponding ideas in our mind. We do not have access to a Platonic world beyond space and time but to a very local and timely set of innate ideas. We can make *a priori* deductions and affirm the objectivity of our conclusions because: (a) God created both the world and our innate ideas, and (b) God is truthful. Or as Descartes put it in the *Discourse on Method*:

I have noticed certain laws which God has so established in nature, and of which he has implanted such notions in our minds, that after adequate

---

[27] *Principles of Philosophy*, Part III, art. 43, A.T., VIII-1, p. 99.

[28] *Ibid.*, Part IV, art. 206, p. 328.

[29] Letter of Descartes to Henry More, 5 February 1649, A.T., V, p. 273.

reflection we cannot doubt that they are exactly observed in everything that exists or is made in the world.[30]

What about the concept of body, my body and the hosts of bodies that impinge upon me, and with which I am in constant contact? Here again Descartes ultimately bases his arguments for our acceptance of the reality of bodies (and matter in general) on God's goodness and power. An almighty and benevolent deity would not allow the deliverances of our senses to be systematically wrong. But if mind and matter both exist, and matter is independent of mind, what is matter?

Matter: Something Extended and Malleable

In the Second Meditation, Descartes investigates the nature of matter with the aid of a piece of wax. I believe he had toyed with such an argument as early as 1629, but it will help to state it here in the extended form in which it was eventually published and became famous:

> Let us consider those things that are generally thought to be most clearly understood of all, namely the bodies which we touch and see; not indeed bodies in general—for such perceptions are usually somewhat more confused—but one in particular. Let us take, for example, this piece of wax. It is very recently taken from the hive; it has not yet lost all the flavour of its honey; it retains some of the smell of the flowers from which it was culled; its colour, shape, and size are obvious; it is hard and cold, it is easily handled, and if you strike it with your finger, it makes a sound; in fact, it seems to have everything that is necessary for a body to be known as distinctly as possible. But now, as I speak, it is brought near the fire: the last of its flavour is removed, the smell evaporates, the colour changes, its shape disappears, its size increases, it becomes liquid and hot, it can scarcely be handled, and now, if you strike it, it makes no sound. Does the same wax remain after all this? It must be admitted that it does; no one denies it, no one thinks otherwise.
>
> What then was it in the wax that was so distinctly understood? Certainly none of the things that I reached by the senses; for all the things that fell under taste or smell or sight or touch or hearing are now changed, but the wax remains.
>
> Perhaps it was what I now think—that the wax itself was not the sweetness of honey, nor the fragrance of flowers, nor the whiteness, nor the shape, nor sound, but a body which a little earlier appeared to me as perceptible by these forms and now by different ones. What then is it precisely that I am imagining? Let us consider, and, removing those things

---

[30] *Discourse on Method*, Fifth Part, A.T., VI, p. 41.

which do not belong to the wax, let us see what remains: obviously only something extended, flexible and changeable.[31]

There is a deceptive simplicity about this analysis. It might easily be read as a straightforward argument that wax cannot consist of its sensible qualities, since all these may change while wax itself remains, whereas it cannot lose its property of extension, i.e., occupying space, without ceasing to exist. As Bernard Williams points out, were the argument primarily about the identity of wax, it would, even for Descartes, be less than overwhelming. Wax has a certain shape and a certain volume, but not necessarily a given shape and a given volume. When heated, it changes its shape, but it never ceases to have *some* shape. It is always extended in some way or other; in other words, it is always flexible and changeable. Even if we were to grant that indeterminate extension is an essential property of wax, this would not rule out that indeterminate color is also a characteristic of wax. A change of color is a change of color, not a change from color to colorlessness. To quote Bernard Williams, "from the fact that a certain quality of a thing changes in certain circumstances, it by no means follows that no reference to that quality can figure in a statement of the thing's essence."[32]

The fact that this difficulty does not seem to have troubled Descartes is an indication that what he was striving to convey was not an insight into the nature of wax but into the nature of *matter*. This is clear from the discussion in the *Principles of Philosophy* in which he goes through a list of sensible qualities, such as color, fragrance, weight, and heat, and dismisses them on the ground that we can conceive of some body or other that lacks one of them.[33]

Descartes began from the notion of a body "that is generally thought to be most clearly understood," and proceeded to show that our initial grasp of the notion was confused. The clear notion of body, namely, that it is "something extended, flexible and changeable," only emerged as the result of a process of clarification. Descartes stressed that it can neither be constructed out of sensory evidence nor adequately represented in the form of images. In the Second Meditation, he concluded:

> I must admit, then, that I in no way imagine what this wax is, but perceive it with my mind alone; and I mean this particular piece of wax, for about wax in general it is even clearer. What then is this wax which is perceived only

[31] Descartes, *Meditations*, A.T., VII, p. 30. English translation from Bernard Williams, *Descartes: the Project of Pure Enquiry* (Harmondsworth: Penguin Books, 1978), p. 214. I am much indebted to this outstanding book. On the *Meditations*, see also Martial Guéroult, *Descartes' Philosophy Interpreted According to the Order of Reasons*; Anthony Kenny, *Descartes, A Study of His Philosophy* (New York: Random House, 1968); J.L. Beck, *The Metaphysics of Descartes: A Study of the Meditations* (Oxford: Clarendon, 1965), and Margaret Dauler Wilson, *Descartes* (London: Routledge & Kegan Paul, 1978).

[32] Bernard Williams, *Descartes: the Project of Pure Inquiry*, p. 217.

[33] Descartes, *Principles of Philosophy*, Part 2, art. 11, A.T., VIII–1, p. 46.

by the mind? It is the very same that I see, and touch, and imagine, the same that I believed to exist from the beginning. But—and this is important—the perception of it is not sight, nor touch, nor imagination, and it never was, however it may have seemed at first; but an inspection of the mind alone, which can be either imperfect and confused, as it was at first, or clear and distinct, as it is now, inasmuch as I attend more or less closely to those things in which it consists.[34]

Innate and Unique

The conception of the extended thing does not depend upon the senses and the imagination (by which Descartes does not deny that bodies are sensed and imagined) because it is an immediate deliverance of the intellect, an innate idea.[35] In the Fifth Meditation, the first part of whose title reads, "The Essence of Material Things," Descartes identifies the innate idea of matter with the innate idea of quantity, defined as length, breadth, and depth, in other words, with spatial volume.

> I clearly imagine that quantity, which philosophers commonly call continuous, or the extension in length, breadth or depth of that quantity or, rather, of a thing that possesses that quantity. I can number several parts in it, and assign to these parts various sizes, shapes, positions, and local motions, and to these motions various durations.[36]

The identification of matter and extension was both easy and attractive. It was *easy* because Descartes assumed that he could discover the essential attribute of matter merely by clarifying the notion of matter that he carried in his head. The clarification itself, as we have seen, was simply a question of inspecting the idea and asking what he was forced to think when he asked what matter is. He had to think of extension, nothing less, but (and here is the rub) nothing more. Since he could not think of matter without thinking of extension, Descartes believed that he had an intuitive warrant for saying that matter is simply extension.

The identification was *attractive* because if extension is the only essential property of matter, then heaven and earth must be formed of the same matter. The old theory that the heavenly bodies are composed of a special kind of matter is excluded. A major problem is solved simply by being dissolved! Furthermore, if properties other than extension, for instance, sound and heat, can be reduced to, or derived from, extension, then the material universe can be adequately described in purely geometrical terms. Physics becomes applied geometry, and the methodology of clear and distinct ideas becomes valid throughout science.

---

[34] Descartes, *Meditations*, A.T., VII, p. 31, from Bernard Williams, *Descartes: the Project of Pure Enquiry*, p. 217.

[35] *Meditations*, Sixth Set of Replies, A.T., VII, p. 441.

[36] *Ibid.*, p. 63.

Primary and Secondary Qualities

It may be helpful to contrast Descartes' treatment of what was subsequently termed secondary qualities (color, sound, heat, and cold) with the one that Galileo gave. The Italian scientist argued that sensations, such as tickling or feeling warmth, are subjective responses to the objective properties of shape, size, and motion of the extended particles that we encounter. Descartes arrived at the same conclusion, but his method was much more radical. It is reason alone, unaided by the senses, that settles the question of the constitution of matter. Sensory evidence of any kind is irrelevant to the discussion. While this casts a shadow over the relevance of experiments, it was not perceived as a disadvantage by Descartes.

Galileo asked the following kind of question: if I pass a feather over the sole of someone's foot and he starts laughing, is the laughter in the feather?[37] Of course not, came the reply, all we find in the feather is a given extension moving at a certain speed! Galileo was interested in identifying the qualities that reside in the objects themselves. So was Descartes, but he posed a different kind of question, namely, what am I compelled to think about when I consider the motion of a material substance? Galileo would have answered that we must think of a whole cluster of qualities, such as shape, size, number, distance, and speed. Descartes' answer is that he is forced to think only of extension. The remaining primary qualities enjoy no more than a secondary status as modes of extension, and do not form part of the essence of a material substance. The intuition of pure reason establishes a hierarchy among the primary qualities, all of which reside in physical bodies, but not all on the same level.

It is clear from the foregoing analysis that Descartes assumed that he had a distinct idea not only of matter in general, but of particular determinations of shapes and sizes, i.e., of concrete things. When he states that he has the idea of a triangle whose "nature, or essence, or form is immutable and eternal and not invented by me,"[38] he makes no difference between the abstract conception of a triangle and a real triangle. But the abstract conception of a triangle, one could object, is not the conception of a *material* object at all! This objection was indeed formulated by the French philosopher Pierre Gassendi, and here is how Descartes summarized it:

> Some first-rate minds [not a flattering phrase coming from Descartes!] think that they see clearly that mathematical extension, which I lay down as the fundamental principle of my physics is nothing but an idea and that it does not exist and cannot exist outside my mind since it is merely an abstraction which I form from physical bodies.

[37] Galileo Galilei, *Il Saggiatore, Opere*, vol. VI, p. 348. Translated by Stillman Drake in S. Drake and C.D. O'Malley, *The Controversy on the Comets of 1618.* (Philadelphia: University of Pennsylvania Press, 1960), pp. 309–310.

[38] Descartes, *Meditations*, A.T., VII, p. 64.

"Here," says Descartes, "is the objection of objections." But he does not proceed to answer it. Rather he mocks it as though it were a denial of rational thought and an invitation to behave "like monkeys and parrots." With a sneer at his simian and psittacine critics, he adds: "At least, I can console myself with the thought that they link my physics with pure mathematics, which above all I hope they resemble."[39] Descartes never wavered in this certainty. A year before his untimely death in Sweden, he wrote to Henry More, who had suggested that his philosophy could stand even if his identification of matter with extension were abandoned,

> I do not admit what you courteously concede, namely that all my other views would hold even if what I wrote about the extension of matter were refuted. It belongs to the main, and to my mind, most certain foundations of my physics.[40]

Descartes could not deny, however, that the correct notion of body or matter required some effort, even the exercise of the imagination. To Princess Elizabeth, of all his correspondents the one who brought out his pedagogical side to best advantage, he confided that although extension can be known by the intellect alone it can be grasped "much better if the intellect is helped by the imagination." He added, significantly, "mathematics, which exercises mainly the imagination in the study of shapes and motions, trains us to form really distinct notions of body."[41] Note that Descartes is not making the weak claim that geometry (in its Euclidean or pictorial sense) helps us to understand the *behavior* of matter, but the much stronger claim that it helps us conceive what matter is. Extension clearly known is extension clearly imagined!

The Privileged Status of Mathematics

Although the object of mathematics may be "nothing but various relations or proportions," Descartes thinks of them as holding between lines "because I did not find anything simpler, nor anything that I could represent more distinctly to my imagination and senses."[42] Intelligibility of the clear and indubitable kind that Descartes wants is provided by embodying, or seeing, proportions in lines, the simplest kind of extension. The proper object of

---

[39] Letter of Descartes to Clerselier in reply to objections raised by Gassendi, 12 January 1646, A.T., IX–1, pp. 212–213. Leibniz and Newton also saw that the geometrical properties of a body are precisely those that leave out what makes it material and, in their own rather different ways, identified this element as force. For Leibniz, see Martial Guéroult, *Leibniz, Dynamique et Métaphysique* (Paris: Aubier-Montaigne, 1968), and Yvon Bélaval, *Leibniz, Critique de Descartes* (Paris: Gallimard, 1960). For Newton, see Ernan McMullin, *Newton on Matter and Activity* (South Bend, Ind.: University of Notre Dame Press, 1978).

[40] Letter of Descartes to Henry More, 5 February 1649, A.T., V, p. 275.

[41] Letter of Descartes to Princess Elizabeth, 28 June 1643, A.T., III, p. 692.

[42] Descartes, *Discourse on Method*, Third Part, A.T., VI, p. 20.

science is therefore extension and comparisons of extensions. As we know from the *Rules for the Direction of the Mind*, we must always ensure "that every problem has been reduced to the point where our sole concern is to discover a certain extension on the basis of a comparison with some other extension which we already know."[43] Gerd Buchdahl suggests that from holding that "a successful scientific treatment of nature *presupposes* its being *considered* under the aspect of extension, Descartes slides into the assertion that (material) nature *is* essentially equivalent to extension, and that this alone justifies us in postulating the existence of genuine science."[44] Descartes may have unconsciously slithered from epistemology to ontology, but this is not how things appeared to him. He saw himself as arguing that *all the attributes* of bodies presuppose extension, just as "shape is not conceivable except in an extended thing, nor motion except in extended space."[45] Extension he considered self-evident to anyone who would think clearly about the matter. His opponents were not merely wrong, they were blind or at least blindfolded.

Descartes' unbounded faith in himself and in his method hinges on the role or mission he felt called upon to fulfill as a natural philosopher. What he hoped to achieve was something that no modern philosopher would wish to entertain even in his wildest dreams. Since Kant, philosophers have taken it for granted that their task is to analyze scientific theories in the light of what they believe to be humanly knowable, and to locate scientific results within the realm of critical knowledge. Descartes would have considered this menial work. He had no wish to explicate current scientific practice but to legislate about future scientific procedure. His goal was to formulate a general program that would yield reliable conclusions within science. As a gifted young mathematician, he had been fascinated by the clarity and certainty of mathematics. By 1619 he had found a new way of trisecting an angle and a new method for generating mean proportionals. In the *Rules for the Direction of the Mind*, he declared that the certainty of mathematics lay in the simplicity of their object and the rigor of their deductions. Hence, "to seek the right path of truth, we ought to concern ourselves only with objects that admit of as much certainty as the demonstrations of arithmetic and geometry."[46] The certainty of mathematics emerged from the crucible of universal doubt as guaranteed by God's goodness and benevolence. The conceptual purity of its object, extension, escaped unscathed.

Unscathed but under Theological Fire

Descartes could poke fun at Gassendi and treat his criticism as mere monkey business, but there was one objection he was bound to take seriously. It was

---

[43] Descartes, *Rules for the Direction of the Mind*, Rule 14, A.T., X, p. 447.

[44] Gerd Buchdahl, *Metaphysics and the Philosophy of Science*, pp. 89–90.

[45] Descartes, *Principles of Philosophy*, Part I, art. 53, A.T., VIII–1, p. 25.

[46] Descartes, *Rules for the Direction of the Mind*, Rule 2, A.T., X, p. 366.

theological in nature and concerned the dogma of transubstantiation that had been defined by the Council of Trent (1545–1563). According to this dogma, at the consecration in the Mass, the substance of the bread and wine is changed into the body and blood of Christ, while the accidents (i.e., the secondary qualities, such as color and taste) of the bread and wine remain. Since, on Descartes' account of matter, corporeal substance is extension and the secondary qualities are merely subjective, no real accidents can remain after the substance of the bread and wine has been changed into the body and blood of Christ. Here is how Antoine Arnauld, the sharpest of Descartes' critics, formulated the objection:

> It is an article of our faith that when the substance of bread is removed from the bread of the Eucharist only the accidents remain: these are extension, shape, colour, smell, taste and the other sensible qualities. Now M. Descartes thinks that there are no qualities but only certain motions of the minute corpuscles that surround us, and by means of which we perceive those different impressions to which we then give the names of colour, taste and smell. What remains is shape, extension and mobility. But the author denies that these properties are intelligible apart from some substance in which they inhere, and hence he holds that they cannot exist without such a substance.[47]

In his reply to Arnauld, Descartes takes the perilous step (for a layman) of interpreting the decree of the Council of Trent. The Council, he observes, employed the word *species* not *accidens*, and *species* means "what can act on the senses." For Descartes this is simply the *surface* of the body, which he considers a thin film of air that, properly speaking, belongs to neither the bread nor the contiguous bodies but is the boundary common to both.[48] When the substance of bread is changed into another substance, so that the second substance is entirely contained within the limits of the bread and wine, "it necessarily follows that the new substance would act on our senses in entirely the same way as that in which the bread and wine would act, if no transubstantiation had occurred."[49] Indeed, Descartes was convinced that his account of matter was a real boon for Catholic theology:

> If I may here speak the truth freely and without offence, I venture to hope that a time will come when the view that there are real accidents will be

---

[47] *Meditations*, Fourth Set of Objections, A.T., VII, pp. 217–218. On Descartes and the physical explanation of the Eucharist, see Jean-Robert Armogathe, *Theologia Cartesiana* (The Hague: Martinus Nijhoff, 1977), pp. 41–81.

[48] "Our conception of the surface should not be based on the external shape of a body that is felt by our fingers, but we should also consider all the tiny gaps that are found between the particles of flour that make up bread . . . . And since bread does not lose its identity despite the fact that the air or some other matter contained in it pores is replaced, it is clear that this matter does not belong to the substance of bread. Hence the surface of the bread is not the immediate superficies of the bread but the one immediately surrounding its individual particles" (*Meditations*, Fourth Set of Replies, A.T., VII, p. 250).

[49] *Ibid.*, p. 251.

exploded by theologians as irrational, incomprehensible, and hazardous to the faith, and that my own will be accepted in its place as certain and indubitable.[50]

Descartes was too sanguine in his hopes. The Council of Trent had indeed used *species* instead of *accidens*, as he had pointed out, but a close reading of the decree makes it clear that the word was intended for real accidents and not merely for what can be said, in some way, to activate the senses. Behind the battle of words loomed the war of ideologies. But Descartes has no wish to become embroiled in a theological controversy, and he was convinced that the road to heaven was as open to the ignorant as to the learned. Nonetheless, he also strongly felt that his philosophy was a safeguard, for learned and ignorant alike, against the cavils of theologians. Straight thinking and true faith went hand in hand. This is why, as he told Franz Burman, he wished "above all, to see scholastic theology eradicated."[51]

The Living Watch

Less theologically sensitive perhaps, but philosophically more pressing, was the problem of the nature of living beings in a world where there are only two kinds of substance: the spiritual, defined as a thing that thinks, and the material, defined as extension. Living bodies can hardly be ascribed to the first class, and if they belong to the second, they cannot be anything but matter in motion, in other words, machines. Descartes believed this was the case, and he expended his energy in showing the implications of this view. In the second part of *The World*, posthumously published as the *Treatise on Man*, he describes the human body as an automaton on the analogy of the hydraulic statues and figurines that appeared to move of their own accord in public gardens.

> Truly we can compare the *nerves* of the machine that I am describing to the *tubes* of the mechanisms of these fountains, its *muscles and tendons* to the various *devices and springs* that make them move, and its *animal spirits* to the *water* that drives them, of which the *heart* is the *source* and the *brain's cavities the water-main*. Moreover, *breathing* and other such ordinary and natural actions that depend on the flow of the spirits, are like the movements of a *clock* or *mill* which the ordinary flow of water can regulate. *External objects*, which by their mere presence act on the organs of sense and by this means determine them to move in various ways, depending on how the parts of the brain are arranged, are *like strangers* who, entering in some of the grottoes of these fountains, unwittingly cause the movement that then occur, since they cannot enter without stepping on certain tiles so arranged. For example, if they approach a Diana bathing they will cause her

---

[50] *Ibid.*, p. 255.

[51] Conversation with Burman, 16 April 1648, A.T., V, p. 176.

Figure 1

to hide in reeds [see Figure 1], and if they pursue her they will cause a Neptune to come forward and threaten them with his trident; or if they go in another direction they will make a marine monster come out and spew water into their face.[52]

Although Descartes did not explicitly say this, he was in fact describing the automated figures in a grotto of the royal gardens at Saint-Germain-en-Laye, either from memory or from the engravings in a book by the

[52] *Treatise of Man* [*Traité de l'Homme*], A.T., XI, pp. 130–131, emphasis added; English translation by Thomas Steele Hall (Cambridge, MA: Harvard University Press, 1972), p. 22. This translation is accompanied by a very useful historical and analytical commentary as well as the French text that appeared in 1664 (Paris: Jacques Le Gras), following the publication of an imperfect Latin translation by Florentius Schuyl two years earlier (Renatus des Cartes, *De homine* (Leyden, Apud Franciscum Moyardum et Petrum Leffen, 1662). The *Treatise of Man* was the second part of his general treatise on *The World*. We know from Descartes' correspondence that he began working on it in the summer of 1632 (see the letter of Descartes to Mersenne written at the end of June 1632, A.T., I, p. 254, and the letter to the same correspondent written in November or December of that year, *ibid.*, p. 263). On Descartes' philosophy of biology, see Richard B. Carter, *Descartes' Medical Philosophy: the Organic Solution to the Mind-Body Problem* (Baltimore: Johns Hopkins University Press, 1983).

engineer Solomon de Caus from which our illustration is taken.[53] Descartes believed that the workings of the human body could be exhaustively explained on the principles that governed the movement of these figures.

But if the body is a machine, how can it be joined to the mind? The obvious answer, since mind and body are distinct substances, would seem to be that the relation can only be external and analogous to one that a driver has to a car, a secretary to a word processor or, less anachronistically, a pilot to a ship. As Antoine Arnauld put it, "the body is merely a vehicle of the spirit, whence follows the definition of man as a spirit which makes use of a body."[54] But Descartes thought this was too little, and he had already stated in the Sixth Meditation that the mind does not simply use the body as an instrument. Nature teaches me that I am united to my body, and whatever she teaches must have some truth in it, since nature "is either God himself or the order and disposition of created things established by God."[55] Furthermore, it is clear from "my sensations of pain, hunger, thirst, and so on," adds Descartes,

> that I am not in my body like a pilot in a ship, but that I am very closely joined and, as it were, intermingled with it, so that I form one whole with it. Otherwise, when my body is hurt, I, who am nothing but a thinking thing, would feel no pain since the wound would be perceived by the intellect alone, just as a sailor perceives with his eyes if something is damaged on his ship.[56]

The mind and the body constitute a unity, and nature will not allow a denial of this empirical fact. But how and where do they interact? Descartes thought he had found the precise point of interaction in the pineal gland. Figure 2 illustrates the process for the case of vision. There is a point-to-point correspondence between the pattern of the object ABC, the pattern on the retinal image 1,3,5, the pattern of the projection of that image on the lining of the brain cavity 2,4,6, and the pattern of the effluence of "animal spirits" through the surface of the pineal gland *a, b, c*. These "animal spirits" are the smallest and most agitated particles of blood that have risen to the brain.

---

[53] Solomon de Caus, *La raison des forces mouvantes avec diverses machines tant utiles que plaisantes ausquelles sont adjoints plusieurs desseings de grotes et fontaines* (Frankfurt: J. Norton, 1615). The engraving is reproduced in the English translation of the *Treatise of Man*, p. iv. In his *Cogitationes Privatae*, written between 1619 and 1621, Descartes considers the case of a puppet dancing on a string and an automated dove (A.T., X, pp. 231–232). Nicolas Poisson, who had access to Descartes' manuscripts, also mentions as "the most ingenious of these devices an artificial partridge that was set in flight by a spaniel" (Nicolas Poisson, *Commentaire ou Remarque sur la Méthode de René Descartes* (Vendôme, 1670), p. 156, quoted in A.T., X, p. 232). For an appraisal of seventeenth-century automata, see Derek J. de Solla Price, "Automata and the Origins of Mechanism and the Mechanistic Philosophy." *Technology and Culture* 5 (1964), pp. 9–42.

[54] *Meditations*, Fourth Set of Objections, A.T., VII, p. 203.

[55] *Ibid.*, p. 80.

[56] *Ibid.*, p. 81.

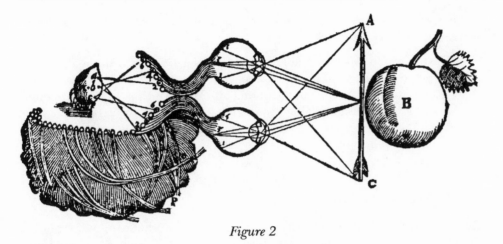

Figure 2

They flow from *a, b, c* to tubes 2,4,6 that were enlarged by the pull exerted on them by the image at 1,3,5.[57]

In the case of volition, when I deliberately turn my eyes, for instance, the mind influences the flow of spirits from the pineal gland, so that some tubes are enlarged, and a pull is exerted on the muscles of the eyes to make them rotate. The mind does not create new movements but merely alters the direction of the animal spirits that are already endowed with motion. In this way, the principle of the conservation of motion is preserved.

Localization of the point of interaction between mind and body can hardly be said to solve the problem arising from the action of an immaterial mind on a material body, since an "idea" is merely a patterned efflux of spirits from the pineal gland, namely, a differentiation of the *res extensa* or matter.[58] This main line of Cartesian thought, namely, that of emphasizing the distinction between mind and body, clashes irremediably with a second line that would save the unity of the person.[59] But Descartes' last word on the

[57] *Treatise of Man,* A.T., XI, pp. 175–176. Descartes had observed the pineal gland in animals, but he was unable to find it in a woman whose brain was being dissected by Adriaan van Walckenburg in an anatomical class that he attended in Leyden in 1637. When Walckenburg told him that he had never been able to see it in humans, Descartes concluded that it decomposed very rapidly after death (letter to Mersenne, 1 April 1640, A.T., III, p. 49). On the pre-Cartesian interpretation of the pineal gland, see Thomas Steele Hall's translation of Descartes' *Treatise of Man,* pp. 86–87, n. 135.

[58] In the *Treatise of Man,* where Descartes is describing the perfect mindless machine, ideas are necessarily material (A.T., XI, pp. 185–186). We are told that "when there shall be a rational soul in this machine it will have its main seat in the brain and will reside there like the turncock" (p. 132), but we are not told how ideas can be dematerialized.

[59] When a young professor at the University of Utrecht, Henri De Roy or Regius, suggested that the Cartesian philosophy implied that the soul and the body were only accidentally joined, Descartes immediately wrote to correct this misapprehension: "Whenever and wherever you have a chance, in public or in private, you must profess that you believe that man is truly *one being and not merely an accidental one* and that mind and body are really and substantially united" (letter to Regius, January 1642, A.T., III, p. 493).

subject, published in the *Passions of the Soul* in 1650, the year of his death, leaves the mystery intact:

> The body of a living man differs from that of a dead man, just as a watch or some other automaton (that is, a machine that moves of itself), when it is wound up and contains in itself the corporeal principle of the movement for which it is designed along with all that is required for its action, differs from the same watch or some other machine when it is broken, and the principle of its movement ceases to act.[60]

The Beast Machine

Descartes' willingness to say that machines are automata follows from his dualism. Where there is no mind, there can only be matter. But what about the evidence that animals are not completely mindless but can learn and communicate? Descartes insists that there is no genuine evidence for ascribing reason to animals. Some animals, like parrots, have organs that enable them to utter sounds, but they do not utter them intelligently in the sense that they think of what they are saying, understand the meaning of the words, or invent new signs to convey their ideas. Animals give signs of their feelings, but these are no more than automatic reflexes. Descartes believed that an automaton with the outward shape of a monkey would deceive us any time, and that the greater dexterity of animals is no indication that they have a mind.[61] "It shows rather," as he puts it in the *Discourse on Method*,

> that they have no reason at all, and that it is nature that acts in them according to the disposition of their organs, just as a clock, which is composed of wheels and weights, is able to tell the hours and measure the time more correctly than we do with all our wisdom.[62]

---

[60] *Passions of the Soul* [*Passions de l'âme*], A.T., XI, pp. 330–331.

[61] See *Discourse on Method*, Fifth Part, A.T., VI, pp. 56–59; the letter to Reneri of April or May 1638, A.T., II, pp. 39–41 (for the addressee and the date, see p. 728); *Meditations*, Fourth Set of Replies, A.T., VII, pp. 219–221; letter to the Marquis of Newcastle, 23 November 1646, A.T., IV, pp. 573–576. When Henry More entered the lists to defend magpies and parrots (letter to Descartes, 11 December 1648, A.T., V, p. 244), Descartes repeated his arguments with one important qualification, namely, he admitted that we cannot strictly prove that birds do not reason and that he was dealing in probabilities, in this case the overwhelming probability that animals have no minds (letter to More, 5 February 1649, A.T., V, pp. 276–277).

[62] *Discourse on Method*, Fifth Part, A.T., VI, p. 59. On Descartes' denial of souls in animals, see Leonora Cohen Rosenfield, *From Beast-Machine to Man-Machine* (New York, Octagon Books, 1968), pp. 4–25. The problem about the beast-machine was clearly the fact of pain. Mersenne asked Descartes how he explained pain in animals if they had no soul. They have no pain, answered Descartes, for pain exists only where there is understanding. Animals merely go through the external motions that in man are symptoms of pain without experiencing the mental sensation (letter to Mersenne, 11 June 1640, A.T., III, p. 85).

We are inclined to think that animals are more than machines because we see them perform actions similar to ours. Since we attribute the movements of our bodies to our minds, we spontaneously assume that animals also have minds or some vital principle. All this proves, according to Descartes, is that we have to curb our rashness in making inferences about alleged animal life. How are we then to judge that the persons we meet are not sophisticated robots in human form? The test for Descartes is language and the ability to create symbols. Even the most stupid people, he says, can arrange words to express thoughts, and dumb people can learn or invent signs to make themselves understood.[63]

The Wonder of Motion

Commentators have usually emphasized the reductive side of Descartes' philosophy of biology. Animals are stripped of their "sensitive souls" and turned into machines that are, at least in principle, fully intelligible. What has not been so often stressed are two interesting consequences of Descartes' radical division between the two worlds of matter and spirit. The first concerns man's position and dignity, the second the use of arguments from design, or final causes, in science. Both are linked to Descartes' ultimately religious vision of the world.

There can be no doubt that Descartes saw his mechanization of animal life as an important aspect of his determination to reassert the unique position of man, since it entailed that the difference between man and animal is not simply one of degree. In the summary of *The Treatise of Man* in the Fifth Part of the *Discourse on Method*, Descartes makes this perfectly clear: "I showed that the rational soul, unlike the other things of which I had spoken, cannot be derived in any way from the potentiality of matter, but must be specially created." "For after the error of those who deny God," he continues,

> there is none that leads weak minds further from the straight path of virtue than that of imagining that souls of beasts are of the same nature as ours, and hence that after this life we have nothing to fear or hope for, any more than flies or ants. But when we realize how much beasts differ from us, we understand much better the reasons that prove that our soul is of a nature that is entirely independent of the body, and consequently that it is not bound to die with it. And since we cannot think of any other cause that destroys the soul, we are naturally led to conclude that it is immortal.[64]

---

[63] *Discourse on Method*, Fifth Part, A.T., VI, pp. 57–58.

[64] *Discourse on Method*, Fifth Part, A.T., VI, pp. 59–60. Libert Froidmont tried to turn the tables on Descartes by claiming that the arguments used to deny that animals had souls could be used to deprive man of his soul (letter of Froidmont to Plempius, 13 September 1637, A.T., I, p. 403). Descartes replied by stating that "the souls of beasts are nothing else but their blood" and quoting Scripture (*Leviticus*, Chapter 17, verse 14, and *Deuteronomy*, Chapter 12, verse 23) as his warrant (letter to Plempius, 3 October 1637, *ibid.*, p. 414).

Descartes did not have a mere theoretical possibility in mind. A letter to the Marquis of Newcastle reveals that he was thinking of the influential writings of Montaigne and Charron.[65] In his *Essais*, Montaigne had suggested that animals communicate among themselves as well as humans, and Charron, in *De la Sagesse*, claimed that the wise man differs from the common man as much as the common man differs from the beasts. Descartes is at pains to show that all signs of mental activity in animals are just the result of clockwork. The exaltation of man requires the downgrading of animals. But the marvel of the mind is purchased at the price of making matter in motion perform feats that are almost miraculous.

The second important consequence of the reduction of the material world to a mechanical system is the elimination of teleological explanations, namely, the explanation of physical structures in terms of their aim or goal. Descartes could have made his own Francis Bacon's regrets "that the handling of final causes in physics has driven out the inquiry of physical ones, and made men rest in specious and shadowy causes, without ever searching in earnest after such as are real and truly physical."[66] As early as the *Rules for the Direction of the Mind*, Descartes gave as an illustration a figure of Tantalus that he once saw on top of a column placed inside a bowl. Tantalus looked as if he longed for a drink and when water was poured into the bowl, it rose until it reached his lips and then suddenly ran out. The feeling of amazement that spectators experienced when this happened was linked to a false impression of teleology or intended goal. It looked as though the running out of the water was in some way connected with Tantalus' lips when, in fact, it had nothing to do with his lips but only with the height the water reached and the location of the concealed conduit. Focusing on the apparently parched lips and the implied thirst only distracted viewers from the quest for the real mechanical causes.[67]

Just as the downplaying of animal life was linked with the exaltation of man, so the demise of teleological considerations is bound with the glorification of God's infinite and inscrutable wisdom. This is what Descartes emphasizes in the Fourth Meditation: "my own nature is very weak and limited, whereas God's nature is immense . . . for this reason alone I consider the search for final causes to be totally useless in physics."[68] When Gassendi objected that we often know *what purpose* a thing serves without knowing *how* it is made (for instance, we know what the valves of the heart are for, even if we do not know the material out of which they are made), Descartes replied that final causality is merely efficient causality disguised.[69] All we can know

---

[65] Letter of Descartes to the Marquis of Newcastle, 23 November 1646, A.T., IV, p. 573.

[66] Francis Bacon, *Dignity and Advancement of Learning*, Book III, Chapter IV in Francis Bacon, *Works*, J. Spedding, R.L. Eslie, *et alii.*, eds. 14 vols. (London, 1857–1874), facsimile (Stuttgart-Bad Canstatt: Frommann, 1963), vol. IV, p. 363. I have revised the translation.

[67] *Rules for the Direction of the Mind*, Rule 13, A.T., X, pp. 435–436.

[68] *Meditations*, A.T., VII, p. 55.

[69] *Ibid.*, pp. 374–375.

about the realm of ends is that God is the efficient and final cause of the universe. To say that "man is the end of creation" or that "the Heavens are made for the Earth and the Earth for me" sounded to Descartes as a gross impertinence.[70] We can only marvel at God's unfathomable decrees and trust in his Providence. The mechanical philosophy makes man unique; it also elevates God beyond the grasp of human analogies.

[70] Letter of Descartes to Princess Elizabeth, 15 September 1645, A.T., IV, p. 292.

Chapter Nine

Unweaving the Rainbow

*D*ESCARTES SPENT MOST OF HIS FIRST NINE MONTHS in the Netherlands working on his treatise of metaphysics. But he was a man of many parts, and his mind frequently reverted to the problems of optics that had been at the center of his interests during the Parisian years. Indeed, he may well have chosen Franeker as his Dutch retreat in 1629 in order to attend the lectures of Adriaen Metius, who had published a couple of books in 1614 in which he reported that his brother, Jacob Metius, had invented the telescope in 1608, a claim that Descartes was to repeat in his *Optics*.[1]

The Artisan Jean Ferrier

We have seen in Chapter Seven how heavily Descartes depended on Mydorge and Ferrier to give the lenses the correct curvature that he had been able to determine in the light of his discovery of the law of refraction. Thanks to Mydorge's superior draughtsmanship and Ferrier's technical skill, a good

---

[1] Adriaen Metius, *Nieuve geographische orderwysinghe* (Franeker, 1614), p. 15, and *Institutiones astronomicae et geographicae. Fondamentale ende grondelijcke orderwysinge van de sterre-konst* (Franeker, 1614), pp. 3–4, cited and translated in Albert Van Helden, *The Invention of the Telescope* (Philadelphia: American Philosophical Society), 1977, p. 48. Descartes speaks of Jacob Metius' discovery as the fortuitous fitting of a concave and a convex lens (*Optics*, A.T., VI, pp. 81–82). Van Helden believes that Jacob Metius and Hans Lipperhey, whom Descartes does not mention, succeeded independently in making a telescope.

hyperbolic lens was produced, but a concave lens proved beyond their reach. This bothered Descartes, and he kept thinking about it long after he left Paris. Metaphysics may be more important than optics, but no one, not even Descartes, can live on that exalted plane for more than a few hours a day.[2] In his leisure time, Descartes toyed with possible improvements in the technique of lens grinding, and on 18 June 1629, he wrote to Ferrier that he had come across a brilliant idea:

> Since I left you, I have learned much about our lenses, so that it is now possible to do something that surpasses what has been seen thus far. It all seems so easy and so certain, that I hardly have any doubts left about the technical side, as I did before.[3]

Descartes' aim was to entice Ferrier to the Netherlands, but he avoided telling him the nature of his discovery on the grounds that practical matters are not easy to convey in writing. Were Ferrier willing to share his "wilderness" for a few months, success could not fail to crown their joint efforts. Descartes asked Ferrier to take his tools and travel to Dort, where he would be provided with ready cash by Isaac Beeckman, the rector of the local college, with whom Descartes was still on good terms. He assured Ferrier that it was safer to journey from Dort to Franeker than to take a stroll through the streets of Paris!

Privacy at All Cost

If Descartes was willing to advance money from the port of arrival, why did he not offer to send Ferrier some money in Paris? The reason lies in Descartes' obsession with privacy (nowadays, he would have an unlisted telephone number and a post office box for his address). "If I could arrange to have money handed over to you in Paris," he wrote to Ferrier, "without disclosing my address (which I do not wish) I would ask you to bring me a small camp-bed, for the beds here have no mattresses and are most uncomfortable." Ferrier was not to tell anyone, not even Mydorge, that Descartes had written, and were he to decide to come to the Netherlands, he must do so in secrecy.[4]

Ferrier did not leap at the opportunity of travelling. Instead, he asked Descartes' help in securing an apartment in the Louvre, an honor that was bestowed on fashionable artists and artisans. Descartes complied and at the end of the summer thanked a Parisian friend for helping Ferrier, "who, I can assure you, is not only a grateful and honest man, but unrivalled in what he undertakes." He then explained what he had hoped to achieve if Ferrier had joined him:

---

[2] Descartes later confided to Princess Elizabeth that he never spent more than "very few hours, per year, on matters that concern the understanding alone" (letter of 28 June 1643, A.T., III, pp. 692–693).

[3] Letter of Descartes to Ferrier, 18 June 1629, A.T., I, p. 13.

[4] *Ibid.*, p. 15.

There is a branch of mathematics that I call the science of miracles because it teaches to use air and light so advisedly that by its means we can produce all the illusions that the magicians are said to perform by the aid of devils. To the best of my knowledge, this science has never been put into practice, and I know of no one but him [Ferrier] who is capable of it. I hold that he could make such things even if I despise them as trifles. I will not hide from you, however, that if I had been able to entice him away from Paris, I would have given him employment here, and passed in his company the hours that I otherwise lose at games or in useless conversations.[5]

The Seclusion of the City

By September, therefore, Descartes was beginning to feel tired of life in a small Dutch provincial town, and to realize that it offered no more privacy than the French towns he had fled. According to his biographer, Adrien Baillet, he moved to Amsterdam as early as October 1629. We know what his sentiments were from a letter that he wrote some time later to his friend Guez de Balzac:

> However charming a house in the country may be, it always lacks most of the conveniences that can be found in a city. Even the seclusion that one looks for is never complete. I am willing to own that you can find a waterway that will inspire the glibbest tongues, and a vale so secluded that it will exalt and transport them, but you cannot so easily avoid a lot of small neighbours, who occasionally bother you, and whose visits are more of a nuisance than the ones you received in Paris. Now in this large city where I live, everyone, except myself, is in business and so keen on increasing his profit, that I could spend my whole life here without anyone ever noticing me.[6]

Since Descartes had moved to Amsterdam, there was no point in maintaining his invitation to Ferrier or in keeping up the pretence that his improvement in lens grinding could only be communicated by word of mouth. As we shall see in the second part of this chapter, Descartes had become interested in the summer of 1629 in a different but related problem of optics, namely, the explanation of the rainbow. Work on this topic left him no time for protracted tinkling with instruments to improve the quality of lenses. On 8 October, he wrote to withdraw his invitation, but he did so in the polite language of a half-disclaimer. After urging Ferrier to get on with the instrument he had been commissioned to do for Jean-Baptiste Morin

---

[5] Letter to an unknown correspondent, dated September 1629, *ibid.*, pp. 19–21. The editor of the correspondence of Mersenne suggests that the letter was written to the Minim Friar in August 1629 (*Correspondance du P. Marin Mersenne*, vol. II, pp. 250–253).

[6] Letter of Descartes to Guez de Balzac, 5 May 1631, A.T., I, p. 203.

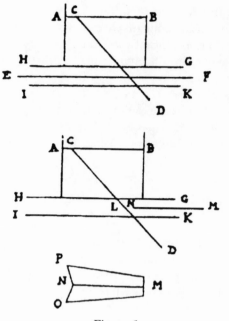

Figure 1

(probably a quadrant equipped with a telescope), he added: "I wish you were here but, from what I know about your own affairs, I cannot hope it. Furthermore, we are in a season that you would find inconvenient, and we would have to wait until next summer."[7]

Grinding Lenses

As far as Descartes' technological breakthrough is concerned, Ferrier now learned that it was merely a modification of the machine that Descartes had told him about in Paris. This consisted of three parts: a roller AB (see Figure 1), a ruler CD that passed through the roller, and a cylinder EF that moved between the planks GH and IK and ground the lens with one of its ends, E or F.

This device had proved unsatisfactory when it was tried in Paris, and Descartes' new idea was to use it not to grind the lens directly but to fashion a blade PNOM, which would then be applied to the lens to give it the desired curvature PNO. In this improved version, the ruler CD that slides through a hole in the roller AB is fixed rigidly to the roller, and the cylinder EF is dispensed with, since CD turning with AB produces at L the desired line. The blade NM is held tightly between the planks GH and IK and pressed against the ruler CD. This confers the shape PNO to the blade, which is then given a cutting edge in a second operation. The blade is now applied to a suitably soft grinding stone to which the curve PNO is transferred. Once this is done, the lens SR (see Figure 2) is applied to the stone and ground to the desired shape.

The Craftsman Insight

Descartes promised to send Ferrier diagrams by the next post, and he ended his letter with a request that Ferrier send him a description in his own words of the procedure that he had just outlined. "Lest," Descartes patronizingly added, "you imagine you understand it when you actually leave out something important."[8] Ferrier complied upon receipt of Descartes' instructions, and his letter is a lesson in Cartesian clarity. He not only recognized that the

---

[7] Letter of Descartes to Ferrier, 8 October 1629, *ibid.*, p. 33. Why travelling in October should be more uncomfortable than in early spring is not obvious. But Ferrier was meant to read between the lines. Descartes wrote to Mersenne on the same day to ask him to find employment for Ferrier in Paris (*ibid.*, pp. 24–25).

[8] Letter of Descartes to Ferrier, 8 October 1629, *ibid.*, p. 36.

curve was a hyperbola (although Descartes had withheld its name), but he offered a description of the instrument that was an improvement on Descartes' own. He was also keenly aware of several practical difficulties about which Descartes was either ignorant or had chosen to remain silent, such as that: (a) two blades are required, since the one used for the concave side of the lens will not do for the convex; (b) if ruler CD is fastened to roller AB, it will only touch point N when it is raised or lowered; (c) one plank or board, not two, as Descartes had suggested, is necessary; (d) the abrasive (sandstone or emery) placed between the grindstone and the lens

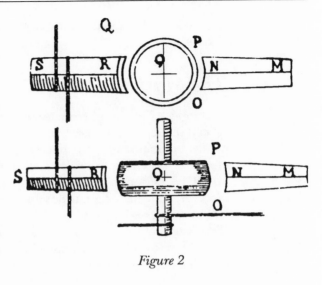

Figure 2

will wear the stone rapidly; and (e) the blade will become dull by rubbing against the stone.

Ferrier displays his real mastery when he proceeds to suggest a number of improvements, including the following: (a) making the grindstone out of iron or brass; (b) placing it above the lens to avoid too rapid a loss of the abrasive; (c) making the grindstone and the axle of one piece; (d) pouring water mixed with oil on the stone to make the abrasive adhere to its surface; (e) avoiding the use of cogs and wheels that can never mesh well enough to avoid minute bumps and dents; and (f) giving the lens the roughly desired shape before grinding it to perfection with Descartes' instrument. Ferrier adds (what Descartes had not mentioned) that the stone to grind the convex side must have the shape of a pulley (i.e., be concave), and that it will not wear down equally.

The letter ends on a note of gossip. It would seem that Mydorge not only taught a method of determining the focal point of a lens but claimed it as his own. "I know," says Ferrier, "that this secret is not unknown to you, and that the aforesaid gentleman only knows what you taught him." This bit of slander may have been inspired by personal resentment against Mydorge who in Ferrier's hearing complained that he could not find a decent lens grinder. Ferrier was deeply wounded and unburdened himself to Descartes:

> He holds me in such low esteem that he does not believe I have enough brains to understand or undertake the slightest thing. He even says it in my presence! I recognize my limitations, but I should be excused since I was never given any instruction except by you, Sir, to whom I am completely indebted. This contempt, however, does not dishearten me to the point that I have lost my desire to grasp, and my ability to enjoy, the genuine scientific knowledge that persons of your excellence might communicate

to me. I have made it my ambition to be known for something above the ordinary.[9]

The Master's Voice

In a long letter dated from Amsterdam on 13 November 1629, Descartes agreed that convex and concave lenses require different blades and that two planks or boards are not necessary. Ferrier had pointed out the inconvenience of fastening the ruler CD to the roller AB and had suggested that it would be better to make it pass through the roller. Descartes believed, however, that his original design could be maintained provided the blade NM were pressed against the ruler with a weight or spring.[10] A crucial point (Descartes calls it, "one of the main secrets of the contrivance") consists in the skillful variation of the speed of rotation of the grindstone and the lathe to which the lens is fixed:

> By making, as need requires, one faster and the other slower, you can render the shapes as perfect as is humanly possible. But the ratio of these motions can only be known through practice, that is to say, even if you were an angel, you would not be able to do as well in the first as in the second year.[11]

The wheel must press constantly against the lens, and should Ferrier fail to find a way of doing this, Descartes brashly promises to provide one, forgetting that he has just admitted that the problem is not only one of design but of skillful craftsmanship. Ferrier is also told not to be surprised if the lenses look almost straight, but to polish them with the utmost care with a piece of wood or leather. We also learn that Descartes planned to use plano-convex and plano-concave lenses for the telescope, since he informs Ferrier that the "flea-lenses" (namely, magnifying lenses) are different and must be ground on both sides. He then instructs Ferrier in the method of tracing a hyperbola with a pair of compasses. This is the mechanical construction that is described in the *Optics*, and Descartes states that it is also, as far as he knows, the one used by Mydorge.[12]

A more ticklish matter (Descartes speaks of "a greater secret") is the

---

[9] Letter of Ferrier to Descartes, 26 October 1629, *ibid.*, p. 51. The letter runs from p. 38 to p. 52.

[10] Letter of Descartes to Ferrier, 13 November 1629, *ibid.*, p. 54. When he wrote his *Optics* a few years later, Descartes realized that Ferrier had been right, and he modified the description of his instrument to allow the ruler to pass through the roller, so that it could move up and down. The weight or spring now presses against the roller instead of against the blade (*Optics*, Discourse X, A.T., VI, p. 217). No mention is made of Ferrier whose touching wish to be "known for something above the ordinary" evoked little sympathy in the heart of a man to whom such a desire was not alien.

[11] *Ibid.*, pp. 59–60.

[12] See above, pp. 153–154.

determination of the angle of inclination of the machine to grind lenses. He communicates his method to Ferrier, but this time with the full realization that satisfactory results cannot be expected in less than a year or two of hard work. Were Ferrier willing to undertake this task, "I would dare to hope," he concludes, "that thanks to you we could see whether there are living beings on the moon."[13] Such were Descartes' high hopes in the power of telescopes fitted with properly ground lenses!

The Craftsman Rebuffed

Ferrier did not acknowledge receipt of Descartes' letter, and on 25 January 1630, Descartes wrote to Mersenne to ask whether he had finished the instrument he was making for the astronomer Jean-Baptiste Morin. Mersenne replied that Ferrier was no longer in Morin's employ but was preparing to leave Paris to join Descartes in the Netherlands! This news gave Descartes what can only be described as a shock. Having left Franeker for the amenities and privacy of a large anonymous city, such as Amsterdam, he had no wish to be encumbered with a lodger. Annoyance robbed him of his philosophical calm, and in a letter to Mersenne he lashed out against Ferrier and castigated him for not replying to his two long letters "that were more like books." This was grossly unfair, since Ferrier had responded to Descartes' first letter with a list of practical suggestions that ran to over 4,000 words. Descartes even claimed that it was Ferrier's reluctance to leave Paris that made him relinquish the lodgings he had taken in Franeker:

> in a small castle, separated by a moat from the town, where Mass was said in safety. If he had come, I would have purchased furniture and rented part of the building to establish our independent household. I had already hired a young man who knew how to cook in the French style, and I was resolved not to move for three years. During that period he would have had leisure to make lenses according to my design and to acquire the proficiency that would, thereafter, have brought him honour and profit. But as soon as I learned that he was not coming, I altered my arrangements, and I am now getting ready to cross over to England in five or six weeks time.[14]

Descartes had in no way intimated to Ferrier that he intended to move or that he proposed to travel to England. When he had written to him on 18 June 1629, he had stated, regardless of Ferrier's own plans: "as for myself, I am so well here, that I do not plan to leave for a long time." Descartes' intended journey was probably a mere excuse, since fear of seeing Ferrier arrive at his doorstep made him add in his letter to Mersenne that even if he stayed in the Netherlands he could not receive Ferrier without inconve-

---

[13] Letter of Descartes to Ferrier, 13 November 1629, A.T., I, p. 69. See above page 108.

[14] Letter of Descartes to Mersenne, 18 March 1630, *ibid.*, pp. 129–130.

nience to himself. "And between us, even if I could, what you tell me about his failure to complete Mr. Morin's instrument would remove any desire to do so." But what Descartes really fears, now that Ferrier has been fully apprised of the difficulties in grinding perfect lenses, is a blemish on his own reputation:

> I would be ashamed if, after keeping him for two or three years, he were to achieve nothing that was above the ordinary. I might be blamed for this failure or, at least, for having summoned him here for nothing.

Descartes' lack of candor becomes even more apparent when he adds:

> It is not necessary to talk to him about this matter or even to mention that I am no longer willing to receive him unless you see that he is getting ready to leave in earnest, in which case, tell him, please, that I told you that I was going out of this country and that he might not find me here.[15]

Should Ferrier think he can get a better job in the Netherlands than in France, Mersenne is to "assure him that life is more expensive here than in Paris," and that virtually no one is interested in instrument making (this in the home of the telescope!). Descartes then proceeds to berate Ferrier for failing to answer queries he had made about the whereabouts of his friends Balzac and Silhon. He concludes his undignified diatribe by saying that he would be only too happy, at no cost to himself, to help the artisan: "After all, I feel very sorry for Mr. Ferrier, and I would like, without too much trouble, to relieve his unlucky streak."[16]

We do not know how much of Descartes' letter Mersenne chose to disclose to Ferrier, but it would seem that he reported to Descartes that the instrument-maker was optimistic about the outcome of his lens grinding. On April 15, Descartes expressed surprise that Ferrier could have such hopes, "since he neglects to write to me. Even if I described in detail the machines required to make the lens, I do not think he can do without me."[17] We cannot escape the suspicion that behind Descartes' brave show of indispensability lurked the fear that Ferrier would, indeed, succeed without his guidance.

Several months later, in a letter of 4 November 1630 to Mersenne, we learn that the diagrams that Descartes had promised to send Ferrier in his letter of 8 October 1629 had indeed reached him, but that Ferrier had found them of little use. Descartes was cut to the quick:

> I should be the one to complain since I paid for them and they cost him nothing. He may well have pretended that he did not receive them to avoid admitting what he owes to me, for I was assured that they had been correctly addressed. I should not be unhappy if it were known that I told

[15] *Ibid.*, p. 130.

[16] *Ibid.*, p. 132.

[17] Letter of Descartes to Mersenne, 15 April 1630, *ibid.*, p. 138.

you that he is a man that I do not consider very highly. He never finishes what he starts and he is mean-minded.[18]

Descartes then informed Mersenne that he had received a letter from Ferrier, who forwarded an invitation to travel to Constantinople with M. de Marcheville, the newly appointed French ambassador. Gassendi was to have been of the party. Descartes passed this off as a jest in bad taste by Ferrier, since he was not even acquainted with de Marcheville. "I laughed at all this for I have no intention of travelling." Yet, six months earlier, in April, Descartes had told Mersenne that he was about to embark for England! Nonetheless, he instructed Mersenne, should the offer prove genuine, to ask Gassendi to assure de Marcheville that, had the proposal been made four or five years earlier, he would have welcomed it as a great stroke of luck. Unfortunately, at the present time, he was too busy to accept: "Furthermore, I would be happy if it were known that I am not, thanks be to God, in need of travelling to seek my fortune . . . and if I travel it is only for my knowledge and pleasure."[19] When de Marcheville eventually left for Constantinople in July 1631, neither Descartes nor Gassendi were part of his entourage.

Mydorge had apparently complained to Mersenne that Descartes wrote to Ferrier and not to him. Descartes, in reply, asked Mersenne to inform Mydorge that he did not always write to those "whom he honoured and esteemed most." If he wrote to Ferrier rather than Mydorge it was because he needed someone to run a few errands.[20] He made it clear to Mersenne, however, that he no longer wished to correspond with Ferrier, not out of a feeling of what he owed to Mydorge, but because he was concerned lest his letters fall into the hands of rivals who would be able to work out the correct law of sines that he wanted to be the first to publish in his *Optics*.[21]

Meanwhile, Ferrier had become genuinely distressed by Descartes' treatment and had requested the intercession of several influential persons. We know that Fr. de Condren, the head of the Oratory, and Fr. Gibieuf,

[18] Letter of Descartes to Mersenne, 4 November 1630, *ibid.*, pp. 172–173.

[19] *Ibid.*, p. 174.

[20] "I would like him to know that the people to whom I write more often are not those whom I esteem and honour the most. I have many close relatives and intimate friends to whom I never write" (*ibid.*, p. 175).

[21] Descartes first voices this fear in a letter to Mersenne on 25 November 1630 (*ibid.*, pp. 178–179), and more explicitly in November or December 1632: "If Ferrier has shown my letters to someone in the least acquainted with mathematics he will very easily have understood how to measure the angle of refraction" (*ibid.*, p. 262). This worry is probably what had decided Descartes to communicate his sine law to Mersenne in June 1632: "Concerning the way of measuring the refraction of light, I compared the sines of the angles of incidence and the angles of refractions, but I would be happy if this were not disclosed, since the first part of my *Optics* will not contain anything else" (*ibid.*, p. 255). Mersenne, however, was the last person to keep anything secret, and he inserted the formulation of the sine law in his *Harmonie Universelle*, stating that Descartes would give the demonstration in his *Optics*. It is the publication of this statement in 1636 that made Descartes hasten the completion of the three essays that appeared with the *Discourse on Method* in 1637.

whom Descartes greatly respected, wrote on his behalf, and that Gassendi sent a note to Reneri, Descartes' disciple and friend, to plead Ferrier's case. Descartes' reaction was to pen a long letter to Ferrier, which he forwarded through Mersenne, to whom he entrusted the prior task of showing it to Gassendi, Gibieuf, and de Condren. He also wrote a skillful letter to de Condren in which he expressed great pity for Ferrier whom he affected to consider as misguided rather than mischievous.[22]

The Craftsman Vindicated

Despite Descartes' poor appreciation of his perseverance, Ferrier continued to work on the improvement of optical lenses and met with success. In his *Perspective Curieuse*, published in Paris in 1638, François Niceron, Mersenne's fellow priest in the Order of the Minims, commends Descartes' *Optics* that had just appeared, and "from which," he says,

> we soon hope to see great things thanks to Mr. Ferrier who is willing to work at it. Indeed, if anyone can succeed with this new invention, he is the right person. He is not only skillful and experienced but acquainted with the secrets of the author. We have an idea of what he is able to do from a sample he showed his friends, namely a looking-glass with a small hyperbolic lens that makes out and enlarges the smallest object.[23]

What Ferrier displayed was a "*lunette à puces*," namely, a simple microscope. But he had not been idle in other fields. Jean-Baptiste Morin praised his technical achievements in fixing telescopic lenses to quadrants and in improving their design. In 1634 he was even asked by Cardinal Richelieu to construct a quadrant to observe the altitudes of two planets at the same time.[24] Ferrier realized that the publication of the *Optics* was an opportunity to reestablish contact with Descartes, and he wrote in 1638 to inform him of the progress of his work. Descartes must have been impressed, since his reply of September 1638 is free of any ill feeling: "Since you do me the favour of letting me know what you have achieved concerning the grinding of hyper-

---

[22] Descartes wrote to Mersenne, on or around 2 December 1639 (*ibid.*, pp. 189–191) enclosing letters for Ferrier (pp. 183–187) and Condren (pp. 188–189). Descartes' treatment of Ferrier can be compared to the one he meted out to Isaac Beeckman (see above pages 79–86). In 1640, the French scientist and craftsman Florimond de Beaune hurt his hand while trying to grind lenses according to Descartes' instructions. When Descartes heard of the accident he wrote to Constantin Huygens: "You might think that I am saddened, but I swear to you that I take pride in the fact that the hands of the best craftsman do not extend as far as my reasoning" (letter of 12 March 1640, A.T., III, p. 747).

[23] François Niceron, *La Perspective curieuse, ou Magie artificielle des effets merveilleux de l'Optique, Catoptrique, Dioptrique . . .* , (Paris, Pierre Billaine, 1638), pp. 100–101, cited in A.T., II, p. 376.

[24] *Correspondance de Mersenne*, vol. II, p. 420.

bolic lenses, I feel obliged to inform you what a turner of Amsterdam did for a friend of mine."[25]

This Dutch artisan had successfully built a polishing lathe, but he had been unable to get the grindstone to keep its shape. The rim of copper would not fit snugly into the wooden rim of the wheel, and the powder used as an abrasive sunk into the copper. Descartes saw no easy solution, but he fully realized that his hopes, if any, lay in Paris: "If anyone can succeed, it is you!"[26] This is the last recorded word of Descartes to Jean Ferrier. It is a touching recognition of the skill of the artisan and an indication that for all his speculative bent Descartes recognized that the crafts had their role to play in the creation of the new mechanical science.[27]

A Sign in the Sky

We must now retrace our steps to the summer of 1629. At that time Descartes was still busy writing his treatise of metaphysics, but he had just had a new idea for grinding better lenses, and had written to Ferrier to invite him to help him bring this insight to fruition. The fact that he was willing to think about optical instruments is an indication that he welcomed a respite from abstract speculation, and it is not surprising that he should have shelved his metaphysics altogether when his interest in optics was definitely rekindled by a sign from the heavens.

Around 2.00 p.m. in Rome on 20 March 1629, the Jesuit astronomer Christoph Scheiner and several friends were startled by the unexpected appearance of four parhelia or "mock suns." This striking optical phenomenon, whose nature was not known at the time, occurs when the sun shines through a thin cloud composed of hexagonal ice crystals falling with their principal axis vertical. The refraction is through a 60° prism and results in the component colors of the solar spectrum being bent through a slightly different angle. The red end of the spectrum, being bent the least, appears on the inside, while the blue, when visible, appears on the outside. There is usually one circle, but in this case three were observed accompanied by four patches of shimmering light, the parhelia, which are refracted images of the sun.

A description of the phenomenon was sent to Nicolas Claude Fabri de Peiresc in the south of France. This wealthy amateur had copies made and he circulated them widely (see Figure 3). Several reached Gassendi who was touring Holland in the summer of 1629, and he gave one to Reneri who

---

[25] Letter of Descartes to Ferrier, September 1638, A.T., II, p. 374. The friend of Descartes is Constantin Huygens who carried on a lengthy correspondence with Descartes on this topic (A.T., I, pp. 317–337).

[26] Letter of Descartes to Ferrier, September 1630, A.T., II, p. 376.

[27] The presentation of Descartes' ideas in the *Optics* ends with the plea that "some of the more curious and skilful persons of our age undertake to put them into practice" (*Optics*, A.T., VI, p. 227).

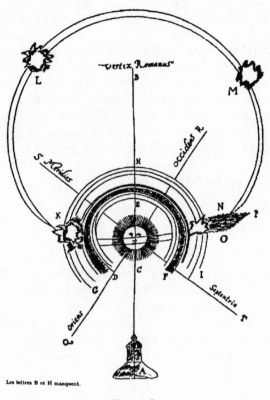

Figure 3

passed it on to Descartes.[28] Descartes was struck by the fact that the first two circles looked like rainbows, and he immediately felt that if he could understand the nature of the rainbow, he would be able to explain not only the parhelia but the whole of optics.

The Lure of the Rainbow

Rainbows are beautiful and awe inspiring. For Descartes and his contemporaries, they also represented an intellectual challenge and were often stud-

[28] Henri Régnier or Reneri (1593–1639) probably met Descartes in Amsterdam in March 1629. On 28 March of that year, he wrote to Constantin Huygens proposing, as his own inventions, several of the optical tricks that are found in della Porta's *Magia Naturalis* and that Descartes had entered in his private notebook, the *Cogitationes Privatae* (see above pp. 107–108). Reneri was probably driven to this because he was in need of a patron after having been disowned by his parents for converting to Protestantism. Although Descartes' senior by some three years, he became his first and most ardent disciple. Reneri's letter to Huygens is printed in A.T., X, pp. 541–542. Figure 3 is taken from Isaac Beeckman's copy (Isaac Beeckman, *Journal*, Cornelis de Waard, ed., 4 vols. (The Hague: Martinus Nijhoff, 1939–1945), vol. IV, p. 150).

ied.[29] For instance, in the popular *Récréation Mathématique*, first published in 1624, the Jesuit Jean Leurechon describes how rainbows can be observed in fountains, the spray raised by oars, a glass of water, soap bubbles, or a triangular prism. Everyone knew that this was a matter of reflection and refraction, but no natural philosopher or mathematician was able "after all these years and so much speculation," wrote Leurechon, to go beyond this vague generalization.[30]

When Descartes returned to Paris in 1625, Mersenne was eagerly sounding out his friends about the properties of the rainbow, and shortly thereafter he wrote an extended essay on the phenomenon that remained in manuscript.[31] In September 1629, he mentioned the parhelia in a letter to Descartes, who replied on 8 October that he had heard about them some two months prior and that, since he could only give his full attention to one thing at a time, he had dropped his essay on metaphysics "to examine in an orderly way all the meteors" (by which he meant atmospheric phenomena in general). "I believe," he added, "that I can now give an account of them, and I have decided to write a small treatise that will include an explanation of the cause of the rainbow, the matter that has given me the greatest difficulty."[32]

Descartes intended to write what he called this "sample of my philosophy" in Latin and to publish it anonymously in Paris. In the meantime, he begged Mersenne not to mention his project, so that he might hide behind his work and listen to what people said about it when it appeared in print.[33]

---

[29] An illuminating study of the history of the rainbow is Carl B. Boyer, *The Rainbow, From Myth to Mathematics* (New York: Thomas Josehoff, 1959). See also William A. Wallace, *The Scientific Methodology of Theodoric of Fribourg* (Fribourg: Fribourg University Press, 1959), and A.C. Crombie, *Robert Grosseteste and the Origins of Experimental Science, 1100–1700.* (Oxford Clarendon Press, 1953).

[30] *Récréation Mathématique* (Pont-à-Mousson: Jean Appier Hanzelet, 1626), pp. 42–43. This is a reprint of the first (also anonymous) edition published in the same locality in 1624. A second edition was published by Robert Boutonné in Paris in 1626. A third edition appeared in the same year with notes by Claude Mydorge, the scientist with whom Descartes discussed optics in Paris. Mydorge claimed that his notes had been published without his consent, and an authorized version (with additional notes by Denis Henrion) was published in 1627 with the title for the first time in the plural, *Récréations Mathématiques.* The 1630 and subsequent editions are entitled *Examen du livre des Récréations Mathématiques* by Claude Mydorge. Descartes refers explicitly to the *Récréations Mathématiques* in a letter to Mersenne of April 1634 (A.T., I, p. 287).

[31] See the letter of Robert Cornier to Mersenne, 29 July 1625, *Correspondance du P. Marin Mersenne,* vol. II, p. 237. Mersenne's essay on the rainbow is printed in the same volume, pp. 649–666 with useful editorial notes, pp. 666–673.

[32] Letter of Descartes to Mersenne, 8 October 1629, A.T., I, p. 23.

[33] *Ibid.,* pp. 23–24. Mersenne would have recognized Descartes' implicit reference to Apelles, the famous painter of the fourth century B.C., who hid behind his paintings to hear the comments of passers-by. When a cobbler, who had pointed out a fault in a sandal went on to criticize the leg, Apelles uttered the famous "*Sutor, ne supra crepidam*" ("Cobbler, don't go beyond the sandal"), which Descartes appropriated for use against his critics. The story of Apelles is told by Pliny, *Natural History,* Book 35, section 36, 84–85 and was a popular conceit in the seventeenth century. For instance, Galileo's Jesuit adversary, Christoph Scheiner,

This took much longer than he had anticipated, and the treatise on the rainbow was only published in 1637 as the Eight Discourse of his *Meteorology*.[34] It was not printed in Paris or in Latin but in the Netherlands and in French. However, a pretence of anonymity was kept up.[35] I believe that this Discourse is substantially the work that Descartes drafted in 1629. If he had revised it before publication, he would surely have stressed the connection with the *Optics*, whereas it appeared as a self-contained study of the rainbow, and was offered as a prime example of his method:

> The rainbow is such a striking marvel of nature, and one that able persons have for so long sought to explain with such care and with so little success, that I could not choose a better subject to show how, with my method, we can come to know what escaped the writers whose works have come down to us.[36]

The rainbow had been widely discussed since Aristotle in antiquity. It is a sign of Descartes' self-confidence, if not his arrogance, that he begins his study as though he had nothing to learn from his predecessors. His experience and his intellect alone are all that he deems necessary to account for this marvel of nature, and he deliberately creates the impression that he was led to his discovery simply by asking himself why rainbows can be observed in the spray of fountains. He saw that the explanation hinges on the action of light on drops of water, and he decided "to make a very big drop by filling a large glass bowl with water."[37] The technique was less novel than Descartes implied and had been used by the medieval physicist and philosopher Witelo (born c. 1230), and the Renaissance Sicilian scientist Francesco Maurolico (1494–1575).[38]

---

published his *Three Letters on the Sunspots* under the pseudonym *Apelles latens post tabulam* (Apelles hiding behind the painting).

[34] *Meteorology* [*Les Météores*], Eighth Discourse, "On the Rainbow," A.T., VI, pp. 325–344.

[35] Descartes' name as the author of the *Discourse on Method*, the *Optics*, the *Meteorology*, and the *Geometry* only appeared on the title page of the posthumous edition of 1650. In the Preface to the Latin translation of the *Discourse*, the *Optics* and the *Meteorology* published in 1644, Descartes stated that he had revised and corrected the text, thereby implying authorship. The Latin translation of the *Geometry* appeared in 1649 and clearly identifies Descartes as the author. Since Descartes personally distributed the 1637 edition to many friends and scholars, there was never any uncertainty about its provenance.

[36] *Meteorology* [*Les Météores*], Eighth Discourse, A.T., VI, p. 325. This work is translated with an introduction by Paul J. Olscamp in René Descartes, *Discourse on Method, Optics, Geometry and Meteorology*, Library of Liberal Arts (Indianapolis: Bobbs-Merrill), 1965.

[37] *Ibid.*

[38] Witelo's *Opticae* became widely known when they were edited and published by F. Risner along with Alhazen's *Opticae Thesaurus* in Basel in 1572. The two treatises are separately paginated. The reference to a round glass full of water through which sunlight is passed occurs in Book X of the *Opticae*, p. 474. Maurolico's *Photismi de lumine et umbra* was published posthumously in Naples in 1611, and again in Lyons in 1613 and 1617 under the title *Theoremata de lumine*. In the English translation by Henry Crew, entitled *The Photismi de*

The Eloquence of a Drop of Water

Descartes held the bowl at arm's length and found that when he moved or rotated it, a bright spot always appeared at a point from which a line drawn to the eye made an angle of 42° with the line that passed through the sun to the eye. This was already a considerable improvement over Maurolico who had estimated the angle at 45°, but Descartes' greatest achievement resulted from the bold generalization he made when he claimed that his experiment was valid for all the drops of water suspended in the air. The boldness lies in assuming, contrary to earlier students of optics, that drops of water are not hopelessly deformed when pressed together in a rainbow. The deceptive simplicity of the idea should not blind us to its daring.

Descartes projected the bowl of glass into the sky (see Figure 4) and used it as a megadrop to explain how light is reflected and refracted to produce the rainbow. In other words, he described his observation of the bowl of water as though he were speaking of one of the thousands of drops of water that make up the rainbow. He could do this because he assumed that he had reproduced in his "laboratory" the experimental conditions that obtain in the atmosphere.

As we have seen, Descartes determined that a bright red spot appeared at D when angle DEM was around 42°. If this angle was slightly increased, the spot vanished, but if it was slightly decreased, it did not disappear immediately but split into "two less bright bands in which yellow, blue, and other colours were perceived."[39] Descartes also observed a fainter red spot at K when angle KEM was around 52°. When this was increased or decreased, the same result as in D was obtained but in the reverse order, i.e., a slight increase yielded other fainter colors; whereas a slight decrease erased all color. Descartes concluded that when the atmosphere is packed with raindrops, red spots must appear on all of them at points that make angles of 42°

---

lumine of Maurolycus. A Chapter in Late Medieval Optics (New York: 1940), the study of refraction in a glass sphere is on pp. 58–75. Descartes refers especially to Maurolico in his *Meteorology* (A.T., VI, p. 340) and to Witelo in his correspondence (A.T., I, p. 239; II, p. 142; III, p. 483). The following passage from Leurechon's *Récréation Mathématique* could also have inspired Descartes: "If you want to see a rainbow that is more stable and permanent in its colours, take a glass of water and let the rays of sunlight that pass through it fall on a shaded place. You will enjoy seeing a lovely rainbow" (*Récréation Mathématique*, p. 42). For early attempts at finding a law of refraction, see A. Mark Smith, "Ptolemy's Search for a Law of Refraction: A Case-Study in the Classical Methodology of 'Saving the Appearances'," *Archive for History of Exact Sciences* 25 (1982), pp. 221–240.

[39] *Meteorology*, A.T., VI, p. 327. Descartes refers to the colors of the rainbows as red, yellow, blue, and "others." Newton picked out what he considered to be the most prominent colors in the spectrum as red, orange, yellow, green, blue, indigo, and violet. It is now customary to refer to six colors, omitting indigo, which most people cannot distinguish. But there is really an infinite number of colors in the rainbow. It is no more possible to say how many colors there are than it is possible to say how many points there are in a line of given length. Moreover, we only have a limited number of names for colors and the word "red," for example, has to cover a wide range of tints.

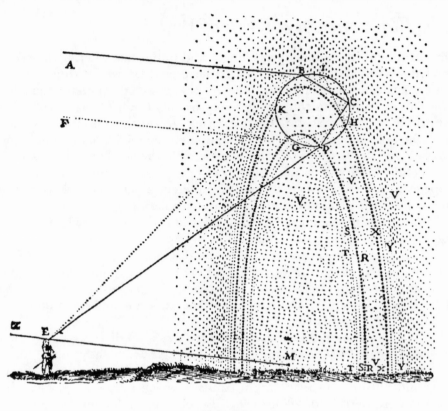

Figure 4

or 52° with line EM, thereby producing a primary rainbow passing through D (with red on its upper side and violet on its lower side) and a higher, fainter secondary rainbow with the colors reversed (red on the lower side and violet on the upper).

The determination of the angle of the inner and outer rainbow was already a considerable improvement over earlier attempts, but the next step was even more crucial. This concerned the path that the incoming ray of light took from B to D when it travelled inside the bowl of water. Again, Descartes made a tacit simplifying assumption: he took for granted that the refraction through the glass wall of the bowl could be neglected, and spoke as though the entire bowl were pure water. He also displayed considerable experimental skill in his investigation, although he does not provide the kind of detailed report that we have come to expect from physicists.

He placed an opaque body between A and B and then between D and E. In both cases, the red spot at D vanished. Since the bowl was opened at the top, he was able to slip an opaque body between B and C, and then between C and D. Again, spot D disappeared. He then covered the whole bowl and found that, provided he left an opening at B and D, the red spot did not fail to become visible. It was then clear to Descartes that the incoming ray AB was *refracted* upon entering the bowl at B, travelled to C where it was internally *reflected* to D, whence it was further *refracted* upon emerging into the air. The interior rainbow was therefore produced by *one reflection and two refractions*. Descartes repeated the same procedure for the spot K and determined that the secondary rainbow resulted from ray FG being *refracted* at G, internally *reflected* at H and I, and finally *refracted* upon reentering the air at K. This time there were *two reflections and two refractions*.

Why Angles of 42° and 52°?

This is brilliant work, but Descartes presented it as a mere propaedeutic to the question: why does a red spot appear only in those parts of the drops from which lines drawn to the eye make an angle of 42° or 52° with EM? In other words, why must they all subtend the same angle and lie on the surface of a cone with the apex at the eye?

Descartes was in the unique position of being able to tackle this problem because he had the tool required to measure not only reflection, which is easy to determine, but refraction, which had eluded all his contemporaries except Snell, who had not thought of applying it to the rainbow. The sine law enabled Descartes to calculate by how much an incident ray would be bent upon entering or leaving a drop of water, but it is symptomatic of his lack of candor that he should not have stated this simply and unequivocally. Instead, he offered a roundabout summary of his actual thought process:

> But the main difficulty still remained, which was to understand why, since there are many other rays that, after two refractions and one or two reflections, can tend toward the eye when the bowl is in a different position, only those of which I have spoken cause certain colours to appear. In order to resolve this difficulty, I looked to see if there were some other subject where they appeared in the same way, so that by comparing them I could better judge their cause. Then remembering that a prism or a triangle of crystal causes similar colours to be seen, I considered one that had the shape MNP [see Figure 5].[40]

Interrogating the Prism

It would have been simpler to say: light passing through a prism is broken up into the colours of the rainbow, so their production can be studied in a prism, especially since the refractive index (namely the value of $\sin i / \sin r$) is known to be 3/2. This is the more surprising because the *Meteorology* follows the *Optics* in which Descartes made his discovery known. The most likely reason, as I have suggested, is that the treatise on the rainbow was written in

---

[40] *Meteorology*, A.T., VI, p. 329. The translation, slightly amended is from Olscamp, *Discourse on Method, Optics, Geometry and Meteorology*, pp. 334–335.

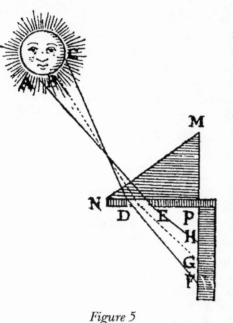

Figure 5

1629 and incorporated without major revisions into the *Meteorology* published in 1637. What was uppermost in Descartes' mind when he wrote the passage we have just quoted was the vindication of the methodology he had advocated in Rule 8 of his *Rules for the Direction of the Mind.* As we have seen in Chapter Seven, Descartes recommended reasoning from analogous instances if direct insight failed to disclose the nature of the case at hand.[41] When he could not immediately see why the rainbow was only produced when the rays were at certain fixed angles, he sought "some other subject" where refraction is also determined by some fixed ratio. Descartes knew full well that this was a prism, although he writes as if he had to dredge it from the recesses of his memory.

The assumption that refraction in a drop of water can, without further ado, be compared with refraction in a different material, such as glass, would not have appeared obvious to most seventeenth-century natural philosophers. But Descartes had already arrived in his *Rules for the Direction of the Mind* at the conclusion that there is only *one* kind of matter whose essential property is geometrical extension. Hence the legitimacy of analogies from one material object to any other material object. In the new realm of quantity, qualities are no longer indicative of substantial differences, and measurement acquires a voice of its own.

The analogous subject is the prism MNP (see Figure 5) through which sunlight is refracted after passing through a narrow slit, DE, on the otherwise darkened face NP. The colors of the rainbow appear on a white screen placed at PHGF, the red being toward F and the blue toward H. From this experiment, Descartes drew a number of conclusions, all applicable to the prismatic role of a drop of water:

1. colors are not caused by the curved surface of the drop, since faces MN and NP of the prism are both plane;

2. reflection is not required, since there is none here;

3. several refractions are not necessary, provided there is at least one and that, in the case of two, the second does not undo the action of the first, as would happen if faces NM and NP were parallel;

4. shade is required, for as soon as the slit DE is made too large, the colors appear only at the edge, and the center is left white. If the slit is made even larger, the colors disappear altogether.[42]

---

[41] See above, pp. 160–162.

[42] *Meteorology*, A.T., VI, pp. 330–331.

But why should red appear at F and blue at H? Here is where the theorizing begins, and it is intimately connected with the development of Descartes' cosmological views. This aspect of Descartes' development is known from *The World* (the full title is *The World or A Treatise on Light*) that also dates from around 1630, although it was only published posthumously in 1664.

Spherical Particles of Light

In *The World*, Descartes reduces the four traditional elements of fire, air, earth, and water to the first three. These are no longer distinguished by intrinsic qualities as they were by Aristotle and his followers for whom fire was hot and dry, air hot and moist, and earth cold and dry. Descartes recognizes only one kind of matter, which varies solely according to the size, shape, arrangement, and speed of its parts. The particles that form earth are large, irregular and sluggish, while those that compose air are small, smooth, and spherical. Fire is made up of particles so minute that they can instantly fill the interstices between the particles of air, which in turn fill the gaps between the particles of earth. It follows that this universe is a *plenum* with no void whatsoever.[43]

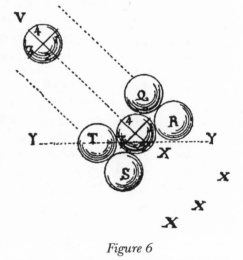

We shall return to the properties of this universe later on, but for the present, all we need consider are the small spherical particles of air through which pressure from a luminous source is transmitted. "These particles," writes Descartes in the section of the *Meteorology* we have been considering, "must be pictured as small balls rolling in the pores of earthly bodies." If the neighboring walls move at the same rate, "their rotation is nearly equal to their motion in a straight line," whereas if the neighboring balls move faster or slower, their rotation is increased or retarded. In other words, Descartes surmises that at the edge of the shade, namely, at D and E in Figure 5, the rotary motion of the balls is altered and that this is what causes the various colors that are observed.

Figure 6

Bearing in mind that all physical and optical phenomena are to be explained in terms of the size, shape, and motion of extended particles, and that the particles of air are all of the same size and shape, the explanation of color can only be sought in their change of speed. Imagine a ball, 1234 (Figure 6) that is pushed obliquely from V to X, and acquires a spin upon striking the surface of the water YY. This happens, says

[43] *The World [Le monde ou Traité de la lumière]*, ch. 5, A.T., XI, pp. 23–31.

[44] *Meteorology*, A.T., VI, p. 331.

Descartes, because on entering the water, part 3 is retarded, while part 1 continues for a brief moment with undiminished speed. As a result, the ball is compelled to rotate clockwise, i.e., in the order 1234. Now imagine it to be surrounded by four other balls Q, R, S, T of which Q and R are still moving with undiminished speed, while S and T have been retarded. According to Descartes, Q, pressing upon the part of the ball marked 1, and S, holding back the one marked 3, increase the ball's spin, while balls R and T do not hinder it because R "is disposed" to move faster and T more slowly towards X than the ball marked 1234.[45]

We may note here a curious oversight. Descartes states that the rotation of the ball in direction 1, 2, 3, 4 is increased by Q and S, whereas the diagram makes it evident that the rotary motion of the ball is augmented by Q and R, not S. That this is not merely a typographical error is clear from the explanation that accompanies the diagram. We have here an instance of Descartes' Gallic temperament. When he had an idea that looked promising, he sketched it out, and having satisfied himself that it could work, let the matter drop. Details did not interest him, as there would always be people willing to carry out the tedious business of experimenting and quantifying.

A careful reading of the *Meteorology* reveals that Descartes does not say in a simple and straightforward way that balls R and T move *faster* or *slower* than the ball 1234 that has just entered the water. Since he assumes that the transmission of light is instantaneous in a *plenum*, he uses (at least in his guarded moments) a terminology that implies that the motion is virtual, yet in such a way that the properties of virtual motion are identified with those of actual motion. This is why, in the passage we are considering, he describes the four balls Q, R, S, T, not simply as moving but as "tending to move," or "being disposed" to move faster or slower. Descartes not only conferred the same essential property of extension upon all matter, he took the even more daring step of endowing virtual and actual motion with the same characteristics. The much derided "potentiality" of the Scholastics is not so much denied as transmogrified into a subspecies of "actuality."[46]

Instantaneous Explanation

There is a Parmenidean undercurrent to much of Descartes' speculation about motion, but the more immediate and obvious connection is with the world of magic in which there is no interval between hearing the magic words and witnessing their spectacular result. We must remember that in repudiating non-mechanistic causal connections, and hence the occult relations postulated by magic, Descartes never disowned instantaneous change. That was not magic somehow. It was wonderful, of course, but it found an explanatory niche in an extended category of reality that was made to embrace whatever is "really" virtual.

[45] *Ibid.*, pp. 331–332.

[46] See pp. 234–235, 273, 329–330.

It is demonstrated quite clearly from all this, it seems to me, that the nature of the colours appearing at F [see Figure 5 above] consists only in the fact that the particles of the subtle matter that transmits the action of light tend more strongly to rotate than to move in a straight line; so that those that have a much stronger tendency to rotate cause the colour red, and those that have only a slightly stronger tendency cause yellow.

"In all this," continues Descartes, "the explanation (*la raison*) agrees so perfectly with experience that I do not believe it possible, after one has grasped both, to doubt that the matter is as I have just explained it." This is self-evident for Descartes, since, on his mechanical assumption, "it is impossible to find in the crystal MNP anything else that can produce colour except the way in which it sends the little parts of subtle matter towards the screen FGH and from there to our eyes."[47]

Appearance and Reality

The mechanical explanation of colors entails their objectivity, and Descartes welcomes the opportunity of taking up a polemical stance: "I don't like the distinction made by philosophers when they say that some colours are true while others are false or merely apparent."[48] He does not identify these philosophers, but the Jesuit authors of the Coimbra Commentary on Aristotle held that there were true and permanent colors, such as white in a swan or black in a crow, and apparent and transitory ones, such as those that appear in the rainbow.[49] On Descartes' view, all colors are "appearances," i.e., physiological responses to the stimuli of the fine particles of matter that possess different linear and rotational velocities. In this sense, "the true nature" of colors, as he puts it, "is to appear," and it would be silly to say "that they are false when they actually appear." Nonetheless, appearances have to be explained coherently and consistently, and there are a number of tensions in Descartes' account that cannot be overlooked. The rents in what Descartes considered the seamless garment of his natural philosophy are hard to conceal.

We can perhaps summarize the nature of the underlying problems as follows. Descartes initially worked out his explanation of colors in terms of the differences between the linear and rotational speeds of spherical particles of subtle matter. When he realized that these particles are so tightly packed that there can be no void, it became apparent to him that light could

---

[47] Descartes, *Meteorology*, A.T., VI, pp. 333–335.

[48] *Ibid.*, p. 335.

[49] *Commentaria in tres libros de Anima Aristotelis* (Coimbra, 1596), Lib. II, cap. 7, qu. 2, art. 2 (for the commentaries of the Jesuit professors in Coimbra, see above pp. 5–6). Descartes was following Kepler who had repudiated the distinction: "Since the colours observed in the rainbow are of the same kind as those found in coloured bodies, they have the same origin" (Kepler, *Ad Vitellionem Paralipomena*, Chapter 1, prop. 15 in *Gesammelte Werke*, vol. 2, p. 23).

only be transmitted instantaneously. He coped with this incongruity by describing the instantaneous transmission of light as virtual or "tendential." This was his first major problem. The second was the need to reconcile the law of the conservation of *rectilinear inertia* (to which we shall return in Chapter Eleven), with the apparent *rotational inertia* of the spherical particles of the subtle matter.

These difficulties surfaced in one guise or another as soon as Descartes' ideas became known and discussed. This is why we shall examine the kind of reaction Descartes' account of color elicited in his reader when it was published in 1637, before proceeding to consider the steps he took in the *Meteorology* to explain why we only see a rainbow composed of rays that make an angle of 42° or 52° with the original direction.

The Response to Descartes' Theory of Colors

Descartes distributed copies of his *Discourse on Method* and the three accompanying treatises to prominent persons in the academic world. He sent three complimentary copies to the Louvain professor of medicine, Vopiscus Fortunatus Plempius, who gave one to Jean Ciermans, a young Jesuit colleague who taught mathematics. When Descartes heard from Plempius that he had passed on the work to a Jesuit he asked for his comments. Ciermans was pleased to comply, but he forwarded his letter to Descartes through Plempius to preserve a semblance of anonymity.

Ciermans says that he read the whole work, namely, the *Optics*, the *Meteorology*, and the *Geometry*, with the exception of the introductory *Discourse on Method*. (The attitude to introductions cannot have been very different in the seventeenth century from what it is today!) Ciermans is fulsome in his praise of the *Geometry*, and he compares its author to a navigator "who leaves familiar coasts to face the challenge of a new world." The other two essays he finds more controversial, and he selects for discussion the account of the rainbow because it is here, he says, that Descartes' "brilliance, above all, appears." This was music in Descartes' ears for the rainbow was the foremost illustration of his method. Usually so touchy about the slightest criticism, Descartes declared himself delighted with Ciermans' choice of a topic, but he surprisingly played down its significance:

> By choosing, from the many passages in my writings that you believe stand in need of more rigour, the passage where I try to explain colours by the rotation of little balls, you show that you are no novice in this kind of warfare. For if there is a place in that essay that is ill defended and exposed to the fire of the enemy, it is, I confess, the one you attack.[52]

---

[50] *Meteorology*, A.T., VI, p. 335.

[51] Letter of Jean Ciermans to Descartes, March 1638, A.T., II, pp. 55–56.

[52] Letter of Descartes to Ciermans, 23 March 1638, *ibid.*, p. 71. Ciermans, of course, had no way of knowing that Descartes' prime example had cost him much labor and was perhaps

The implication is that Descartes' methodological fortress would still be well garrisoned were this particular outpost to be overrun. Descartes' courteous treatment of Ciermans may also have something to do with his hope of gaining the Jesuits to his cause, and the fact that Ciermans did not attempt to criticize Descartes' views from the vantage point of some other philosophy but in the light of his own assumptions.

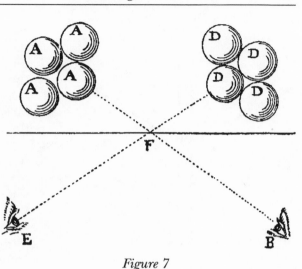

Figure 7

A Case for Interference

Basing himself on a straightforward reading of Descartes' published text, which implied that the *actual* rotation of the balls of fine matter caused the various colors, Ciermans concluded that interference would preclude seeing colors clearly and distinctly. The situation that he imagined was the following. Spheres of a ray of red light (labelled A) are travelling towards an observer at B (see Figure 7), while spheres of another color, say blue (labelled D), are moving towards an observer at E. Since the rays cross at F, the faster rotating red spheres will be retarded by the slower rotating blue ones, and, as a result, neither the observer at B nor the one at E will have a perception of pure red or pure blue.

Ciermans anticipated Descartes' answer that small spheres of fine matter do not interfere with one another. But then, he asked, how can they be used to explain the speeding up or slowing down of light as it emerges from a prism? If spheres of fine matter collide in the air without any apparent effect, why should they behave differently upon entering or emerging from a prism of glass?

An Analogy from Sound

Unbeknown to Ciermans, Descartes had already wrestled with this problem in *The World* in which he claimed that the particles of the second element, namely, air, can receive and transmit "many different motions at the same time." He provided the following illustration (see Figure 8): three pipes

---

less entrenched than it sounded. In October 1629, Descartes had confided to Mersenne, "the explanation of the colours of the rainbow has given me more trouble than all the rest" (A.T., I, p. 23).

53 Letter of Ciermans to Descartes, March 1638, A.T., II, pp. 58–59.

54 *The World*, A.T., XI, p. 101.

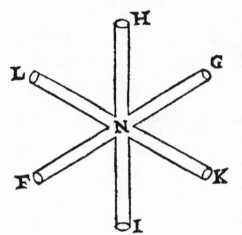

Figure 8

Figure 9

meet half-way at N, and the air that is blown in at openings, F, H, and K is unimpeded on its way to G, I, and L. If the air is pushed much more vigorously through F than through H and K, the air will only reach G. "This very comparison," according to Descartes, "can serve to explain how strong light impedes the action of light from a weaker source."[55]

Without being in the least acquainted with Descartes' unpublished *The World*, the French physicist and astronomer Jean-Baptiste Morin raised the same difficulty that Ciermans had pointed out with the aid of a diagram that is virtually the same as Descartes' own. Take, says Morin, a globe of air or water, ABCD (see Figure 9), and place two luminous sources of the same intensity at A and B. According to Descartes' principles, the light coming from A will be seen at C if the particles of fine matter at the center, E, are pushed towards C. But since the same argument applies to light streaming from B to D, we have a paradoxical situation where the material particles at E are required to move in two different directions at the same time![56]

Morin's criticism gave rise to an interesting if inconclusive correspondence. In a letter of July 1638, Descartes used Morin's diagram (see Figure 9), but he spoke of air rather than light being transmitted through pipes AC, BD, and FG, and he avoided mentioning that a stronger stream from A would interfere with weaker ones coming from B and F. Instead, he offered an explanation where velocities are combined as though they were merely scalar and not vectorial quantities (i.e., as though they could be simply added regardless of their direction). While Descartes recognized that the particles of fine matter at the intersection of the pipes at E could not move in three directions at once, he mentioned that it was enough "if some move towards C, some towards D, and some towards F at *three times* the speed of the other particles in the pipes."[57] How one-third of the particles could be accelerated to three times their initial velocity is a question that is left in abeyance.

We can hardly blame Morin for being skeptical, and in a second letter, he wondered how a particle of matter at E, pushed with equal force from the equidistant points A, B, and F, could move at all. Would it not be immobilized under the action of three identical and equally distributed forces?

[55] *Ibid.*, p. 102.

[56] Letter of Jean-Baptiste Morin to Descartes, 22 February 1638, A.T., I, p. 556.

[57] Letter of Descartes to Morin, 13 July 1638, A.T., II, pp. 219–220, emphasis added.

Morin suggested a feline experiment that was in keeping with seventeenth-century science, for which the eyes of cats were not only receptors but sources of light.[58] Place the eye of a cat (let us call him Tabby) at one end of tube AC, and the eye of a second cat (say Tommy) at the other. Tabby will see Tommy if the light streams from Tommy's eye to his own, and the same can be said of Tommy, but *on Descartes' theory*, this would require that particles of fine matter move in diametrically opposed directions at the same time![59]

An Analogy from Wine

Descartes' line of defence in his correspondence with both Ciermans and Morin was to reiterate his distinction between inclination to motion and actual motion.[60] In his letter of 23 March 1638 to Ciermans, he referred to the illustration in the *Optics* where the transmission of light is compared to the downward tendency exerted by half-pressed grapes at several points on the bottom of a vat (see Figure 10):

> The wine that is at C tends towards B, but it does not impede the wine at E from tending towards A, nor each of its parts from inclining to descend towards several different parts, although they can only move towards one at a time. I have mentioned in several places that what I understand by light is not the motion itself but an inclination or propensity to motion.[61]

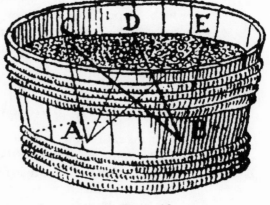

Figure 10

The analogy of the vat is now modified to answer Ciermans' objection that the mutual interference of spheres of red and blue light would render colors indistinct (see Figure 7 above). Just as a fish swimming in the must would not alter the downward propensities at C, D, and E (see Figure 10), currents in a vat filled with air would not influence the visibility of colors at C, D, and E.[62] How convincing is this analogy? Air is transparent; fishes, however small, are not. But then everything hinges on Descartes' theory of light, which, as he repeats to Ciermans, he had not wished to explain in the *Optics* or the *Meteorology*.

---

[58] See above p. 116.

[59] Letter of Morin to Descartes, 12 August 1638, A.T., II, p. 303.

[60] "The action or inclination to motion is enough, without motion, to make us perceive light" (letter to Descartes to Morin, 12 September 1638, *ibid.*, p. 372).

[61] Letter of Descartes to Ciermans, 23 March 1638, *ibid.*, p. 72. The diagram is from the *Optics*, A.T., VI, p. 86.

[62] Letter of Descartes to Ciermans, 23 March 1638, A.T., II, pp. 72–73.

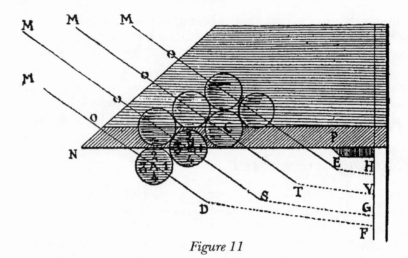

Figure 11

Even the fear of being misunderstood as reintroducing qualities and forms, which he professes to abhor, is not enough to shake Descartes from his resolve. Like the rest of impatient mankind, Ciermans is made to hold his peace until Descartes' will deign to reveal his complete system to an expectant world.[63]

The Rolling Spheres

Ciermans raised a second objection that was equally devastating. Even if we were to grant, he says, that the speed of rotation of the spheres of celestial matter is changed upon leaving the prism, the results could not be as Descartes described.

As we have seen, on Descartes' analogy, the ball 1234 (see Figure 6 above) has only translational motion until it impinges upon the surface of the water YY and begins to rotate. This rotation is increased by faster moving spheres of fine matter, such as Q, and retarded by slower moving ones, such as S. "This explains," writes Descartes, "the action of ray DF"[64] [see figure 5]. Now examine, says in turn Ciermans, what this analogy implies if we consider light passing through a prism, bearing in mind Descartes' assertion in the *Optics* that the spheres of fine matter have greater ease of passage (and hence "move" more swiftly) through a dense medium than through a rare one. In Figure 11, sphere A leaves the denser medium of glass for the rarer medium of air, whereas in Descartes' example, the ball 1234 (see Figure 6 above) leaves the rarer medium of air for the denser one of water. Descartes assumed that the cases were identical.

---

[63] *Ibid.*, p. 74. Descartes assured Mersenne that all questions concerning the physics of light are "very easily" explained in the *World* but "unintelligible" otherwise (letter to Mersenne, 15 November 1638, *ibid.*, p. 437).

[64] *Meteorology*, A.T., VI, p. 333.

If we look more closely, says Ciermans, we shall see that this is not the case. Ball A, which is part of the red ray DF, is just emerging into the air, and its speed of rotation is hindered by the more sluggish spheres of air. Sphere B, just above it, is being pressed by a faster rotating sphere of fine matter still in the prism, and hence will be made to rotate faster. As a result, the spheres that reach H will be rotating faster than those that arrive at F. But the color red appears at F and hence is produced by spheres that rotate slower, *not faster*, as Descartes had claimed![65] The same objection was urged independently, by Jean-Baptiste Morin, and Descartes was made to realize that something was wrong with his analogy. Replying to Morin in July 1638, he tried to recast his argument:

> I am not talking about particles of fine matter, but about balls of wood (or some other visible material) that are being pushed towards the water. This is obvious since I make them rotate in a different direction from that of the particles of fine matter, and I compare the rotation they acquire when they come out of the air and enter the water to the one that the particles of subtle matter acquire when they leave water or glass and enter the air.[66]

Understandably, Morin was not convinced. Why bring in balls of wood, he asked, if they do not behave like the small spheres of fine celestial matter?[67] Descartes' rejoinder is noteworthy for the way it shifts the argument from theoretical considerations to the requirements of experimental control: "I had to use balls that can be seen rather than particles of fine matter that are invisible in order to submit my arguments to an empirical test [*à l'examen des sens*] as I always try to do."[68] Again, Morin was unimpressed. Replying to Descartes, he pointed out that there was no indication in the *Meteorology* that Descartes was thinking of balls of wood. But even if he was, the experimental claim was a hollow one, "since no one in the world could make the experiment you suggest."[69] No surprise therefore that after this the correspondence with Morin lapsed!

Descartes never squarely faced Ciermans' stricture that he was muddled about the rotation of the spheres of fine matter that produce red and blue (namely, by claiming that the faster produce red). Instead, he made a rhetorical claim for independent experiments that would confirm his position:

> I would not have you believe, from the slight and limited number of arguments that I published [in the *Meteorology*], that it is from one experiment alone that I was moved to assert that the colour red consists, I do not say in the more frequent agitation, but in the greater tendency to circular

[65] Letter of Ciermans to Descartes, March 1638, A.T., II, pp. 59–61.

[66] Letter of Descartes to Morin, 13 July 1638, *ibid.*, p. 208.

[67] Letter of Morin to Descartes, 12 August 1638, *ibid.*, pp. 293–294.

[68] Letter of Descartes to Morin, 12 September 1638, *ibid.*, p. 366.

[69] Letter of Morin to Descartes, October 1638, *ibid.*, p. 418.

motion. Although I do not believe that there is a better proof than the one I adduced, there are a hundred more [literally "*six hundred more*"] that I could give were I considering the parts of physics to which they belong. When discussing animals, I would explain why blood is red, elsewhere I would explain why quicksilver and other substances become red through the action of fire alone, and so on. If I came across a single instance, in the whole realm of nature, that was at variance with my opinion, I would suspend assent until I had satisfied myself that I was right. But are there no other experiments that confirm my view in the *Meteorology*? For instance, on page 272 and the following where I discuss the red colour of clouds, the blueness of the sky and the sea, and so on.[70]

Descartes doth protest too much, as we can see if we consider the passage in the *Meteorology* to which he refers. It occurs in the chapter that follows the one on the rainbow, and merely repeats that blue is perceived when small spheres of fine matter rotate slowly, and red when they rotate faster.[71] As far as blood is concerned, Descartes does broach the subject in a biological manuscript that he wrote much later, but all we are told is that blood is red because the small spheres of fine matter at the surface of the blood "rotate much faster."[72]

Rectilinear and Circular Inertia

Ciermans marvelled that the spheres of fine matter, which he assumed flowed from the sun, did not lose their speed as they journeyed through distant regions of space. He was not aware of Descartes' law of inertia, which was still unpublished, but Descartes assumed that this was what he had in mind. The question then became: if rectilinear motion is inertial, what accounts for the persistance of rotary motion? Descartes' reply to Ciermans reveals that he had not fully grasped the implications of his own principle, since he professed to see no difficulty in maintaining both *rectilinear inertia* (what, after Newton, we simply call inertial motion) and *circular inertia* (which, after Newton, we consider to be non-inertial, i.e., requiring the constant application of an outside force):

> I do not see why it seems to you that the particles of celestial matter do not maintain the rotation that gives rise to colours as well as the motion in a straight line in which light consists. We can grasp both equally well through our reasoning. I am convinced that, as far as natural events are concerned,

[70] Letter of Descartes to Ciermans, 23 March 1638, *ibid.*, p. 75.

[71] *Meteorology*, A.T., VI, pp. 346–347.

[72] *La Description du Corps Humain*, A.T., XI, p. 256. Descartes equates his interpretation of facts with the facts themselves when he writes, "we have sensory awareness [*nous pouvons sentir*] of two kinds of motion which these balls have: one whereby they approach our eyes in a straight line, which gives us the sensation of light, the other whereby they turn about their centres" (*ibid.*, pp. 255–256). This work was written around 1648.

we cannot think of anything more accurate, namely that better answers the rigour of mathematical computation.[73]

Descartes' bold pronouncements on the rigor of mathematics add nothing to the entirely qualitative nature of his explanation. What we are said to grasp "through our reasoning" is no more than the possibility that colors are caused by the various speeds of rotation of the particles that reach our eye. Descartes never suspected that the prism broke up white light into its constituent parts, and he offered a mechanical explanation of color in terms of motion alone. None of his colors is intrinsically different, and they arise simply from the greater or lesser speed of rotation. Fortunately, Descartes' claim to fame in optics does not rest on his explanation of color, but on his discovery of the law of refraction, and his brilliant analysis of the rainbow to which we now return.

Privileged Angles

We had left in abeyance the crucial question: why is the main rainbow formed exclusively by rays that make an angle of about 42°? Descartes saw that the answer lay in calculating the path of the rays that fall on various points of a drop of water in order to determine under what angles they come toward our eyes. He ascertained that, after one reflection and two refractions, many more rays can be seen under an angle of about 42° than under lesser ones, and that no ray can be seen under a larger angle. Analogous calculations for two reflections and two refractions revealed that many more rays came toward the eye under an angle of about 52° than under any larger one, and that no ray came under a lesser. These calculations were only possible because Descartes had discovered that when light passes from one medium to another, the sine of the angle of incidence bears a constant ratio to the sine of the angle of refraction. This had enabled him to determine the value of sin i/sin r (what we call the refractive index) from air to water at a little over 4/3, namely, at 250/187, which is excellent in experimental terms.

Descartes illustrated his procedure with the aid of Figure 12.[74] All the rays coming from the sun (located at the bottom of the figure on the side of S) are parallel but they are refracted, like ray EF, upon entering the drop of water. As was customary in his day, and to avoid fractions, the radius of the drop is taken as 10,000 units. The angle of incidence of the ray EF is not given in degrees, but is determined by the magnitude of the distance FH between the ray and a parallel ray passing through the center of the drop. The ratio FH/FC is, therefore, the sine of the angle of incidence i of the ray. For FH = 0, the ray coincides with the central ray AH, and the angle of incidence is zero; for FH = 10,000, the ray just grazes the drop, and the angle of incidence is 90°. If ray EF penetrates the drop and is reflected at K, it can

[73] Letter of Descartes to Ciermans, 23 March 1638, A.T., II, p. 74.

[74] *Meteorology*, A.T., VI, pp. 337–340.

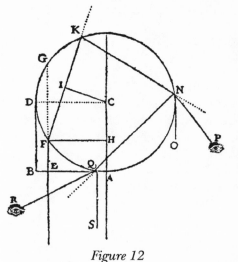

Figure 12

either exit at N and travel to the eye at P, or be reflected and proceed to Q and thence to R. In the first case, it will reach the eye after one reflection and two refractions, in the second after two reflections and two refractions.

Descartes saw that he had to determine the size of the angle ONP for the primary bow and of the angle SQR for the secondary one. He calculated, for values of FH from 1,000 to 10,000, the corresponding angle ONP, that is, the angle between the emergent ray and the direct rays from the sun. The computation is based on the deviation from a straight line when the ray is refracted or reflected. At F, the deviation is measured by angle GFK, which is equal to $i - r$, where i is the angle of incidence and r the angle of refraction. At K where the ray is internally reflected, there is a second deviation of $180° - 2r$, and at N, upon leaving the drop, a third deviation of $i - r$. The total deviation therefore is $D = 180° + 2i - 4r$. ON is parallel to EF, so that angle ONP is equal to $180° - D$, namely $180° - (180° + 2i - 4r) = 4r + 2i$. For FH = 8000, which is the ray Descartes uses as an illustration, i is $40°44'$. The angle of refraction, r, is easily found from the refractive index of air to water, i.e., $\sin i / \sin r = 4/3$. An analogous procedure yields the value of angle SQR.[75]

Eloquent Tables

The result of Descartes computations are as follows:

line FH	line CI	arc FG	angle arc FK	angle ONP	SQR
1,000	748	168°30'	171°25'	5°40'	165°45'
2,000	1,496	156°55'	162°48'	11°19'	151°29'
3,000	2,244	145°4'	154°4'	17°56'	136°8'
4,000	2,992	132°50'	145°10'	22°30'	122°4'
5,000	3,740	120°	136°4'	27°52'	108°12'
6,000	4,488	106°16'	126°40'	32°56'	93°44'
7,000	5,236	91°8'	116°51'	37°26'	79°25'
8,000	5,984	73°44'	106°30'	40°44'	65°46'
9,000	6,732	51°41'	95°22'	40°57'	54°25'
10,000	7,480	0	83°10'	13°40'	69°30'

Table 1

75 For a lucid summary of Descartes' procedure, see Carl B. Boyer, *The Rainbow*, pp. 200–219.

line FH	line CI	arc FG	arc FK	angle ONP	angle SQR
8,000	5,984	73°44'	106°30'	40°44'	65°46'
8,100	6,058	71°48'	105°25'	40°58'	64°37'
8,200	6,133	69°50'	104°20'	41°10'	63°10'
8,300	6,208	67°48'	103°14'	41°20'	62°54'
8,400	6,283	65°44'	102°9'	41°26'	61°43'
8,500	6,358	63°34'	101°2'	41°30'	60°32'
8,600	6,432	61°22'	99°56'	41°30'	58°26'
8,700	6,507	59°4'	98°48'	41°28'	57°20'
8,800	6,582	56°42'	97°40'	41°22'	56°18'
8,900	6,657	54°16'	96°32'	41°12'	55°20'
9,000	6,732	51°41'	95°22'	40°57'	54°25'
9,100	6,806	49°	94°12'	40°36'	53°36'
9,200	6,881	46°8'	93°2'	40°4'	52°58'
9,300	6,956	43°8'	91°51'	39°26'	52°25'
9,400	7,031	39°54'	90°38'	38°38'	52°
9,500	7,106	36°24'	89°26'	37°32'	51°54'
9,600	7,180	32°30'	88°12'	36°6'	52°6'
9,700	7,255	28°8'	86°58'	34°12'	52°46'
9,800	7,330	22°57'	85°43'	31°31'	54°12'

Table 2

The striking revelation of this table is that whatever the angle at which the ray enters the drop, the angle at which it exits will not make an angle greater than 40°57', with its original direction. It is also the case that a large number of rays (those for which FH lies between 8,000 and 9,000) are refracted at an angle of about 40°. To determine the clustering more accurately, Descartes then computed the paths for values ranging from FH = 8,000 to FH = 10,000 (Table 2).

These computations showed the conjunction of many rays in the neighbourhood of 41°30'. Allowing 17' for the apparent radius of the sun, Descartes placed the *maximum* angle of the interior rainbow at 41°47', and the *minimum* angle of the outer one at 51°37'.[76]

The values that Descartes arrived at explain not only why the bows appear at angles of about 42° and 52°, but also why the outer boundary of the primary rainbow is more sharply defined than the inner edge of the secondary one. No light is returned, after the indicated reflection and refractions, at an angle greater than about 46°30', although there is an appreciable number of rays at slightly less than this angle. In the case of the secondary rainbow, however, there is a clustering of rays at slightly larger angles than

[76] Tables 1 and 2 are found in the *Meteorology*, A.T., VI, pp. 338–339.

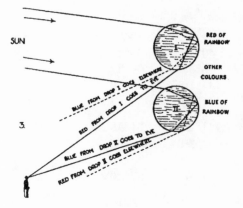

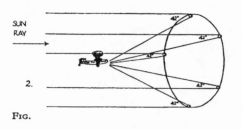

Figure 13

Figure 14

51°37', but no rays return to the eye at smaller angles. Descartes merely alluded to this important fact. What he wished to stress was that his scientific method enabled him to correct observational reports. Experience unbacked by theory is unreliable and with unbecoming censoriousness, he pointed a finger at Francesco Maurolico, who had stated that angle ONP was around 45° and angle SQR around 56°. "This shows," wrote Descartes, "how little faith we must have in observations that are not accompanied by the correct explanation."[77]

Descartes' calculations reveal that only the narrow, tightly packed beams that emerge from drops that suspend an angle of about 42° with the direction of the sun are sufficiently intense to affect the eye. Since they all subtend the same angle, they must lie on the surface of a cone with the apex at the eye. Hence the rainbow appears in the shape of a bow. It is clear that if a number of persons stand in a line they will all see a different rainbow, for a different set of raindrops will lie in the appropriate direction for each person (see Figure 13). If they stand on the ground, the part of the circle which is below them will be cut off, although from an airplane a complete circular bow might be seen (see Figure 14). But Descartes does not seem to have considered the theoretical possibility, say of an angel perched on a cloud and admiring a rainbow, since he interpreted reports of inverted rainbows as resulting from the reflection of rays of the sun from the surface of a lake to the drops of rain, the direct rays being cut off by an intervening cloud (see Figure 15).

A Triumph of Insight . . . and Rhetoric

Descartes' explanation of the rainbow is indeed a triumph of his scientific method. His observations are telling, and his mathematical deductions profoundly illuminating. But when he points out that observations that remain unexplained are not to be trusted, he seems oblivious of the fact that observations are only made in areas where theory leads one to expect that they will be meaningful. Descartes never bothered, for instance, to measure accurately the width of the rainbow because his theory in no way encouraged the notion that white light was dispersed into its component parts.

Descartes denied qualitative change in the Aristotelian sense, but he retained the idea that light was qualitatively modified when it passed from

[77] *Ibid.*, p. 340.

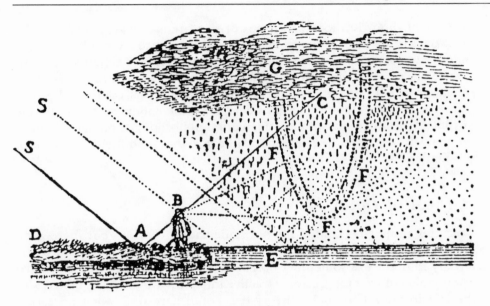

Figure 15

one medium to another even if he interpreted the phenomenon in mechanical terms. When the particles of fine matter tend to turn more vigorously than to travel in a straight line, the result is red light; when the rotation is less pronounced, yellow is seen; and when the rotation is even slighter, green or blue is observed. The reversal of the order of the colors in the secondary rainbow posed a serious challenge to this interpretation. Descartes faced it with a mixture of rhetoric ("I have had no trouble"), and an arbitrary manipulation of the shapes of the invisible particles of matter whose properties were assumed to be identical with those of macroscopic objects:

> Moreover, I have had no trouble understanding why red appears on the *outside* of the interior rainbow and on the *inside* of the external one. What causes red to be seen near F rather than H after passing through the crystal MNP [see Figure 5 above] also causes the eye, when it is placed at FGH, to see red towards the *thicker* part MP, and blue toward N. The reason is that the red-tinted ray that goes to F comes from C, the part of the sun closes to MP. For the same reason, when the centre of the drops of water (and hence their *thickest* part) is on the outside with respect to the coloured points forming the interior rainbow, red must appear on the outside.[79]

In spite of the banner of "ease" under which this explanation is made to sail, it does not partake of the clarity that is Descartes' vaunt. What he seems to be saying is that the reversal of the order of the colors results from an

[78] *Ibid.*, p. 342.
[79] *Ibid.*, pp. 340–341, emphasis added.

inversion of the prism to which drops of rain are assimilated, and that the *thickness* is somehow responsible for the appearance of red. A material sphere can rotate on its axis or move in a straight line. The latter accounts for the law of refraction, the former for the production of colors. Because Descartes admits no other kind of motion and treats color as the only property of the rainbow, he considers his explanation as the only one possible. With the self-assurance of a natural philosopher who has the key to the marvels of nature, he concludes: "I believe that no difficulty remains in this matter."[80]

A Host of Bows

Descartes cannot be faulted for not anticipating Newton, but there is an interesting step that he could have taken if he had pondered reports that a tertiary rainbow was sometimes observed. He assumed that this happened when grains of ice of a greater refractive index than water were mixed with the raindrops. Yet he had a theory that could have done what no earlier hypothesis was in a position to achieve: predict where one should look for the tertiary rainbow, if it existed, as well as the fourth, fifth, or sixth. As Carl Boyer has pointed out, all Descartes had to do was continue to add an internal reflection to generate possible paths for new rainbows. This is illustrated in Figure 16 where *r*, the number of internal reflections, indicates the order of the bow.[81]

Neither Descartes nor Newton bothered to carry out calculations for cases above two internal reflections. Halley, the British astronomer and friend of Newton, seems to have been the first to carry out calculations on the tertiary rainbow, and as can be seen from Figure 16 above, the result was a surprise. The third rainbow has an angular radius of 40°20', and appears not opposite to the sun but as a circle around the sun itself. It is invisible not because of the weakness of its light but because of the brightness of the sun. Halley also found that in the case of the fourth bow, the ray had undergone a deviation of 405°33', and that this bow is a circle of radius 45°33' about the sun. The fifth bow very nearly coincides with the second but with the colors in the reverse order, and this contributes to the difficulty of observation. The sixth lies with the primary and has never been observed

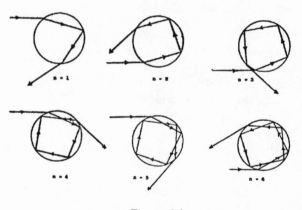

Figure 16

[80] *Ibid.*, p. 341.

[81] See Carl B. Boyer, *The Rainbow*, p. 250.

outside laboratory conditions where more than 18 rainbows have been observed, all confirming Descartes' theory.

A New Covenant

Descartes could indeed be proud. He had conquered one of the most potent
symbols of nature with his mechanical philosophy. After the flood, God
made the rainbow an everlasting covenant "between himself and every living
creature" (*Genesis* 9, 13), and in the *Iliad*, Homer writes that Aphrodite,
wounded by Diomedes, fled from the field of battle to Olympus along the
rainbow route, carried as swiftly as the wind by the goddess Iris, whose name
in Greek means rainbow.[82]

Like the ancient Greeks and Hebrews, Descartes rejoiced in the rainbow, which put the seal of God's pleasure upon his work. It will come as no
surprise, therefore, that he closed his chapter on the rainbow by showing
that his method could not only explain marvels but produce them as well. To
provide a display of natural magic that went beyond della Porta's meager
efforts, Descartes suggested mixing liquids of varying refractive indices with
the spray of a fountain, thus making it possible to cause "the shape of a cross,
or a column, or some other such thing which gives cause for wonder."[83]
Little could he foresee what Keats was to write almost two centuries later
when the marvels of the mechanical philosophy had lost their appeal:

> Do not all charms fly
> At the mere touch of cold philosophy
> There was an awful rainbow once in heaven
> We know her woof, her texture; she is given
> In the dull catalogue of common things.
> Philosophy will clip an Angel's wings,
> Conquer all mysteries by rule and line,
> Empty the haunted air, and gnomed mine—
> Unweave a rainbow . . . .[84]

---

[82] *Iliad*, V, 350. In Virgil Juno sends Iris down from heaven to breathe fair winds on the Ilian
fleet (*Aeneid*, V, 606–607).

[83] *Meteorology*, A.T., VI, p. 344.

[84] John Keats, *Lamia*, Part II, vv. 229–237, in *Complete Poems*, Jack Stillingfleet, ed. (Cambridge,
MA: Harvard University Press, 1978), p. 357.

Chapter Ten

The Action of Light

W E HAVE SEEN THAT before Descartes could finish the metaphysical treatise he had been working on for the first nine months after his return to the Netherlands, he was interrupted by an urgent request to explain the appearance of parhelia. In order to offer a satisfactory answer, he resumed the work on refraction that he had laid aside when he left Paris. This in turn led to an investigation of the nature of the rainbow and a new theory of colors. He published his results in the *Meteorology*, the second of the three scientific treatises that were published with the *Discourse on Method*. The first of these treatises entitled *Optics* [in French *La Dioptrique*] was not intended as a theoretical treatise but as a practical handbook for craftsmen, such as Jean Ferrier, who wanted to make better telescopes. At the very outset, Descartes states that he wishes to make himself "intelligible to everyone," and he promises not to use any notion that would require prior knowledge of another science. Indeed, he claims that an exact knowledge of the nature of light is not required:

> Now since the only reason for speaking of light here is to explain how its rays enter into the eye, and how they may be deflected by the various bodies they encounter, I need not attempt to say what is its true nature. It will, I think, suffice if I use two or three comparisons in order to facilitate the conception of light which seems most suitable for explaining all those of its properties that we know through experience, and deducing all the others that we cannot observe so easily. In this I am imitating the astrono-

mers, whose assumptions are almost all false or uncertain, but who nevertheless draw many very true and certain consequences from them because they are related to various observations.[1]

Descartes did not wish to discuss the nature of light because craftsmen were unlikely to be interested. Although he believed that his laws of optics could ultimately be derived from the basic properties of matter, he felt that this could not be clearly conveyed without explaining the whole of his metaphysics or at least that part of it that dealt with natural philosophy. A full understanding of light, for Descartes, implied a grasp of the underlying structure of the material universe. This is why the complete title of his posthumous cosmological essay is *The World or Treatise on Light.*

Models and Analogies

One feature of light that was particularly problematic, inasmuch as it did not appear to result from straightforward intuition, was its instantaneity. We cannot focus directly on instantaneous motion because we have no ways of working with infinite speed. All we can do is try to understand it by analogy with some "natural power" with which we are familiar. Descartes had already addressed this problem in Rule 9 of his *Rules for the Direction of the Mind*:

> If, for example, I wish to inquire whether a natural power can travel instantaneously to a distant place, passing through the whole intervening space, I shall not immediately turn my attention to magnetic force, or the influence of the stars, or even the speed of light, to see whether actions such as these might occur instantaneously; for I would find it more difficult to settle that sort of question than the one at issue. I shall, rather, reflect upon the local motions of bodies, since there can be nothing in this whole area that is more readily perceivable by the senses. And I shall realize that, while a stone cannot pass instantaneously from one place to another, since it is a body, a power similar to the one which moves the stone must be transmitted instantaneously if it is to pass, in its bare state, from one object to another. For instance, if I move one end of a stick, however long it may be, I can easily conceive that the power which moves that part of the stick necessarily moves every other part of it instantaneously, because it is the bare power which is transmitted at that moment, and not the power as it exists in some body, such as the stone that carries it along.[2]

The stick or cane will become the first of three analogies that Descartes considers in the *Optics*. The other two are a vat of fermenting wine and a tennis ball. We shall examine each in turn in this chapter. But before we proceed, we must note the attempt that Descartes makes to justify his method

---

[1] *Optics* [*La Dioptrique*], A.T., VI, p. 83.

[2] *Rules for the Direction of the Mind*, Rule 9, A.T., X, p. 402.

in the passage we have quoted above where he compares his procedure to that of astronomers "whose assumptions are almost all false or uncertain, but who nonetheless draw many true and certain consequences because they are related to various observations that they have made."[3]

The appeal to analogies creates no major problem in a context that is defined as practical and propaedeutic. What is troublesome is the reference to computing devices that are *known* to be false. Descartes is thinking here of the epicycles and deferents of Ptolemaic astronomy that were used to determine the position of celestial bodies but which were not considered physically true. The acknowledged arbitrariness—and hence falsity—of the astronomical models has greatly exercised Cartesian scholarship. What Descartes seems to be saying is that although light does not literally move like a cane, or wine in a vat, or a tennis ball, these models can nonetheless enable us to work out the path of a ray of light, even if we fall short of understanding the actual process of illumination. We cannot avoid the impression, however, that Descartes was hoping that his analogies would convey much more to his perceptive readers.

The passage from Rule 9 of the *Rules for the Direction of the Mind* that was quoted at the beginning of this chapter stresses that the appeal is to "local motion" (namely, change of place), the kind of motion that is most readily and easily perceived.[4] In this he is following his own injunction in Rule 2 of the *Rules for the Direction of the Mind*: "We should attend only to those objects of which our minds seem capable of having certain and indubitable cognition."[5] Local motion, for Descartes, is the object of such certain and indubitable knowledge, and hence the starting point of scientific investigation. It also appeared to him that it could, in some instances, be instantaneous.

The Blind Man's Cane

This is brought home in the first comparison of the action of light with the motion of a cane with which a blind man not only feels his way around obstacles, but comes to recognize objects with such uncanny precision that he can be said to "see with his hands." On Descartes' analysis, the object is perceived at the very instant that the end of the cane touches it. In other words, the transmission of information is instantaneous. "In order to draw a comparison from this," writes Descartes,

[3] *Optics*, A.T., VI, p. 83. This echoes what he had written in Rule 12 of the *Rules for the Direction of the Mind*: "Certain assumptions must be made that perhaps not everyone will accept. But even if they are thought to be no more real than the imaginary circles that astronomers use to describe the phenomena, this matters little, provided they help discern what might be true from what might be false" (A.T., X, p. 417).

[4] According to Aristotle, local motion is prior to all other kinds of change (*Physics*, Book VIII, Ch. 7).

[5] *Rules for the Direction of the Mind*, Rule 2, A.T., X, p. 362.

I want you to consider that light, in bodies we call luminous, is nothing but a certain motion or a very rapid and lively action that passes to our eyes by means of the air and other transparent bodies, in the same way that the motion or the resistance of bodies encountered by a blind man passes to his hand by means of his cane.[6]

The claim that the transmission of light is instantaneous strikes a modern reader as unwarranted, especially when it is made to rest on the analogy of touching an object with a wooden cane. The compression of the parts (however swift) is not timeless. For Descartes and his contemporaries, however, the idea that light travelled instantaneously and could be compared to touch was much less difficult to entertain. The theories of vision elaborated by the ancients, and still widely discussed in the seventeenth century, enable us to see why this was the case.

As early as the fifth century B.C., Empedocles had tried to explain vision by recourse to "ocular beams" that flowed from the eye to the object, so that the sensation of sight was comparable to that of touch. Aristotle had criticized Empedocles for maintaining that light took time to go from one place to another, and had offered an alternative explanation on the assumption that light is not a material stream of particles flowing from a luminous object to the eye, but a state or quality that the medium acquires *all at once* from the light source, just as water can freeze in all its parts simultaneously.[7] While at variance with Aristotle, Kepler and Descartes both accepted the doctrine of instantaneous transmission.[8] The novelty of Descartes' approach lies in assuming that the instantaneous transmission of local motion is sufficient to explain the action of light.

---

[6] *Optics*, A.T., VI, p. 84. In the *Rules for the Direction of the Mind*, Descartes had given an even more striking example of what he had in mind when he asked his reader to think of the motion of a pen whose nib cannot move without the cap at the other end moving at the same time (A.T., X, p. 414).

[7] For an excellent brief summary of the state of the art before Descartes, see David C. Lindberg, "The Science of Optics" in David C. Lindberg, ed., *Science in the Middle Ages* (Chicago and London: University of Chicago Press, 1978), pp. 338–368. A more detailed account will be found in the same author's *Theories of Vision from al-Kindi to Kepler* (Chicago and London: University of Chicago Press, 1976). For Aristotles' theory, see his *On the Soul*, Book 2, Ch. 7, 418a26–419a25, and *On Sense and Sensible Objects* (*De Sensu*), Ch. 2–3, 437a18–439b18; the analogy with freezing water occurs in Ch. 6, 447a3 ff. On Descartes' strategy, see John Hyman, "The Cartesian Theory of Vision," *Ratio* XXVII (1986), pp. 149–167, and Peter Galison, "Model and Reality in Descartes' Theory of Light," *Synthesis* 4 (1979), pp. 2–23.

[8] Johann Kepler, *Ad Vitellionem Paralipomena, quibus Astronomiae Pars Optica Traditur*, Chapter 1, Proposition 5 (Frankfurt, 1614) in *Gesammelte Werke* Max Caspar, Franz Hammer *et alii*, eds, 20 vols. to date (Munich: C.H. Beck, 1948–) vol. 2, p. 21. For Kepler's views, see the richly annotated French translation of Catherine Chevalley, *Paralipomènes à Vitellion* (Paris: Vrin, 1980), pp. 32–41. The only notable opponent of instantaneous transmission in the Middle Ages was Ibn al-Haytham (died *c.* 1039), known as Alhazen, who asserted that the movement of light requires a finite, though imperceptible, interval of time. Descartes could have read Alhazen in F. Risner's popular collection of optical texts, the *Opticae Thesaurus* (Basel, 1572), facsimile (New York: Johnson Reprint, 1972), p. 37 (this is Alhazen's *Optics*, II, 21).

No Flitting Images

Descartes is insistent that nothing is transmitted beyond motion. The blind man perceives differences in objects virtually as well as one who can see, "and yet," writes Descartes, "in all these bodies the differences are nothing but the various ways of moving the cane or resisting its movements." From this he would have us conclude "that there is no need to suppose that something material passes from the object to our eye to make us see colours and light."[9] So the main point of the analogy is not so much instantaneity, which does not greatly exercise Descartes, but the purely mechanical transmission of information. He underscores this by singling out for scorn the "intentional forms" that Aristotelians invoked to explain how the image of an object travels to the sense that receives it:

> By this means, your mind will be delivered from all those little images called *intentional forms*, that flit through the air, and exercise the imagination of philosophers. You will even find it easy to settle the current philosophical debate concerning the origin of the action that causes visual perception.[10]

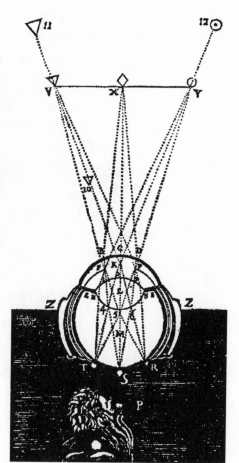

Figure 1

The last sentence refers to an ongoing debate in the seventeenth century about the origin of visual rays. The two contending theories are usually called "extramission," if the rays come from the object, and "intromission," if the rays are sent out from the observer's eye to "feel" the object. Kepler had dealt the *coup de grâce* to the theory of intromission when he showed that the eye can be treated as a *camera obscura*, and that the incoming rays form an inverted image on the retina. Descartes verified this experimentally with the eye of a bull and published his results in the *Optics* (see Figure 1).[11]

It is all the more surprising that in the opening chapter of the *Optics*,

---

[9] *Optics*, A.T., VI, p. 85. It is interesting to compare this statement with what Aristotle wrote in *De Sensu*: "but whether light or air is the medium between the visible object and the eye, motion through the medium is what produces vision" (*De Sensu* ch. 3, 438b3–4).

[10] *Optics*, A.T., VI, p. 85. The *Conimbricenses* and Eustache de Saint Paul defended the view that intentional species are necessary (see Etienne Gilson, *Index Scolastico-Cartésien*, 2nd ed. (Paris: Vrin, 1979), pp. 97–98). For the relevance of these Aristotelian commentaries to Descartes' early education, see above pp. 5–6.

[11] *Optics*, A.T., VI, p. 119.

which we have been considering, Descartes maintains extramission and intromission as though both followed from his analogy with a cane:

> For just as our blind man can feel the bodies around him not only through their action when they move against his cane, but also through the action of his hand when the bodies do nothing but resist the cane, so we must acknowledge that objects of sight can be perceived not only by means of the action in them which tends towards our eyes, but also by the action in our eyes which tends towards them.[12]

Descartes believed that the eyes of cats functioned like spotlights, but his conclusive evidence for intromission is one that he does not mention in the *Optics*. This is his own personal experience as he recorded it in the account of his celebrated dream.[13] He makes no attempt to explain the optics of intramission, however, and it is difficult to see how it could be reconciled with the mechanism he takes for granted in his published *Optics*.

An Inclination to Motion: the Lesson from Wine

If nothing is physically transmitted and the event is instantaneous, we have, properly speaking, and inclination or tendency to motion rather than motion itself. This is what the analogy with a vat will help us understand. The first comparison of light with a blind man's cane had linked two sets of operations:

(1)   hand → cane → motion or resistance to motion → feeling objects

(2)   eye → air → action or tendency to motion → seeing colors

It is symptomatic that whereas we see the weakness of this analogy in the implausability of instantaneous propagation, and the difference between physical contact in (1) and sensory awareness in (2), Descartes saw it in the discrepancy between the opacity of the cane and the transparency of air. Hence the need of a second analogy—that of a vat full of fermenting grapes. At first blush, the new comparison is not a perspicuous example of transparency, but Descartes believed that the *grapes* in the vat could be compared to the rounded particles or small spheres of matter that make up air and transparent bodies, while the *juice* or *must* stood for the fine matter that fills the interstices between these spheres. It appeared unproblematic to Descartes that all the fluid matter in the vat tended to move in a straight line towards all the openings at the bottom. Here is how he developed the analogy with the aid of a diagram (Figure 2):

> Consider a wine-vat at harvest time, full to the brim with half-pressed grapes, in the bottom of which are one or two holes, such as A and B,

---

[12] *Optics*, A.T., VI, pp. 85–86.

[13] See above p. 116.

through which the unfermented wine can flow
... *you will easily understand* how the parts of
wine, for instance those at C, *tend* to go down in
a straight line through the hole A *at the very instant* it is opened and, at the same time, through
hole B, while those parts that are at D and E also
tend, at the same time, to go down through
these two holes, without these actions being impeded by each other or by the resistance of the
bunches of grapes in the vat. This happens even
though the bunches of grapes support each
other, and so do not tend in the least to go
down through the holes A and B, as does the
wine, but can even be moved in several different

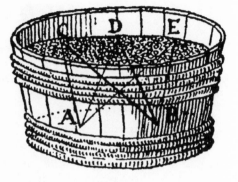

Figure 2

ways by those who press them. *In the same way*, all the parts of fine matter
that are touched by the side of the rim facing us *tend in a straight line towards our eyes at the very instant they are opened*, without these parts impeding
one another, and even without being impeded by the coarser parts of the
transparent bodies which lie between them.[14]

Let us see what is at stake in this procedure. First, it is clear that for
Descartes the parts of the fluid at C receive an instantaneous tendency to
move towards both holes A and B as soon as they are opened. The point is
that even before they start moving, they have a real tendency to move. This is
consistent with what Descartes wrote to Mersenne when commenting on the
law of falling bodies: the weight of a body must be considered at the initial
instant of fall, not when it is actually in the process of falling.[15] This view
originated in the treatise on hydrostatics that he wrote for Beeckman in 1618
and that we examined in Chapter Two,[16] but Descartes does not address the
question that follows in its wake, namely, since the "tendency" begins at the
very instant that hole A is opened, did the wine at C have no tendency
downward before the hole was made? In other words, is the mere fact of
making a hole at the bottom of the vat enough to cause a tendency at the
surface?

Second, why should the fluid at C tend equally towards A and B?
Descartes seems to imply that this is the case simply because it is as easy to
trace a straight line from C to B as from C to A. He completely disregards the
fact that the distance from C to B is greater than from C to A, and that weight
or pressure is exerted downward. In other words, he seems unconcerned
about the concrete physical situation and only interested in the pictorial
suggestiveness of straight lines drawn across the vat.

---

[14] *Optics*, A.T., VI, pp. 86–87, emphasis added.

[15] See p. 29 above.

[16] See pp. 29–33 above.

A Theory-Laden Description

In the comparison with a cane, the description of light was modelled on the probing action of the cane, but in the analogy with a vat, it is Descartes' notion of light that governs the account of the behavior of the liquid. The telling sentence is, "In the same way, all the parts of fine matter . . . tend in a straight line towards our eyes." Descartes knows that rays of light do not impede one another (for instance, the rays coming from two candlesticks can cross without visible interference), and he foists this consideration upon the vat of fermenting grapes. Behind this move is probably the notion that light is the archetypal natural phenomenon.[17] What happens in the case of light must occur elsewhere even if it is not so manifest, or even if it does not seem to apply.

If we try to tease out Descartes' implicit reasoning, I believe we get the following. The fluid at C can come out through the opening at A or the opening at B. The easiest way to either A or B is a straight line. Therefore the fluid at C tends in a straight line towards A and B. What *actually* happens to the juice, namely, whether it comes out through A or B, is merely a practical matter that does not alter the geometry (and hence the physics, since matter is mere extension) of the situation. "Note here," writes Descartes, rehearsing the by now familiar distinction,

> that it is necessary to distinguish between the movement and the action or tendency to move. For we can very easily conceive that the wine at C tends towards holes A and B even though it cannot actually move towards both holes at the same time, and that it tends exactly in a straight line towards A and B, even though it cannot move exactly in a straight line because of the bunches of grapes which are between them. In the same way, considering that the light of a luminous body must be regarded as being not so much its movement as its action, you must think of the rays of light as nothing other than the lines along which this action tends.[18]

The "tendency to go down" or "action" of the wine is characterized as: (1) *rectilinear* (the law of inertia is invoked but not explained), (2) *multi-directional* (it tends towards both A and B), (3) *instantaneous*, and (4) *uninhibited*. Now these are the properties that Descartes assumes, from the outset, to be typical of light. This is why the concluding sentence of the text I have just quoted enjoins the reader to "think of the rays of light as *nothing other* than the lines along which the action leads." That infinitely many rays should tend from a light source is said to follow from the analogy with the vat where we

---

[17] The Preface to the first (1664) edition of *The World* mentions that the original title was simply *Treatise of Light* (A.T., XI, p. viii). On the crucial role played by the metaphysics of light before Galileo, see A.C. Crombie, *Roger Crosseteste and the Origins of Experimental Science* (Oxford: Oxford University Press, 1953).

[18] *Optics*, A.T., VI, p. 88.

"imagine an infinity of straight lines along which the action coming from all the points of the surface of the wine tends towards one hole."[19] But whether we be thinking of light or wine, the criterion of intelligibility is purely geometrical or, better still, diagrammatic.

Tennis Balls and the Grand Slam

Descartes allegedly introduced his second analogy because of the difference in transparency between a wooden cane and an expanse of air. In fact, he was mainly concerned with the instantaneous and rectilinear features of the propagation of light, and the dark and turbid liquid in the vat can hardly be said to have served his purpose. This is why he introduces a third analogy, which is meant to illuminate both transparency and colors. Rays of light, that meet bodies that are not uniformly transparent,

> are liable to be deflected or dampened by them in the same way that the motion of a ball or a stone thrown in the air is deflected by the bodies it encounters. For *it is easy to believe* that the *action or tendency to motion*, which, as I have said, should be taken for light, *must follow* in this *the same laws as motion*.[20]

Despite the alleged ease of comprehension, it is not immediately obvious how an instantaneous tendency can follow the same laws as the temporal motion of a ball or stone. I shall return to this presently, but first let us consider how Descartes develops his analogy. The stone is promptly forgotten, and we are asked to consider a tennis ball struck by a racquet. The ball moves forward, but it can also be made to rotate or spin when grazed or cut. The surface that the ball strikes will alter these motions in varying degrees. Analogously, black bodies "dampen the rays of light and take all their strength away," while others reflect them in the order in which they arrive (plane mirrors) or in different directions (curved mirrors). Furthermore,

> some bodies, namely, those that we call white, reflect these rays without bringing about any other change in their action, while others, namely those that are red, yellow, blue or some other colour, produce a change similar to that which the motion of a ball receives when we graze it.

Descartes adds, as if to reassure his readers that the analogy is not as tenuous as might appear: "I believe I can determine the nature of each of the colours and demonstrate this experimentally [*le faire voir par expérience*], but it goes beyond the limits of my subject."[21] As we know from our study of the rainbow, Descartes offers an explanation of colors in Chapter Eight of the

[19] *Ibid.*

[20] *Ibid.*, pp. 88–89, emphasis added.

[21] *Ibid.*, p. 92.

Meteorology, published between the same covers as the *Optics*, and it is surprising that he should not refer to that development. The reason is that he wrote the *Optics* first and did not revise it after completing the *Meteorology*.[22]

Idealizations and A Priori Knowledge

The assumption that underlies all of Descartes' comparisons is that an "inclination or tendency to motion" follows the laws of motion. Descartes takes this for granted and uses it as a warrant for studying the nature of light, not by investigating actual optical phenomena, but by considering the *reflected* and *refracted* motion of a tennis ball. But before proceeding to an analysis of reflection, Descartes introduces three additional abstractions or idealizations.[23] The first is that the surface that the ball strikes is perfectly hard and smooth. This may not seem particularly daring because we are familiar with modern physics textbooks in which perfectly round spheres roll on completely frictionless rigid surfaces. In the seventeenth century, however, such mathematical abstractions were usually considered a denial rather than an elucidation of physics. The second of Descartes' idealizations is that we can also disregard weight, size, and shape, and here we begin to see how difficult it is to stop on the slippery path of abstraction. With the third idealization, namely, that the speed of the ball is the same *before and after impact*, we find ourselves in a world in which a change of direction is not really a change at all.

Descartes' idealizations are less an attempt at simplification, in the belief that the main factors can be isolated, than the assertion that a number of factors are known, *a priori*, to be irrelevant. In other words, Cartesian idealization is not linked to *contrivance* or the determination to test under suitable conditions. In the case that we are considering, it is the result of a dogmatic belief that the main features of light are known upon simple and direct inspection.

Descartes distinguishes between the "force" that impels the ball and the "position" of the racquet that determines its trajectory: "the power [*puissance*], whatever it may be, that makes the motion of the ball continue, is different from the power that determines it to move in one direction rather than in another." The former depends on how hard the ball is hit, the latter on the position of the racquet at the moment of impact. After striking the ground, the ball bounces back in a different direction "without any change occurring in the force of its motion."[24] Here again, while Descartes appears to be appealing to an analogy from tennis, he is really describing the collision of a ball with a racquet in a language that fits his assumptions about the action of light. What he has in mind is the apparently "effort-less" way light

[22] In the *Meteorology*, he explicitly refers to the *Optics*, e.g., *ibid.*, p. 331.

[23] *Optics*, A.T., VI, pp. 93–94.

[24] *Ibid.*, p. 94.

bounces off a mirror. Since the "determination" and "the force of motion" are distinct, they can be considered independent variables. The direction can be changed without the speed being affected.

Quies Media

Descartes' analysis is governed by what he takes to be the nature of light, but it is also related to the notorious medieval problem of the *quies media*, or the notion that there is always an interval of rest between two successive motions. A ball that strikes the floor and bounces back does not stop before reverting, "for if its motion were once interrupted, no cause could be found to start it again."[25] Elasticity is excluded from the outset because the ball and the surface are assumed to be perfectly rigid. The same interpretation applies to the collision of two balls. Replying to a query by Mersenne in 1640, Descartes writes:

> When two metal balls meet and, as often happens, one of them rebounds, it does so in virtue of the same force that made it move forward: for the force and the direction of motion are completely different as I said in my *Optics*.[26]

A few months later, Mersenne passed on Hobbes' objection that when a ball strikes the ground both the surface of the ground and the surface of the ball curve inward upon impact and then regain their shape. Descartes conceded the empirical fact but refused to see it as an objection to his theory. Far from agreeing that reflection would be impossible if colliding bodies were incompressible, he affirmed that compressibility only results in distorting the effect of reflection, so that the angle of incidence and the angle of refraction are no longer equal.[27] Hence incompressibility appeared necessary to Descartes in order to treat collision mathematically. How elusive the notion of elasticity remained for Descartes' contemporaries can be seen in the reply that Descartes made to Mersenne, who was trying to understand it under the anthropomorphic category of "gathering up force":

[25] *Ibid.* The problem was raised by Aristotle who concluded that the motion of a body that turns back upon a straight line must stop (*Physics*, book 8, ch. 8, 262b24–263a4). This was denied by Galileo who claimed that there was no interval of rest (Galileo Galilei, *De Motu, Opere*, vol. I, pp. 323–328, or in the translation by I.E. Drabkin in Galileo Galilei, *On Motion and On Mechanics* (Madison: University of Wisconsin Press, 1960), pp. 94–100). Isaac Beeckman agrees with Aristotle in his *Journal*, vol. 2, p. 23, while Marin Mersenne gives the arguments for and against but does not take sides in his *Harmonie Universelle* (Paris, 1636), facsimile (Paris: C.N.R.S., 1975), vol. III, pp. 163–165.

[26] Letter of Descartes to Mersenne, 11 March 1640, A.T., III, p. 37. Earlier in 1630, when he was writing the *Optics*, Descartes had applied his denial of an interval of rest to the case of a vibrating string arguing that it could never revert to its original position if it stopped before turning back (letters to Mersenne of 4 and 25 November 1630, A.T., I, pp. 172, 181; see also a letter written in 1630 or possibly later, A.T., IV, p. 687).

[27] Letter of Descartes to Mersenne for Hobbes, 21 January 1641, A.T., III, p. 289.

I do not agree that the speed of a hammer stroke takes nature by surprise, so that it has no time to gather its forces in order to resist. Nature has no force to gather, *nor does it need time for that, since, in everything, it acts mathematically.*[28]

When Hobbes returned to the charge, Descartes replied with what he thought a telling argument: if rebound were due to compression and elasticity, it should be possible to make a ball bounce up merely by pressing it down hard.[29] It is clear that for Descartes time is irrelevant to the analysis of collision and rebound, and that allowing elastic recoil would be tantamount to abandoning a truly mathematical interpretation of the world. Mathematics is indeed timeless, and so is instantaneous motion!

The Analysis of Reflection

If we now turn to Descartes' analysis of reflection, we find that he introduces a further assumption about the divisibility of the "determination" or direction of the motion: "it must be noted that the determination to move in a certain direction, as well as motion and in general any kind of quantity, can be divided among all the parts of which we can imagine that it is composed."[30]

For reasons that are not explicitly stated, out of all the parts of motion that "can be imagined" in AB (see Figure 3), Descartes chooses the determinations or directions AC perpendicular to the surface, and AF, parallel to it. At the moment of impact, the surface hinders the first "determination" but not the second. In other words, the downward motion AC is impeded while the parallel one AF remains unaffected.

In the light of this assumption, Descartes finds the path the ball will follow after striking the surface by drawing a circle with B as center and AB as radius (Figure 3). Since the speed of the ball is unchanged, it will move from B to a point F on the circumference of the circle in the same time it would have proceeded to D in the absence of a reflecting surface. The point F is found by noting that the parallel "determination" remains unchanged after impact, so that it must be equidistant from H, and lie along the line FD parallel to HB and AC. It is also clear from the diagram that angles ABC and FBE made with the surface are equal. These Descartes calls the angle of incidence and the angle of reflection, whereas we refer to angle ABH as the angle of incidence, and angle FBH as the angle of reflection. The difference is

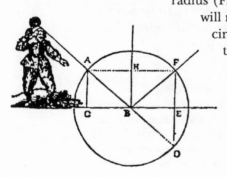

Figure 3

[28] Letter of Descartes to Mersenne, 11 March 1649, *ibid.*, p. 37, emphasis added.

[29] Letter of Descartes to Mersenne, 18 March 1641, *ibid.*, p. 338.

[30] *Optics*, A.T., VI, pp. 94–95.

merely terminological: Descartes usually refers to the line AH (= CB), which is, letting the radius AB = 1, the sine of angle ABH.

Descartes' *Optics* was passed on to Fermat who was puzzled by Descartes' argument. If the "determination" could be divided into all the parts of which it could be imagined to be composed, why privilege the determinations AH and AC? Descartes replied that motion can indeed be divided into an infinite number of different components, but that a "real" (by which he meant a physical) surface, such as CBE, impedes the downward but not the lateral motion of a ball.[31] In other words, a hard surface will not allow the ball to pass through it. But if this is the case, Descartes' argument boils down to the assertion that the geometry of the situation is disclosed in experience. It is simply a matter of everyday observation that a hard even surface impedes downward and not sideways motion, and that the ball bounces in such a way that the angle of reflection is equal to the angle of incidence. What are we to make therefore of the alleged possibility of deducing the law of reflection from its abstract mathematical features? The appeal to experience may be necessary, but it is not warranted on Descartes' own premises. Yet about this Descartes is silent.

On to Refraction

The ensuing discussion of refraction is introduced with a further modification of the tennis ball analogy. Imagine, says Descartes, that the tennis ball strikes not the ground but a frail canvas, which it breaks through, losing half its speed. Bearing in mind that "the motion of the ball is entirely different from its determination to move in one direction rather than another," the path of the ball is found by tracing a circle AFB, and drawing three straight lines AC, HB, and FE at right angles with CBE, such that the distance between FE and HB is twice that between HB and AC (see Figure 4). This reveales that the ball must tend to point I:

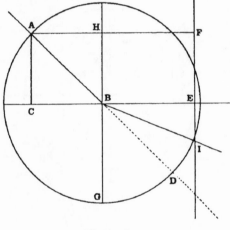

Figure 4

> For, since the ball loses half of its speed in going through the canvas CBE, in order to travel below from B to any point on the circumference of the circle AFD, it must employ twice the time it took above the canvas from A to B. And since it loses nothing whatsoever of its former determination to advance in the right hand direction, in twice the time which it employed to go from the line AC to HB, it must cover twice the distance in the same

[31] Letter of Descartes to Mersenne for Fermat, 5 October 1637, A.T., I, p. 452. Fermat's objections were formulated in a letter he wrote to Mersenne in April or May of the same year, *ibid.*, pp. 358–359.

direction, and consequently arrive at a point on the straight line FE at the same moment as it reaches a point on the circumference of the circle ADF. But this would be impossible if it did not proceed towards I, as this is the only point below the canvas CBE where the circle AFD and the straight line EF intersect.[32]

If we now replace the canvas by water and assume that the speed of the ball is reduced by half, the same considerations will apply. The ball will be deflected towards I: "For the water can open up to let it pass just as easily on one side as on the other, at least if we assume, as we always do, that the ball's course is not altered by its heaviness, lightness, size, shape, or any other extraneous cause."[33]

This is the first step in Descartes' argument about reflection, and we shall return later to consider some of its features, especially the halving of the speed. But let us now proceed to the second step or the application of the model to the action of light. This involves yet more tinkering to make the model conform to the experimental fact that the deflection of a light ray upon entering a denser medium (say water) is not away from the normal (the line HG) but towards it.

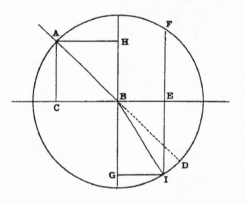

Figure 5

To account for this deflection, Descartes assumes that the ball, on reaching the surface at B, is again given a smash by the racquet CBE, so that "the force of its motion" is increased by one-third, and that it now covers in two moments the distance it had previously covered in three (see Figure 5). Descartes boldly claims that "the same effect would be produced if the ball encountered at B a body of such a nature that it would pass through its surface CBE a third more easily than through air."[34] The actual path of the refracted ray BI is then determined by taking BE = 2/3 BC, and drawing the perpendicular FE which, when prolonged, cuts the circle at I. Here is the implication as Descartes saw it:

Since the ball, which comes in a straight line from A to B, is deflected at point B and moves towards I, this means that the force or ease with which it penetrates the body CBEI is to that with which it leaves the body ACBE as the distance between AC and HB is to that between HB and FI, that is, as the line CB is to BE.[35]

[32] *Optics*, A.T., VI, pp. 97–98.

[33] *Ibid.*, p. 99.

[34] *Ibid.*, p. 100.

[35] *Ibid.*

The Law of Refraction

The ratio CB/BE is the sine law as it appears in the *Optics*. The modern form sin $i = n$ sin r (where i is the angle of incidence, r the angle of refraction, and n a constant specific to the refractive medium) easily follows, as we can see from our diagram (Figure 5) in which ABH is the angle of incidence and IBG the angle of refraction. Sin i = AH/AB, and sin r = GI/BI. But AB = BI = 1, hence sin i = AH and sin r = GI. Now AH = CB, and GI = BE. Hence the legitimate comparison that Descartes institutes between CB and BE. Descartes probably chose this way of formulating the sine law to enable artisans, such as Ferrier, to see directly from the diagram what lines had to be measured. To Mersenne, however, he had expressed the law in the form sin i = n sin r, and this is how Mersenne had made it known in his *Harmonie Universelle* in 1636. But in whatever form we consider the law, the proof that Descartes adduces is far from carrying immediate and intuitive conviction. If I have quoted him at length, it is in order to examine his reasoning more closely.

As we have seen above, the first step in Descartes' argument involved reducing by half the speed of the ball when it crashed through the canvas or entered the water. This is already fraught with ambiguity. On the one hand, Descartes states that the horizontal component of motion remains unaltered, and that only that part of the "determination" that makes the ball "tend downward" is changed. On the other hand, a few lines later, he interprets the decrease in speed as occurring along the *actual* path of the ball under the surface *CBE* (see Figure 6). He writes that the ball, having lost "half its speed in going through the canvas CBE, must employ twice the time it took above the canvas from A to B to travel below from B to any point on

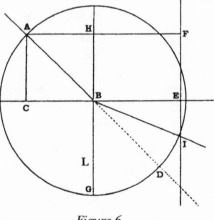

Figure 6

the circumference of the circle AFD."[36] To be consistent, Descartes should have written that it would take twice the time to descend not along the actual path BI, but along the vertical distance BL (equal to HB)!

What is going on? I believe that the answer is obvious if we bear in mind that the whole exercise rests on Descartes' prior knowledge of the law. In other words, what he is offering is not a process of discovery but a piece of justification. As we know from our discussion of the rainbow in Chapter Nine, Descartes was aware of the sine law before he began writing his *Optics*. What he wanted to show was how it could be deduced from geometrical considerations.

[36] *Ibid.*, pp. 97–98.

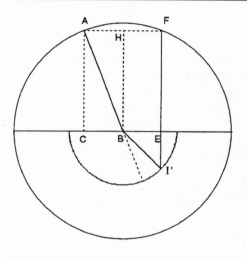

Figure 7

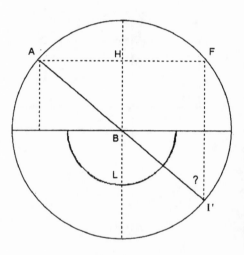

Figure 8

Geometry Invoked

Let us look at the first step of the geometrical proof of the law of reflection, which simply says that the angle of incidence is equal to the angle of reflection. Here Descartes has no problem in describing a circle of radius AB because the ball bounces back from B to F in the same time it took to go from A to B (see Figure 3 above). Since AB = BF, the speed is unaltered. What Descartes does not seem to have noticed is that when the speed is changed as in the case of refraction, the size of the circle should also be changed. Hence when the speed below the surface CBE is reduced by half, a second smaller circle of radius 1/2 AB should be drawn below the surface CBE, as in Figure 7.

Since the horizontal speed is constant, AH = HF, and the path below CBE will lie along BI', where I' is the point where the smaller circle and the perpendicular FI' intersect. As we can see from Figure 8, this would not work when the angle of incidence is above 30° because FI' would fall outside the smaller circle.

Descartes does not introduce a second circle in the *Optics*, but the smash of the racquet increases "the force of the motion by one-third, so that it can cover in two moments the distance it previously covered in three."[37] FE is drawn such that CB = 3/2 BE (see Figure 9), and Descartes concludes that the ball will head towards I, the point where the extended perpendicular FE and the circle intersect. But there is a sleight of hand here. By making CB = 3/2 BE, Descartes has, in fact, made the lateral speed *before* the impact of the racquet one-third less than after, whereas we would expect the force to be increased by one-third *after* the smash. But this would have yielded a different ratio when Descartes *already knows* that 3/2 is the correct ratio for refraction from air to glass!

A Curious Coincidence

What if we were to follow the line of reasoning that appears more logical and draw the second larger circle? Given that AH = HF, we take Descartes' ratio

---

[37] *Ibid.*, p. 100.

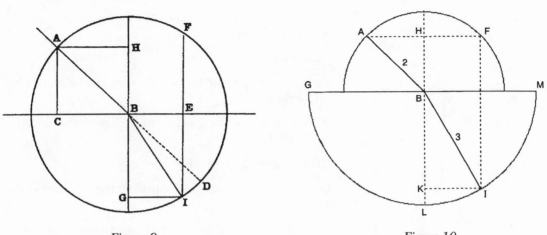

Figure 9   Figure 10

3/2, and assume that the refracted ray BI covers three units of distance when the incident ray AB only covers two (see Figure 10). We then trace semicircle GLH whose radius BL is to radius BC of the smaller circle as three is to two.

Drop IK perpendicular to BL. The angle of incidence is ABH, and the angle of refraction is IBL.

Thus,
$$\frac{\sin i}{\sin r} = \frac{AH/AB \ (AH/\text{ radius of small circle})}{IK/BI \ (IK/\text{ radius of large circle})}$$

$$= \frac{AH/\ 2}{IK/\ 3}$$

Now, since AH = IK, therefore, $\sin i / \sin r = 3/2$

In other words, the same result as Descartes obtains in the *Optics*!

It is fascinating to compare this hypothetical line of argument with the one that Claude Mydorge actually followed in Paris some time between 1626 and 1631.[38] Mydorge considers a situation in which a ray of light FE is refracted at E in the direction EG (see Figure 11), and he seeks to determine the path that the ray HE will follow when it is refracted in turn.

---

[38] Mydorge's text was copied by Mersenne and is printed in Marin Mersenne, *Correspondance*, vol. I, p. 405, where it is presumed to have originated in a letter written by Mydorge to Mersenne in February or March 1630 (p. 404). Pierre Costabel believes that it is posterior to Mydorge's work on conic sections, which he wrote in 1631 (René Descartes, *Règles utiles et claires pour la direction de l'esprit en la recherche de la vérité* Jean-Luc Marion, trans., with notes by Pierre Costabel (The Hague: Martinus Nijhoff, 1977), p. 318. Mydorge's proof is discussed in A. Mark Smith, "Descartes' Theory of Light and Refraction: A Discourse on Method," *Transactions of the American Philosophical Society*, 77, part 3 (1987), pp. 27–29.

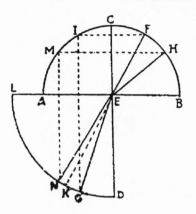

Figure 11

Draw semicircle ACB with center E and radius EB. F and H lie on its circumference.

Draw FI parallel to AEB.

Drop perpendicular IG intersecting the refracted ray HEG at G.

With E as centre and EG as radius, describe quarter-circle DGL.

Draw HM parallel to AEB.

Drop perpendicular MN cutting the quarter-circle at N.

Join EN, which will be the path of refracted ray HE.

The procedure is essentially the one we outlined above, since EG/EF = radius of large circle/radius of small circle. Mydorge proceeded, therefore, the way Descartes might have done. But even if Descartes initially used this approach, he may have decided to use only one circle in the *Optics* because this has the advantage of displaying the law clearly, since AH and GI (see Figure 9 above) are referred to the same radius.

Clear for illustrative purposes, the diagram used by Descartes is less successful in providing a rational explanation, since it masks the assumptions that: (1) the horizontal component of the speed remains unvaried, and (2) the ratio of the speed above to the speed below the surface of the medium is constant.

The Smash

In order to bend the ray towards the normal after it enters the water, Descartes postulates that the ball is struck a second time as it passes through the surface, and is speeded up in such a way that it traverses in two moments the distance it formerly covered in three. This is perhaps the least persuasive aspect of the tennis ball analogy. The smash of the racquet seems far-fetched, and even if the ball were suddenly accelerated, it is not obvious why all the change should take place at the surface, so that once the ball enters the water it travels without further variation of speed through a resisting medium. Descartes is aware of these difficulties and tries to circumvent them.

The sudden increase in speed at the surface is not explained by a mechanical cause similar to the racquet. Rather it is interpreted as resulting from the greater ease of penetration into the denser medium. The second stroke of the racquet has the same effect "as if the ball met at B a body of such a nature that it could pass through the surface CBE [see Figure 9 above] one-third more easily than through air."[39] The problem here is that, even if the

[39] *Optics*, A.T., VI, p. 100.

denser medium offered no resistance whatsoever, it does not follow that the ball would be accelerated upon entering, unless the force of the ball were previously dissipated by some counter-prevailing force. Descartes recognizes that his analogy is strained. His reader, as he puts it, "will perhaps find it strange" that light is bent toward the normal upon entering a denser medium whereas a ball, on entering water, is deflected away. In other words, whereas the ray tends towards I (see Figure 12), a ball would move towards V. But Descartes is undeterred. All the reader has to do is recollect that: (a) light is "nothing but a certain movement or an action received in the very fine matter that fills the pores of other bodies," and (b) that a ball "loses more of its motion in striking a soft body than a hard one, and rolls less easily on a carpet than on a completely bare table."[40]

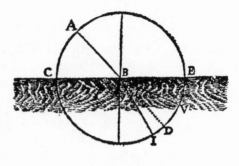

Figure 12

The comparison with a rolling ball is unlikely to satisfy the modern reader. It is true that a hard ball is arrested by a cushion, whereas it bounces back when it strikes another hard ball, but we do not consider the rebound a simple continuation of the original motion. We explain the occurrence in terms of elasticity. The initial speed is destroyed, and speed in the opposite direction is generated. If the collision were totally inelastic, the two colliding balls would simply be flattened out. Descartes, however, operated under the assumption that the "determination" or direction of the ball can be changed without the motion itself being altered. The change of direction is instantaneous and involves no gain or loss of momentum. The ball never comes to a rest, however infinitesimal in duration, for if it were once stopped there would be no reason for it to start moving again. In Descartes' terminology, the same force operates throughout. Since he holds that the transmission of light is instantaneous, he does not worry overmuch about the niceties of impulse or force acting over a period of time. He believes, nonetheless, and this is what we find surprising, that instantaneous transmission is achieved with greater or lesser ease! He reasons as follows: light is an action upon the fine matter that fills the pores of material bodies, and when the pores are soft and ill-joined as is the case with air, the action of light is less easily transmitted than through the more tightly-packed pores of a denser medium.[41]

---

[40] *Ibid.*, p. 103.

[41] It is surprising that Descartes does not mention the case of sound, which travels faster in water than in air. It was well known, for instance, that the sound of horse hoofs can be heard by pressing one's ear to the ground long before they reach the ear through the air. A modern version of what Descartes had in mind might run as follows: I have pressed the accelerator of my car to the bottom, and I am only inching forward on soft ground, when suddenly my wheels touch a hard surface, and I'm off at a terrific speed.

The Persistence of Juvenile Dreams

The conviction that light passes more readily through a denser medium is not a well-thought-out, mature scientific position. It is a point of view that harks back to what we have described as Descartes' Rosicrucian phase. As early as 1619–1621, he jotted down in his notebook:

> Since light can only be produced in matter, where there is more matter, it is produced more easily, other things being equal; therefore, it penetrates more easily through a dense than through a rare medium. This is why refraction is made away from the perpendicular in the latter, and towards the perpendicular in the former.[42]

Almost 20 years later, the *Optics* of 1637 declare that the sine law is a measure of the ease of penetration in a dense medium.[43] Whatever the merits of the idea that a ball is accelerated upon entering a denser medium, it does not dispel the surprise attending upon the further claim that the ball moves at a *uniform* speed through the medium. Descartes knew as well as the next man that if a stick is thrust into a pile of sand, its speed is dampened, and it soon comes to a halt. Neither could it have escaped him that when arrows are shot into bales of hay they are slowed down and stopped. Yet he believed, as we have already noted, that water offers little or no resistance to motion.[44] His description is modelled on a theoretical ball whose motion is in no way affected by weight, size, or shape. Again we are back to instantaneous, diagrammatic, and hence (for Descartes) unproblematic motion.

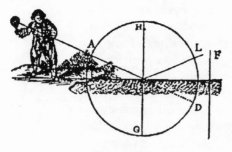

Figure 13

A Theory and its Consequences

Descartes did not always pursue the implications of his theory beyond their practical relevance to optics. But there is one consequence of his analysis that he stressed because of its near lethal consequences: a ball can be struck at such an oblique angle that it will not go through the water but bounce off "just as if it had struck the earth [see Figure 13]. This has unfortunately been experimented when cannon balls fired for amusement's sake towards the bottom of the river wounded bystanders on the other side."[45]

---

[42] *Cogitationes Privatae*, A.T., X, pp. 242–243.

[43] "the force or ease . . . is like CB to BE" (*Optics*, A.T., VI, p. 100).

[44] See above p. 240. Galileo was also convinced that "water offers no resistance whatever to being divided" (Galileo Galilei, *Fragments Related to the Treatise on Floating Bodies* [1610–1612], *Opere*, vol. IV, p. 27).

[45] *Optics*, A.T., VI, p. 99.

Descartes' motivation (beyond public spirit) in conveying this information was probably to reassure the reader that he had worked out the quantitative implications of his views. In fact, he had been remarkably desultory in doing so. One striking case is the diagram (see Figure 14) that Descartes uses to illustrate what would happen if a tennis ball struck a canvas that reduced its speed by half so that it proceeded to a point I on the circumference of the circle, where I is said to be determined by letting HF = 2 AH, and dropping the perpendicular FI. In the diagram published in the *Optics*, AH = 10.5 mm, and AF = 14 mm

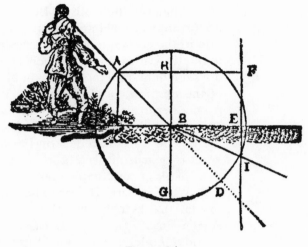

Figure 14

instead of 21 mm, as his law required. The reason is clear. Since the radius AB is only 15 mm, AF, drawn to scale, would have lain outside the circle, and we would have the case of the cannon ball in Figure 13. Indeed, it can easily be computed that if the angle of incidence ABH is greater than 32°, FE will lie beyond the circle. In Figure 14, the angle ABH is 44°!

The discrepancy between the wording of the text and the diagram was spotted by Hobbes, who brought it to Descartes' attention in a letter of 30 March 1641 that was forwarded by Mersenne.[46] Descartes' immediate reaction was an outburst of indignation. How could any reader be "so stupid" as to impute to him the mistakes of the printer! "If, in the diagram, the line HF is not exactly twice the length of AH, it is the printer's fault, not my own," he expostulated.[47] The truth is that the diagram was not prepared by the printer but by Franz Van Schooten under Descartes' vigilant eye.[48] Descartes could not make his point about refraction if the line FE fell outside the circle, and this is the real reason why he tailored the diagram to fit his illustrative purposes. Eighteen months later, writing to Mersenne in a less passionate vein, he shifted his ground, and explained the diagram as follows:

> I used the ratio 2:1 on pages 17 and 18 of my Discourse [*Optics*, A.T., VI, p. 98] because it is the simplest, and I wanted to make myself clear, *but I had them print* a diagram with a smaller ratio to show that what I said applied to all kinds of ratios, and also to make it closer to what is experienced.[49]

[46] Letter of Hobbes to Mersenne for Descartes, 30 March 1641, A.T., III, p. 348.

[47] Letter of Descartes to Mersenne, 21 April 1641, *ibid.*, p. 356.

[48] Descartes wrote to Constantin Huygens on 13 July 1636 that Franz Van Schooten the Younger was drawing *all* the figures of the *Optics* to his complete satisfaction, A.T., I, p. 611.

[49] Letter of Descartes to Mersenne, 20 October 1642 A.T., III, pp. 589–590. See also his letter to Mersenne of 13 October 1642, *ibid.*, p. 583.

Whatever the truth of Descartes' gloss on his mistake, he missed the opportunity of making a useful discovery. Had he paid a modicum of attention to the consequences of his assumption that AF = 2 AH, he would have found the critical angle at which a ray of light coming from a denser medium does not penetrate the surface but is refracted along the top. From his study of the rainbow, Descartes had accurately determined the refractive index from water to air as 3/4. The critical angle is, therefore, 3/4 = 0.75 = 48° 35'. The reason Descartes was not led to this consideration is probably because there is no internal reflection in the case of a ray going from air to water. What is clear is his lack of interest in extending the mathematical implications of his general statements.

While in Paris, Descartes had secured experimental confirmation of his sine law thanks to the draughtsmanship of Mydorge and the practical skills of Ferrier. In the *Optics*, he arrives at the formulation of his law by reasoning round a model in geometrical fashion. How does this square with his insistence that all knowledge must be grounded on intuitive starting points? Even if we allowed Descartes that local motion is intuitively obvious, such a status could hardly be bestowed upon the idea that light is "a tendency to move." It would seem that all Descartes has is a set of analogies (the blind man's cane, the vat, and the tennis ball), and that his explanations of optics are no more than hypotheses. When Descartes came to write the *Discourse on Method*, he recognized the difficulty and ascribed to his readers a "shock" that may well have been his own:

> Should anyone *be shocked* at first by some of the statements I make at the beginning of the Optics and the *Meteorology* because I call them 'suppositions' and do not seem to care about proving them, let him have the patience to read the whole book attentively, and I trust that he will be satisfied. For I take my reasonings to be so closely interconnected that just as the last are proved by the first, which are their causes, so the first are proved by the last, which are their effects. It must not be supposed that I am here committing the fallacy that the logicians call 'arguing in a circle'. For as experience makes most of these effects quite certain, the causes from which I deduce them serve not so much to prove them as to explain them; indeed, quite to the contrary, it is the causes which are proved by the effects. And I have called them 'suppositions' simply to make it known that *I think I can deduce them from the primary truths I have expounded above*; but I have deliberately avoided carrying out these deductions in order to prevent certain ingenious persons from taking the opportunity to construct, on what they believe to be my principles, some extravagant philosophy for which I shall be blamed.[50]

We must bear in mind that Descartes is not offering in this passage a statement about what scientific method should be, but that he is anticipating objections and inventing (on the spur of the Preface, as it were) some kind of

[50] *Discourse on Method*, A.T., VI, p. 76, emphasis added.

reply. If the effects prove the cause, as he claims, then knowledge of the truth of the consequences is not axiomatic but empirical. This may be enough for an empiricist, but Descartes expected better and more intuitive grounds for his science. It is not enough for him that hypotheses should yield observed consequences that can be invoked as evidence for their truth. His hypotheses or "suppositions" possess a far superior epistemological warrant. They can be deduced, he writes, "from the primary truths I have expounded above," but we are not told whether he intends the *cogito ergo sum*, the existence, goodness, and omnipotence of God, the concept of extension, or the laws of motion. Actually, what he has in mind is his treatise *The World*, which he had summarized in the Fifth Part of the *Discourse on Method*.

Descartes' explanation did not dispel the difficulties but merely served to highlight them. Fr. Vatier, a professor at La Flèche to whom Descartes had sent a copy of his book, expressed surprise at a method that promised rational intuition but only provided a series of empirical models. Descartes replied that he had offered an *a posteriori* proof because an *a priori* one would have required a complete exposition of his physics. He claimed that he could have deduced all his suppositions from the first principles of his metaphysics, but that he had chosen instead to let the truth speak for itself. "I wanted to see," he wrote, "whether the mere statement of the truth would be enough to carry conviction."[51] A few days later, however, he took a different tack in a letter to Mersenne. He now declared that he had "demonstrated refraction geometrically and *a priori*."[52] When the Minim Friar reminded him that he had only used models and analogies, Descartes hastily retreated to his earlier position. "To require from me," he wrote, "geometrical demonstrations in a question which concerns physics is to ask for what is impossible."[53] Mersenne was left to marvel in silence . . . .

---

[51] Letter of Descartes to Vatier, 22 February, 1638, A.T., I, p. 563. Antoine Vatier (1596–1659) was born the same year as Descartes and taught at La Flèche from 1618 to 1642 except for two brief periods when he was in Paris (1626–1628), where he may have met Descartes, and Bourges (1632–1634).

[52] Letter of Descartes to Mersenne, 1 March 1638, A.T., II, p. 31.

[53] Letter of Descartes to Mersenne, 27 May 1638, *ibid.*, p. 142.

Chapter Eleven

Matter and Motion in a New World

*T*HE WORK THAT DESCARTES considered the embodiment of his system of natural philosophy, and to which he referred with proprietorial pride as "my World",[1] was written between 1630 and 1632. It contains the new cosmology that was demanded by his concept of matter and his understanding of motion. We have seen in Chapter Eight how Descartes' metaphysical starting point, the analysis of the *Cogito*, led him to conclude that mind and matter were radically separate and distinct. He identified matter with extension and claimed that all its characteristics were reducible to this one single property. Hence the task of showing how weight, impenetrability, hardness, and other apparent properties of matter are derived from extension alone. However logical this project might look, it clearly runs counter to common sense and everyday experience, for if the physical universe is everywhere extended, as Descartes contends, then there is matter everywhere, a vacuum is impossible, and places that are apparently empty are ontologically (i.e., really) full. The difference between a stone and an equal volume of empty space is no longer a difference of kind but merely one of density.

Not a Matter of Feeling

With such a concept of matter, it is clear that Descartes can no longer trust the disclosure of his senses, and it is to forestall a reliance on sensation that

---

[1] "Mon monde" (letter to Mersenne, 4 November 1630, A.T., I, p. 176).

The World opens with a chapter entitled, "On the Difference between Our Sensations and the Things that Produce Them," which would otherwise seem out of place in a scientific treatise. Descartes' point is not that we should disbelieve what we see, hear, or touch, but rather that we should not assume that the objects of sight, hearing, and touch are similar to the sensations through which they come to the known. Words are sound waves that bear no similarity to the meanings they evoke in our mind. Indeed, as Descartes observes, not only do we grasp an idea without noticing the sound that brings it to our attention, but if we speak more than one language, we may be at a loss to say in which language we first heard of an idea. The case is analogous with other senses. We see a smiling or a worried face, when what our eyes perceive are upturned lips or a furrowed brow, and we describe a feather as tickling, when there is nothing in the feather beyond extension and motion. Descartes uses the illustration of a soldier who returns from the fray and thinks he has been wounded. He is rushed to the doctor, his armor is removed and . . . a strap or a buckle is found to be pressing on his ribs. "If his sense of touch, in making him feel this strap, had imprinted an image of it in his mind, there would have been no need for a doctor to tell him what he felt."[2]

We can see why Descartes was anxious to stress the difference between the nature of our sensations and the ontological reality of the objects that cause them. He was coming to terms with the epistemology that his analysis of matter had made mandatory. What he does not say in *The World* is that this represents a radical break with the analysis of sensation that he had offered in *The Rules for the Direction of the Mind* in which he had argued that physical objects impress their form on the imagination, thereby guaranteeing the objectivity of the disclosure of our senses.[3] It is because he is arguing against his former self that Descartes is almost tedious in his insistence that we do not know the physical world by examining a faithful snapshot on our retina or recording a telling sound on our eardrums. Descartes is anxious lest his readers be arrested, as it were, at the stage at which he had found himself some three years earlier.

Celestial Flame and Terrestrial Fire

Having cleared the epistemological air, Descartes turns to fire, of which he says he knows only two sources: the stars in the heavens above and ordinary fire on the earth below. Since the stars are out of reach, let us look, he suggests, at a piece of burning wood. In the light of what Descartes has just told us about the treachery of our senses, we would expect him to carry out a rigorously experimental and quantitative analysis of the modes of combustion. Instead, we find him appealing to what we *see*, and inferring that what

---

[2] *The World* [*Le monde*], A.T., XI, p. 6.

[3] See above p. pp. 144–146.

lies below the threshold of vision is of like nature. When fire burns wood, he tells us,

> we see *at a glance* that it moves small particles of this wood . . . . Someone else, if he pleases, may imagine in this wood the form of fire, the quality of heat, and the action that burns it as different things; as for me, who am afraid of deceiving myself if I suppose anything more to be there than what I *see* must necessarily be present, I am content with conceiving the movement of its parts.[4]

In other words, motion is not only a necessary but a necessary and sufficient condition for fire. But all this must be understood against the background of seventeenth-century science. For Descartes and his contemporaries—indeed, for everyone until Lavoisier at the end of the eighteenth century—fire was a genuine physical substance like water or air. Where we see a process of oxidation, namely, the combination of oxygen with another substance and the concomitant release of light and heat, they saw a manifestation of the properties of fire. This is why Descartes goes on to say that the motion of the small parts of wood must be caused by very small and swift particles of fire. They may be invisible, but because there is only one kind of matter, they can in principle be exhaustively described in the vocabulary proper to large bodies in motion. Descartes recognized, however, that the small particles of fire must have considerable speed "to compensate for their lack of size." This would seem to invite a determination of the quantitative relation between their *size* and their *velocity* in order to determine their *direction*. But all we find is a repetition of the claim made in the *Optics* that speed and direction are completely independent variables:

> I add nothing about the direction in which each part moves, for if you consider that the power to move, and the power that determines in what direction motion must take place are entirely different, and that one can exist without the other (as I explained in the *Optics*), you will easily understand that each part moves in the way that is easier for it given the arrangement of the neighbouring bodies.[5]

This passage is interesting for two reasons. First, we are told that the distinction between motion and direction was explained in the *Optics*, and second, we are assured that with this distinction in mind we shall experience no difficulty in understanding that a flame goes up rather than down merely because the neighboring bodies make it easier for it to rise. As far as the first point is concerned, we were indeed told of the distinction in the *Optics*, but it was merely stated, not justified. On the contrary, we were left with the distinct impression that it hinged upon a general account of Cartesian physics to be given in *The World*. It would seem, therefore, that Descartes is treating us to the professorial merry-go-round: in course 101, we are told that

---

4 *The World*, A.T., XI, p. 7.

5 *Ibid.*, pp. 8–9.

x will be explained in course 201, and in course 201, we are reminded that *x* was already explained in course 101! The second point, namely, the assertion that fire is extruded by neighbouring bodies, also stands in need of explanation. Since direction is not directly linked to size and speed, we have to be shown why vertical motion is easier than horizontal motion, but Descartes postpones a discussion of this question until his analysis of weight at the end of *The World*.

Hard and Soft

For the time being, Descartes prefers in Chapter Three of *The World* to develop his concept of matter on the assumption that not only particles of fire, but every particle of matter is moving (in some way and to some extent), and that this universal motion is conserved because it is grounded in God's immutability, which he will consider later on in Chapter Seven. The first thing he would have us examine is the difference between liquids and solids. "Think" (we would say "assume"),

> that each body can be divided into extremely small parts. I do not wish to determine if the parts are infinite or not, but this much at least is certain: as far as our knowledge is concerned, it is indefinite, and we can suppose that there are several millions in the smallest grain of sand that is still visible.[6]

If two small parts lie motionless side by side, they can only be separated by being pushed, whereas if they are moving and only touch accidentally, very little force is required to separate them. Indeed, no force at all will be required if "the motion with which they can separate of their own accord is equal or greater than the one with which we want to separate them."[7] Therefore hard bodies are those whose parts are at rest, fluid ones those whose parts are agitated. This line of argument only makes sense if we suppose with Descartes that the speed of a moving body is a purely *scalar* quantity, i.e., that it has only magnitude, not direction. A modern reader cannot escape the feeling that the ease with which Descartes solves the problem of hardness is purchased at too great a price, but Descartes himself thought he had found a brilliant solution to the problem of the coherence of materials without invoking any "glue or cement" as he assumed everyone else had to do.[8] Bodies are hard just because their parts are at rest side by side. But if motion is all that is required to make a body a fluid and to cause the

---

[6] *Ibid.*, p. 12.

[7] *Ibid.*, p. 13.

[8] *Ibid.* By a sudden reversal of perspective, which is one of the ironies of history, Newton later scoffed at Descartes for telling us "that Bodies are glued together by rest, that is, by an occult Quality, or rather by nothing" (Isaac Newton, *Opticks.* (London, 1704), reprint (New York: Dover, 1952), p. 388).

sensation of fire, why aren't we scorched by the breeze? To this rhetorical question, Descartes replies that

> we must consider not only the speed but the size of the moving parts. The smaller ones produce the more fluid bodies, but the larger ones have more power to burn and, generally speaking, to act upon other bodies.[9]

No quantative development is offered, and the reader is left to puzzle out for himself what larger means in this context, and why larger bodies have more penetrating power when they are heavier. The impression one has here and throughout the *World* is that Descartes is interested in understanding change in general, but that a quantitative mechanics remains peripheral to his concern.

Facing the Void

Motion would seem to suppose room to move. But for Descartes matter is extension, and extension is merely space, from which it follows that any particular extended thing is merely a part of the *one extended thing*. Another way of putting this is to say that where there is space, there is extension and hence matter. Since we are unable to imagine an unextended place, the idea of a void or perfect vacuum is impossible on purely metaphysical grounds. Strictly speaking, bodies are not *in space*, but only among other bodies. This is central to Descartes' physics. He stresses it in Chapter Four of *The World*, and takes it up again in the *Principles of Philosophy* where he argues that if God removed everything that is contained in a vase the sides would touch because there would no longer be anything between them. *Nothing* can have no properties and hence no dimensions; therefore, two objects separated by *nothing* are really in contact.[10] An empty vessel is not a vessel at all! But couldn't God, asked Mersenne, remove all the air in a room without replacing it by anything else? This, replied Descartes, would be like suggesting that God could level the mountains and leave the valleys![11] But how can we have change of place when there is apparently no place to change? Descartes thought he had the answer:

> I would have been uneasy about replying had I not learned, through various observations [*expériences*] that all the motions that take place in the world are in some way *circular*. That is, when a body leaves its place, it always takes the place of some other body, and this one that of another,

[9] *The World*, A.T., XI, p. 15.

[10] *Principles of Philosophy*, Part II, art. 18, A.T., VIII–1, p. 50.

[11] Letter of Descartes to Mersenne, 9 January 1639, A.T., II, p. 482. Shortly thereafter, Descartes asserted in the *Meditations* in 1641 that God can indeed create mountains without valleys (A.T., VIII, p. 224), but he reverted to the wording of his letter of 9 January 1639 in the *Principles of Philosophy* published in 1644 (Part II, art. 18; A.T., VIII–1, p. 50).

and so on, so that the last body occupies at the same instant the place vacated by the first.[12]

If there is no empty space and the world is literally full of homogeneous matter, one part cannot be displaced without some other one taking its place at the very same instant. The *instantaneity* and *circularity* of motion are necessary consequences of the assumption (for Descartes, the intuitive certainty) that matter is a homogeneous quantity. The warrant is said to be experiential. For instance, if we open the bottom of a barrel of wine, the liquid will not flow unless a hole is punched at the top. When the hole is made, the wine flows, not out of any anthropomorphic "fear" of the void, but because air takes its place.

Unnoticed but Pervasive

The fact that we seldom observe these circular motions is not an objection for Descartes, who would have us think of fish in an aquarium. They flap their tails and gills, and flit about without so much as causing a ripple on the surface of the water! But the consequences of the theory are startling. A vase full of gold does not contain more matter than an empty one! Descartes admits that this sounds strange, but this is only because people confuse perceiving with thinking, and slip unawares into assuming that physical reality is coextensive with sensed reality. As instances of unfelt physical reality, we are reminded of the great heat of our heart (for Descartes, the organ we think of as a pump was a furnace) and the weight of our clothes.[13]

A more interesting application of Descartes' theory is found in a letter to his disciple Reneri written when he was drafting *The World*. Descartes was asked why a test-tube full of mercury does not run down when inverted. "Imagine," he replied, "air to be like wool and the aether in its pores to be like whirlwinds moving about in the wool" (see Figure 1).[14] The air at the bottom is pressed down by the layers of air on top and is therefore much heavier, but this weight goes unnoticed: "If we push the air at E towards, F, the air at F will move in a circle in the direction GHI and return to E, so that its weight is not felt, *just as the weight of a rotating wheel is not felt if it is perfectly*

---

[12] *The World*, A.T., XI, p. 19, emphasis added. The source of instantaneous circular motion is to be found in Plato's *Timaeus* where περιωτισ ("circular thrust") is invoked to explain respiration. Our breadth is a sort of projectile fired from our mouth. Since it does not issue forth into empty space, it must dislodge the air near the mouth without leaving empty space inside the mouth. Here is how Plato puts it: "Since there is no void into which any moving body could enter, and our breath moves outward, the consequence is plain to anyone: the breadth does not go out into the void but pushes the neighbouring body out of its place, and the body thus displaced in turn drives out the next . . . all this takes place *simultaneously like a revolving wheel because there is no void*" (*Timaeus* 79B).

[13] *The World*, A.T., XI, pp. 19–21.

[14] Letter of Descartes to Reneri, 2 June 1631, A.T., I, p. 205. The diagram is on p. 206.

balanced on its axle."[15] Why the air that is pushed upward should revolve in this way is not further specified, and the analogy of a wheel is employed as though it were sufficient by itself to carry conviction.

So much for the general principle. Now for the application to the inverted tube of mercury (OR in our diagram). The liquid can only fall if the wool (= air) that is at R pushes the wool at O, which in turn pushes the wool along P and Q, namely, along "the entire heavy line OPQ." But the tube is sealed at D, and no air can enter at that end. Hence the air around R remains stationary. But what about the little "whirlwinds" that are the analogue of the "aether" and fill the interstices between the particles of air? Descartes admits that they could penetrate through the glass, but since the neighbouring aether already fills the pores of the circumambient air, any additional aether would have to come from the celestial region above the air, and this could only occur if air rose to take its place.[16] Again the answer rests on broad cosmological considerations, and no attempt is made to determine the weight of the air that would have to be displaced.

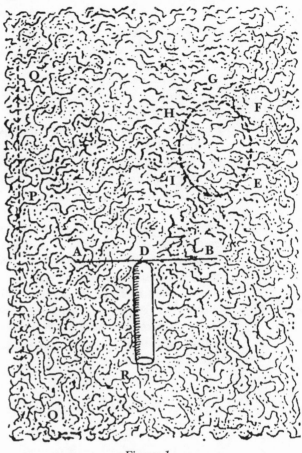

Figure 1

One Matter but Three Elements

In Chapter Five of *The World*, Descartes seeks to reconcile the notion of one homogeneous matter with the traditional division into the four elements of fire, air, water, and air. He does not deny the macroscopic differences that led to this classification, but he sees them as resulting merely from variations in the size, figure, and speed of the parts of matter. The smallest and fastest particles constitute the element of fire that is not only found in the sun and the stars but is present in all bodies, where it fills the interstices between the

---

[15] *Ibid.*, p. 206, emphasis added. Note the similarity with the passage from the *Timaeus* mentioned above, p. 256, n. 12.

[16] *Ibid.*, pp. 206–207.

larger round particles of the element air and the bulkier particles of the element earth. Water loses its status as an element and is assimilated to the fluid element of air.

This exercise is merely a concession to the nomenclature current in the seventeenth century, since Descartes insists that the fire, air, and earth that he calls elements are not to be identified with the bodies that we sense. Not only are these elements exceedingly small and fast, but *in order to preclude the possibility of a void*, they have "no determinate size or shape," and so are able to slip into the interstices of any body. But since a body is nothing more than extended substance, it cannot really alter its size. It may appear to expand and increase in bulk, but such an increase does not mean increased extension, and hence increased matter. The particles have merely been driven further apart, and their interstices filled with smaller bodies. Descartes' analogy is that of a sponge that swells when placed in water. The apparent increase is due to the addition of another body, in this case water. For Descartes the parts of the sponge are not more extended or stretched, they are simply pushed further away.[17]

In the following chapters of *The World*, Descartes proceeds to describe a new world composed exclusively of his new kind of matter, but before we follow him on this interesting journey, let us examine more closely three main features of this new matter, namely, its infinite divisibility, its impenetrability, and its mobility.

Division without End

Descartes believed that the intrinsic divisibility of matter followed immediately from the definition of matter as extension. As he wrote to his early mentor Fr. Gibieuf, "we cannot have the idea of an extended thing without also having the idea of its half, or its third and, hence, without conceiving it divisible in 2 or 3."[18] The *physical* divisibility of matter is as clear and necessary as the *geometrical* truth that the sum of the interior angles of a triangle is equal to two right angles.[19] It is also implied by the essentially circular nature of matter in motion. In order for bodies to move in a universe where there is

---

[17] *The World*, A.T., XI, pp. 23–31. The sponge analogy occurs on p. 31 and is repeated in *The Principles of Philosophy*, Part II, art. 6. See also the letters to Mersenne of 25 February 1630 and 11 October 1638, A.T., I, p. 119, and II, p. 384. In the first of these letters Descartes informs Mersenne that he has reached precisely this point (i.e., Chapter Four) in writing *The World* (A.T., I, p. 120). See John W. Lynes, "Descartes' Theory of Elements: From *Le Monde* to the *Principes*," *Journal of the History of Ideas*, 43 (1982), pp. 55–72.

[18] Letter of Descartes to Gibieuf, 19 January 1642, A.T., III, p. 477.

[19] "For example, the fact that its three angles are equal to two right angles is contained in the nature of a triangle; and divisibility is contained in the nature of body, or of an extended thing (for we cannot conceive of any extended thing which is so small that we cannot divide it, at least in our thought). And because of these facts it can be truly asserted that the three angles of every triangle are equal to two right angles and that every body is divisible" (Second Set of Replies to the Objections to the *Meditations*, A.T., VIII, p. 163).

no void, matter must be infinitely divisible. This can best be shown by employing Descartes' own example in the *Principles of Philosophy*.

Assume that very fine matter is revolving clockwise around an eccentric body EFGH (see Figure 2), and that the space above G is four times the size of the one below E, and hence that it contains four times as much matter, since there is no void and no contraction or condensation of matter. Furthermore, because no matter can move without all matter moving, the matter above G cannot move towards E without the matter below E moving out *at the same time.* But since the space under E is four times narrower than the space above E, the matter coming from above G will have to move four times faster to squeeze through. Such an instantaneous increase in speed seemed to Descartes to require an equally instantaneous division of matter "into infinitely or indefinitely small parts."[20]

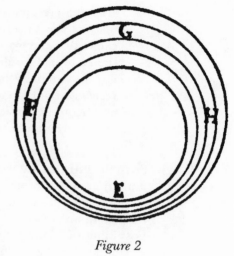

Figure 2

The situation is paradoxical. Descartes had assumed that space was full of bodies so accommodated to the space they occupied that they could not fill a larger space or be squeezed into a smaller one. If moved, they would have to displace other bodies, but there is no reason to believe that they would undergo a radical quantitative change. Now we are told, however, that there are cases of compression in which circular motion can only be understood if matter is somehow made to undergo a process of infinite division to enable all the matter to move at the same instant. But isn't this an argument against the very attempt at explaining motion without allowing empty space? Not so! replies Descartes. All we have is an instance of the limits of human knowledge: "I confess that we find in this motion something that our mind perceives to be true but is unable to comprehend."[21] Note that what Descartes fails to comprehend is not how bodies can move when there is no void (empty space has been tossed out of court!) but the unending divisibility that motion in a plenum requires.

Finite Minds and Infinite Space

If matter is pure extension, we are compelled to think of it as infinitely extended as well as infinitely divisible. This has cosmological implications as Descartes explained to his friend Hector-Pierre Chanut in 1647:

> If we suppose that the world is finite, we have to imagine that beyond its boundaries are spaces with their three dimensions, and hence that they

[20] *Principles of Philosophy*, Part II, arts. 33–34, A.T., VIII–1, pp. 59–60.

[21] *Ibid.*, p. 59.

are not merely imaginary, as the Philosophers call them, but contain some matter. Now since this matter cannot be elsewhere but in the world, this shows that the world extends beyond the boundaries that had been assigned to it. Therefore, since I have no argument to prove that the world has boundaries (indeed I cannot even conceive that it does) I call it *indefinite*. But I cannot deny that some may be known to God although they are incomprehensible to us, and this is why I do not say that the world is absolutely infinite.[22]

Descartes would really have liked to assert that matter is infinitely divisible and that the world is infinitely extended. The argument from the limitation of the human intellect is not altogether convincing when it comes from the mouth of someone who professes that the logical consequences of his system are invariably true. Indeed, Descartes had initially explored the possibility of plainly stating what followed from his theory of matter. In December 1629, when he was about to begin writing *The World*, he had asked Mersenne:

> Please let me know if anything is determined in religion concerning the extension of created things, namely whether it is finite or infinite, and whether there are real, created bodies in what is called imaginary space. Although I have no wish to broach this question, I believe that I shall nonetheless be compelled to prove it.[23]

We do not have Mersenne's reply, but he must have urged caution. Several years later, Queen Christina of Sweden voiced the latent theological concern when she expressed her fear that an infinite universe would be eternal (a position condemned by the Church) and would abolish man's special place in creation. Playing the sage about to be summoned to court, Descartes replied that the world was indefinite, not infinite, and hence that there was no cause for worry.[24] Indeed, as he told Frans Burman a few months later, he had invented the distinction himself.[25] But was it a distinction without a difference? I would rather suggest that it was a distinction that Descartes believed he had to make on theological grounds. But having said this, I hasten to add that Descartes was convinced that sound science cannot be at variance with good theology. However unwelcome, the distinction had

---

[22] Letter of Descartes to Chanut, 6 June 1647, A.T., V, p. 52. On Descartes' view of space, see Maurizio Mamiani, *Teorie dello spazio da Descartes a Newton* (Milan: Franco Angeli, 1979).

[23] Letter of Descartes to Mersenne, 18 December 1629, A.T., I, p. 86.

[24] "The Cardinal of Cusa and several other Doctors supposed that the world was infinite without having been reprimanded by the Church. On the contrary, it is considered worthy of God to conceive of his work as immense. And my opinion is easier to accept than theirs because I do not state that the world is *infinite* but only *indefinite*" (letter of Descartes to Chanut, who had transmitted Queen Christina's query, 6 June 1647, A.T., V, p. 52). To the second objection, Descartes simply replied: "I do not think that we have to believe that man is the end in creation" (*ibid.*, p. 53).

[25] Conversation with Burman, 16 April 1648, *ibid.*, p. 167.

to be made to work. The task was not easy and had repercussions beyond cosmology. The theory that matter is infinitely divisible seemed to undermine the Scholastic principle that "there is no infinite regress in the order of causes" upon which rested the Thomistic demonstration of the existence of God. Descartes saw this clearly, and in his *Meditations* he offered a proof of God's existence that did not appeal to this principle but to a revised version of the ontological argument. In the First Set of Replies to the *Meditations*, he commented:

> I did not base my argument [for the existence of God] on the fact that I observed an order or succession of efficient causes among the objects perceived by the senses . . . I did not think that such a succession of causes could lead me anywhere except to a recognition of the imperfection of my intellect, since an infinite chain of such successive causes from eternity without any first cause is beyond my grasp. And my inability to grasp it certainly does not entail that there must be a first cause, any more than my inability to grasp the infinite number of divisions in a finite quantity entails that there is an ultimate division beyond which any further division is impossible. All that follows is that my intellect, which is finite, does not encompass the infinite.[26]

The fact that we cannot comprehend an infinite number of divisions in a finite quantity of matter reveals that a finite intellect cannot grasp the infinite. In the Second Set of Replies to the *Meditations*, the argument is carried one step further. The idea of an infinite number is now seen to depend upon an infinitely perfect being:

> from the mere fact that when I count I cannot reach the largest of all numbers, I recognise that there is something in the process of counting that exceeds my powers. I maintain that from this alone it necessarily follows, not that an infinite number exists, or *is implied*, as you say, but that the power of conceiving that there is a thinkable number that is larger than any number that I can think of comes, not from myself, but from some other being more perfect than myself.[27]

Properly speaking, God alone is *infinite* because "in Him alone, not only do we not recognise any limits whatsoever, but we understand positively that there are none."[28] The idea of infinity would appear therefore to be clear and distinct only when applied to God. In all other cases, it is blurred.

---

[26] First Set of Replies to the Objections to the *Meditations*, A.T., VII, pp. 106–107. The second of Thomas Aquinas' celebrated five proofs for the existence of God rests on the impossibility to proceed to infinity in the series of efficient causes (Thomas Aquinas, *Summa Theologica*, Part I, Question 2, art. 3). For a summary of Aquinas' views, see Frederick Copleston, *A History of Philosophy* (Vol. 2): *Medieval Philosophy, Part II, Albert the Great to Duns Scotus* (Garden City, N.Y.: Doubleday, 1962), pp. 55–65.

[27] Second Set of Replies to the Objections to the *Meditations*, A.T., VII, p. 139.

[28] *Principles of Philosophy*, part I, art. 27, A.T., VIII-1, p. 15.

Indeed, Descartes himself is not always distinct, since at times he claims that the idea of infinity is reached by negating finitude while at other times he holds (consistently with the passage on numbers that we have quoted) that we conceive finiteness by negating the prior idea of the infinite.[29] The idea is clear enough, however, for Descartes to rule out the possibility of atomism, on the grounds that "anything we can divide in thought must, for that very reason, be divisible."[30] Even if God were to create parts of matter that are indivisible (such is the etymology of atom), He could not deprive himself of the power of subdividing them should He so choose.[31] The warrant for this is once again the self-authenticating character of mathematical insight.

So much for the endless divisibility of matter, but physical bodies have at least two other properties that cannot be so easily derived from the purely mathematical notion of extension. The first is that they are impenetrable, namely, they exclude matter from occupying the same space, and, second, unlike geometrical figures, they can move and be moved. To these features we must now turn.

Impenetrable, Incompressible, and Mobile

The same extension in length, breadth, and thickness that constitutes space, constitutes body. It follows, for Descartes, that any extended thing that completely occupies a given space excludes any other extended thing from occupying that space.[32] Parts of matter simply cannot interpenetrate.[33] This is completely at variance with the geometrical notion of matter because we can easily think of two geometrical solids as occupying parts of the same space, for instance, two polyhedra built on the same base. Matter's property of excluding other extended things does not automatically follow, as Descartes would have us believe, from the identification of matter and geometrical extension, but from the identification of matter and substance. But once the absolute continuity and impenetrability of matter is accepted, it follows that it is absolutely incompressible. If it were compressible, it could occupy less space than before without something having to move out to make room for it. What looks like compression is really displacement. When air is

---

[29] Contrast, for instance, in the *Meditations*, A.T., VII, p. 45, lines 223–226, with p. 113, lines 9–17. See "Infini" in Etienne Gilson, *Index scolastico-cartésien*, 2nd. ed. (Paris, Vrin, 1979), pp. 142–150.

[30] *Principles of Philosophy*, Part II, art. 20, A.T., VIII–1, p. 51.

[31] *Ibid.* In the same work, Part I, art. 60, Descartes makes a similar point when discussing the real distinction between mind and body. Even if God were to join the two as closely as can be conceived, they would remain really distinct because God cannot forsake his power of dividing them (A.T., VIII–1, p. 29). See also his letter to More, 5 January 1649, A.T., V, p. 273.

[32] *The World*, A.T., XI, p. 33; letter to Elizabeth, 28 June 1643, A.T., III, p. 694.

[33] In the Sixth Set of Replies to Objections to the *Meditations*, Descartes repudiates the notion that parts of matter can interpenetrate, A.T., VII, p. 442.

compressed, its parts come closer because the particles of fine matter in its pores are squeezed out. Since air is normally compressed in hard metal cylinders, it follows that the fine matter can pass through them with relative ease, a consequence that does not seem to have embarrassed Descartes in the least.[34]

Moving Shapes

In the Aristotelian tradition in which Descartes was trained at La Flèche, extension in length, breadth, and depth is not the conception of a material object at all. It is a geometrical abstraction, and abstractions cannot move. It would be a categorical mistake to say of any idea—be it the idea of love or shape—that it is subject to motion. But Descartes' notion of extension, as we have seen, is not that of pure plane or solid geometry. His allegedly *distinct* idea includes *particular matter, matter on the move.* The "object of the geometer," as he puts it in the *Discourse on Method,* "is a continuous body, or a space indefinitely extended" whose parts "can be transposed in every way." The paradox is that Descartes recognises that the mobility of geometrical objects is mental, since he adds, "I noted also that there was nothing at all in these [geometrical] demonstrations that assured me of the existence of their object."[35] The idea of extension does not of itself imply the concept of motion. The geometrical conception of corporeal substance belongs to a static world, and there can be no physics without an explanation of how extended bodies are set in motion. At this point Descartes introduces his cosmogony but under the unexpected form of a scientific myth.

Science Fiction: the Handmaid of Science

The man, who wrote in his early notebook, "When I appear on the world's stage, I am masked,"[36] was a revolutionary who had no desire to be hailed as one. He was anxious to avoid conflict with the official philosophy, and much exercised over the way of doing this without compromising his own viewpoint.[37] In modern terms, Descartes' concern for social order makes him a conservative, but then modern terms hardly apply. Descartes wished to see a more "natural" philosophy prevail, but he did not believe that the existing order should be shattered to accomplish this. Once the generality of man-

---

[34] See, for instance, his letter to Mersenne of 25 February 1630 where he asserts that the fine matter passes through "gold, diamonds and any other body, however solid" (A.T., I, p. 119).

[35] *Discourse on Method,* Fourth Part, A.T., VI, p. 36.

[36] *Cogitationes Privatae,* A.T., X, p. 213.

[37] In the Third Part of the *Discourse on Method,* before embarking on the application of his method, Descartes set out a provisional ethic whose first maxim enjoined to obey the laws and customs of the land, to remain a Catholic, and to follow the views of moderate and sensible men (A.T., VI, p. 23).

kind had been brought to see things clearly and distinctly as they are, Descartes believed that the necessary changes would follow in due course, easily and without fanfare. Ordered and accurate thought would replace the confused and disjointed system of the Scholastics.

The problem was to get people to listen and walk in his footsteps without pointless preambles and justifications. Descartes believed that if he could avoid giving offence, he would easily persuade an unbiased reader that he was right. How to do this worried him for several months until he struck upon the idea of writing what he terms "a fable," what we would call a piece of science fiction. Descartes asks his reader to allow his thought "to leave the world for a wholly new one that I shall cause to rise before you in imaginary spaces."[38] These "imaginary spaces" that surround the closed world of the Scholastics are summoned only to be ridiculed: "Philosophers tell us that these spaces are infinite, and well should they be believed since they made them themselves."[39] As we have seen, the Cartesian identification of space and matter entailed the infinite extension and divisibility of space, but theological misgivings had led Descartes to rein in his imagination. The new world does not exceed the solar system in size, but it is replete with matter, which we are to conceive

> as a real and perfectly solid body, which uniformly fills the entire length, breadth and depth of this huge space in the midst of which we have brought our mind to rest. Thus, each of its parts always occupies a part of that space which it fits so exactly that it could neither fill a larger one nor squeeze into a smaller; nor could it, while remaining there allow another body to find a place there.[40]

A perfectly solid and homogeneous matter, as Leibniz later remarked, would not give rise to any change whatsoever.[41] For motion to spread and produce a division in matter, matter would already have to be divided and in a fluid state. But then matter can only become fluid through motion! The circularity in the reasoning is only apparent, according to Descartes, because God creates matter and sets it in motion at the very same instant. Nonetheless, we find Descartes speaking of matter as an inert block: "If we consider the state that matter could have been in before God set it in motion, we must imagine it as the hardest and most solid body in the world." But this is a

---

[38] *The World*, Ch. 6, A.T., XI, p. 31. The idea occurred to Descartes at the end of 1629. Around 13 November, he wrote to Mersenne, "I think I have found a way of conveying my ideas that will please some people without offending anyone" (A.T., I, p. 70). The expression "the fable of my world" first appears in a letter to the same correspondent around 5 November 1630 (*ibid.*, p. 179).

[39] *The World*, Ch. 6, A.T., XI, pp. 31–32.

[40] *Ibid.*, p. 33.

[41] Gottfried Wilhelm Leibniz, "De ipsa natura sive de vi insita actionibusque Creaturarum, pro Dynamicis suis confirmandis illustrandisque," in *Die philosophischen Schriften*, C.J. Gerhardt, ed., 7 vols. (Berlin, 1875–1890); reprint (Hildesheim: Olms, 1978), vol. IV, pp. 512–514.

pedagogical fiction because Descartes immediately adds that God gave motion to matter "at the same instant."[42] We are left, however, with a serious problem because a purely postulated homogeneous block (a fiction within a fiction) loses much of its interest. Why Descartes spoke of hardness prior to motion is easier to understand when we recall that in Chapter Three of *The World* he had defined hardness or solidity as the mere absence of motion.[43]

From Chaos to Cosmos

God, therefore, imparts motion to matter, extension, or space (all synonymous for Descartes), but we need not concern ourselves over the initial state, be it "a chaos as confused and muddled as any of the poets could describe," because "the ordinary laws of nature are sufficient to cause the parts of this chaos to disentangle and arrange themselves in such good order that they will have the form of a very perfect world," one in which we will be able to observe "not only light but all the other things, general as well as particular, which appear in the real world."[44]

This fable (with its beginning at some unspecified point in time) enabled Descartes to avoid any problem that might arise from the generally received biblical chronology that fixed the date of creation some five or six thousand years ago.[45] As he put it in the *Discourse on Method*: "I wished to be free to say what I thought about them without having either to follow or to refute the accepted opinions of the learned. So I decided to leave our world wholly for them to argue about, and to speak solely of what would happen in a new world."[46] The irony is heavy-handed. The so-called real world is left to the sterile disputations of the philosophers while the imaginary one is investigated scientifically.

Avoiding direct confrontation with the prevalent views of his time was not the only reason for inventing a new world in outer space. Descartes' other reason was less intrinsic to his method and may be expressed by saying that the question: what is it? is best answered by asking: how did it come about? Descartes fashions his own world out of a matter that is *perfectly intel-*

---

[42] *The World*, Ch. 8, A.T., XI, p. 49.

[43] "It is enough if the parts are motionless and touch without there being any intervening space" (*ibid.*, p. 13). In the *Meteorology*, Descartes introduced the further notion of intertwining parts. Nearly all bodies are now considered to have "very irregular and rough shapes, so that they need be only slightly intertwined in order to become hooked and bound to each other, as are the various branches of bushes that grow together in a hedgerow. And when they are bound together in this way, they compose hard bodies" (A.T., VI, pp. 233–234).

[44] *The World*, ch. 6, A.T., XI, pp. 34–35.

[45] Descartes' contemporary Jacques Gaffarel (1601–1680) provides a table of estimates that range between 6310 and 3760 B.C. (Jacques Gaffarel, *Curiosités Inouïes* (Paris, 1650), p. 37, quoted in Geneviève Rodis-Lewis, *L'oeuvre de Descartes* (Paris: Vrin, 1971), p. 494, n. 18).

[46] *Discourse on Method*, Fifth Part, A.T., VI, p. 42.

ligible, and hence unproblematic. This, of course, is pure extension whose knowledge "is so natural to us that we could not even pretend to ignore it."[47] Matter and the laws of motion (which we shall examine later in this chapter) are all that Descartes needs to deduce a new universe that turns out to be so remarkably like our own that we would be mistaken had we not been told it was a figment of Descartes' imagination.

Let There Be Light

In a Christian society in which the biblical account of creation was still normative, a cosmological novel avoided a head-on collision. Nonetheless, Descartes would have been happy if some kind of concordance had been forthcoming, and he made an attempt in this direction. The problem was twofold: the first concerns the *order* of creation, the second the *state of perfection* in which the creatures appear in the book of Genesis.

God's first words in the Bible are, "Let there be light!", and Descartes was justifiably pleased at the centrality of the notion of light in his system. But in *Genesis*, God creates light before the firmament and the heavenly bodies, whereas in Descartes' *World* light is the result of the action of celestial bodies. Descartes was aware of the discrepancy as early as 1630 when he wrote to Mersenne:

> I am now ordering the chaos to produce light. This is one of the highest and most difficult tasks that I could face because it involves virtually the whole of physics. I have to think of a thousand different things at the same time in order to find a way of stating the truth without shocking someone or offending received opinions. I want to take a month or two to think of nothing else.[48]

The outcome was a rough concordance: (a) in the first verse of the Bible, God creates the heavens and the earth; in the Cartesian *World*, He first creates matter; (b) in the Bible, "the earth was formless" (*Gen.* 1,2); in *The World* it is "a chaos",[49] (c) all things are ordered by God in the first chapter of *Genesis*; in the *World* He "establishes everything in number, weight, and measure."[50] The fit was less than perfect, but when Descartes decided to publish a revised version of *The World* in 1641, he thought that it was so good that he wrote to Mersenne that his *Principles of Philosophy* would contain an explanation of the first chapter of *Genesis*.[51] It is probably at this time that he wrote to an unidentified correspondent:

---

47 *Ibid.*, p. 43.

48 Letter of Descartes to Mersenne, around 23 December 1630, A.T., I, p. 194.

49 *The World*, A.T., XI, p. 34.

50 *Ibid.*, p. 47. This is itself a quotation from the book of *Wisdom*, Ch. 11, verse 21.

51 Letter of Descartes to Mersenne, around 28 January 1641, A.T., III, p. 296.

I am not moving fast, but I am moving. I am now describing the origins of the world in which I hope to include most of my physics. Rereading the first chapter of the book of *Genesis*, I was astonished to discover that it can be completely explained on my view, and much better, it seems to me, than on any other view. I had never dared to hope for so much before, and I am now resolved, after giving an account of my new philosophy, to clearly show how all the truths of Faith agree much better with my philosophy than with that of Aristotle.[52]

Descartes even made an attempt at learning Hebrew, although he did not get very far. In a seventeenth-century memoir, Descartes is said to have called on Anna-Maria Van Schuurman (1607–1678), a prodigy who knew most European languages, including Latin and Greek, as well as Syriac, Chaldean, Arabic, and Turkish. On this particular morning, around 1640, Descartes found her reading the Scriptures in Hebrew. He expressed surprise that she should be wasting her time "on such a trifling matter." When Miss Schuurman remonstrated and tried to show him that the word of God should be read in the original, he replied that he had once had the same notion and had begun "to read the first chapter of *Genesis* on the creation of the world, but think about it as he might, he could not find anything clear and distinct, nothing that he could grasp *clare et distincte.*"[53]

In 1648, Descartes was visited at Egmond by a 20-year-old admirer named Frans Burman. He entertained the young man at dinner and gave frank and lively answers to his questions. One touched on the topic of concordance, and Descartes replied that he had tried to fit his account to the story of *Genesis* but had decided to give it up and leave the whole thing to the theologians, since the correct interpretation might well be metaphorical, as would seem to be the case with the six days of creation.[54]

---

[52] The date of this letter is uncertain. A.T., IV, p. 698 gives the text of the Latin edition of 1700. The French text published by Clerselier, which may be the original, is printed in Marin Mersenne, *Correspondance*, vol. II, p. 618, where 14 October 1630 is indicated as a possible date. Etienne Gilson makes a strong case for assigning it to 1641 (René Descartes, *Discours de la méthode*, with a commentary by Etienne Gilson, 4th edition (Paris: Vrin, 1967), pp. 381–382). The other "truth of Faith" that Descartes has in mind is the dogma of transubstantiation "which is perfectly clear and easy when explained by my principles" (letter to Mersenne, around 28 January 1641, A.T., III, p. 296).

[53] This anecdote appeared in the anonymous *Vie de Jean Labadie* (Paris 1670), quoted in A.T., IV, pp. 700–701.

[54] Conversation with Burman, 16 April 1648, A.T., V, pp. 168–169. When Descartes used a couple of Hebrew words for illustrative purposes, he managed to get both wrong (p. 169, n. a). Despite Descartes' withdrawal from the lists, the battle continued after his death. In 1668 an anonymous book appeared with the title: *Copie d'une Lettre écrite à un sçavant religieux de la Compagnie de Jésus, pour montrer: I. Que le Système de Monsieur Descartes et son opinion touchant les bestes n'ont rien de dangereux. II. Et que tout ce qu'il en a écrit semble estre tiré du premier chapitre de la Genèse.* The 67-page booklet bears no place and no name of printer. A year later in the Netherlands, Johann Amerpoel published *Cartesius Mosaïzans, seu Evidens et facilis conciliatio Philosophiae Cartesii cum historia Creationis primo capite Geneseos per Moysem tradita* (Groningen: Leovardiae, pro haeredibus Thomas Luyrtsma, 1669). Malebranche also says

Perfection From the Start

Whatever the sequence of events in the history of creation, the Bible clearly affirms that things were created in their state of perfection. Descartes had no wish to see his opponents accuse him of following Lucretius and the atomists rather than Moses and, in the *Discourse on Method*, he clearly stated that the world was created as we actually find it. In the *Principles of Philosophy*, he was even more explicit. The sun, the stars, and the living plants appeared in all their perfection. Adam and Eve were created as adults, for such is "the doctrine of the Christian faith, and our natural reason convinces us that it was so." Given the infinite power of God, we cannot think that he ever created anything that was not wholly perfect in its kind. "Nevertheless," continues Descartes,

> if we want to understand the nature of plants or of men, it is much better to consider how they can gradually grow from seeds than to consider how they were created by God at the very beginning of the world. Thus we may be able to think up certain very simple and easily known principles which can serve, as it were, as the seeds from which we can demonstrate that the stars, the earth and indeed everything we observe in this visible world could have sprung. For although we know for sure that they never did arise in this way, we shall be able to provide a much better explanation of their nature by this method than if we merely described them as they now are.[55]

This passage poses the whole problem of the status of Descartes' account. Was he merely playing a game with the censors? Did he really believe that his hypothesis on the formation of the planets was only a philosophical speculation? It is difficult, on the one hand, to believe that Descartes did not consider his theory to be true. On the other, there is no reason for doubting his faith in the tenets of Christianity common to his day. Yet how can we reason *genetically* when there is really no development, but things are created in their full perfection?

Descartes' answer lies in his conviction that the laws that govern the present world would be true in any conceivable world. While there may be an infinite number of possible states for a world made of matter and motion, there is only one state of equilibrium: the one we witness. The text of the *Discourse* is explicit:

> It is certain, and it is an opinion commonly accepted among theologians, that the act by which God now preserves it is just the same as that by which he created it. So even if in the beginning God had given the world only the

---

that Descartes' system agrees with the account in Genesis (Nicolas Malebranche, *The Search After Truth*, Book VI, second part, Ch. 4, Thomas M. Lennon and Paul J. Olscamp, trans. (Columbus: Ohio University Press, 1988), pp. 463–466. The work was first published in 1674–1675).

55 *Principles of Philosophy*, Part I, art. 45, A.T., VIII–1, p. 100.

form of a chaos, provided that he established the laws of nature and then lent his concurrence to enable nature to operate as it normally does, we may believe, without calling the miracle of creation in question, that by this means alone all purely material things could, in the course of time, have come to be just as we now see them. And their nature is much easier to conceive if we see them develop gradually in this way than if we consider them only in their completed form.[56]

For Descartes, even if Adam and Eve were created as adults, it is still methodologically sound to consider them as slowly evolving. This is the insight that is embodied in the Third of his famous Four Rules:

> to direct my thoughts in an orderly manner, by beginning with the simplest and most easily known objects in order to ascend little by little, step by step, to knowledge of the most complex, and by *supposing some order even among objects that have no natural order of precedence.*[57]

The Laws of Motion

In the *Discourse on Method*, Descartes defined the "object of the geometers" as a body "extended in length, breadth and height . . . that can be moved."[58] Geometrical bodies are of and by themselves capable of motion. This is a crucial consequence of Descartes' understanding of the rule of clarity, and it runs counter to the Aristotelian notion of mathematics prevalent in his day. For Aristotle, mathematical entities were abstractions incapable of motion, which he considered the essential characteristic of physical objects, and he repudiated the Pythagorean identification of the geometrical solid with the sensible body.[59] Descartes approached the problem of matter in the light of his convictions about the realism of intuitive ideas. Because we can clearly combine points to make lines, lines to make surfaces, and surfaces to make solids, we have no reason to hesitate, once we have arrived at a solid geometrical figure, to cross the boundary into the physical world. Motion is adequately represented by a straight line and is fully intelligible without the added notions of speed or direction. As Descartes contemplated the trajectory of a moving body on a sheet of paper, it seemed clear to him that it could be fully grasped regardless of the speed with which the distance was traversed or the direction along which it travelled. This appeared so overwhelmingly clear to Descartes that he neglected to consider velocity. In a letter to Florimond de Beaune, who was planning a book on mechanics, he wrote:

---

[56] *Discourse on Method*, Fifth Part, A.T., VI, p. 45.

[57] *Ibid.*, pp. 18–19.

[58] *Ibid.*, p. 36.

[59] Aristotle, *Metaphysics*, Book I, Ch. 8, 989b29–990a35.

I would like to answer you suitably concerning your work on mechanics but, although all my physics is nothing but mechanics, *I have never closely examined problems that depend on the determination of speed.* Your way of distinguishing different dimensions in motion and of *representing them by lines* is undoubtedly the best possible.[60]

The notion of motion like that of extension is intuitively obvious. It need not be defined, merely inspected. Indeed, as Descartes explained to Mersenne, "if we attempt to define things that are very simple and naturally known, such as shape, size, motion, place, time, etc., we obscure them and just get them confused." In a passage that is reminiscent of Johnson's celebrated refutation of Berkeley, Descartes goes on to dismiss the Aristotelian definition of motion by appealing to everyday experience: "a person walking up and down a room gives a better idea of what motion is than one who says: *est actus entis in potentia prout in potentia.*"[61] This traditional definition of motion is the frequent butt of Descartes' sarcasm. He quotes it in Rule 12 of the *Rules for the Direction of the Mind* as an instance of "finding a difficulty where none exists," and in Chapter Seven of *The World*, as passing comprehension:

> these words are so obscure that I am compelled to leave them in Latin because I cannot interpret them . . . . By contrast, the nature of the motion I mean to speak of here is so easy to know that geometers, among all men the most concerned to conceive very distinctly what they study, have judged it simpler and more intelligible than the nature of surfaces and lines—as is shown by the fact that they have explained "line" as the motion of a point, and "surface" as the motion of a line.[62]

Descartes needed a double philosophical warrant to use his notion of motion, however intuitive it might appear. The first is the epistemological correspondence between the laws of nature and innate ideas, the second the ontological grounding of these laws. Descartes had no problem with the first: the God who created the world also created minds capable of knowing it. As he put it in one of his first letters to Mersenne after settling in the Netherlands, "God is the one who established the laws of nature . . . . There is none that we cannot understand if we will but consider them for they are all *mentibus nostris ingenitae.*"[63] As far as the ontological grounding is concerned, this is laid out in Chapter Seven of *The World* in which Descartes states that the laws of nature (or as he prefers to call them, the laws of matter) derive from God's constancy or immutability. Although he does not say explicitly that God's immutability is a clear and distinct innate idea, he suggests as much and draws the "easy" inference that God "always acts in the same way."

[60] Letter of Descartes to Florimond de Beaune, around 30 April 1639, A.T., II, p. 542, emphasis added.

[61] Letter of Descartes to Mersenne, 16 October 1639, *ibid.*, p. 597.

[62] *The World*, Chapter 7, A.T., XI, p. 39.

[63] Letter of Descartes to Mersenne, 15 April 1630, A.T., I, p. 145.

From this it is an equally easy step to "two or three principal rules." *The First Law* (or Rule, Descartes uses the words indiscriminately) is expressed as follows:

> each individual part of matter always remains in the same state so long as collision with others does not compel it to change that state. That is to say, if it has some size, it will never become smaller unless others divide it; if it is round or square, it will never change unless others force it to; if it is brought to rest in some place, it will never leave that place unless others drive it out; and if it has once begun to move, it will always keep on moving with an equal force until others stop or retard it.[64]

It is at this point in *The World* that Descartes introduces the notion that motion is easier to understand than a geometrical line, since it accounts for its genesis. A geometrical line does not change because it is not a dynamic reality, a force operating in time. It is, in a sense, *timeless*. So is motion. The next, or *Second Law*, reads:

> when a body pushes another it cannot give it any motion unless it loses as much of its own motion at the same time, nor can it take away any of the other's motion unless its own is increased by as much.[65]

The First Law therefore, postulates *the conservation of any state of matter*, the second, the *conservation of motion*. They both "follow manifestly from the mere fact that God is immutable and that, acting always in the same way, he always produces the same effect."[66] This is a crucial step in the direction that will eventually lead to Newton's laws of motion, but an essential component of Newton's First Law is still missing: the *rectilinearity* of inertial motion. This is expressed almost as an afterthought in the *Third Law*:

> when a body is moving, even though its motion for the most part takes place along a curved path . . . yet each of its individual parts tends to continue its motion in a straight line. And so their action, that is the tendency they have to move, is different from their motion.[67]

Experiment shows this to be the case, says Descartes. If a stone is released from a sling, it does not continue to move in a circle but flies off along the tangent. From our post-Newtonian perspective, this is a good illustration, but its significance is obscured by what Descartes immediately adds, namely, that while the stone is still in the sling "it presses against the middle and causes the string to stretch."[68] In other words, before the stone is released, it exerts a pull at right angles to the tangential path that it will follow when it flies off. This second radial tugging away from the center of

---

[64] *The World*, A.T., XI, p. 39.

[65] *Ibid.*, p. 41.

[66] *Ibid.*, p. 43.

[67] *Ibid.*, p. 44.

[68] *Ibid.*

revolution is what Huygens was to term "the centrifugal force." But in an inertial system, the centrifugal force is non-physical, that is to say, it arises from kinematics and is not due to physical interaction. This was a serious problem for Newtonians, but it did not arise for Descartes because he did not consider *direction* an essential part of the concept of motion. All Descartes saw was that regardless of direction motion tended to continue in a straight line. Given the importance of circular motion, we shall consider it in more detail in the next chapter, but here we must mention one aspect of the problem that Descartes sidestepped. The rectilinear motion that he calls natural can only obtain in a perfect void, and a perfect void for Descartes is not only a fiction but an impossibility. How can a cosmos whose basic laws are incapable of realization be an ordered cosmos? But this objection never struck Descartes for a twofold reason: (a) he never entertained the possibility of motion in a void, and (b) his main concern was to show that the Third Law is grounded in God's immutability like the first two.

Cartesian motion is neither dynamic (involving consideration of force) nor kinematic (involving only consideration of space and time) but merely diagrammatic (involving only consideration of space). God who is eternal—above and outside time—conserves what he creates "as it is at the very instant that he conserves it."[69] This role played by God's instantaneous action helps to understand why Descartes felt that the *Meditations*, in which he demonstrated the existence of God, provided the rationale for his science. To Mersenne, he wrote that it contained "all the principles" and "all the foundations" of his physics.[70] If we ask: what is being preserved in this way, i.e., at this instant? we find that Descartes' answer is purely epistemological. For what is conserved is what can be clearly and distinctly understood to exist at the instant, and "only motion in a straight line is entirely simple and has a nature which may be wholly grasped in an instant."[71] Descartes claims that this is not the case with circular motion, which can only be conceived if two of its instants and their mutual relation are taken into consideration. Descartes believed that he was contrasting rectilinear and circular motion, but in the absence of any reference to force, he was really comparing a geometrical line (which he implicitly reduced to a point) with a circle (a locus of coplanar points equidistant from a center of which at least two have to be known in order to determine the nature of the circle).

The theological standpoint is clear from the conclusion of the argument in favor of the Third Law:

> According to this Rule, it must be said that God alone is the Author of all the motions in the world insofar as they exist and insofar as they are rectilinear, and that it is the various dispositions of matter that make them

[69] *Ibid.*, p. 44.

[70] Letters of Descartes to Mersenne of 11 November 1640 and 28 January 1641, A.T., III, pp. 233, 298.

[71] *The World*, A.T., XI, p. 45.

curved and irregular. Likewise, theologians teach that God is the Author of all our actions, insofar as they exist and insofar as they have some goodness, and that it is the various dispositions of our wills that can render them evil.[72]

Two things are arresting here. First, Descartes uses the theological doctrine that God is the cause of everything to explain not only *being* but *becoming*. Second, the *disposition* of the will is compared to the *direction* of motion. The analogy does not proceed from the natural to the supernatural but the other way round: the perspicuity of Christian dogma is used to shed light on the obscurities of physical motion.

The theology to which Descartes is appealing was devised to save God's omnipotence without making him responsible for sin. For instance, theologians affirmed that the physical reality of any action (say releasing an arrow) ultimately rests on God's creative power, but that the intention (harming another human being) depends on man's will. The ontological status of the act was distinguished from its *rectitude* or *crookedness*, and it was considered fully intelligible without reference to its moral or immoral orientation. Likewise, Descartes would have us believe that motion is perfectly clear without specifying its actual direction beyond saying that it is naturally straight. The problem with this analogy is that it smuggles in the very notion of "potency" that Descartes found reprehensible in Aristotle. It is not quite the Aristotelian concept, of course, since direction is a geometrical condition that is added to motion, but Descartes' motion is nonetheless intelligible prior to actualization, and it is precisely because of this prior intelligibility that it can be distinguished from direction. If real motion always has direction, it is hard to escape the conclusion that motion without direction is some kind of "potential" energy.[73]

The Advantages of a Purely Geometrical Notion of Motion

The drawbacks of Descartes' concept of motion have often been pointed out, but we should not be blind to the important role it played in simplifying the analysis of motion. I shall briefly indicate six areas in which Descartes felt that his clearer notion was fruitful, and this will help us, incidentally, to sum up much of what we have discussed.

The first and most spectacular advantage of Descartes' concept of motion as naturally rectilinear is the solution it provides to the vexed prob-

---

[72] *Ibid.*, pp. 46–47.

[73] Descartes' opposition to the notion of potency stemmed in part at least from the fact that it appeared to grant more reality to motion than to rest (See Pierre Costabel, "Essai critique sur quelques concepts de la mécanique cartésienne," *Archives Internationales d'Histoire des Sciences* 20 (1967), pp. 235–252, reprinted in Pierre Costabel, *Démarches originales de Descartes savant* (Paris: Vrin, 1982), pp. 141–158).

lem of projectile motion. Indeed, it dissolves the problem entirely by show-ing that it rests on false premises. Since antiquity, and more prominently from the sixteenth century onwards, natural philosophers had investigated the nature and cause of the motion of arrows and other projectiles once they were in flight. In the light of his new conception of motion, Descartes no longer asked: why does the projectile continue to move? but, why does it eventually cease to move? And he answered: because of the resistance of the air. From a Newtonian point of view, this is usually expressed by saying that we have to account not for motion but for change of motion. Descartes had not travelled that far, since he did not consider that a change of direction was a change of motion but merely an alternative actualization of the same motion, but we can see that he effectively opened a new avenue for specula-tion about the nature of projectile motion.

Second, Descartes believed that his notion solved the problem of the hardness of bodies without invoking some kind of glue or force between their particles. Here again he could claim that earlier research had been misguided. Hardness needs no explanation beyond plain rest; what has to be explained is the internal agitation that renders some bodies less solid. Since direction is not part of the concept of motion, Descartes could claim that a body whose internal parts are in motion is less resistant to breaking than one whose parts are at a complete standstill.

Third, Descartes' "quantized" explanation of motion, namely, its re-duction to a succession of divine instantaneous creative acts, enabled Des-cartes to account for sudden transitions in nature. Whereas Galileo had identified rest with an infinite degree of slowness and had argued that bodies that are accelerated pass through all the degrees of speed, Descartes neither saw the necessity nor the utility of Galileo's continuum. Although space and time are infinitely divisible, there is no ontological connection between the successive instants of a being's existence outside God's will. In the *Third Meditation*, Descartes makes this point about the self, but it is relevant to all created entities, including motion:

> For a lifespan can be divided into countless parts, each completely inde-pendent of the others, so that it does not follow from the fact that I existed a little while ago that I must exist now, unless there is some cause which, as it were, creates me afresh at this moment.[74]

The radical discontinuity of time and the metaphysical gap between existential instants enabled Descartes to explain cases of collision in a way he believed the continuists were unable to elucidate. His prime example was a large cannonball encountering a very small stationary ball in full flight. Assuming that both balls are "extremely hard," we have an instance of inelastic collision, and Descartes claimed that it was ridiculous to say that the

---

[74] *Meditations*, A.T., VII, pp. 48–49.

small ball is continuously accelerated and has to go through all the degrees of speed until it reaches the velocity of the cannonball.[75]

Fourth, Descartes' notion of motion proved useful in resolving ambiguities in statics, and at the request of his friend Constantin Huygens, he wrote a short treatise on simple machines in 1637.[76] The basic ratios between force and resistance were known, and there was nothing to add to what Archimedes had written. The ambiguity to be dispelled lay in the use of velocity and displacement as though these were simply interchangeable. For instance, in the case of the lever, since both ends move in identical time without acceleration, it is immaterial whether one uses the virtual velocities of the two weights or their virtual displacements. But this holds only for the lever and similar devices where a mechanical connection ensures that each body moves in the same time and where, because of equilibrium, there is no real but only virtual motion. Descartes' geometrical concept of notion enabled him to see (what escaped Galileo) that only the ratios of the displacement explain why the force and the resistance vary as they do: "it is not the difference of velocity which determines that one of these weights must be double the other, but the difference of space [i.e., displacement]." Consideration of speed, he adds in the same letter, would only obscure the issue, since it cannot be explained without explaining what weight is, and this would require a knowledge of the whole system of the world.[77] Descartes seems to imply that since speed is not a clear motion, it can be dispensed with in accounting for the working of nature.

Fifth, the law of refraction (what English textbooks call Snell's and French textbooks Descartes' Law) is justified by Descartes on the assumption that light "is an action, or a virtue, that follows the same laws as local motion," as he wrote to Mersenne on 27 May 1638.[78] A couple of months earlier, he had written to the same correspondent, "Please note that I demonstrated the refractions [i.e., the sine law] geometrically and *a priori* in my *Optics*."[79] Matters were unfortunately less clear to Descartes' readers than they were to himself, and the abiding perplexity about his explanation of refraction can be seen in the conflicting interpretations of three distinguished contemporary historians of science: I.B. Sabra believes that what is being offered is a proof of the law; Gerd Buchdahl thinks that it is rather a

---

[75] Letter of Descartes to Mersenne, 17 November 1642, A.T., III, pp. 592–593.

[76] Letter of Descartes to Huygens, 5 October 1637, A.T., I, pp. 435–447; for a revised version, see Descartes' letter to Mersenne, 13 July 1638, A.T., II, pp. 222–245. For a discussion of Descartes' treatment of simple machines, see R.S. Westfall, *Force in Newton's Physics* (London: Macdonald, 1971), pp. 72–78.

[77] Letter of Descartes to Mersenne, 12 September 1638, A.T., II, pp. 354–355.

[78] Letter of Descartes to Mersenne, around 27 May 1638, *ibid.*, p. 143.

[79] Letter of Descartes to Mersenne, around March 1638, *ibid.*, p. 31.

method of discovery; and Bruce Eastwood finds it a rhetorical device.[80] Eastwood does not believe that the metaphysical underpinnings of the *Meditations* are necessary to understand the argument in the *Optics*. "Surely Descartes' sense of his audience," he writes, "was not so dull that he would have published a treatise requiring a knowledge of works that were unavailable to the reader."[81] Reading Descartes' mind is a notoriously difficult exercise, but Descartes frequently repeated in his correspondence that his physical explanations were incomplete without a grasp of the metaphysics they presupposed. For instance, he wrote to his former teacher Antoine Vatier: "all my opinions are so intimately connected and depend so much on one another, that one cannot be grasped without knowing them all." But despite such declarations, Descartes also maintained that what he wrote about refraction could be grasped without a prior knowledge of the nature of light. In the same letter, he stated that the conclusions arrived at in his *Optics* and his *Meteors* could be "deduced in an orderly fashion from the first principles of my metaphysics," but that he had "wanted to see if the mere exposition of truth would be sufficient."[82] Descartes believed that his notion of motion was not only true but intuitive and, indeed, true because intuitive. When people objected to his analysis, he did not suspect that he might be wrong but assumed that they were blind or painfully shortsighted.

A sixth advantage that Descartes could claim for his idea of motion and, more specifically, for the distinction he drew between motion and direction, was that it enabled him to explain how mind could act on matter without upsetting the principle of the conservation of matter. Since God always preserves the same amount of motion in the world, it might be objected that the immaterial soul cannot act on material objects (its own body as well as other corporeal substances) without introducing new motion into the world. On Descartes' theory, however, the soul merely redirects the motion of bodies that are already moving. In the case of an act of volition (for instance, deciding to reach out for a glass), the mind simply sends the "animal spirits" along the nerves that are conceived as channels or funnels through which these material particles flow. In principle, there is no loss or gain of the motion first imparted by God when the universe was fashioned. I say in principle because Descartes never provided the detailed account that would have put his mechanism to the test.[83]

[80] I.B. Sabra, *Theories of Light from Descartes to Newton* (London: Oldbourne, 1967), pp. 29–33; Gerd Buchdahl, *Metaphysics and the Philosophy of Science* (Oxford: Blackwell, 1969), pp. 141–142; Bruce S. Eastwood, "Descartes on Refraction," *Isis* 75 (1984), p. 483.

[81] Eastwood, "Descartes on Refraction," p. 483.

[82] Letter of Descartes to Vatier, around 22 February 1638, A.T., I, pp. 562–563.

[83] In the *Principles of Philosophy*, Part II, art. 40, published in 1644, Descartes promised to explain how minds can act of bodies in a sequel entitled *On Man*, presumably a revised version of the *Treatise on Man* that he wrote in 1632 (A.T., VIII–1, p. 65). According to Antoine Legrand (+ 1704), Descartes was working on this problem when he died in 1650 (from a

Although these advantages did not all materialize, and several were to belie Descartes' expectations, they were important in strengthening his conviction that he had found the key to the clockwork machinery of the universe. In this mechanical world, circular motion plays an admittedly different role from the one it had in the geocentric cosmos of Aristotle and Ptolemy, but it is nonetheless essential. This is why we must consider it at the beginning of the next chapter before proceeding to a fuller description of Descartes' world.

---

manuscript note in Legrand's copy of the French version of the *Principles,* A.T., IX, p. 64, n. c). In his last published work, *The Passions of the Soul,* Part I, art. 43, Descartes mentions that the will has the power to make the pineal gland move in such a way that the animal spirits are pushed towards the muscles (A.T., XI, p. 361).

Chapter Twelve

The Laws and Rules of Motion

A COMBINATION OF THE FIRST AND THIRD LAW OF MOTION in *The World* affirms that the motion that is preserved (or inertial, as we would say) is motion in a straight line. These two laws were fused into one by Newton and enshrined in his celebrated First Law: every body continues in its state of rest, or of uniform motion in a straight line, unless it is compelled to change that state by forces impressed upon it. Following Newton, we see this law as implying that circular motion is not inertial but constrained, namely that it does not go on by itself but requires the application of an external force. We have seen in Chapter Eleven that Descartes added rectilinearity as an after-thought, and in the form of a separate Third Law. This reveals that he had not fully anticipated Newton, largely because of the cosmological necessity of circular motion in a universe that is a plenum in which nothing can move unless everything moves. When God imparted motion to matter, no part could be displaced without the whole of matter rearranging itself in a loosely circular fashion.

This Great Whirlpool of a World

The importance of circular motion cannot be dissociated from the "myth of circularity" or the pervasive belief that circular motion is more perfect and

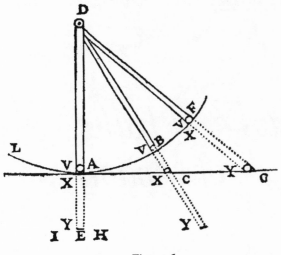

Figure 1

more enduring than any other form of motion,[1] but we must not neglect a natural phenomenon that greatly impressed Descartes: the circulating movement of water in an eddy or whirlpool. When Descartes considered the whirling of a straw or a small piece of wood in an eddy, he thought it could be compared to the motion of a stone in a sling, and here is the analysis he offered in Chapter Seven of *The World*. At the very instant that the stone arrives at point A on its way to B (see Figure 1), its instantaneous tendency is towards C along the tangent to the circle, and there is nothing that would make its motion circular:

> So much so that if you suppose that it begins there and then to leave the sling and that God conserves it as it is at that moment, it is certain that He will not conserve it with its tendency to move in a circle along the curve AB but with one to go straight towards the point C.[2]

In this passage, Descartes focuses on the fact that the stone upon leaving the sling flies off at a tangent, and he sees this as implying that rectilinear motion is conserved. But there is another equally important, if apparently antagonistic, observation, namely, the tugging on the string that is felt when the sling is whirled round. Hence there would appear to be two virtual motions at right angles to each other: one along the tangent (the path the stone will follow when released), the other radially outward from the center (the direction in which we feel the pull of the stone). The problem is to reconcile these motions, and this is what Descartes attempts in Chapter Thirteen of *The World* where he decomposes the motion of the stone into three "tendencies": (a) along the tangent AC, if we consider only the stone's "agitation"; (b) along the circle AF, if we consider it as attached to the string; and (c) along the radius DA, if we consider that part of its "agitation" that is impeded by the string. Descartes tells us that we shall "understand this last point distinctly," if we imagine

> the tendency that the stone has to move from A towards C as if it were composed of two others, one to turn along the circle AB, and the other to recede in a straight line along VXY. . . . Then, since you know that one of the parts of its inclination, namely the one that carries it along the circle AB is *in no way impeded* by the sling, you will see that resistance is exerted

---

1 See Marjorie H. Nicolson, *The Breaking of the Circle*, revised edition (Oxford: Oxford University Press, 1960).

2 *The World*, Chapter 7, A.T., XI, p. 46.

only on the other part, namely the one that would make it move in the direction DVXY if it were not impeded. Therefore, the stone only tends (i.e., only strives) to move away in a straight line from the centre D.[3]

We are to imagine, therefore, that the tendency along the tangent is composed of two other tendencies, one along the circle and the other radially outward from the center. The sling cannot impede the circular component because it is itself revolving in a circle; it can only hinder the radial tendency away from the center. In the *Principles of Philosophy*, the same analysis is repeated with two further illustrations. In the first, a ruler rotates about one end while an ant crawls outward along it (see Figure 2).[4] In the second example, a ball placed in a hollow tube moves downward as the tube turns around a fixed center (Figure 3).[5] It is perhaps here that we see most clearly Descartes' conceptualization of the problem. The ball inside the rotating tube is receding from the center, and should the tube suddenly break, the ball will fly off at a tangent.

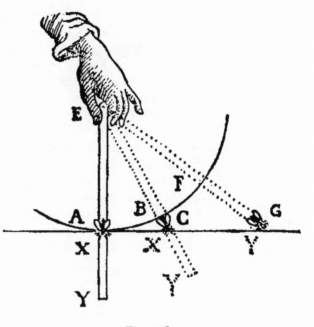

Figure 2

The Mechanics of Circular Motion

The modern reader will find much to marvel at in Descartes' analysis of circular motion. Since Descartes clearly states (Law I and Law II combined) that inertial motion is rectilinear, it follows that a body must be constrained to move in a circle. Descartes knows this and states it unequivocally. But he also states in the last passage we have quoted from *The World* that the circular component of the mo-

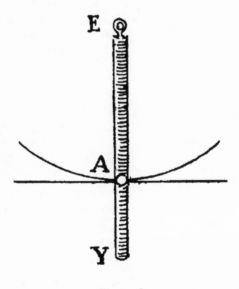

Figure 3

---

[3] *Ibid.*, Chapter 13, pp. 85–86, emphasis added.

[4] *Principles of Philosophy*, Part III, art. 58, A.T., VIII–1, pp. 109–111.

[5] *Ibid.*, art. 59, pp. 111–112.

tion of the stone is "in no way impeded," hence inertial. As R.S. Westfall puts it, Descartes "returned unconsciously virtually to embrace the idea of a natural circular motion."[6] Descartes felt that the *de facto* eternal circulatory motion of his cosmos was in this way accommodated in his inertial physics, and he did not expect that a detailed quantitative treatment would alter the picture in any significant way.

Descartes' failure, as well as that of his immediate successors, to see the implication of his own law of inertia can perhaps be understood in terms of focus. After Newton, we say that the First Law of Motion invites us to attend to the external constraint or force that turns bodies away from their rectilinear path and makes them move in a circle. Descartes focused on the *internal* effort of the body thus constrained, in other words, *on the force away from the center*, what came to be called *centrifugal force*. Newton was the first to realize that the situation was more aptly conceptualized if attention was shifted to the *centripetal force* that must be applied to produce and maintain circular motion.

Although the descriptions of circular motion in terms of centripetal or centrifugal force are quantitatively identical, since the centripetal and the centrifugal force are always equal, they are conceptually poles apart.[7] We shall return to this point when we examine the rules of impact that Descartes eventually derived from his laws of motions and published in the *Principles of Philosophy* in 1644. But in *The World*, Descartes does not go beyond assuring his readers that he could provide such rules. What he wants to stress is the superiority of his method:

> I shall content myself with telling you that, apart from the three laws that I have explained, I do not wish to suppose any others but those which follow infallibly from the eternal truths on which mathematicians are accustomed to base their most certain and most evident demonstrations—the truths, I say, according to which God himself has taught us that he has arranged all things in number, weight and measure. The knowledge of these truths is so natural to our souls that we cannot but judge them infallible when we conceive them distinctly, nor doubt that if God had created many worlds, they would be as true in each of them as in this one. Thus those who are able to examine sufficiently the consequences of these truths and of our rules will be able to recognize effects by their causes. To express myself in scholastic terms, they will be able to have *a priori* demonstrations of everything that can be produced in this new world.[8]

[6] R.S. Westfall, *Force in Newton's Physics* (London: Macdonald, 1971), p. 82. I am much indebted to Westfall's penetrating analysis of motion in the seventeenth century.

[7] The ambiguity survived well into the nineteenth century. It led Hegel astray as William Whewell had to show as late as 1849 (William Whewell, "On Hegel's Criticism of Newton's *Principia*," *Transactions of the Cambridge Philosophical Society* VIII (1849), p. 698, cited in William R. Shea, "The Young Hegel's Quest for a Philosophy of Science, or Pitting Kepler Against Newton," in *Scientific Philosophy Today*, J. Agassi and R.S. Cohen, eds., (Dordrecht and Boston: D. Reidel, 1982), p. 388).

[8] *The World*, Chapter 7, A.T., XI, p. 47.

The last sentence is striking and becomes even more remarkable when read in conjunction with the enthusiastic letter that Descartes wrote to Mersenne in 1632:

> In the last two or three months, I have penetrated so far into the heavens, and have satisfied myself so well about its nature and that of the stars that we see (as well as about many other things that I would not even have dared to hope a few years ago) that I have now become bold enough to dare to seek the cause of the location of each star. For although they appear haphazardly scattered in the sky, I do not doubt that there is some natural, regular and fixed order among them. Knowledge of this order is the key and the foundation of the highest and most perfect science that men can have touching material things, for by its means we could know *a priori* all the different forms and essences of terrestrial bodies, whereas without it we have to satisfy ourselves with guessing what they are *a posteriori*, and by their effects.[9]

No Rosicrucian could have asked for more, and it is in this optimistic frame of mind that Descartes moves on, in the next chapter of *The World*, to show how his laws of motion and his analysis of vortices unlock the mysteries of the universe.

A System of Vortices

Descartes' new world began with the instantaneous breaking up of matter into roughly equal parts that immediately started to move in circles. Over time this primitive matter, through repeated collision, rubbing, and grinding, attained the three different forms of the elements. First the sharp edges of the fragments of matter were progressively blunted and became rounded like grains of sand. These small spheres are what Descartes calls the *second element*. The spaces between them were then filled by the filings or scrapings that accommodate themselves at every instant to the space available, so that there is never any void. These filings are the *first element*. Finally the parts of matter that are bulkier, coarser, and slower make up the *third element*. In this way, Descartes accounted for the genesis of the elements of water, fire, and earth that he had listed in Chapter Five of *The World*. The next step is to assume, on the analogy of eddies in a stream, that all this celestial matter revolves in a series of contiguous vortices as in Figure 4.

The center of one of these vortices is the sun, S, which is composed of the first element or the excess filings of matter that settle in the center of the vortex because the small spherical particles of the second element are greater in size and have a greater tendency to recede to the outskirts. The earth and the planets consist of the third element, and the celestial matter of the whirling heavens is mainly composed of tightly packed small spheres of the

[9] Letter of Descartes to Mersenne, around 10 May 1632, A.T., I, pp. 250–251.

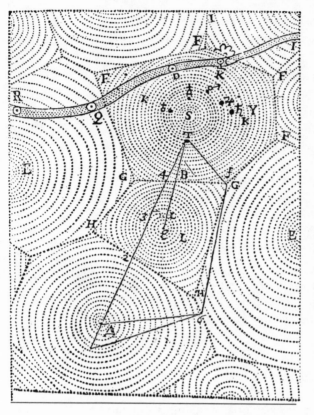

Figure 4

second element whose interstices are filled with the minute particles of the first element.[10]

The Solar System

The heavens are divided into several vortices, for instance, those whose centers are S, E, and A (Figure 4). Their number is indefinite, but they are all similar to the solar system, S, that is surrounded by planets that are identical with those with which we are familiar. What is crucial is the role played by the small spheres of celestial matter. They carry the planets around; they will also, as Descartes "warns us in advance," serve to explain the action of light. The spheres at the outer rim of the vortex (those near F and G in Figure 4) move faster, and their speed gradually decreases as we move towards the center, S, but only down to K where Saturn is located. Thereafter, the spheres become smaller and faster. This arbitrary reversal of speed is dictated by the fact that Saturn revolves more slowly than Mercury. In *The World*, Descartes glossed over this difficulty and merely stated that the spheres in contact with the sun are smaller than those further away, for if they had the same size they would have more centrifugal force and would rise.[11] When he revised his text for inclusion in *The Principles of Philosophy*, he attempted to meet an objection that stemmed from the recent discovery of sunspots by Galileo. These provided evidence for the sun's rotation, but their speed was found to be slower than any of the planets. This ran counter to Descartes' hypothesis that the sun rotated very rapidly, but he found a way of insulating the sun, and hence his theory, by postulating a solar atmosphere that slowed down the spots and extended as far as Mercury.[12]

Whatever their initial location, the planets eventually reached the layer

---

[10] *The World*, chapter 8, A.T., XI, pp. 49–53. The illustration is on p. 55.

[11] *Ibid.*, pp. 53–56.

[12] *Principles of Philosophy*, Part III, art. 1448, A.T., VIII-1, pp. 196–197. On the discovery of comets, see William R. Shea, *Galileo's Intellectual Revolution*, revised edition (New York: Science History Publications, 1975), pp. 75–108.

where the fluid material of the second element has the same force to persevere in motion. If the planet descended, it would be surrounded by smaller and faster small spheres that would push it up; likewise, if it rose, it would meet larger spheres that would slow it down and compel it to sink again.[13] The stability of the solar system was assured, therefore, by the state of equilibrium that particles of the second and the third elements enjoyed because they shared the same density: the closer the planet to the central body, the smaller its density. In the *Principles of Philosophy*, Descartes extended this explanation to the moon, and claimed that the moon always turns the same side to the earth because that side is less dense.[14] The huge planetary clumps of the third element normally find a state of equilibrium, but there are cases when their motion is great enough to carry them beyond their vortex. They then become comets and cut across a whole series of vortices like the comet in Figure 4 that moves along the path CDR.

In Figure 5, which is taken from the Third Part of *The Principles of Phi-*

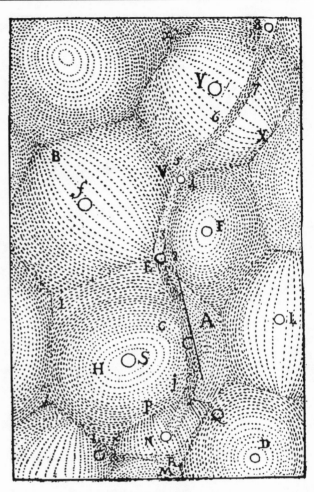

Figure 5

losophy, we see that the vortices are so disposed that they turn without obstructing one another. For instance, if the first vortex with S as center is carried from A to E and I, the adjacent vortex with center F will rotate in the opposite direction from A to E and V.[15] Nonetheless, the pressure of the neighbouring vortices is not everywhere equal, and this results in a distortion of the whirlpools. The solar vortex is flattened, but Descartes never refers to it as elliptical, and it would seem that like his contemporary Galileo he was ignorant of Kepler's discovery that the orbit of the planets is an ellipse.[16]

---

[13] *The World*, Chapter 10, A.T., XI, p. 64.

[14] *Principles of Philosophy*, Part III, art. 152, A.T., VIII-1, p. 198.

[15] *Ibid.*, art. 115, pp. 162–163.

[16] Descartes describes the path of the moon as "coming close to that of an ellipse," but he does not extend this observation to the planets or attempt to use the geometry of the ellipse to determine the actual position of the moon in its orbit (*ibid.*, art. 153, p. 200).

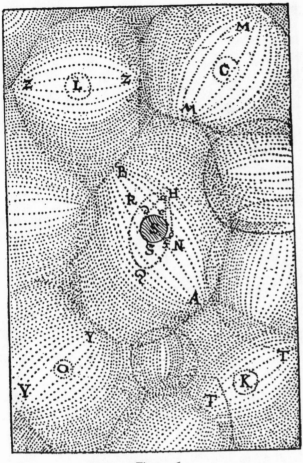

Figure 6

Matter in a Whirl

The extremely mobile and plastic parts of the first element are continuously entering the vortex by the poles and being flung out at the equators. This is illustrated in Figure 6, which is also taken from the Third Part of the *Principles of Philosophy*.[17] The solar vortex AYBM rotates on its axis AB, while the neighbouring vortices K, O, L, C rotate on their axes TT, YY, ZZ, MM. It is clear from Figure 6 that the matter from vortices K and L will be able to enter at the poles A and B, whereas the matter that is spun around axis AB will tend to exit at Y and M, and pass on to O and C. These particles of the first element have to pass through the small spheres of the second element as they wind their way to the star at the center of the vortex. Some particles become hollowed as they are squeezed through the tightly packed spheres and are twisted into grooved threads that Descartes calls channelled particles. When they reach the center of the vortex, they are ejected by the finer and faster moving particles of the first element and combine to form a froth that solidifies and acquires the properties of the third element. In this way, Descartes explains the formation of spots on the sun. They have irregular and changing shapes, but they can come to cover the whole surface of the central star, which then ceases to be able to maintain its whirlpool and is sucked into another vortex where it becomes a planet, or continues its journey beyond as a new comet. The whirlpool itself can be captured, the sun becoming a planet and its planets satellites. This was the origin of our earth and its moon.[18]

Eddies within Eddies

In *The World*, Descartes takes it for granted that the circulation of the celestial fluid will carry the planets just as boats are dragged along by the current in a

---

[17] *Principles of Philosophy*, Part III, art. 69, A.T., VIII–1, p. 120.

[18] *Ibid.*, art. 146, p. 195.

terrestrial bodies downward."[24] If we now return to *The World*, we shall find Descartes eschewing a quantitative treatment of the problem and pressing on to disclose another triumph of his theory.

The Tides Vanquished

The increased importance of navigation made the explanation of the tides not only important but fashionable in the sixteenth and seventeenth centuries.[25] It is the linchpin of Galileo's defence of the heliocentric theory, and although it plays a less important role in Descartes' system, it is still one of the prize illustrations of his theory. Four cycles had to be accounted for: (1) the *daily cycle* with high and low tides recurring at intervals of twelve hours; (2) the *monthly cycle* whereby the tides lag behind 50 minutes each day until they have gone round the clock and are back to their original position; (3) the *half-monthly cycle* with high tides at new and full moon and

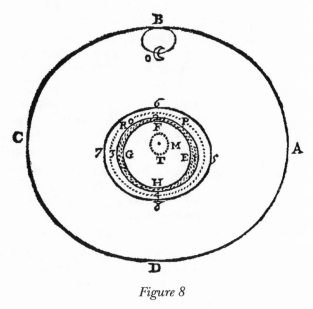

Figure 8

low tides at quadratures; and finally (4) the *half-yearly cycle* with greater tides at the equinoxes than at the solstices. For Descartes all this followed from the motion of the vortex around the earth.

Suppose that the moon is located at the top of the whirlpool ABCD that surrounds the earth (see Figure 8). Suppose further that the whole surface of the earth is covered by water 1, 2, 3, 4, which is in turn enveloped by air, 5, 6, 7, 8. Because there is less space between O and 6, the rotating celestial matter moves faster and depresses the air and water at 6 and 2, and thereby pushes the earth from the center M of the vortex downward to a new position T. This brings the earth closer to D, and since the celestial matter has less room to pass between 8 and D, the air and water will be depressed at 8 and 4, as well as at 6 and 2. The surface of the sea will therefore be flattened at 6, 2 and 8, 4 and bulge at 7, 3 and 5, 1. Since the earth rotates once every 24 hours, the humps move across the clock, and Descartes accounts in this way for the two high and the two low tides of the daily cycle.[26]

Since the earth rotates counterclockwise from E to F and G, namely,

---

[24] *Ibid.*, p. 57. Huygens modified Descartes' experiment by constraining a small globe to move between two strings to the centre of the vortex (*ibid.*, pp. 76–78).

[25] See Shea, *Galileo's Intellectual Revolution*, pp. 172–189.

[26] *The World*, Chapter 12, A.T., XI, pp. 80–82.

from west to east, the bulge moves in the opposite direction, that is, from east to west. Descartes claimed that this was confirmed by sailors, who reported that "navigation is much easier in our seas from east to west than from west to east."[27] Descartes' theory also accounts for the monthly cycle, since the moon moves in the same direction as the earth and completes one revolution each month. In six hours it describes roughly 1/120th of its circuit, so that the place of high tide advances by about 3° and is therefore delayed by twelve minutes each time. In 24 hours, this will make up the 50 minutes that are observed. For the half-monthly cycle, Descartes unveils a new property of the whirlpool: its shape is not perfectly spherical because the axis BD is shorter than AC. This is why the moon moves more rapidly at B and D (when it is full or new) than at A and C (when it is at quadrature).[28] The fourth, half-yearly cycle, is only mentioned in the *Principles of Philosophy* where Descartes correctly states that higher tides occur at the equinoxes.[29]

After completing the section on the tides, Descartes heard that the *Dialogue on the Two Chief World Systems*, which Galileo had originally thought of calling *The Dialogue on the Tides*, had appeared. "I would like to know," he asked Mersenne, "what he writes about the tides for it is one of the things that has given me most trouble to solve, and although I think I was successful, I am not clear about some of the details."[30] When he finally had the opportunity of examining a copy of the *Dialogue*, he declared that he found Galileo's theory "a bit far-fetched," a compliment that Galileo would gladly have repaid.[31]

Light Illuminated

The full title of *The World* is *The World or Treatise of Light*, and its climax is the explanation of the nature of light in Chapters Thirteen and Fourteen. The three modifications of primitive matter initially characterized as fire, air, and earth, following the traditional nomenclature, should really be understood as the constitutive elements of the sun, the sky, and the planets inasmuch as they produce, transmit, or reflect light.[32] We have seen in our discussion of refraction in Chapter Nine how Descartes repeatedly insisted that the nature of light could only be grasped within the framework of his cosmological system. This system has now been spelt out and shown (at least to Descartes'

---

[27] *Ibid.*, p. 82. The prevailing winds are actually from the west, but Descartes' error was common at the time and was shared by Galileo (Galileo, *Dialogue on the Two Chief World Systems, Opere*, A. Favaro ed., 20 vols. (Florence: Barbèra, 1890–1909), vol. VII, p. 466).

[28] *The World*, Chapter 12, A.T., XI, pp. 82–83.

[29] *Principles of Philosophy*, Part IV, art. 52, A.T., VIII–1, p. 236.

[30] Letter of Descartes to Mersenne, November or December 1632, A.T., I, p. 261.

[31] Letter of Descartes to Mersenne, 14 August 1634, *ibid.*, p. 304. Galileo died in 1642, two years before the publication of Descartes' *Principles of Philosophy*.

[32] *Principles of Philosophy*, Part III, art. 52, A.T., VIII–1, p. 105.

satisfaction) to account not only for the formation of the sun and planets but also for such important physical phenomena as weight and the action of the tides. It is high time that we were told what light is.

The explanation turns out to be an application of the analysis of circular motion that we summarized above on pages 280–282. We are asked to consider each of the small spheres of the second element that compose the fluid matter of the heavens as if it were a stone in a sling. For instance, the spheres that are near E (see Figure 9):

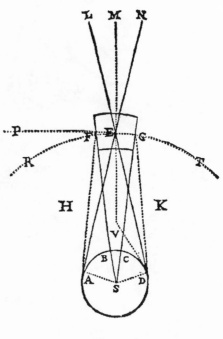

> tend, by their own inclination, only towards P, but the resistance of the other parts of the heavens that are above makes them tend, that is, disposes them, to move along the circle ER. Furthermore, this resistance, which is contrary to their inclination to continue their motion in a straight line, makes them tend, that is, is the reason why they strive to move towards M. Applying the same reasoning to all the parts of the second element, you will see in what sense we can say that they tend towards points diametrically opposed to the centre of the heavens they compose.[33]

Figure 9

The celestial matter beyond E restrains the small spheres of celestial matter like the sling restrains the stone. This is what causes the centrifugal force of the small spheres at E. This force is increased by the action of the lower spheres as well as by the rotation of the central body at S. Not by all the lower spheres, however, for it appeared to Descartes that only those in the cone AED could push a sphere at E. The argument for excluding the action of other spheres around H and K involves a thought-experiment. Imagine that the matter at E is suddenly removed, and ask yourself what neighboring particles of the second element will rush in to fill the void. For Descartes, the answer can only be the celestial matter in the cone AED. His reason is as remarkable as the sudden appearance of a void, however hypothetical, in a world where all action is by contact. The celestial matter outside the cone AED does not tend towards E because "all motions continue, as far as possible, in a straight line and, consequently, when nature has many ways of arriving at the same result, it inevitably follows the shortest."[34] For Descartes the least circuitous way of filling the void at E was for the matter in cone AED

[33] *The World*, Chapter 13, A.T., XI, p. 86.

[34] *Ibid.*, p. 89.

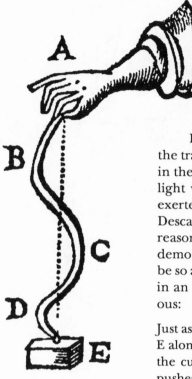

Figure 10

to instantly occupy the empty space just above it. Light is just this pressure exerted by the small spheres of the second element or celestial matter:

> Now you should know that the inhabitants of this new world will have such a nature that, when their eyes are pushed in this way, they will have a sensation that is just like the one we have of light.[35]

But what can pushing mean, since Descartes holds that the transmission of light is instantaneous? The answer is found in the analogies we have considered in Chapter Nine in which light was compared to the action of a cane or the pressure exerted by must fermenting in a vat. Again we are reminded of Descartes' early work in hydrostatics and his willingness to reason round a model without offering a rigorous geometrical demonstration. How the small spheres of celestial matter can be so arranged as to transmit a rectilinear tendency is answered in an essentially pictorial fashion, which is alleged to be obvious:

> Just as you can easily understand that the hand A pushes the body E along the straight line AE even though it pushes it by means of the curved stick BCD [see Figure 10]. Likewise, ball number 1 pushes ball number 7 in a straight line by means of ball number 5 just as much as by balls number 2, 3, 4 and 6 [see Figure 11].[36]

An Experimental Proof of the Instantaneous Transmission of Light

Descartes seldom sought the company of others to test his ideas in the crucible of scholarly discussion. He gladly expounded his views to the high and mighty, such as Queen Christina or Princess Elizabeth, or to the docile and promising, such as Henri Reneri, but he found it difficult to acknowledge anyone as his equal.[37] Isaac Beeckman is the only person with whom he

---

[35] *Ibid.*, p. 97.

[36] *Ibid.*, p. 100.

[37] Those who took at face value the invitation that Descartes issued at the end of the *Discourse on Method* and sent him their objections came in for contumely greatly at variance with his much vaunted good breeding. The French mathematicians who criticized his *Geometry* were dismissed as "two or three flies" (letter to Constantin Huygens, 19 August 1638, A.T., II, p. 671); Roberval is described as "less than a rational animal" (letter to Mersenne, around 29 June 1638, *ibid.*, p. 190); Pierre Petit as "a little dog" (letter to Mersenne, 27 July 1638, *ibid.*, p. 267, and 30 April 1639, *ibid.*, p. 533); and Hobbes as "extremely contemptible" (letter to Mersenne, 4 March 1641, A.T., III, p. 326). Jean de Beaugrand's letters are only good to be used as "toilet paper" (letter to Mersenne, around September 1641, *ibid.*, p. 437), while

had genuine scientific discussions for a brief period in 1618–1619, and their friendship was shipwrecked on the shoals of Descartes' susceptibilities in 1629. Fortunately, Beeckman was the most forgiving of men, and as we have seen in Chapter Four, he made peace with Descartes and visited him in Amsterdam in August 1634. It was on this occasion that Descartes explained his theory of light and the necessity of its instantaneous transmission.[38] Beeckman demurred on the grounds that nothing corporeal can move at infinite speed, and he proposed an experiment to determine the velocity of light. This consisted in noting the time elapsed between sending a flash of light and receiving its reflection from a mirror at a distance of a quarter of a mile.[39] Beeckman was so confident of the outcome that he was prepared to stake the whole of his physics on the experiment. Descartes accepted the wager and replied that if the slightest interval of time were detected "his entire philosophy would be completely subverted."[40] They then discussed the experiment without being able to agree on its feasibility. This was on Saturday, 12 August. The next day, Descartes declared that the question of the speed of light could easily be settled by "an experiment that thousands and thousands of persons have verified with great care,"[41] by which he meant the observation of lunar eclipses.

Figure 11

On the preceding evening, Beeckman had suggested that light might take one pulse beat to travel to and from a mirror situated a quarter of a mile away. With studied magnanimity, Descartes proposed to increase this value 24 times to 1/24th of a pulse beat for a quarter of a mile, or 1/6th for one mile! This apparently arbitrary value was actually chosen to simplify the calculations that now follow. Assume, says Descartes, that the moon is at a distance of 50 earth-radii and that the radius of the earth is 600 miles. A

Fermat's work is plain "shit," a word hardly softened for being in Latin (letter to Mersenne, around December 1638, A.T., II, p. 464). He expressed his contempt for his opponents by having his erstwhile servant Gillot answer their queries (e.g., *ibid.*, pp. 179, 195–196, 275). He returned unread Fermat's *Isagoge ad locos solidos*, one of the great mathematical works of the seventeenth century, because he believed that it could only repeat what he had already published in his *Geometry* (letter to Mersenne, 9 February 1639, *ibid.*, p. 495).

[38] Beeckman arrived in Amsterdam on Saturday, 12 August, and left on the following Monday morning (see Descartes' letter to Mersenne, 14 August 1634, A.T., I, p. 303). Shortly thereafter he wrote to Descartes who replied in a letter dated 22 August 1634, in which he summarized the discussion and clarified his position (A.T., II, pp. 307–312). Clerselier, who first published the letter, does not give the name of the addressee, but Pierre Costabel has shown it was intended for Beeckman (Pierre Costabel, *Démarches originales de Descartes savant* (Paris: Vrin, 1982), p. 81).

[39] Letter to Beeckman, 22 August 1634, A.T., I, p. 308. Cornelis de Waard points out that Beeckman normally used the Dutch mile, which is equal to 7.4074 kilometers or 4.6029 miles. A quarter of this distance gives us therefore a little over 1 English mile (Isaac Beeckman, *Journal*, C. de Waard, ed., 4 vols. (The Hague: Martinus Nijhof, 1939–1945), vol. III, p. 287, n. 1).

[40] Letter to Beeckman, 22 August 1634, A.T., I, p. 308.

[41] *Ibid.*

simple calculation yields 5,000 pulse beats for the time it would take light to travel from the earth to the moon and back, and this could hardly be less than an hour.[42]

A	B	C

Along the line ABC, let A, B, and C represent the positions of the sun, the earth, and the moon respectively, and suppose that from the earth at B the moon is being eclipsed at C. The eclipse must appear at the moment when the light emitted by the sun at A and reflected by the moon at C would have arrived at B if it had not been interrupted by the earth. On the assumption that it takes one hour for light to make the return journey from B to C, the eclipse should be seen one hour after the light from the sun reaches the earth at B. In other words, the eclipse should not be observed from the earth until one hour after the sun has been seen at A. But this is false because when the moon is eclipsed at C, the sun does not arrive at A an hour earlier but at the same moment as the eclipse. "Hence," Descartes concluded, "your experiment is useless." "And your argument," retorted Beeckman, "begs the question."[43] We do not know exactly how Beeckman developed his counter-argument, but there is something less than obvious in Descartes' experimental proof.[44] The problem is to determine the actual from the apparent place of the moon when it is eclipsed by the sun, since whenever an eclipse occurs, the *images* of the sun and the moon will lie along the same line. For his argument to be valid, Descartes would need some way of determining when the earth emits the shadow that eclipses the moon, and this he cannot do without knowing the velocity of light.

Light is now known to take about 2.57 seconds to travel from the earth to the moon and back, a detectable time. The problem with Descartes' procedure is that it requires a prior knowledge of the speed of light to be valid, for whenever we *see* an eclipse, we have an angle of 180° between the sun and the moon. Descartes never wavered in his belief that he had found an overwhelming experimental proof of the instantaneity of light. When he was asked by Mersenne to comment on Galileo's new book, the *Two New Sciences*, in 1638, he noted that the Italian scientist had suggested determining the speed of light by having two persons signal to one another from a distance of a few miles. The idea was to measure the time elapsed between sending a light signal and receiving a light signal in return. Descartes pronounced the experiment "useless," and declared that the matter was entirely settled by eclipses of the moon.[45] He does not seem to have been aware that

---

[42] 5000 pulse beats per hour are roughly 83.3 per minute, close to the average for women.

[43] Letter of Descartes to Beeckman, 22 August 1634, A.T., I, p. 310.

[44] See Spyros Sakellariadis, "Descartes" Experimental Proof of the Infinite Velocity of Light and Huygens' Rejoinder," *Archive for History of Exact Sciences* 26 (1982), pp. 1–12.

[45] Letter of Descartes to Mersenne, around 11 November 1638, A.T., II, p. 384. Galileo's experiment is described in the First Day of his *Discourses on Two New Sciences*, in *Opere*, vol. VIII, pp. 88–89.

Beeckman proposed a similar experiment in his *Journal* in an entry dated 19 March 1629, in which two men with identical synchronized watches face one another across a distance of a few miles. One fires a cannon and makes a note of the exact time of firing; the other sees the flash and jots down the time. The men then exchange watches and repeat the experiment several times. The slightest discrepancy in the recorded times would indicate that light travels at a finite speed.[46]

Spelling Out the Laws of Motion

The reworking of *The World* into *The Principles of Philosophy* was largely a matter of reducing the material to articles along the lines of a textbook. There is, however, one clear improvement and two major developments. The improvement concerns the ordering of the laws of motion. The Third Law (regarding rectilinearity) becomes the Second, so that the First, "each thing in particular continues to be in the same state, by its own force (*quantum in se est*) and only changes it by colliding with others," is now followed by the law that says, "each part of matter by itself never tends to move along curved but along straight lines."[47] The two improvements are: (a) the formulation of secondary rules that cover various cases of collision, and (b) the explanation of magnetism to which we shall return after examining the rules.

The Third Law of motion (formerly the Second) is explicated as follows:

> When a moving body strikes another, if it has less force to continue to move in a straight line then the other has to resist it, it is turned back in the opposite direction without losing any of its motion, and if it has more force, it moves the other body with it and loses as much of its motion as it gives to the other.[48]

Descartes never took the decisive step of identifying change in direction with change in motion. In other words, motion has no sign attached to it, and this explains why the seven rules that he considered applications of his three laws are generally unsatisfactory. They are conveniently summarized in Figure 12 below where v stands for speed and m for size. The two colliding bodies are assumed to be perfectly hard.[49]

Perhaps the best way of examining these rules and seeing what is wrong with them is to remind ourselves of the principle of the conservation of

---

[46] Isaac Beeckman, *Journal*, vol. III, p. 112, quoted in A.T., X, p. 552.

[47] *Principles of Philosophy*, Part II, art. 37, (First Law), art. 39 (Second Law), art. 40 (Third Law), A.T., VIII–1, pp. 62–65. On the meaning of the phrase "*quantum in se est*" in the First Law, and its classical origin in the Roman writer Lucretius, see I. Bernard Cohen, "*Quantum in se est*: Newton's Concept of Inertia in Relation to Descartes and Lucretius," *Notes and Records of the Royal Society of London* 19 (1964), pp. 131–155.

[48] *Principles of Philosophy*, Part II, art. 40, A.T., VIII–1, p. 65.

[49] Figure 12 is taken from Aiton, *The Vortex Theory of Planetary Motions*, p. 36. The seven rules are listed in the *Principles of Philosophy*, Part 2, arts. 46–52, A.T., VIII–1, pp. 68–69.

momentum, and the difference between elastic and inelastic collision, two aspects of the mechanical situation that escaped Descartes despite his passion for clear ideas and coherent propositions. Momentum (mv) is the product of the mass of a body by its velocity, and the principle of the conservation of momentum states that if no external force acts on a system, the total momentum of a system remains unchanged. In applying this principle, one must remember that momentum is a vector quantity; if the direction of the velocity is reversed, the momentum of a body changes sign.

Collisions are either *inelastic* when the bodies do not rebound but stick together or *elastic* when they do. In this second case, the bodies are compressed for the brief moment they are in contact. At the instant of maximum compression, they both have zero velocity, and energy is stored in the elastic bodies as in a compressed spring. This energy is immediately released, and the bodies fly apart. If very little energy is dissipated as heat and vibrational energy, the velocities of rebound are practically equal to the initial velocities.

Descartes' difficulties in formulating his seven rules can be seen to result from: (a) his failure to recognize that direction is essential to momentum, and (b) his denial that bodies rebound because they are compressed, i.e., elastic. The colliding bodies are assumed to be perfectly hard. The paradox is that his first rule is perfectly correct for the case of *elastic* collision. Two objects of equal mass, coming together with the same speed, will bounce back at the same speed (see Figure 12). But Descartes is emphatic that this has nothing to do with elasticity: if the speed is not altered, this is because a change of direction can neither increase nor decrease the existing motion. (The correct solution for an *inelastic* collision is that the two objects will stop).

Rule 2 provides the correct form for inelastic collision, but Descartes neglects the direction of motion ($+m_2v_2$ should read $-m_2v_2$), and the result is the surprising claim that the speed is not reduced and that the balls move together after collision at the speed they had before impact. Rule 3 suffers from the same neglect of sign, and would only be correct if the speed after impact read $(v_1-v_2)/2$. Rule 4 has the extraordinary feature of precluding the possibility of a small body moving a larger one whatever the smaller body's speed! Rule 5 is correct. Rule 6 is an interesting interpolation between Rules 4 and 5 and guesswork. This interpolation can best be illustrated with Descartes' own numerical example in which a ball in motion approaches one at rest with four degrees of speed. It appeared to Descartes that the moving ball communicates one degree to the stationary one before turning back with the three remaining degrees. He arrived at this conclusion by reasoning as follows: since the moving ball *is not smaller* than the one at rest, there is a case for saying that it will act as in Rule 5 and transfer half its speed to the ball at rest, so that both will move thereafter with a speed of two. However, since it is equally true that the moving ball *is not larger* than the one at rest, it is also the case that it should be reflected with its full speed of four degrees. But there is no reason for preferring one of the two possibilities. Descartes concludes that the effects must be equally shared, namely, that the moving

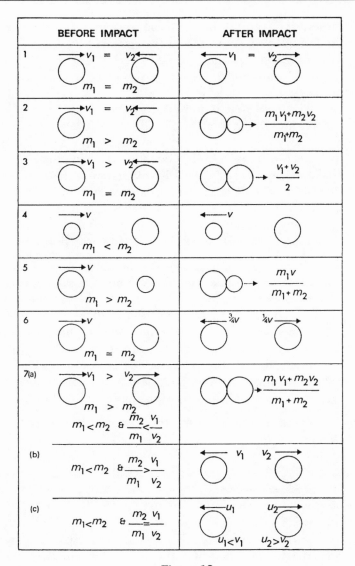

Figure 12

ball must transfer one degree of speed to the ball at rest and turn back with the remaining three.

Rule 7(a) is correct, and Rule 7(b) is an application of Rule 4, since m_1 cannot overcome the resistance of a larger body when $m_2 m_1, > v_1/v_2$, i.e., when $m_2 v_2 > m_1 v_1$. Rule 7(c) is analogous to Rule 6 and is an interpolation between Rule 7(a) and 7(b). Descartes does not determine the amount by which the new speed u_1 falls short of v_1, or u_2 is greater than v_2, but he illustrates Rule 7(a) with a numerical example, and sums up in the Latin edition with these words: "Similar cases are to be dealt with in a similar way. And these things require no proof because they are obvious in themselves."[50] In the French version, this is amended to read: "And the demonstrations of all this are so certain that, even if experience seemed to show us the contrary, we would nonetheless be obliged to place more trust in our reason than in our senses."[51]

The rule that is most severely rebuked by experience is the fourth which states that a small body cannot move a body at rest no matter how fast it collides with it. It is not only our everyday experience that runs counter to the rule. Our reason finds it equally surprising because it implies that matter resists motion as such. This is at variance with Descartes' determination to cleanse matter of all organic features and all internal force. In several of Descartes' pronouncements, matter is wholly inert and cannot have a force to resist motion. The idea that matter contains such resistance is a prejudice, "founded," as Descartes explained to a correspondent,

> on our preoccupation with our senses, and derives from the fact that having tried since our infancy to move bodies that are hard and heavy, and having always experienced difficulty, we have been persuaded since then that the difficulty proceeds from matter and is, consequently, common to all bodies. It was easier for us to suppose this than to realise that it was only the weight of the bodies we tried to move which prevented us from lifting them, and the hardness and unevenness of their parts which prevented us from dragging them and, hence, it does not follow that the same thing must happen with bodies that have neither hardness nor weight.[52]

A consequence of the indifference of matter to motion is drawn by Descartes when he states that bodies have to move with a finite velocity. Motion and rest are discontinuous, and a body starting to move does not pass through all the degrees of speed as Galileo maintained. In practice, however, Descartes was faced with the fact, as he himself recognized, that "size is always opposed to speed."[53] But if matter is wholly inert, how can size oppose velocity? The problem was not raised in *The World*, but it was thrust to the fore in the *Principles of Philosophy* when Descartes sought to formulate the rules that govern motion in the light of his guiding principle that motion is a state and not a process. The result was Rule 4. The relative size of the two bodies determines whether the first can move the second. If the second, say

---

[50] *Principles of Philosophy*, Part II, art. 52, A.T., VIII–1, p. 70.

[51] *Principes de la philosophie*, 2ᵉ partie, art. 52, A.T., IX–2, p. 93. This French translation was made by Descartes' friend, the Abbé Claude Picot, and appeared in Paris in 1647. It was revised by Descartes who added a number of developments, such as the one just quoted. For the uncertainty concerning the extent of Descartes' revision, see the Foreword to the French translation in *ibid.*, pp. IX–XX, and the analysis of R.P. Miller and Valentine Rodger Miller, "Descartes" *Principia Philosophiae*: Some Problems of Translation and Interpretation," *Studia Cartesiana* 2 (1981), pp. 143–154.

[52] Letter of Descartes to Morin, 13 July 1638, A.T., II, pp. 212–213.

[53] *The World*, Chapter VIII, A.T., XI, p. 51.

B, is larger by any amount whatever, the first, *A*, will not be able to move it. At this point, the natural thought occurred that *B* at rest remains a constant factor whereas the force of *A* can increase indefinitely as its velocity increases. The more he examined the problem, however, the more Descartes was convinced that *A* can never move *B* whatever *A*'s velocity. In the Latin edition of the *Principles of Philosophy*, he merely stated the rule. In the French translation that appeared three years later in 1647, he explained the reasoning behind it: *A* cannot push *B* without making it go as swiftly as *A* itself would go afterwards, and *B* must resist so much the more as *A* comes towards it more swiftly. Thus, for example, if *B* is twice as large as *A*, and *A* has 3 degrees of speed, *A* can only push *B* if it transfers two-thirds of its speed to *B*. If *A* has 30 degrees of speed, it must transfer 20 to *B*; if 300, it must give 200, and so on. But since *B* is at rest, it resists the reception of 20 degrees 10 times more than 2, and 200 degrees 100 times more. So the greater the speed of *A*, the more resistance it finds in *B*.[54]

Since Descartes treated the change of motion as instantaneous, the resistance he attributed to matter had to be resistance to motion itself and not merely to change of motion. The resistance to motion that Descartes admitted cannot be reconciled with the inertness that he considered an essential property of matter. The fact that this incompatibility escaped Descartes gives us an idea of the magnitude of the conceptual change involved in the ontological identification of motion and rest. In his *First Law of Nature*, Descartes affirmed that motion like rest is a *state* not a *process*, and hence that motion continues uninterrupted unless forced to change by some outside agent. Combined with his *Second Law of Nature*, "that all motion is of itself straight," we have—in all appearance—a clear statement of the principle of inertia. That this is not the case is clear from Rule 4.

Radical Discontinuities

A comparison of Rules 4, 5, and 6 leads to another startling conclusion: a barely perceptible change in size can alter the entire outcome of the head-on collision of two bodies! The situation described in Rule 4 (see Figure 12 above) remains unaltered if the smaller incoming body, m_1, is slowly increased in size until it is almost, but not quite, the size of the larger body, m_2, at rest. But when m_1 is increased by an additional amount (however small) and is made equal to m_2, the situation is dramatically changed, and Rule 6 obtains. The second body, m_2, no longer resists motion but sets off with one-quarter of the original speed of m_1, while m_1 turns back with the remaining motion. An equally spectacular change occurs if m_1 is made only slightly larger than m_2. Both bodies now move together in the direction of the incoming body, and we have Rule 5!

These quantitative leaps were one of the reasons that made Leibniz

---

[54] *Principes de la philosophie*, 2ᵉ partie, art. 49, A.T., IX–2, pp. 90–91.

skeptical about the general validity of Descartes' rules, but Descartes himself was unperturbed.[55] As we have seen, his ontology of creative acts was radically discontinuist, and his opposition to Aristotelian physics made him reject all virtuality, all dynamism. Motion is not a flowing dynamical continuity. This denial of virtuality and the insistence on complete actuality led Descartes to consider each instant of motion at the instant when it occurs, and to consider each instant as self-sufficient. The individual instants of time are geometrical relations that define the instantaneous static positions of bodies with respect to each other. At each instant we have different geometrical states, the instantaneous motion that is defined by this state (compared to the previous one) is not motion at all. But, on the other hand, the instant of motion is also the instantaneous creation by God of this *state*.

God recreates the world at each instant. The subsequent acts of creation are identical with the first and are merely notionally different. But there is no intrinsic, dynamic relation between one state and the next. The regularity we observe expresses the will of God, who chose to produce the world according to rules that we are empowered (ultimately through innate ideas) to interpret. The second state is, like the first, the expression of God's free act of creation. But there is no passage, transition, or flow from one state to the next. What we have is a series of new instaurations, a repetition of free creations. This is why Descartes felt that Galileo was a superficial philosopher when he appealed to the infinite divisibility of time to account for the infinite decrease of speed. Descartes considered that an instant cannot be decreased. Hence elementary speed is also indivisible, and motion is made up of a series of these indivisibles. "You must know," he writes to Mersenne,

> in spite of what Galileo and others say to the contrary, that bodies that begin to fall, or move in any way whatsoever, do not pass through all the degrees of slowness but have a definite speed from the very first instant.[56]

Motion and rest, as well as different degrees of speed, are discontinuous, and a body starting from rest does not pass through all the degrees of speed as Galileo maintained.

The Voice of Experience

Descartes may have thought he had justified his seven rules before the tribunal of reason, but he knew that their application was severely limited. They were formulated for the ideal case of two perfectly hard bodies in a closed system. In the real world, several bodies impinge upon one another,

---

[55] Leibniz, "Animadversiones in partem generalem Principiorum Cartesianorum," in G.W. Leibniz, *Die Philosophischen Schriften*, C.J. Gerhardt, ed., 7 vols. (Berlin, 1875–1890); reprint (Hildesheim: Olms, 1978), vol. IV, pp. 376–380.

[56] Letter of Descartes to Mersenne, 25 December 1639, A.T., II, p. 630. See also the letter to Mersenne of 11 October 1638, *ibid.*, p. 399, and p. 380 where he complains of Galileo's lack of depth.

and what is more important, they are invariably part of a whirlpool of fluid matter. Planets float in celestial matter, and ordinary heavy objects fall because they are displaced by lighter particles of this matter. Motion is invariably motion through a fluid, and when Descartes investigated how bodies move through water, it appeared to him that this was because the parts of the liquid readily gave way:

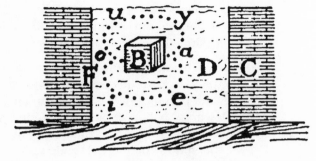

Figure 13

> And upon further investigation why some bodies give up their place to others, while others do not, we *easily* notice that those that are already in motion do not impede other bodies from occupying the places which they spontaneously leave, whereas those that are at rest cannot be driven from their place without some force. From this we may conclude that bodies that are divided into minute particles, which are agitated by diverse movements are fluid, while those whose continuous particles are all at rest are solid.[57]

This is consistent with Descartes' view that the hardness of bodies consists solely in the state of rest of the parts relative to each other. The fact that water and air offer resistance to bodies, particularly fast-moving ones, is explained by the presence of impurities that render them imperfect fluids.

A body at rest in a fluid is pushed equally on all sides and cannot move unless it receives some additional impulse. This can come either from some external force or from the current of the fluid in which the solid is immersed. In the light of his definition of a fluid, Descartes argues that "an immersed solid can be determined to move by the least force."[58] This would appear to violate the fourth rule, and despite Descartes' protestations that this is not the case, his explanation is more clever than convincing. Assume, says Descartes, that body B (see Figure 13) is placed in a fluid that has some of its particles moving clockwise along the circular paths *o u y a* and *o a e i*. If the solid B is placed between *o* and *a*, what happens? Here is how Descartes saw the outcome:

> The particles *a e i o* will be prevented by B from moving from *o* toward *a* to complete a circle and, similarly, the particles *o u y a* will be prevented from continuing from *a* toward *o*. Those coming from *i* toward *o* will drive B toward C, while those coming from *y* toward *a* will drive it back equally toward F. As a result, these particles alone will have no force to move B, but will be driven back from *o* toward *u*, and from *a* toward *e*, and one circulation will be formed by the two, following the order of the letters *a e i o u y a*.

[57] *Principles of Philosophy*, Part II, art. 54, A.T., VIII–1, pp. 70–71, emphasis added.

[58] *Ibid.*, art. 56, p. 71.

Thus, collision with the body B will not in any way interrupt their motion but will only change their direction, so that they will not move along such straight lines (or so nearly straight) as if they had not impinged on B.[59]

This state of equilibrium can be changed by the slightest external force applied to B in the direction BC because it will join the force already exerted by the particles of the fluid coming from *i* toward *o*. In this ingenious way, Descartes believed he had avoided a contradiction with his fourth rule, according to which a small force cannot move a large body. But he failed to explain how the inertial tendency of the body to persevere in its state of rest had been overcome, and as E.J. Aiton remarks, by invoking the complementary force of the circle *a e i o*, Descartes was surreptitiously reintroducing the Platonic theory of *antiperistasis*, which explained projectile motion by having the air compressed in front of the moving body circulate to the rear to push it again.[60]

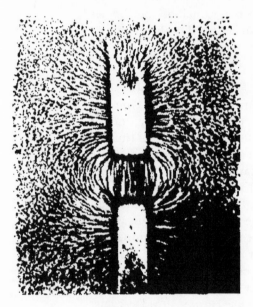

Figure 14

Magnetism Explained

The expansion of the Third Law of motion into seven rules was the first major development of the *Principles of Philosophy*. The second was the explanation of magnetism, a topic that had been fashionable since the publication of William Gilbert's *De Magnete* in 1600. Gilbert had considered a number of experiments, but these were used to buttress his contention that the magnetic form is animate and comparable to the human soul. For Gilbert, the "effluxions" from the magnet are clearly incorporeal because they penetrate dense bodies and magnetize a needle without adding to its weight.[61]

To rescue magnetism from the occult could only be a triumph, but Descartes did not apply himself seriously to the problem before

[59] *Ibid.*, art. 57, pp. 73–74.

[60] Aiton, *The Vortex Theory of Planetary Motions*, pp. 40–41. See Plato's *Timaeus* 79E–80A.

[61] William Gilbert, *De Magnete*, P. Fleury Mottelay, trans. (New York: Dover, 1958), Book 2, Ch. 4, pp. 106–109. Gilbert believed that the magnetic force "is there in an instant, and is not introduced in any interval of time nor successively, as when heat enters iron, for the moment the iron is touched by the loadstone it is excited throughout" (Book 3, Ch. 3, p. 191). On similarities between Descartes and Gilbert and the claim that Descartes' vortex theory owes much to Gilbert, see Marie-Luise Hoppe, *Die Abhängigkeit der Wirbeltheorie des Descartes von William Gilberts Lehre vom Magnetismus* (Halle a S.: C.A. Kaemmerer, 1914).

1640. The suggestiveness of a simple experiment provided a clue. When iron filings are sprinkled on a piece of cardboard resting on a horizontal bar magnet, the filings arrange themselves in a pattern that suggests a vortex (see Figure 14). Following Gilbert, Descartes used a spherical loadstone, and what he observed were filings settling themselves around the North and South Poles in the shape of small curved tubes.[62] Descartes leapt to the conclusion that these were indeed tubes or conduits through which matter moved. But what kind of matter? The large particles of the third element were too big. Small spheres of the second element were possible, but Descartes thought that particles of the first element were more likely, especially if they had been channelled or grooved. The shaded portion of Figures 15 and 16 show how "channelled parts" could be formed as the third element is squeezed through the spherical particles of the second. Like toothpaste being pushed out of a tube, the channelled parts rotate upon emerging, and since they are grooved, they acquire the shape of right-handed or left-handed headless cylindrical screws.[63]

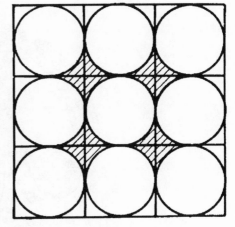

Figure 15

The channelled parts enter the sun along the axis of the vortex, and are expelled at the circumference in the plane of the equator where the centrifugal force is at a maximum. But what is crucial is that they approach the central body from the North or the South Pole. Since the whole vortex rotates in one direction on its axis, "it is obvious," writes Descartes, "that those coming from the South Pole must be twisted in exactly the opposite direction

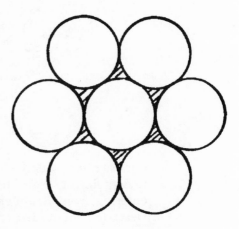

Figure 16

from those coming from the North."[64] When the central star or sun cools down and becomes a planet like the earth, the grooved particles continue to enter from the North or the South Pole and proceed from one hemisphere to the other along pores that are threaded to give passage to right- or left-handed particles, but not both. The channelled particles, pictured as small snail-shells (see Figure 17), traverse the earth ABCD. Those that enter at the South Pole, A, are so threaded that they can pass in a straight line to the

---

62 Magnetism is not considered in *The World* but is discussed at length in the *Principles of Philosophy*, Part IV, arts. 133–188, A.T., VIII–1, pp. 275–315.

63 Figures 15 and 16 are taken from the excellent study of John L. Heilbron, *Elements of Early Modern Physics* (Berkeley: University of California Press, 1982), p. 24.

64 *Principles of Philosophy*, Part III, art. 91, A.T., VIII–1, p. 145.

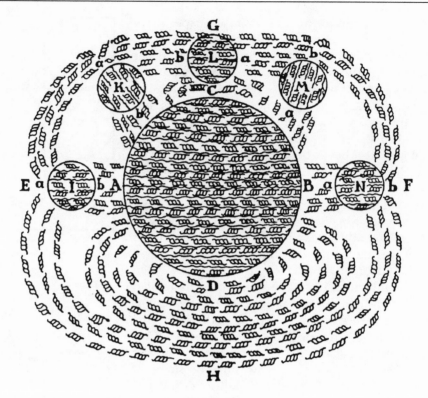

Figure 17

opposite hemisphere CBD where they emerge to return through the air to their point of origin, thereby creating a kind of vortex. Channelled parts entering from B undergo a similar journey in the opposite direction.[65] Descartes' interesting conjecture is that the channelled parts pass through the earth with ease because the interior of the earth is conveniently lined with grooved pores. This is why metals that are extracted from the bowels of the earth, for instance, iron, are easily magnetized.

Why unlike poles attract one another is explained with the aid of Figure 18 in which channelled parts flowing through magnet O move in the direction AB or BA. When they emerge, they continue in a straight line up to R or S when the resistance of the air is great enough to deflect them. The space RVSV constitutes the vortex described by the channelled particles and is "the sphere of force or activity of the magnet O."[66] Likewise, the sphere of force of magnet P is TXSX. When the spheres of activity are brought into contact, so that the North Pole of one magnet faces the South Pole of the other, the channelled particles flowing from O to S continue in a straight line to P, and those coming from P toward S proceed to O, so that the two magnets will behave as one. If like poles face one another, however, the magnets will be

[65] *Ibid.*, Part IV, art. 146, p. 287–288.

[66] *Ibid.*, art. 153, p. 293. The figure appears on p. 292.

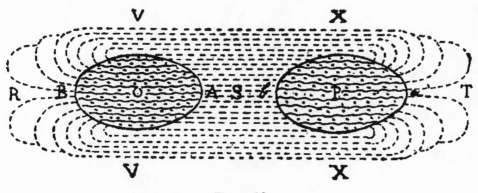

Figure 18

repelled, since the channelled particles are now unable to enter because the tubes or conduits are threaded the wrong way.

It appeared to Descartes that channelled particles could be invoked each and every time a case of attraction or repulsion occurred. This included electrical phenomena and "innumerable other marvelous effects." Equally important, their operation was fully intelligible in terms of size, shape, and motion alone. "I have described the earth and the entire visible universe," concluded Descartes, "on the model of a machine, without considering anything beyond figures and motions."[67] The mechanical philosophy was an unqualified success . . . at least in the mind of its author.

What about Living Organisms?

We have already seen, in chapter eight, how Descartes compared the body to a machine in the *Treatise on Man*, the work that was intended as the second part of *The World*, but suffered the same fate and was only published posthumously in 1664. In the Fifth Part of the *Discourse on Method*, however, Descartes offered a summary of his anatomical views, and expressed regret that he could not offer for living organisms the kind of genetical explanation that he had supplied for the physical universe,

> namely, by demonstrating effects from causes and showing from what seeds and in what manner nature must produce them. So I contented myself with supposing that God formed the body of a man exactly like our own both in the outward shape of its limbs and in the external arrangement of its organs, using for its composition nothing but the matter that I had described.[68]

What Descartes chooses to emphasize is his explanation of the heart, and in order to appreciate its import, let us briefly recall the correct physi-

---

[67] *Ibid.*, art. 187, p. 314.

[68] *Discourse on Method*, Fifth Part, A.T., VI, pp. 45–46.

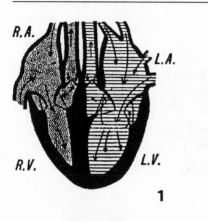

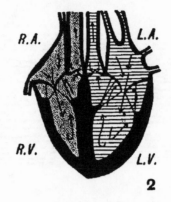

1

2

3

Figure 9

ological account that has become familiar since the work of William Harvey. The heart is essentially a pair of pumps. In principle, it is simply two bags that contract and expand, and that are equipped with an inlet and an outlet valve, made of flaps of tissue so arranged that the pressure of blood in one direction forces them apart and in the other direction forces them together. Figure 19 shows how it works. In stage 1 the inlet valves are open, and the heart is expanding as the blood pours in. At stage 2 the heart has begun to contract from the top downward. The right auricle (R.A.) and the left auricle (L.A.) are contracting the forcing the blood they contain into the right ventricle (R.V.) and the left ventricle (L.V.). At stage 3 the ventricles contract, and the blood is forced through the outlet valves. From the right side, it goes to the lungs, from the left to the rest of the body. While this is happening, the auricles are receiving a fresh supply of blood from the veins. So the action of the heart is a wave of contraction (systole) starting from the auricles and passing down to the ventricles, followed by an expansion (diastole).

Descartes had heard of Harvey's discovery of the circulation of the blood, probably as early as 1628 when he was in Paris, and he had no difficulty in accepting Harvey's demonstration.[69] Where he found himself at variance with the English anatomist was in the choice of an appropriate mechanical analogy. Where Harvey perceived a pump, Descartes saw a sort of steam engine. The heart for him was a flask or retort in which the blood is heated to such a degree that its expansion forces it out of the body. The heat that powers the engine of the heart is assimilated to other cases of "fire without light," such as the spontaneous combustion of damp hay or the fermentation of grapes.[70] The vaporized blood is forced out at diastole, when the heart expands, and fresh blood flows in at systole, when the heart

---

[69] Harvey's *De Motu Cordis* appeared in 1628. At the end of 1632, Descartes referred to the work as having been mentioned to him by Mersenne "in the past" (presumably when he was in Paris in 1628), but he insisted that he had not looked at the work before drafting his *Treatise of Man* (letter to Mersenne, November or December 1632, A.T., I, p. 263).

[70] *Discourse on Method*, Fifth Part, A.T., VI, p. 46.

contracts, the exact reverse of what Harvey maintained, and what turned out to be the case.

Descartes offers no explanation of the source of the heart's beat or how it is maintained. Nor does this seem to have bothered him. In what must be one of his boldest exercises in propaganda, he declares that his account of the movement of the heart has the rigor of a mathematical demonstration, the perspicuity of sensory evidence, and the simplicity of clockwork:

> Now those who are ignorant of the force of mathematical demonstrations, and unaccustomed to distinguish true from merely probable arguments may be tempted to reject what has been said without examining it. To prevent this, let me say that the movement I have just explained follows from the arrangement of the parts of the heart that we see, the pulse that we feel with our hands, and the nature of blood that we know from experience, just as necessarily as the movement of a clock follows from the force, position, and shape of its wheels' counterweights.[71]

A Physician Takes a Second Look

Not everyone saw the heart with Descartes' eyes. The physician Vopiscus Fortunatus Plemp intimated as much when he acknowledged receipt of three complimentary copies of the *Discourse of Method*. When Descartes pressed him for his comments, he complied with a series of objections of which the most telling is the following: when the heart is removed from the lungs it continues to pulsate long after the supply of blood has been cut off.[72] In his reply Descartes does not deny the experimental fact, indeed, he states that he has himself observed that the excised heart of a fish beats longer than that of any terrestrial animal. But this, he adds, is because there are always a few drops of blood left, and these are sufficient to feed the furnace of the heart.[73] To the further objection that the heart of a fish is never very hot, Descartes replies that some liquids can boil without being brought to any great heat.[74] In any case what other explanation can there be if motion is to be explained on mechanical principles alone!

---

[71] *Ibid.*, p. 50.

[72] Plemp thanked Descartes for the *Discourse on Method* and mentioned that he might raise objections in his letter of 15 September 1637 (A.T., I, pp. 399–400). Descartes reminded him of this in a letter of 20 December (*ibid.*, p. 477) and Plemp replied in January 1638 (*ibid.*, pp. 497–499).

[73] Descartes' lengthy rely is contained in a letter of 15 February 1638, *ibid.*, pp. 521–534. Extracts were published by Plemp in his *De Fundamentis Medicinae Libri VI* (Louvain, 1638). When Henri de Roy, a disciple of Descartes, protested, Plemp gave the full text in the second edition entitled *Fundamenta Medicinae* in 1644. Descartes claimed that drops of blood remaining in the auricles fell into the ventricles where they were evaporated by the heat (*ibid.*, p. 523).

[74] *Ibid.*, pp. 529–530. Descartes stresses that the rarefaction of the blood is *instantaneous*, and he compares it to the sudden action of yeast in flour. See also, *Discourse on Method*, Fifth Part, A.T., VI, pp. 48–49.

Plemp had pointed out that Descartes' theory of the heart as an internal combustion engine had already been suggested by Aristotle. The claim that his brilliant insight had originated with the ancients galled Descartes who brooded over it for years. In the *Description of the Human Body*, written ten years later, he sought to dismiss Aristotle's conjecture as a vague guess, essentially different from his own scientific hypothesis:

> It has always been known that there is more heat in the heart than in the rest of the body, and that blood can be rarefied by heat. This is why I am surprised that hitherto no one has pointed out that it is the rarefaction of the blood that is the only cause of the motion of the heart. Although it might seem that Aristotle thought of it when he wrote in chapter 20 of *On Breath*: "This motion is similar to the action of a liquid that heat brings to a boil" . . . it is only by mere chance that he happened to say something that is nearly the truth, but of which he had no certain knowledge. [75]

If Aristotle made a lucky, but untimely and unfruitful, guess, Harvey's experimental evidence for assimilating the heart to a pump "merely shows that experiments can lead us astray when we do not examine their causes with sufficient care."[76] Harvey had argued that the blood was pushed out at systole (contraction), and he had pointed out that if we practice an incision, the blood shoots out when the heart contracts. Descartes claimed that the evidence was unclear, but his main objection was philosophical:

> If we suppose that the heart beats the way Harvey describes it, we would have to imagine some faculty that causes this motion, and the nature of this faculty would be much more difficult to understand than what it claims to explain.[77]

We would also, adds Descartes, need other faculties to explain how the properties of the blood are altered by passing through the heart, whereas "we *see clearly* that dilatation alone is sufficient to explain the motion of the heart as I have explained it, as well the change in the blood."[78] On this obvious theory, which had been adumbrated in the *Discourse on Method*, the "animal spirits," defined as "a very pure and very fine kind of flame," rise from the heart to the brain and from there reach the muscles through the nerves and set the limbs in motion. According to Descartes, all this proceeds "according to the rules of mechanics, which are those of Nature,"[79] but we are vouchsafed little more than the promise that numbers and motion will unlock the marvels of the organic world after conquering the material universe.

[75] *Description of the Human Body*, A.T., XI, pp. 244–245. This work was written in 1647–1648 but was only published posthumously in 1664.

[76] *Ibid.*, p. 242. Descartes makes similar remarks elsewhere, e.g., A.T., VI, p. 340; XI, p. 654.

[77] *Description of the Human Body*, A.T., XI, p. 243.

[78] *Ibid.*, p. 244, emphasis added.

[79] *Discourse on Method*, Fifth Part, A.T., VI, p. 54.

When Descartes offered a summary of his views on man in the *Discourse on Method*, he felt that it was still unable to offer a genetical account of the formation of living substances. In 1639 he told Mersenne that he now knew how to proceed, but nearly ten years later, in 1648, he had not moved much beyond dreaming of success, as we see from the following passage from the *Description of the Human Body*:

> If we had extensive knowledge of all the parts of the seed of some living organism, for instance man, we could deduce, in an entirely rigorous and mathematical way, the shape and structure of each of its organs. Likewise, from a detailed knowledge of the structure, we could deduce what the seed is like.[80]

The human body and all life forms are automata. In principle explaining how they work is merely a matter of accounting for the way they are put together. Descartes is drawing a blank check on the inexhaustable wealth of his mechanical philosophy. The possibility that living organisms grow after a fashion that is far removed from the mere addition of parts to make bigger and better machines is not considered.

Back to Galileo, Falling Bodies and Falling Water

We have seen in Chapter Two how Descartes analyzed the motion of freely falling bodies and how in 1629 he arrived not at the correct law, which states that the distance is proportional to the square of the time elapsed ($s \propto t^2$), but at a different law that would have bodies fall faster than they actually do.[81] Yet five years later in 1634, we find Descartes writing to Mersenne that he has just come across some of his *own* ideas in Galileo's *Dialogue on the Two Chief World Systems*, for instance, the law of free fall, whereby "the distances that heavy bodies traverse when they fall are to each other as the squares of the times."[82]

How can we account for Descartes' lapse of memory? Part of the answer lies in the conceptual revolution that took place in his mind between 1629 and 1634. Up to 1629, his discussion of free fall presupposed: (a) the possibility of the void, and (b) the legitimacy of analyzing the acceleration without committing himself to a determination of the nature of gravity. All that was required was the assumption that the action of gravity (whatever its

---

[80] *Description of the Human Body*, A.T., XI, p. 277. On 20 February 1639, Descartes had informed Mersenne that he believed he could account for the genesis of living bodies (A.T., II, p. 525), but in May 1646, he confided to Princess Elizabeth that he had not got much beyond general principles (A.T., IV, p. 407). See also Descartes' conversation with Burman, 16 April 1648, A.T., V, pp. 170–171.

[81] See above, pp. 26–27.

[82] Letter of Descartes to Mersenne, 14 August 1634, A.T., I, p. 304.

physical nature) was constant and always identical.[83] This was Galileo's position in the *Dialogue* when he replied to the Aristotelian Simplicio, who asserted that gravity was the obvious cause of falling bodies:

> You are wrong, Simplicio; what you ought to say is that every one knows that it is called 'gravity'. What I am asking you for is not the name of the thing, but its essence, of which you know not a bit more than you know about the essence of whatever moves the stars around . . . we do not really understand what principle or what force it is that moves stones downward.[84]

For Descartes the quest for true and certain causes led to a dissatisfaction with merely plausible hypotheses. Around 1630, he saw that he must forego the piecemeal approach of thinkers, such as Mersenne and Galileo, for a more systematic and rigorous approach. In *The World*, he eschewed concepts that could not be defined clearly or were incompatible with contact action, the simple cause that governed all physical change. He rejected the notion of a void as unscientific because it entailed the obscure and magical notion of action at a distance, and he offered a mechanical explanation of gravity or weight. No longer an intrinsic property of matter as the Aristotelians held, nor the result of the attraction of the earth as Beeckman surmised, weight is the result of the pressure exerted by the fine matter that whirls around the earth. The mechanism of free fall is entirely accounted by contact action: there is no occult pushing or pulling.

Free Fall in a Plenum

This conceptual shift invalidated whatever progress had been achieved in the quantitative determination of free fall. With the void went the law that presupposed its possibility. In 1631 Descartes explained the Mersenne: "I do not disown what I said concerning the speed of bodies falling in a void: for given a void, as everyone imagines, the rest can be demonstrated, but I believe it is wrong to suppose a void."[85] Nonetheless, he was confident that he could work out the correct law: "But I believe that I could determine the rate of increase of the speed of a stone not *in vacuo*, but *in hoc vero aere*."[86] This is why when he saw the Galilean law of free fall ($s \propto t^2$) and rashly concluded that it was identical with the one he had formulated in 1629, he felt no urge to pursue the matter but dismissed it as involving the false assumption that the void is possible. He was nonetheless committed to finding the

---

[83] See the letter of Descartes to Mersenne, October or November 1631, *ibid.*, p. 230.

[84] Galileo Galilei, *Dialogue on the Two Chief World Systems*, Second Day, *Opere*, vol. VII, pp. 260–261.

[85] Letter to Mersenne, October or November 1631, A.T., I, p. 228.

[86] *Ibid.*, p. 231.

real law. Several years later in 1637, it still eluded him, and he excused himself to Mersenne by saying:

> it is something that depends on so many others that I could not give you an adequate account in a letter. All I can say is that neither Galileo nor anyone else can determine anything concerning this that will be clear and demonstrative if he does not first know what weight is, and what the true principles of physics are.[87]

But by 1637 Descartes knows what weight is! An entire chapter of *The World* explains it in terms of vortex motion. A terrestrial object is said to have weight because if it is released above the surface of the earth it will be pushed downward by the celestial matter that has greater whirling motion, i.e., greater centrifugal force.[88] But Descartes could not determine the velocity of the celestial whirlpools. In 1640, he confided to Mersenne that the problem was mathematically intractable: "I cannot determine the speed with which each heavy body descends at the beginning for this is merely a factual question that depends on the speed of the fine matter."[89]

Galileo Again

If Descartes never had Galileo's *Dialogue* for more than a couple of days, he acquired his own copy of the *Two New Sciences*. This does not evince a change of heart towards the Italian scientist. Descartes was merely responding to questions that Mersenne had raised. On 29 June 1638, he wrote: "I'll get hold of the book as soon as it is on sale, but only in order to be able to send you my annotated copy, if it is worth it, or at least my comments."[90] By August 23, Descartes had decided that it was not worth it:

> I also have Galileo's book, and I spent a couple of hours leafing through it, but I find so little to fill the margins that I believe I can put all my comments in a very brief letter, and there is no point in sending you my copy.[91]

The promised letter was written in October. The opening paragraph sets the tone for the ensuing remarks:

> I find that in general he philosophizes much better than the usual lot, for he discards as much as possible the errors of the School and strives to examine physical matters with mathematical reasons. In this I am com-

---

87 Letter to Mersenne, June 1637, *ibid.*, p. 392.

88 The action of the twirling celestial matter is described in Chapter Eleven of *The World* (A.T., XI, pp. 72–80), and in Part IV of the *Principles of Philosophy* (A.T., VIII, pp. 212–217). See above, pp. 283–292.

89 Letter to Mersenne, 11 March 1640, A.T., III, p. 36.

90 Letter to Mersenne, around 29 June 1638, A.T., II, p. 194.

91 Letter to Mersenne, 23 August 1638, A.T., III, p. 336.

pletely in agreement with him, and I hold that there is no other way of finding the truth. But I see a serious deficiency in his constant digressions and his failure to stop and explain a question fully. This shows that he has not examined them in order and that, without considering the first causes of nature, he has merely looked for the causes of some particular effects, and so has built without any foundation.

More specifically, what Galileo writes about

> the speed of bodies falling in a void, *etc.* is built without foundation, for he should have determined beforehand what weight is, and if he had done so, he would know that it is nil in a void.[92]

Descartes was more deeply impressed by the *Two New Sciences* than he was willing to let on. Galileo's analysis of motion insinuated itself into his mind, and we shall see it surface in his last fling at the problem of free fall in 1643.

Galilean . . . by Half

Mersenne, who was interested in the mechanical efficiency of water pumps, asked Descartes in 1642 to determine how far water will travel when it is converted into a horizontal jet after falling from a given height. Descartes initially pleaded that he lacked experimental data,[93] but when Huygens joined his entreaties to Mersenne's, he carried out his own experiments in water pipes that he designed for this purpose.[94] He found that when water comes out of a four-foot pipe it goes all the way from B to D (see Figure 20), whereas when it falls from F, one quarter of the original height, it only reaches C. This means that the speed varies as the square root of the height from which it falls (viz. $v \propto s$), and Descartes immediately saw that this implies that $s \propto t^2$.

> It follows that the distance traversed is almost the square of the time, namely, if it falls through one foot in the first minute, it will fall through four feet in the first and second minute taken together.[95]

This statement is followed by a lucid summary of the proof using triangle ABC (see Figure 21) where time is plotted along the axis AB, and speed along the axis BC, with the resulting area, ABC, providing the distance covered. If anything, Descartes' demonstration is more straightforward than Galileo's because he has no hesitation about representing a distance (the height through which the body falls) by an area (the surface of triangle

[92] Letter to Mersenne, 11 October 1638, A.T., II, pp. 380, 385.

[93] Letter of Descartes to Mersenne, 20 October 1642, A.T., III, p. 590.

[94] Letter of Descartes to Huygens, 18 February 1643, *ibid.*, pp. 805–807. See Antonio Nardi, "Descartes 'presque' galiléen: 18 févier 1643," *Revue d'histoire des sciences* 39 (1986), pp. 3–16.

[95] Letter of Descartes to Huygens, 18 February 1643, A.T., III, p. 807.

ABC).[96] It is one of the ironies of the history of science that Descartes' line of reasoning is exactly the one that Beeckman, way back in 1619, read into Descartes' first and infelicitous attempt at finding the law of free fall.[97]

Equally striking is Descartes' acknowledgment that the paths BD and BC (in Figure 20) are parabolas, "as Galileo correctly observed."[98] This is a complete reversal of what he had written to Mersenne in 1638 when he had dismissed Galileo's description of the parabolic trajectory as "idle talk".[99] But his conversion is neither public nor complete. As Descartes develops his explanation, we find him backsliding and unable to dissociate the acceleration of free-falling bodies from the action of weight and surface area. The incriminating passage runs as follows:

> I also notice that from the instant when they begin to descend the cylinders of water (or of any other material) move faster the longer they are, and that their speed is proportional to the square root of their length. This means that a four-foot cylinder will move twice as fast as a one-foot one, and a nine-foot cylinder three times as fast. The same ratio holds for all bodies, namely the greater their diameter, in the direction in which they are descending, the greater their speed. For when the first drop of water comes out of the hole B, the whole cylinder of water FB or AB drops at the same instant, and the latter descends twice as fast as the former. This does not alter the ratios of the triangle [Figure 21] that I considered above, but instead of considering it as a simple surface, we must give it some thickness such as AI or BK [see Figure 22] that stands for the speed that each body has at the first instant of fall. So that if the body is a cylinder four feet long. We must make the side AI twice as broad as if the cylinder were only one foot long, and bear in mind that it covers twice the distance when it falls. The same holds for a drop of water whose diameter is four times that of another drop, namely it will fall twice as fast.[100]

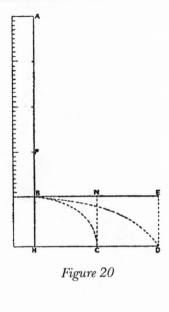

Figure 20

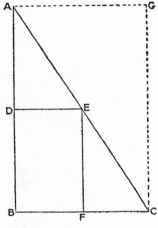

Figure 21

96 *Ibid.*, pp. 807–808. Galileo's demonstration is in the Third Day of his *Two New Sciences* (*Opere*, vol. VIII, pp. 208–212).

97 See above pp. 16–19.

98 Letter of Descartes to Huygens, 18 February 1643, A.T., III, p. 811. This is the only mention of Galileo in the letter.

99 "Il a tout basti en l'air" (letter to Mersenne, 11 October 1638, A.T., II, p. 388).

100 Letter of Descartes to Huygens, 18 February 1643, A.T., III, pp. 809–910.

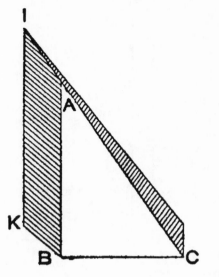

Figure 22

Could the advocate of clarity sail through a denser conceptual fog? Descartes adds a third dimension to the triangle that illustrates free fall, and subverts the principle that $s \propto t^2$ by reintroducing size as a factor in the acceleration of falling bodies. This is at variance with the Galilean Law of Free Fall that he professed to embrace, but it is consistent with his earlier stance, as he had expressed it to Mersenne in 1632:

> What you have sent me about Galileo's calculation of the speed of falling bodies has nothing to do with my philosophy, which maintains that two balls of lead, say of 1 lb. and 100 lbs., would not fall in the same ratio as two balls of wood, also of 1 and 100 lbs., or two balls of lead weighing 2 and 200 lbs. respectively. Galileo does not draw these distinctions which lead me to suspect that he has not arrived at the truth.[101]

Clarity Desired . . . Ambiguity Acquired

Huygens communicated Descartes' letter of 18 February 1643 to Mersenne, who immediately wrote to ask for further clarification. Mersenne's letter is lost, but we can guess what his question was from Descartes' reply in which he reaffirms that size and hence weight play a role in the acceleration of falling bodies:

> I do not believe that a cylinder of wood that is four times as long as another will fall at the same speed (assuming they remain straight when falling). But since this can vary in the air, it would be better to make the experiment with two balls of wood: a large and a smaller one whose diameter is a quarter of the first, and whose weight is one-sixty-fourth. I believe that the small ball will take twice as much time to fall.[102]

Descartes has in mind Proposition 18 of Book 12 of Euclid's *Elements* in which it is demonstrated that the volumes of two spheres stand in the same ratio as the cubes of their diameters ($V_1/V_2 = D^3_1/D^3_2$). This means that when the bodies are homogeneous, as in this case, where both are made of wood, we can neglect the density and only consider the weight. The small ball, whose diameter is as one, weighs 64 times less than the larger ball whose diameter is as four, and takes "twice as much time to fall." Descartes has decidedly veered away from the correct law that says that bodies fall at the same acceleration *regardless of their weight*. Why? The attempt to determine

[101] Letter of Descartes to Mersenne, November or December 1632, A.T., I, p. 261.

[102] Letter of Descartes to Mersenne, 23 March 1643, A.T., III, p. 643.

the speed by appealing to the size or surface of the falling body gives us the clue. Descartes is trying, by hook or by crook, to combine the Galilean Law of Free Fall with his interpretation of weight as the downward motion produced by the impact of the small spheres of the vortex that surrounds the earth. But the mathematics of free fall is at variance with the physics of a plenum. What one part of Descartes' system demands, the other rejects. The result is not only a loss of clarity, but a physics that has forsaken its claim to rigorous mathematization.

Chapter Thirteen

Publish or Perish

ON 22 JULY 1633, Descartes informed Mersenne that *The World* was almost ready for publication, but instead of the book, which he had been promised as a Christmas present, Mersenne received a second letter in December in which he learned that Descartes was thinking of consigning his manuscript to the flames! Descartes' change of heart came after hearing that Galileo's long-awaited book on the motion of the earth had been published, and that all the copies had been seized and burnt.[1] "This surprised me so much," wrote Descartes, "that I have almost decided to burn my papers, or at least to let no one see them."[2] If an Italian, who was close to the Pope, had such treatment meted out to him, what could a Frenchman living among heretics expect? "If the motion of the earth is wrong," pursued Descartes,

> the very foundations of my philosophy are also false, because it obviously follows from them [il se *demonstre par eux evidemment*]. And it is so closely

---

[1] Galileo's *Dialogue on the Two Chief World Systems* issued from the press on 21 February 1632, and was withdrawn from circulation in August of that year, but we do not know how many of the 1,000 copies printed were actually confiscated. Descartes refers to the work as "Galileo's *System of the World*," which is the provisional title that Galileo had given in his *Sidereus Nuncius* of 1610 (Galileo Galilei, *Opere*, A. Favaro, ed. (Florence: Barbèra, 1890–1909), vol. III, pp. 75, 96). Galileo was summoned to Rome, put on trial, compelled to abjure his "errors," and sentenced to imprisonment on 22 June 1633.

[2] Letter of Descartes to Mersenne, end of November 1633, A.T., I, pp. 270–271.

tied to all the other parts of my treatise, that I could not remove it without damaging the rest.[3]

Descartes was convinced that his entire philosophy was a system from which no part could be removed without causing irreparable damage to the whole.[4] The motion of the earth was not merely an important theory, it was entailed by the general circulation of matter in vortices. As he had put it in *The World*: "the matter of the Heavens must not only make the planets rotate around the sun, but also around their own centre."[5] Denying that the earth revolved around the sun was tantamount to arresting all the whirlpools of matter and grinding the universe to a halt.

Descartes' shock and perplexity were heightened by the fact that no copy of Galileo's *Dialogue* had reached the Netherlands by the Summer of 1633. The first copy arrived in the summer of the following year, and was lent by the Amsterdam professor Hortensius to Beeckman, who showed it to Descartes when he visited him over the weekend of 12–14 August 1634.[6] Notification of Galileo's condemnation was given in a document dated from Liège on 20 September 1633, signed by the Nuncio to Cologne and Lower Germany. It declared that the Cardinal Inquisitors had judged that the motion of the earth was "opposed to Scripture," and that Galileo was "vehemently suspect of heresy" for teaching it.[7] At the beginning of 1634, Descartes heard from Mersenne that his last letters had not reached him, and he wrote again repeating the distressing news about Galileo, but no longer suggesting that he might burn his own work. He was resolved, however, "never to show it to anyone," since the motion of the earth was part and

---

[3] *Ibid.*, p. 271.

[4] "My theories are so closely joined and depend so much on one another, that one cannot be understood without knowing them all" (letter of Descartes to Fr. Vatier, around 22 February 1638, *ibid.*, p. 562); "if what I have written about that [the circulation of the blood], or refraction, or anything about which I have published more than three lines, is wrong, then I am willing to have people say that the rest of my philosophy is worthless" (letter to Mersenne, 9 February 1639, A.T., II, p. 501).

[5] *The World*, Ch. 10, A.T., XI, p. 69.

[6] On 13 August 1633, Gassendi wrote to Hortensius (Martin van den Hove), a professor of mathematics and astronomy in Amsterdam, "no copy of the book has reached you, and there is little hope that one will soon do" (Pierre Gassendi, *Opera*, 6 vols. (Lyon, 1658), facsimile (Stuttgart-Bad Cannstatt: Olms, 1964), vol. 6, p. 64*b*). Nicolas-Claude Fabri de Peiresc promised Hortensius a copy on 24 January 1634, but he had not yet received it when he wrote to Peiresc on 2 June 1634 (see Marin Mersenne, *Correspondance*, 17 vols. (Paris: CNRS, 1933–1988), vol. II, p. 165). Beeckman in the Summer of 1634 made frequent trips from Dordrecht to Amsterdam to improve his skill in polishing lenses. This is how, working with an English spectacle-maker in Amsterdam, close to the Dam, he called on Descartes on 12 August 1634. "Mr. Beeckman," Descartes wrote to Mersenne on 14 August, "came here Saturday evening and let me have Galileo's book, but he took it back to Dort this morning so that I only had it in my hands for 30 hours" (A.T., I, pp. 303–304).

[7] The document is quoted in Descartes' letter to Mersenne of 14 August 1634, A.T., I, p. 306.

parcel of his natural philosophy, and if it was wrong, the everything was wrong.[8]

The Price of Peace and Quiet

The condemnation of Galileo distressed Descartes for personal, religious, and philosophical reasons. Having chosen the privacy and seclusion of life in a foreign country, he dreaded being drawn into a prolonged and probably indecisive argument over the heliocentric theory. "My motto," he told Mersenne, is, "He who lives in obscurity, lives happily,"[9] and he insisted that all he wished was "peace and quiet."[10] But beyond his desire to avoid the unpleasantness of public controversy, Descartes was actuated by genuine religious scruples. No sooner had he heard that the motion of the earth had been censured that he wrote to Mersenne, "for nothing in the world would I wish to write something in which even one word was disapproved by the Church,"[11] and we find him repeating the same sentiment in several of his letters.[12] But the real difficulty was philosophical. His physics was allegedly based on self-evident principles, and the rug had been pulled from under his feet. There was no point in publishing yet another arbitrary conjecture: "There are already so many plausible philosophical opinions over which one can argue, that if my own are not more certain and cannot be accepted without discussion, I do not want them ever to be published."[13]

But Descartes was not so fainthearted as to abandon his *World* without a fight. Is an injunction emanating from the Holy Office in Rome really binding? he asked Mersenne:

> To the best of my knowledge neither the Pope nor a Council has ratified the condemnation that was made by the Congregation of Cardinals established to censor books. I would be happy to know what view is held in France, and whether their authority was enough to make it an article of faith.[14]

Descartes had, nonetheless, been trained by the Jesuits, and he did not share the Gallican leanings of many of his contemporaries, including Pascal. He would have considered it against his convictions, as well as beneath his dignity, to play games with the spiritual authority of the Church. When

---

[8] Letter of Descartes to Mersenne, around February 1634, *ibid.*, p. 285.

[9] *"bene vixit, bene qui latuit"* (*ibid.*, p. 286).

[10] Letters to Mersenne, around February 1634, *ibid.*, pp. 212, 285–286.

[11] Letter to Mersenne, end of November 1633, *ibid.*, p. 271.

[12] For instance, Descartes writes that he wishes "to obey the Church in all things" (letter to Mersenne, around February 1634, *ibid.*, p. 281). See also *ibid.*, p. 285; A.T., V, pp. 544, 550.

[13] Letter of Descartes to Mersenne, end of November 1633, A.T., I, pp. 271–272.

[14] Letter to Mersenne, around February 1634, *ibid.*, p. 281. The Council that Descartes has in mind is an Ecumenical Council.

Mersenne reported how lightly some French scientists took the matter, Descartes made this clear:

> I know that it can be said that what the Roman Inquisitors have decided is not automatically an article of faith, and that it requires the approval of the Council. But I am not so fond of my own ideas that I would be willing to make such excuses to go on maintaining them.[15]

For several years Descartes thought that silence was the more prudent and honorable course. In the *Discourse on Method* published in 1637, he did not breathe a word about the motion of the earth. To Mersenne, he confided that he hoped that it would turn out to be like the antipodes, once condemned, and now quite uncontroversial.[16]

Towards a Peaceful Compromise

Silence weighed heavily on Descartes, and in 1640 when he began revising *The World* for publication in textbook form as the *Principles of Philosophy*, he renewed his enquiries in the hope that the opposition of some Protestants to the motion of the earth might persuade Catholics that it was right. Unwilling to appear too anxious or too concerned, Descartes used Mersenne to elicit information from Rome. Cardinal Giovanni Francesco Guidi di Bagno, whom Descartes had met in Paris in 1627, had taken Gabriel Naudé to the Eternal City, and Descartes requested Mersenne to inform Naudé that the only thing that had stopped him from publishing his physics was the prohibition of the movement of the earth. Would Naudé, he asked,

> please sound the Cardinal on this topic, because I am his humble servant and would be most unhappy to give him any displeasure, just as I am very zealous for the Catholic religion and reverence all its leaders. I do not add that I have no desire to risk their censure, for I do not fear that one truth can clash with another, and I believe most firmly both in the infallibility of the Church and the validity of my arguments.[17]

[15] Letter to Mersenne, around February 1634, *ibid.*, p. 285. Priests, such as Pierre Gassendi and Ismaël Boulliau (a convert from Protestantism), were Copernicans. In a letter to Mersenne on 16 December 1644, Boulliau considers the condemnation of the motion of the earth a purely Italian affair (Marin Mersenne, *Correspondance*, vol. XIII, p. 20).

[16] Letter to Mersenne, around February 1634, A.T., I, p. 288. At the beginning of the fourth century, Lactantius, tutor to the son of the Emperor Constantine, devoted a chapter of his *Divine Institutions* to heaping ridicule on the existence of the antipodes, and the silly idea that there are people whose feet are above their heads, or places where rain and snow fall upwards. Lactantius' cosmology never became official Church doctrine, but it was given notoriety by being quoted (as an instance of naive beliefs) in Copernicus' prefatory letter to his *De Revolutionibus Orbium Caelestium* of 1543 (see J.L.E. Dreyer, *A History of Astronomy from Thales to Kepler* (Cambridge, 1906), reprint (New York: Dover, 1953), p. 209).

[17] Letter of Descartes to Mersenne, December 1640, A.T., III, pp. 258–259. It is in this letter that Descartes writes: "I am not unhappy that some [Protestant] minorities thunder against

In another letter we learn that Descartes was also awaiting a reply from "a Cardinal, my friend from many years back, who was a member of the Congregation that condemned Galileo."[18] This was Cardinal Francesco Barberini, the nephew of Urban VIII, who had been Papal Legate to France during Descartes' Parisian years.[19]

Relativizing Motion . . . and Its Censors

We do not know what Cardinal Guidi di Bagno or Cardinal Francesco Barberini replied to Descartes' queries, but they probably confirmed that the Copernican theory could be used as a working hypothesis provided it was not endorsed as physically true. This may not have been enough for Descartes the scientist, but it gave Descartes the epistemologist a clue. In a world where everything is on the move, rest (but also motion) is relativized. In 1641 or shortly thereafter, Descartes realized that this enabled him to reformulate his astronomical hypothesis in a way that the censors (assuming that they were not over-zealous) would allow to slip by.

We have already seen that motion for Descartes is local motion, commonly described as "the action by which a body passes from one place to another."[20] But this definition, argues Descartes, is infelicitous because it introduces the idea of action as though "more action is required for motion than for rest," which is a serious prejudice. We must eliminate the obscure notions of force and action, and use only the perfectly intelligible one of translation or displacement. Hence a second, more correct and more rigorous definition of motion reads:

> the translation of a part of matter or of a body from the neighbourhood of those that touch it immediately, and which we may consider as at rest, into the neighbourhood of some others . . . . And I emphasize the *translation*, not the force or action that transports, to show that it is always in the body that is being moved, not in the one that moves.[21]

It is difficult not to agree with Alexandre Koyré that Descartes framed this relativistic definition of motion at least partly to reconcile the mobility of

---

the motion of the earth; this may convince our preachers that it is right" (p. 258). Earlier, in a letter of 16 October 1639 to the same correspondent, he had written: "I have to complain that the Huguenots hate me as a Papist, and that those of Rome do not love me because they think I am tainted with the heresy of the movement of the earth" (A.T., II, p. 593).

18 Letter of Descartes, undated, to an unknown correspondent, A.T., V, p. 544.

19 Francesco Barberini (1597–1679) was the *legato a latere* in France in 1624–1625 to discuss terms of peace during the war of the Valtellina. He was a member of the Congregation of ten Cardinals that condemned Galileo, but his signature does not appear on the sentence.

20 *Principles of Philosophy*, Part II, art. 24, A.T., VIII–1, p. 53.

21 *Ibid.*, art. 25, pp. 53–54.

the earth with the official doctrine of the Church,[22] but it can also be seen, more interestingly, as a logical development of one side of his philosophy. Since matter is extension, and extension is space, matter is not *in* space but *is* space. Descartes expresses this by identifying material substance with *internal* place.[23] But this does not preclude a consideration of bodies as they are related to other, *external* places. In this sense, a body can share in several motions, for instance, a watch, whose cog-wheels are moving according to their own laws, can be carried by someone pacing the deck of a ship that is sailing on the ocean of a moving earth. "All these movements," writes Descartes,

> are really in the cog-wheels, but because it is not easy to understand so many together, or even to know how many there are, it is enough if we consider only the motion that is proper to each body.[24]

This proper motion is by definition the one that we observe against the background of the neighboring bodies that we choose as our arbitrary point of reference. But we could just as well consider the body at rest and the neighboring bodies to be in motion. There are no fixed points in the universe except those that we decide upon. If we then ask what meaning we can attach to the phrase, "the earth moves around the sun," in the light of the foregoing analysis, we can truthfully reply that the earth and the planets *rest* in their fluid skies, but that the skies themselves are moving "just like a boat that has lifted anchor (and is moved by neither wind nor oars) rests in the sea although it is insensibly carried along by the tide."[25]

Having contented the censors, Descartes did not go on to satisfy the physicists by showing how his new and entirely relative definition of motion agreed with the laws and rules of motion in Part III of his *Principles of Philosophy*. If all motion is relative and all translation reciprocal, we have the curious situation that Rule 4 (see Figure 12 in Chapter Twelve above, p. 297) can be converted into Rule 7(a) by a simple and legitimate change of frame of reference. Instead of having body m_1 bounce off stationary body m_2, both will now move in the same direction. What is changed is not only the description of the phenomena but the phenomena themselves! Neither Descartes nor any of his contemporaries saw matters as clearly, but Henry More was sufficiently intrigued to ask Descartes to comment on wind blowing through the open windows of a tower. What would it mean in this case to

---

[22] Alexandre Koyré, *Galileo Studies*, John Mepham, trans. (Atlantic Highlands, New Jersey: Humanities Press, 1978), p. 265.

[23] "In the thing itself, there is no difference between space or internal place and the corporeal substance that is contained in it. The difference is entirely in the way we conceive them" (*Principles of Philosophy*, Part II, art. 10, A.T., VIII-1, p. 45).

[24] *Ibid.*, art. 31, p. 57.

[25] *Ibid.*, Part III, art. 26, p. 90. The Latin text merely says "a hidden motion" of the sea. The French version specifies the action of the tides. (A.T., IX-2, p. 113).

speak of the reciprocity of translation, or to say that the motion of the wind is relative? Descartes' unease may be surmised from his avoidance of More's example in his reply. Instead, he shifts the argument by proposing an illustration of his own. Let us consider, he says, a small boat trapped in the mud near the shore with one person on board. A friend offers to push *from* the shore while the person in the boat pushes *against* the shore:

> If the strength (*vires*) of these men is equal, the effort of the man on the shore (who is therefore connected to the land) does not contribute less to the motion of the boat than the effort of the other man who is transported with the boat. Hence it is clear that the action whereby the boat recedes from the shore is as much in the land as in the boat.[26]

Descartes has, perhaps unwittingly, shifted the discussion from the motion to the force (*vires*) or action that produces it. He seems to have forgotten that he had introduced his definition of motion to eliminate the obscure notion of force in favor of the perfectly intelligible one of translation or displacement.[27] When More pressed him, Descartes interpreted the moving force (*vis movens*) as ultimately the "force of God himself conserving as much translation in matter as he put it in at the first instant of creation," something he claims to have shied away from stating in his published works, "lest I should appear to favour the opinion of those who consider God as the cosmic soul that is joined to matter."[28] However laudable we may find this theological delicacy, it does little or nothing to explain how the relativity of motion can be made consistent with the principle of conservation of motion, since the amount of motion depends on the purely arbitrary frame of reference that is chosen.

Rest Force

Matters are further complicated by Descartes' attempt in the *Principles of Philosophy* to spell out the implications of his First Law and the notion of matter as inert. The notion of a "rest-force" does not appear as such in *The World* except as an implicit consequence of the First Law and a tacit element in the theory of hardness presented in Chapter Three.[29] Descartes does not specify in *The World* how the force maintaining a body at rest is to be measured or even understood. The first explicit mention of a force to remain at rest occurs in 1640 in a letter to Mersenne:

[26] Letter of Descartes to Henry More, 15 April 1649, A.T., V, p. 346, replying to More's letter of 5 March 1649, *ibid.*, p. 312.

[27] "I am talking about the translation, not about the force or action that transports" (*Principles of Philosophy*, Part II, art. 25, A.T., VIII–1, p. 54).

[28] Draft of letter of Descartes to More, around August, 1649, A.T., V, pp. 403–404, replying to More's letter of 23 July 1649, *ibid.*, p. 384.

[29] *The World*, Ch. 3, A.T., XI, pp. 12–13. See pp. 254–255 above.

it is certain that from the sole fact that a body has begun to move, it has in it the force to continue to move, and also, from the sole fact that it has stopped in a certain place, it has the force to remain there.[30]

After stating the three laws of motion in Part II of the *Principles of Philosophy*, Descartes devotes a special article (art. 43) to show "In what consists the force of each body to act and to resist." Rest is a state on the same ontological level as motion. A quiescent body, he writes, has "a certain force" that makes it persevere in its state of rest and consequently resist any attempt to set it in motion. How that force can be measured is indicated in the last sentence of article 43:

> That force can be estimated from the size of the body in which it is, the surface separating the body from another, the speed of motion, and the nature and contrariety of the ways in which different bodies collide with one another.[31]

The notion of a "rest force" leads to such absurdities as Rule 4 and the claim that a smaller body can never move a larger one, but article 43 also contains Descartes' closest approximation to a recognition of the vectorial aspect of motion. Indeed, he writes that a *body at rest* has a force to persevere in its state of rest, and a *moving body* a force "to persevere in its state, that is, in motion at the same speed and *towards the same direction*."[32] The notion of direction never gains more than this fleeting acknowledgment, and "rest-force" and "motion-force" are measured in the same way as the product of size *x* speed. The word size in itself offers difficulties, since it cannot be identified with Newton's concept of mass, and it is ambiguous because of Descartes' identification of matter and extension. He sometimes speaks as though it could be measured by the quantity of the third element or tangible matter, but he also says as in article 43 that the surface has to be taken into consideration. Crucial is the notion of the "inertia" or natural sluggishness of matter that Descartes had to reinterpret to preclude the possibility that matter resists motion as such. To a correspondent he wrote in 1648:

> And since, if two unequal bodies both receive the same amount of motion, the equal quantity of motion does not give as much speed to the larger as it gives to the smaller, we can say in this sense that the more matter a body contains the more natural inertia it has; to which we can add that a body which is large can transfer its motion to other bodies more easily than a small one, and that it can be moved by them less easily. So that there is a

[30] Letter to Mersenne, 28 October 1640, A.T., III, p. 213.

[31] *Principles of Philosophy*, Part II, art. 43, A.T., VIII–1, p. 67. On the profusion and polysemanticity of "force" in Descartes' writings, see R.S. Westfall, *Force in Newton's Physics*, Appendix B: Descartes' Usage of Force (London: Macdonald, 1971), pp. 529–534.

[32] *Principles of Philosophy*, Part II, art. 43, A.T., VIII–1, pp. 66–67, emphasis added.

sort of inertia which depends on the quantity of matter, and another which depends on the extension of its surface.[33]

In other words, the reality behind the usage of a word, such as "inertia," is not a natural resistance to motion but the role played by the quantity of matter in transmitting or receiving motion. But the solution, as R.S. Westfall points out, ignores dynamic considerations, and when Descartes turned to cases of impact, as in the notorious Rule 4, he surreptitiously reintroduced a resistance to motion that cannot be reconciled with the complete inertness of matter.[34]

Life in the Netherlands

The Roman decision to ban books on the motion of the earth was a hard blow, but the Netherlands were geographically and theologically at a safe distance from Rome, and Descartes was free to continue the life of leisurely research that he had embarked upon.[35]

When the French artisan Ferrier had declined to join Descartes in Franeker, Descartes moved to Amsterdam and then to Leyden where he met Jacob Gool or Golius, who had recently returned from a four-year trip to the Middle East to take up the chair of mathematics vacated by Snell at his death in 1626. Golius exercised a profound influence on the shape Descartes' mathematics was to take by drawing his attention to an unsolved problem in the Greek mathematician Pappus. Descartes found the solution to this problem, and it became the centerpiece and prize illustration of his *Geometry* when it was published in 1637. Descartes also struck up a friendship with another professor of mathematics at the University of Leyden, Frans Van Schooten, whose son, also called Frans, was to draw the diagrams for Des-

---

[33] Letter to an unknown correspondent, probably in March or April 1648, A.T., V, p. 136, emphasis added. The addressee could be the Marquis of Newcastle as suggested in *ibid.*, p. 133, but Jean de Silhon is a more likely candidate as is argued in *ibid.*, p. 660.

[34] Westfall, *Force in Newton's Physics*, p. 69. For a succinct account of Newton's subsequent transformation of Cartesian inertia, see I. Bernard Cohen, *The Newtonian Revolution* (Cambridge: Cambridge University Press, 1980), pp. 182–193.

[35] The main source of information about Descartes' life in Holland are the numerous letters that he wrote mainly to French correspondents. These are collected in the first five volumes of A.T. The reprint (Paris: Vrin, 1969–1974) contains several letters of Constantin Huygens that were only discovered after the first edition. Adrien Baillet, *La Vie de Monsieur Des-Cartes*, 2 vols., (Paris, 1691: reprint, Geneva: Slatkine, 1970) is indispensable. In the twentieth century, Charles Adam, *Vie et Oeuvres de Descartes* (Vol. XII of the *Oeuvres de Descartes*), Gustave Cohen, *Ecrivains Français en Hollande dans la première moitié du XVIIe siècle* (Paris: Champion, 1920), and Cornelia Louis Thijssen-Schoute, *Nederlands Cartesianisme* (Amsterdam: N.V. Noord-Hollandsche Uitgevers Maatschappij, 1954) have shed additional light on Descartes and his Dutch friends and foes. A collection of useful essays is to be found in *Descartes et le cartésianisme hollandais* (Paris: Presses Universitaires de France, and Amsterdam: Editions Françaises d'Amsterdam, 1950).

cartes' *Optics* and translate the *Geometry* into Latin. Later, Descartes became acquainted with the professor of medicine and botany, Adolfus Vorstius, the Professor of Hebrew, Constantin L'Empereur, and two professors of theology, Adriaan Heereboord and Abraham Heidanus. A Catholic physician who tended the sick without charge, Cornelius Hogelande, became a close friend and dedicated to Descartes his treatise on God and the immortality of the soul. In 1632, at the home of Golius, Descartes met Constantin Huygens, the secretary of the Prince of Orange, and he was subsequently a frequent guest of Huygens at The Hague. The two men became intimate and carried on an important correspondence on scientific matters.

In Huygens' house, Descartes made several acquaintances, notably Huygens' sister Constantia and her husband David le Leu de Wilhem, who became Descartes' financial adviser. He must have been a shrewd businessman because Descartes' affairs were managed in such a way that he was able to live in what for a modern university professor would be opulence. Descartes was also introduced to Huygens' five children. The second Christiaan, was to become one of the greatest scientists of the second half of the century, and Descartes was quick to recognize his exceptional gifts and declare that he was "of his kin."[36]

In 1631 or 1632, Descartes took up lodgings in the Kalverstraat in Amsterdam. He was interested in medicine, and he was delighted when the physician Johann Elichman introduced him to Vopiscus-Fortunatus Plemp or Plempius, who was soon to be appointed professor of anatomy, and subsequently became rector of the University of Louvain. Six years later, when he resided in Santpoort, Descartes made dissections of eels, cods, dogs, and rabbits. He used the results of his study of the anatomy of the eye of a bull in his *Optics*. He also took great interest in botany and planted rare seeds sent to him by French correspondents. Although Descartes had yet to publish, his reputation was growing, and he began to have disciples. The first was Henri Régnier or Reneri, who was three years his senior. Reneri, who was born near Liège, had been compelled to teach for his livelihood when his family disowned him after his conversion from Catholicism to Protestantism. Descartes placed high hopes in him, and when Reneri was appointed professor of philosophy at the College of Deventer, Descartes went to live in the same town from May or June 1632 until the end of 1633 when he returned to Amsterdam. In 1634, Reneri was promoted to a chair of philosophy at the Academy of Utrecht (which became a university two years later), and the following year Descartes moved to that city to be close to him.

On 7 August 1635 Descartes returned to Deventer for the christening of his daughter, Francine, born on the nineteenth of the previous month. We know little of the mother beyond the fact that she was called Hijlena Jans, and that she was a Protestant since the child was baptised in the local Calvinist church. Baillet quotes a manuscript in Descartes' handwriting, which was subsequently lost, in which he recorded that Francine was con-

[36] Letter of Constantin Huygens to Princess Elizabeth, 31 December 1653, A.T., X, p. 651.

ceived in Amsterdam on Sunday, 20 October 1634.[37] In all likelihood Hijlena or Hélène, as he calls her, was his housekeeper. Descartes was greatly attached to his daughter, whom he referred to as his "niece,"[38] and the saddest moment of his life was her untimely death at the tender age of five on 7 September 1640. Nothing is known of what subsequently happened to the mother of the little girl.

Publishing . . . . a Little

As we have seen, in 1634 Descartes was shocked by the news of the condemnation of Galileo, and he resolved to keep mum, at least as far as the motion of the earth was concerned. He was anxious, however, to publish the law of refraction that he had communicated to Golius and Mersenne as early as 1632.[39] He detached his *Optics* from his general treatise, revised it, and read part of it to Huygens when he visited him in the Spring of 1635.[40] During the summer he decided to add his explanation of the rainbow and an account of atmospheric phenomena, such as lightning and clouds, in a treatise that he called by the customary name of *Meteorology* [*Les météores*]. In October 1635 Huygens suggested that Descartes contact the publishing house of the Elzeviers or that of William Jansz Blaeu.[41] The Elzeviers had just published a Latin translation of Galileo's *Dialogue on the Two Chief World Systems*, but the printing had been carried out in Strasbourg not in their headquarters in Leyden. Indeed, Leyden was unsafe throughout 1635: between 23 June and 31 December, 14,582 persons died of the plague there. The Elzeviers made themselves difficult ("they wanted to be begged"),[42] and Descartes finally reached an agreement with another Leyden publisher, Jan Maire.

Descartes originally intended to publish only the *Optics* and the *Meteorology*, but by March 1636, he had decided to add the *Geometry*, which he only wrote, however, when the *Meteorology* was in press at the end of 1636.[43] He apprised Mersenne that the general title of the book was to be: *"The Plan of a Universal Science which Is Capable of Raising our Nature to Its Highest Degree of*

---

[37] Adrien Baillet, *La Vie de Monsieur Des-Cartes*, vol. II, pp. 89–90.

[38] Letter of Descartes to an unknown correspondent, 30 August 1637, A.T., I, p. 393. Descartes had seven nieces; the three daughters of his eldest brother, Pierre, and the four daughters of his sister married to Roger du Crévy. They all resided in France and never visited their uncle, but the word niece was useful as a cloak.

[39] See Descartes' letter to Mersenne, June 1632, A.T., I, pp. 255–256, and to Golius, around 2 February 1632, *ibid.*, pp. 237–242.

[40] Letter of Descartes to Golius, 16 April 1635, A.T., I, p. 315, and to Huygens, 1 November 1635, *ibid.*, p. 591. Huygens was in Amsterdam from 29 March to 6 April.

[41] Letter of Huygens to Descartes, 28 October 1635, *ibid.*, pp. 588–589.

[42] Letter of Descartes to Mersenne, around March 1636, *ibid.*, p. 338.

[43] "I practically composed the treatise while the *Meteorology* was being printed, and I even discovered part of it at the time" (letter of Descartes to a priest, perhaps Fr. Jean Derienes, S.J., in the Autumn of 1637 or in February 1638, *ibid.*, p. 456).

Perfection, with the Optics, the Meteorology, and the Geometry, in which the Author, to Give Proof of the Universal Science that He Proposes, Explains the Most Singular Topics He Could Choose in Such a Way that Even Those Who Have Never Studied Can Understand Them. "[44] When Mersenne raised objections, Descartes modified the title and gave a fuller account of his intent:

> I did not put *Treatise on Method* but *Discourse on Method*, which amounts to the same as *Preface* or *Note Concerning the Method*, in order to show that I do not intend to teach a method but only to speak about one. For, as can be seen from what I say, it consists much more in practice than in theory. I call the treatises following it *Essays in this Method* because I claim that what they contain could not have been discovered without it, and they enable us to recognize its value. And I have included a certain amount of metaphysics, physics and medicine in the introductory Discourse in order to show that the method extends to every kind of subject-matter.[45]

Despite his claim that the three treatises illustrate the methodology proposed in the *Discourse on Method*, the explanation of the rainbow is the only concrete instance where Descartes states that his results are the direct outcome of the application of his method.

Descartes spent the best part of 1636 and the first months of 1637 supervising the drawing of the numerous figures and seeing the book through the press. Claude Saumaise, a fellow expatriate, wrote to a correspondent in Paris that Descartes was in hiding and seldom showed himself.[46] Little did he realise that Descartes still had to write the *Geometry* and the *Discourse on Method* after the *Optics* was finally sent to the printer's in the Summer of 1636.[47] In the contract that he signed with Jan Maire, Descartes agreed to obtain a "privilege" or copyright for the book in France.[48] On 1 January 1637, he asked Huygens, as his New Year gift, to forward some galleys to Mersenne in the diplomatic pouch to avoid delays.[49] All Descartes wanted was to protect the interest of his Dutch publisher, and he intended

---

[44] Letter of Descartes to Mersenne, around March 1636, *ibid.*, p. 339.

[45] Letter of Descartes to Mersenne, March or April 1637, *ibid.*, p. 349.

[46] Letter of Claude de Saumaise to Jacques du Puy, 4 April 1637, *ibid.*, p. 365, note.

[47] At the beginning of March 1637, Descartes informed Huygens that he had not finished writing the *Discourse on Method, ibid.*, p. 623). It was printed, however, by 22 March (*ibid.*, p. 624). The treatises have a continuous pagination: *Optics* (pp. 1–153), *Meteorology* (pp. 155–294), and *Geometry* (pp. 295–413). The *Discourse*, although placed at the beginning is paginated separately (pp. 1–78). The table of contents at the end of the book only refers to the three treatises. The *Discourse* is not mentioned.

[48] The contract that was signed between Descartes and Jan Maire is published in Gustave Cohen, *Ecrivains français en Hollande* (Paris: Edouard Champion, 1920), pp. 503–504.

[49] Letter of Descartes to Huygens, 1 January 1637, A.T., I, pp. 615–616. We learn from this letter that Descartes feared postal delays of up to three months. The normal time would seem to have been ten to twelve days for letters coming from Paris (*ibid.*, pp. 128, 135–136).

the book to be anonymous. Mersenne, who had already given the work advance publicity in his *Harmonie Universelle*, saw things in a different light and requested a "privilege" that not only named Descartes but contained a fulsome praise of his achievements, and called upon him to publish more. All this took time, and the copyright was only granted on 4 May 1637 with the result that the book, which was ready at the end of March, only appeared on 8 June 1637. Descartes had excised his name from the copyright, and the pretense (however hollow) of anonymity was kept up.

Descartes, now 41 years old, held his first book in his hands, and he promptly despatched the 200 free copies he had received to dignitaries and high officials as well as scientists and philosophers. Cartesianism was launched! But all was not to be plain sailing. For one thing, the Jesuits, from whom Descartes expected warm approval, greeted the book with rather cautious praise, obviously conditioned by fear of seeming to approve a whole new system of philosophy when they had only been shown a small part.[50] A Roman bookseller agreed to purchase a dozen copies provided "the motion of the earth was not mentioned," but as soon as he saw them, he wanted to send them back.[51] Descartes had been sanguine in his expectations. The contract stipulated that Jan Maire could publish up to 3,000 copies in two successive runs, but Descartes took all the risks, since he agreed to buy the unsold copies. We do not know how many copies were actually printed, but Descartes admitted to Mersenne in January 1639 that few had been sold.[52] He had probably swamped the market with the 200 copies he distributed. Nonetheless, he had the *Discourse on Method*, the *Optics*, and the *Meteorology* translated into Latin by Etienne de Courcelles, a French Protestant minister who lived in Amsterdam. These appeared along with the *Principles of Philosophy* in 1644. The *Geometry*, translated by Franz Van Schooten the Younger, was only published in 1649.

Odium Mathematicum

Descartes was sensitive to any criticism, however implied, of his *Geometry*. He was particularly annoyed by Johan Jansz Stampioen (called de Jonghe (the Young) because he bore the same name as his father) with whom he had had a short passage of arms as early as 1633.[53] In 1638 Stampioen published a placard containing a mathematical problem and challenging mathematicians, as was the wont, to solve it. In further placards he gave his own

---

[50] Descartes expressed his disappointment to Mersenne: "The excuse of those who tell you that they cannot make objections because I do not state my principles is a mere pretext and not a valid reason" (letter to Mersenne, 15 November 1638, A.T., II, pp. 424–425).

[51] Letter of Descartes to Mersenne, 19 June 1639, *ibid.*, p. 565.

[52] Letter of Descartes to Mersenne, 9 January 1639, *ibid.*, p. 481.

[53] Letter of Descartes to Stampioen, end of 1633, A.T., I, pp. 275–279.

solution, which he claimed to be the only one possible, and he announced the imminent publication of his *Algebra or New Method* in which the general method of the extraction of cube-roots would be demonstrated.[54] Descartes took umbrage at the title and interpreted Stampioen's book as a challenge to his own *Discourse on Method*. He was so upset that he spent more than a year putting Stampioen down, and even threatened to leave the Netherlands should he fail.[55] Descartes helped a young mathematician from Utrecht, Jacob Van Wassenaer, write a damning review of Stampioen's book when it appeared at the end of 1638. Stampioen replied by challenging Wassenaer to solve a test problem for a forfeit of 600 gulden. Wassenaer, with Descartes' financial backing, accepted the wager. The problem was solved by Descartes and copied by Wassenaer, but the four professors who had been appointed as judges were in no great haste to decide on the matter. "Why, the whole thing could be settled in less than fifteen minutes!" fumed Descartes.[56] Wassenaer was finally declared the victor in May 1639, and Descartes proceeded to publish (in Dutch and always under Wassenaer's name) what he considered an indispensable vindication of his honor. It bore the contemptuous title, *The Ignorant Mathematician: I. I. Stampioen Exposed*.[57] Nonetheless Stampioen was far from being a "charlatan" as Descartes called him. He was a gifted mathematician and a first-rate teacher, who was preceptor to the future Prince William II, to Princess Elizabeth of Bohemia, and later to the sons of Constantin Huygens, Descartes' intimate friend.

A New Home

After the publication of the *Discourse on Method*, Descartes left Leyden for Alkmaar, then for Santport near Haarlem where he rented a house with a garden. He spent much of his leisure experimenting on plants and dissecting animals. Through Huygens, a devout Protestant, Descartes, a practicing Catholic, was put in touch with two priests of the neighboring city of Haarlem: Johann Albert Ban (Bannius) and Augustin Bloemaert. They were interested in musical theory and invited Descartes to choral and instrumental concerts in Haarlem. Huygens encouraged their research as part of his

---

[54] Stampioen D'Ionghe, *Algebra ofte Nieuve Stel-Regel, waer door alles ghevanden wordt, inde Wis-Konst, wat vindtbaer ist. Novt door desen bekendt* (The Hague, 1639). The book was printed by the author.

[55] Descartes was taken up by the Stampioen Affair from October 1639, if not earlier, until October 1640 (A.T., II, pp. 611–613, II, p. 16, and p. 200, *n. b*). Huygens, in a letter of 14 August 1640, took Descartes' "disgust" so seriously that he wrote to entreat him not to leave the Netherlands (A.T., III, p. 756). On 27 August, Descartes reassured him of his fondness for the Dutch with whom he hoped to pass not only this life but the next (*ibid.*, p. 759). For an account of the involved dispute, see Bierens de Haan, *Bouwstoffen Voor de Geschiedenis der Wis-en Natuurkundige Wetenschappen in de Nederlanden* (Leyden, 1887), vol. II, pp. 383–433.

[56] Letter of Descartes to Golius, 3 April 1640, A.T., III, p. 58.

[57] *Der on-wissen Wis-konstenaer I.-I. Stampioenus ontdeckt* (Leyden, 1640).

program of enhancing church music. He was himself a strong advocate of organs in Protestant churches and sent Descartes his pamphlet on the subject.[58]

Descartes was as reticent as ever about giving his address to correspondents who might pass it on to others without authorization. He even declined to give it to Mersenne (whose forte was not discretion), and asked that all his letters be sent to Bloemaert. Descartes' house was not located at any great distance, since one day, as he was sealing a letter, he decided to find out first whether any letters had arrived for him. He despatched a servant to Haarlem and upon his return had time to reply on the same day to the three letters that had been brought.[59]

In 1641 Descartes took up residence in the Castle of Endegeest, in Oegstgeest, just outside Leyden. Here he was visited in 1642 by another French expatriate, Samuel Sorbière, who has left us a vivid description of the location and of Descartes' life-style:

> He lived in a small castle, pleasantly situated, at the door of a large and fine University, three leagues from the Court, and less than two hours from the Sea. He had a sufficient number of well-trained and comely servants, an attractive garden at the end of which was an orchard, and fields all around. Spires of varying heights could be seen in the distance dwindling to mere points on the horizon. A day's journey by boat on the canals took him to Utrecht, Delft, Roterdam, Dordrecht, Haarlem, and occasionally Amsterdam where he had two thousand pounds in the bank. He could spend half the day at The Hague, and return home by the most beautiful road in the world, passing fields and summer houses, and then a forest that borders the town.[60]

Friends and Pupils

Descartes was never a perfect recluse. In Santport he had played host to Huygens, Reneri, and several others including his former servant, Jean Gillot, to whom he had taught his new geometry and who became, in Descartes' own words, one of the few who understood it perfectly. Gillot taught mathematics at the Engineering School of Leyden and was frequently commissioned by Descartes to answer critics of his *Geometry*. At one point he was considered for a position in Paris (to the horror of his devout Huguenot parents), and Descartes sent the following testimonial:

> He is entirely trustworthy, very bright, and naturally pleasant. He speaks French and Flemish and knows some Latin and English. He has a thor-

---

[58] Letter of Huygens to Descartes, 114 August 1640, A.T., III, pp. 756–757. The work was published by the Elzeviers in Leyden on the following year as *Gebruyck of ongebruvck van 't Orgel in de Kerken der Vereenighde Nederlanden.*

[59] Letter of Descartes to Mersenne, 15 November 1638, A.T., II, pp. 437–438.

[60] Quoted in A.T., III, p. 351.

ough grasp of mathematics and understands enough of my method to teach himself whatever he does not yet know in other branches of mathematics. But one should not expect him to behave like a servant: he has always lived with his betters and been treated as an equal.[61]

This tells much about Descartes' attitude to his retainers. Nor was Gillot an isolated case. Gerard von Gutschoven, who was also in his employ, became a professor at the University of Louvain, and Henry Schlutter, who was his last manservant, acquired considerable proficiency in mathematics. The most remarkable case is that of Dirck Rembrantsz, a poor shoemaker from the town of Nierop. Twice he was refused admission by Descartes' servants who thought he was too shabbily dressed to be anything but a beggar. To make him desist, Descartes sent him a small sum of money which he refused with great dignity saying he hoped the philosopher would see him at some later time. Descartes welcomed him on his third visit and on numerous other occasions. Indeed, he became a pupil and eventually a competent mathematician and astronomer who published several textbooks in Dutch.[62]

An equally gifted, but much higher-ranking disciple, was the Princess Elizabeth, the eldest daughter of the exiled Elector Palatine, who was then living with her mother, the Queen of Bohemia, at The Hague. The princess was a genuine scholar who had a command of English (her mother was Elizabeth Stuart, the sister of Charles I), French, German, Dutch, Latin, and even Italian, since she proposed to Descartes that they study the works of Machiavelli together. She knew enough mathematics to solve a tricky problem Descartes sent her, and she understood recent advances in telescopic observations. She could also raise intelligent objections to Descartes' explanation of the magnet. She was 23 years old when she first wrote to Descartes in 1642 to express her admiration of his recently published *Meditations*. Descartes was flattered and kept up a steady correspondence with her. The orphaned Elizabeth (the Elector Palatine had died in 1632) was young enough to be his daughter, and he became a surrogate father to her. Her letters are full not only of lively philosophical and scientific queries but also of questions about her health. She consulted Descartes about her minor ailments such as her occasional constipation and the rash on her hands. The philosopher, usually so guarded and reserved in his letters, was drawn out by the confidence she bestowed on him, and revealed to her more about his own personal life than to any other correspondent. He told her of his childhood illnesses and the way he managed to get rid of bad dreams. Above all he praised a life of leisure:

the main rule that I always followed in my studies and that I believe helped me most in acquiring knowledge is to never give more than a few hours, per day, to thoughts that occupy the imagination [i.e., mathematics and

[61] Letter of Descartes to Mersenne, around 27 May 1638, A.T., II, pp. 149–150.

[62] Adrien Baillet, *La Vie de Monsieur Des-Cartes*, 2 vols. (Paris, 1691), facsimile (Geneva: Slatkine, 1970), vol. II, pp. 553–555, quoted in A.T., V, pp. 265–267.

physics], and very few hours, per year, to those that occupy the under-standing only [i.e., metaphysics]: the rest of my time I relaxed and gave my mind a rest.[63]

Odium Theologium

The Stampioen incident had caused Descartes much bitterness, but he was soon to become embroiled in an affair of far greater consequence. Gisbert Voet or Voetius, the professor of theology at the University of Utrecht and a pillar of the Protestant Establishment, had found upon reading Descartes' *Discourse* that his ideas were dangerously subversive. To doubt the existence of God, even with the avowed intention of establishing it on a surer basis, appeared to Voetius a threat to religion. What could be worse than a Papist with liberal ideas? Voetius saw an opportunity to voice his disquiet in March 1639 when a colleague at the University of Utrecht, Antoon Aemilius, pro-nounced the funeral oration of Reneri who had just died. Aemilius praised Reneri's friendship for Descartes, "the Atlas and unique Archimedes of our century."[64] Worse still, the town council printed the oration, thereby giving it an official seal of approval. Voetius raised a cry of alarm and warned his colleagues of the atheism latent in Descartes' philosophy. But he had to contend with Aemilius and with Henry de Roy or Regius, the scion of a rich family of Utrecht brewers, who had been appointed extraordinary professor (we would say today associate professor) of theoretical medicine and botany in 1638, and ordinary professor the next year. Regius had been introduced to Descartes by Reneri and had become an enthusiastic Cartesian.

In June and July 1639, the end of term debates that were part of the normal curriculum enabled Voetius to mount an attack on a series of theses that were described as atheistic but rested in fact on the methodical doubt advocated by Descartes, whose name, however, was never pronounced. Regius replied by organizing a debate on Harvey's theory of the circulation of the blood that Descartes had praised in his *Discourse* (although he dis-agreed with him on the mechanism of the circulation). When Descartes was shown the text that Regius intended to have read by a student, he suggested that a less belligerent tone would achieve better results. His advice was disregarded: Regius, as Descartes was later to learn at his expense, was a man who positively enjoyed a quarrel. Harvey's theory was therefore presented and energetically defended against opponents on 20 June 1640. Voetius was up in arms. At a distance of over three centuries, we may well ask how a theologian could be so strenuously opposed to the circulation of the blood? The reason is that the theory seemed to do away with the notion of "sub-stantial form," a concept that was held to be essential to the traditional explanation of the immortality of the soul and the relation of the body to the

[63] Letter of Descartes to Elizabeth, 28 June 1643, A.T., II, pp. 692–693.

[64] Quoted in Descartes' letter to the magistrates of Utrecht, A.T., VIII–2, p. 203.

soul. Regius had his theses published, only to have them immediately impunged by an English physician from Hull, John Primerose, whose *Remarks* were published by Jan Maire in Leyden in 1640. Before the year was out, Regius had retorted with a pamphlet whose title reads in part, *A Sponge to Wash Away the Dirt of Primerose's Remarks.*

In the meantime Voetius became rector and organized a new public debate, with a student, Lambert Van den Waterlaet, as his mouthpiece.[65] This time the motion of the earth, which Descartes was known to entertain, was criticized. By February 1642 Regius' rebuttal was in print, but it was couched in such abusive language that Voetius had no difficulty in having him censured by the town council and the senate of the university. The 130 unsold copies of Regius' rejoinder were impounded, and he was ordered to stick to medicine and botany in his teaching. But Voetius was not satisfied. Having gagged the disciple, he had yet to fetter his master. He wrote to Marin Mersenne in Paris in the hope of enlisting him in a crusade against Descartes' novel and pernicious ideas, but the Minim Friar replied that Voetius should reserve his judgment until Descartes had published his entire philosophical system. He also informed Descartes of Voetius' design. Descartes then decided to expose Voetius in an open letter to his former teacher, Fr. Jacques Dinet, now Provincial (i.e., Head) of the Jesuit Province of France. Descartes, always anxious to win the Jesuits to his cause, described himself as an aggrieved and unjustly persecuted Catholic. Voetius is not mentioned by name, but since he is referred to as the rector of the university, identification was beyond doubt. This open letter was printed at the end of the second edition of the *Meditations* that appeared in the spring of 1642.

Voetius waxed indignant and convinced the town council that a reply was in order. Voetius' own son, Paul, was asked to draft a resolution, but since it had to be officially discussed, approved, and sanctioned, it was only fifteen months later, in September 1643, that it was finally published. Voetius senior could not be patient for so long, and he decided upon a shaft of his own devising. In August 1642 he was visited by a former student, Martin Schook, whom he enlisted as his spokesman. Schook was set the task of attacking Descartes in a work entitled *The Admirable Method of the New Philosophy of René Descartes.*[66] His hand was guided from the beginning by Voetius, and manuscript sheets were sent in installments to an Utrecht publisher, Jan van Waesberge, in order to speed up the process of printing. Descartes had friends in Utrecht, however, and the galley-proofs were surreptitiously passed on to him. He was thus able to work at his reply while his adversaries were still correcting the proofs of their own work. After the first six quires (144 pages), however, the printing stopped. Foul play had not been discovered; Voetius

---

[65] The protracted quarrel between Voetius and Descartes is discussed at length in the second volume of A.C. Duker's monumental *Gisbertus Voetius*, 4 vols. (Leyden: Brill, 1897–1915).

[66] The original in Latin is now available in a French translation along with other documents relative to the incident in: René Descartes and Martin Schook, *La querelle d'Utrecht*, Theo Verbeck, ed. (Paris: Les impressions nouvelles, 1988).

simply had more pressing matters on his hands. He had been called upon to pronounce on a delicate matter of conscience at Bois-le-Duc ('S Hertogenbosch). The incident is revealing of the man and his age, and as we shall see, it was to involve him in a quarrel with another Protestant pastor, Samuel Desmarets, who thus became Descartes' ally.

Strange Bedfellows

Desmarets was a French Huguenot who had been invited to settle in the Netherlands and had been assigned pastoral charges in regions with mixed religious populations on the reconquered borders of the country. He had been posted in Maestricht and later in Bois-le-Duc, considered the Rome of the Netherlands, the way Utrecht was recognized as its Geneva. He was strictly orthodox in his Calvinist outlook, but he was able to get along with the Catholics. Now an ancient "Confraternity of our Blessed Lady," dating from 1318, was one of the chief ornaments of Bois-le-Duc. It still helped the poor, but it had evolved into an association of wealthy merchants, who prided themselves on the high gastronomical standards of their dinner parties. It was both an honor and a pleasure to belong to such a company. In 1642, the governor of Breda and several Protestant notables requested admission. The statutes were revised to allow non-Catholics, and fourteen prominent Protestants of Bois-le-Duc applied for membership. This caused an uproar among their more conservatively minded or merely envious coreligionists, and insult was added to injury when they were officially received into the Confraternity on a Catholic feastday at which fish was served. Recourse was made to Voetius, who was known for his militant anti-Catholicism, and he leapt into the fray with glee. He interrupted his attack on Descartes to compose a violent diatribe against the Confraternity. Descartes, who had not made the acquaintance of Desmarets, got in touch with him, and they agreed to make a common front against their mutual enemy.

Descartes had been preparing a rejoinder to Voetius' *The Admirable Method of the New Philosophy of René Descartes*, now on sale, and he decided to add a reply to the theologian's attack on the Confraternity. His *Letter to Gisbert Voetius* was published in May 1643 and ran to 282 pages.[67] This may seem long, but it was half the length of Voetius' *A Specimen of the Somewhat Ambiguous or Lubricous, and Somewhat Perilous Statements Contained in a Recently Published Tract for the Members of the Confraternity of the Blessed Lady*, which numbered 511 pages of small print. Voetius sought civil redress, and on June 23 1643, the town councillors of Utrecht had the bells of the town hall solemnly rung as a citation was nailed to the wall ordering Descartes to appear before them. Descartes refused the summons, but he sent on 6 July 1643 an open letter in Dutch in which he claimed that since he was not a citizen of Utrecht

---

[67] *Epistola ad Celeberrimum Virum D. Gisbertum Voetium* (Amsterdam: Louis Elzevier, 1643), in A.T., VIII-2, pp. 1–194, with the French translation, pp. 199–273. For the Marian Confraternity Controversy, see pp. 64–107.

the city had no right to ask him to account for himself. On 13 September 1643, the town council passed a vote of censure on Descartes, and forbade the sale of both his *Letter to Fr. Dinet* and his *Letter to Gilbert Voetius* as libellous.[68] Descartes was alarmed. Although he resided in Egmond in the province of Holland, an agreement between the provinces of Holland and Utrecht stipulated that a decree rendered in one province was applicable in the other. Descartes appealed to his powerful friends at The Hague, and he was able through the good offices of Constantin Huygens to arrange for a secretary of the Prince of Orange to write to the town council of Utrecht.

The French ambassador, Gaspard Cognet de la Thuillerie, also intervened, and the proceedings against Descartes were immediately dropped. Matters would have probably rested there had Descartes not decided to be vindicated. *The Admirable Method of the New Philosophy of René Descartes* had appeared anonymously, and Descartes was bent on showing that Voetius, and not Martin Schoock, was the author. Schook was a professor at Groningen, and Descartes lodged a formal complaint with the university. Since Schoock was rector that year, the protest can hardly be called well-timed. Furthermore, Desmarets had recently been appointed professor of theology at Groningen, and there was the added risk of a conflict between a professor and his rector. The university wisely delayed taking any action until the end of Schoock's term of office on 26 August 1644. An enquiry was opened, and Schoock admitted that Voetius had not only suggested that he write against Descartes but had provided the arguments. The printed text contained a number of personal attacks and insults that were plainly absent from Schoock's own copy. Who had added them? Schoock had entrusted his manuscript to van den Waterlaet, Voetius' student, but van den Waterlaet denied having seen the proofs. It was hard to escape the conclusion that Voetius was responsible for the defamatory passages.

On 20 April 1645, the University of Groningen submitted its report in which it was made clear that both Schoock and Voetius had behaved with less than academic propriety. Descartes forwarded the report to the town council of Utrecht. By this time, the councillors were thoroughly fed up with the petty squabbling of university professors, and they approved on 12 June 1645 a motion prohibiting the publication of any writing for or against Cartesian philosophy. Descartes, who had hoped for a complete victory, wrote an indignant letter in Latin to the town council followed by a lengthy apologetic writing in both French and Dutch. Matters were not helped by the rector of the Theological College, Jacob Revius, who had a long-standing distrust of Descartes. When they had met in Deventer several years earlier, Revius had sought to convert Descartes to Protestantism. Descartes politely replied that he intended to remain faithful to the religion of his king. When Revius tactlessly persisted, Descartes added that he wished to keep the faith of his wet-nurse. The Frenchman's irony was lost on the grave Dutchman, who

---

[68] Register of the Town Council (Vroedschap) of Utrecht, quoted in A.T., IV, p. 23.

never forgave him for appealing to such unphilosophical reasons for refusing the higher light of Calvinism.[69]

An Unruly Disciple

Descartes was so incensed by the attitude of the academic establishment that he once more considered leaving Holland. He travelled to France in June 1647, and lodged in Paris with the Abbé Picot who was completing the French translation of his *Principles of Philosophy*. He saw Mersenne and made the acquaintance of Blaise Pascal, but the rumblings of civil war and the vague and ineffectual promises that he received made him realize the blessings of life in the Netherlands. By the end of September, he was back in his philosophical harbor at Egmond. Unfortunately, these waters were soon to be ruffled again. The cause this time was his hitherto disciple in Utrecht, the young professor Henri de Roy or Regius.[70] The storm had been gathering since 1645 when Regius had submitted to Descartes the manuscript of his *Foundations of Physics* in which he purported to develop Descartes' ideas. Of the twelve chapters contained in Regius' work, the first six follow more or less the outline of Descartes' *Principles*, but the next six discuss plants and animals as well as human anatomy and physiology, the very topics Descartes was working on in view of a sequel to his book. Descartes was annoyed, partly because Regius was rushing into print before he had managed to state his own position on these difficult and controversial subjects, and partly because Regius made a mess of the whole matter. On the question of muscles, for instance, Regius had culled his information from Descartes' manuscript notes, but he had not seen the diagrams, and those he drew revealed that he had not grasped the nature of Descartes' explanation.

But there were more substantive issues. Descartes had opened his *Principles of Philosophy* with a summary of his metaphysics in order to stress that his science had a solid foundation. Regius considered this irrelevant and moved the summary to the end, thereby implying that Cartesian physics was independent of metaphysics. Descartes considered this a subversion of his thought. A second difficulty concerned the unity of man, a dogma that was expressed in both Catholic and Protestant theology by saying that the soul and the body are one natural substance. Regius had swallowed Cartesian dualism whole and felt that mind alone was the real man. Hence his original description of the union of body and soul as *accidental*, a term he subsequently deleted at Descartes' request, but only to claim that the soul is a *mode* of the body, and that Scripture alone tells us that the soul is a substance. This meant that Cartesian philosophy was at variance with Holy Writ. Descartes

---

[69] The incident is recorded in Dirck Rembrandsz, *Des Aertrycks Beueging en de Sonne Stilstant* (Amsterdam, 1661), p. 49, quoted in Charles Adam, *Vie et Oeuvres de Descartes* (Paris: Léopold Cerf, 1910), p. 345*n*.

[70] For Regius, see M.J.A. De Vrijer, *Henricus Regius, een "Cartesiaansch" hoogleeraar aan de Utrechtsche hoogeschool* (The Hague: M. Nijhoff, 1917).

protested that he had never meant such a thing, and he urged Regius not to publish. But Regius thought he had outgrown his master and sent his *Foundations* to Elzevier, who had published Descartes' *Principles of Philosophy*, and who used, without Descartes' knowledge or consent, some of the woodcuts that had been made for that work. Descartes felt betrayed and complained in letters to several friends, including Huygens. Regius retorted by printing a broadsheet and having it posted on notice boards in Utrecht. It was headed *Programma* and listed 21 theses that Regius was prepared to defend. It ended with a quotation from Descartes that Regius turned against its author: "No one acquires a great reputation for piety as easily as the hypocrite and the superstitious."[71] This was the welcome Descartes received upon his return to Holland! He saw the need to vindicate himself, and in December 1647, the Elzeviers published his *Remarks on a Certain Program*.[72] Regius was silenced for the time being, but after Descartes' death, he published a second edition of his *Foundations of Physics* in which he made it clear that he had not recanted.

French Passions

Descartes' trip to France in 1647 had not been altogether without success. On 6 September 1647, he had been awarded an annual pension of three thousand livres, but some service to the Crown was probably expected, since Descartes was invited back to Paris in the following year. He arrived in the French capital early in May and within a few days regretted leaving Holland. The conflict between Mazarin and the Parlement was coming to a head, and Parisians were mobilizing for war not philosophy. Descartes had been invited by friends to a dinner party only to find, as he later put it, "their kitchen in disorder and their pans overturned."[73] Descartes does not seem to have realized the extreme gravity of the situation until insurrection broke out on 26 August. Paris was no longer safe, and Descartes beat a hasty and undignified retreat back to the Netherlands.

During these periods of bitter feud in Holland and no less bitter disappointments in France, Descartes was not philosophically idle. In the intervals between writing polemical pamphlets, he busied himself with a treatise on the passions. The moral stance he advocated is a form of Stoicism akin to the ideal proposed by his contemporary Pierre Corneille in his famous tragedies. The work was completed in 1649, and dedicated to Princess Elizabeth whose questions had prompted several developments.[74]

---

[71] The sentence is lifted from Descartes' Preface to his *Principles of Philosophy*, A.T., VIII–1, p. 2. Regius' broadsheet was reprinted by Descartes in his *Remarks on a Certain Program*, A.T., VIII–2, pp. 342–346.

[72] *Notae in Programma Quoddam* (Amsterdam: Louis Elzevier, 1643), A.T., VIII–2, pp. 337–369.

[73] Letter of Descartes to Chanut, 26 February 1649, A.T., V, p. 292.

[74] *Les Passions de l'Ame* (Paris: Henry le Gros, 1649), A.T., XI, pp. 301–497.

Swedish Blandishments

Descartes would have been happy to spend the rest of his days in Holland, but he was enticed to make yet another trip abroad by the flattering invitation he received from the young Queen Christina of Sweden. She expressed the desire of becoming his pupil, and even sent the admiral Claudius Flemming to fetch him in a warship in April. But Descartes could not make up his mind. As he put it to his friend Brasset:

> For a man born in the garden of Touraine, and living in a land where, if there is less honey than in the one promised by God to the Israelites, there is more milk, it is no easy thing to leave for the country of bears, and live amidst rocks and ice.[75]

Nevertheless, Descartes eventually made up his mind and left for Stockholm at the beginning of September. Two days before embarking he paid a farewell call on Brasset at The Hague. The French diplomat was amused at Descartes' sartorial elegance and penned the following description of the travelling philosopher:

> I confirm that when he came to say goodby with his hair curled, wearing shoes that ended in a crescent and gloves decorated with white fur, I was reminded of that Plato, who was not so divine as not to wish to know what human nature was like, and I thought to myself that the departure from Egmond meant the arrival in Stockholm of a full-dressed and well-shod courtier.[76]

Descartes landed in Sweden after a trip that lasted over a month and was warmly received by the young Queen. She suggested that they meet three times a week to study his philosophy. This much Descartes had expected; what came to him as a surprise was the hour she named: five o'clock in the morning! Descartes was in the habit of staying in bed until noon, but he accepted with good grace. These early risings and the drive in a cold carriage from the French embassy to the Royal Palace were the cause of the pneumonia that he caught in February 1650. After a brief illness he died on 11 February. His personal papers had been left behind in Leyden where he had entrusted them to his friend Cornelius Hogelande, who made an inventory of the contents of the chest left in his custody. Descartes had empowered him to burn whatever he saw fit, but Hogelande preserved most of the documents that were later forwarded to Descartes' heirs, and reached Paris by the water route that we described in the Introduction.

---

[75] Letter of Descartes to Brasset, 23 April 1649, A.T., V, p. 349.

[76] Letter of Brasset to Chanut, 7 September 1649, *ibid.*, p. 411.

Conclusion

I quote Descartes. Indeed, I do more:
I dedicate my book to him.
I write against a bad philosophy
and I recall a good one.

S UCH DECLARATIONS ARE NOT UNCOMMON—especially in France—not only in the seventeenth and eighteenth century, but in the nineteenth and twentieth as well. The one just quoted appeared in 1863 in Philippe Flourens' *On Phrenology*,[1] a work that praises Descartes' scientific method and claims to have successfully applied it to the bumps on our heads! We may have misgivings about the depth of Flourens' probing of the Cartesian mind, but he is a typical representative of a large class of scientists who were left with the impression that Descartes had provided them with an infallible crank to turn out mechanical truths about the world. In England, even after the publication of Newton's *Principia Mathematica*, Descartes long received the same adulation. Witness what Joseph Addison had to say about his achievement in an address delivered in Oxford in 1693: "He solved the difficulties of the universe, almost as well as if he had been its architect."[2] Addison was not thinking, of course, of the details of Descartes' physics but of the fundamental thrust of his natural philosophy, and of his demonstration of the possibility of the mechanical causation of phenomena.

---

[1] Phillippe Flourens, *De la Phrénologie* (Paris: Garnier, 1863).

[2] Joseph Addison, "Nova Philosophia Veteri Praeferenda Est," in *Works*, Richard Hurd, ed., new edition, 6 vols. (London: George Bell & Sons, 1889–1890), vol. 6, p. 608. The scientific heyday of Cartesianism extended well into the eighteenth century. See William R. Shea, "The Unfinished Revolution: Johann Bernoulli (1667–1748) and the Debate between the Cartesians and the Newtonians," in W.R. Shea, ed., *Revolutions in Science: Their Meaning and Relevance* (Canton, MA: Science History Publications, 1988), pp. 70–92.

Addison's words invite me by way of conclusion to add a few words on the contrast between Descartes' methodological ideal and his actual scientific procedure. We must recollect first of all that Descartes passionately believed that his method was right and that it had received overwhelming empirical confirmation. There are several passages in his writings in which he seems willing to predicate his method on the results of actual observations. The best known is a letter written to Isaac Beeckman in 1634 in which he takes objection to his friend's claim that the velocity of light is finite, and argues that it is instantaneous:

> You have such confidence in your observation that you would hold your philosophy false if there was no perceptible delay between sending and receiving a pulse of light. I say, on the contrary, that if such a delay were perceived, the whole foundations of my philosophy would be completely overturned.[3]

Although Descartes feared no such overturning, the passage is a forceful reminder of the centrality of the instantaneous transmission of light in his system. "I am so certain of this," he says, "that if it could be shown to be false, I would have to confess that I know nothing in philosophy."[4] But his claim to absolute certainty was not restricted to the case of the velocity of light. When writing to Mersenne about the circulation of the blood, he boldly asserted: "If what I have written on this, on refraction, or on any topic that I have treated in more than three lines in my published works is false, all the rest of my philosophy is worthless."[5] This declaration was intended for public consumption, since letters to Mersenne were copied and distributed as soon as they reached their recipient. It was much like sending a letter to one of our daily newspapers. Descartes' claim is even more startling when we remember that he had appropriated Harvey's discovery of the circulation of the blood only as an illustration of the general principle that everything moves in a closed circuit. When he examined the heart, he turned it not into a pump but into a teakettle, in order to derive its heat from known mechanical causes. Whereas Harvey had established the fundamental role of the systole, Descartes' vaporization model led him to argue that it was in diastole that the blood left the heart. He mechanized Harvey's discovery, but lost the mechanical explanation of cardiac motion in the process! It was indeed shaky ground on which to rest his entire philosophy, but Descartes was convinced that a true method could only yield assured results. We are put in mind of Galileo's sweeping claim that all celestial discoveries had been vouchsafed to him, and him alone.[6]

---

[3] Letter of Descartes to Beeckman, 22 August 1634, A.T., I, p. 308.

[4] *Ibid.*

[5] Letter of Descartes to Mersenne, 9 February 1639, A.T., II, p. 501.

[6] Galileo, *Opere*, Antonio Favaro, ed., 20 vols. (Florence: Barbèra, 1890–1909), vol. VI, p. 383, n. 13.

Galileo and Descartes had a singular notion of the scientific cooperation they professed to encourage. This attitude is explained in part at least by
the fact that they did not ask as we do: what is involved in the mathematical
description of nature? But the related question: how do we obtain outside
mathematics the certainty we enjoy within mathematics? Their common
answer rested on the denial of the inside/outside dichotomy. There is
nothing outside mathematics in the real world. As Descartes put it: "All my
physics is nothing but mathematics."[7] To the obvious objection that if physics
is geometry, it is no more than a clever mental construction, Descartes
replied that the mathematical style is the very style of nature. But not all
physical necessity can be reduced to mathematical rigor, and Descartes had
to appeal to other considerations. Why the instantaneous transmission of
light, for instance? One reason is that the universe is a plenum, and actual
motion must result in a complete ring of bodies moving together. If light had
a finite motion, it would be necessary to abandon the law of rectilinear
motion, and the whole of Cartesian physics would be threatened. It follows
that to obey the law of rectilinear propagation, light cannot be an *actual*
motion but what Descartes calls "an inclination to motion," an instantaneously transmitted pressure in the inelastic medium.

Let us call this argument cosmological. With a higher theological warrant, to which we shall return, it seemed overwhelming. The problem is that
Descartes could not work with infinite speeds. In actual scientific practice, he
was driven to employ models that he compared to the epicycles and eccen-
trics of Ptolemaic astronomy while claiming for them a much higher epistemological status. The model that he introduced in the *Optics* to explain refraction is a tennis ball that strikes the surface of water. Velocity is supposed
to be greater in a denser medium, and the ball speeds up as it enters the
water. All the change in velocity takes place at the surface, and exclusively in
the vertical direction. From these premises Descartes was able to show that
for all angles of incidence at which light is refracted into a second medium,
the sine of the angle of incidence is proportional to the sine of the angle of
refraction. The result is spectacular, but what of the argument? To some it
has appeared "preposterous,"[8] and this on two grounds. First, since Descartes asserts that light is "a tendency to motion" transmitted instantaneously,
how can he compare it with the successive motion of a projectile? Or for that
matter, how can he say that it travels at different velocities in different
media? Second, in the case in which the motion is assumed to be swifter in
the second medium, Descartes has to imagine that the tennis ball receives a
second stroke when it touches the surface, a device for which an optical
counterpart is difficult to find.

Descartes believed that he could overcome the first difficulty by postulating that the tendency to motion follows the same laws as motion itself.

---

[7] Letter of Descartes to Mersenne, 27 July 1638 A.T., II, p. 268.

[8] Richard S. Westfall, *The Construction of Modern Science* (New York: John Wiley & Sons, 1971),
p. 55.

This is why in investigating optical reflection and refraction he conveniently forgot about the theoretical mechanism of light, and studied the reflection and refraction of actually moving bodies. As he put it in the *Optics*:

> Now since I shall treat of light only to explain how its rays enter the eye, and how they can be deflected by various bodies they encounter, there is no need for me to say what its true nature is. I believe it is enough if I use two or three comparisons that will help us understand it in what seems to me the most convenient way, in order to explain all those of its properties that experience has made known to us, and then deduce all the others that are not so easily noticed. In this I imitate the astronomers who, although their assumptions are almost all false or uncertain, yet, because they refer to various observations they have made they draw many conclusions that are true and well-assured.[9]

Descartes and his readers were perfectly aware that ancient descriptive geometry had found various ways of reconciling observations with conflicting hypotheses. But it is equally clear that Descartes was not merely offering an instrumentalist account of the nature of refraction. As Gerd Buchdahl points out:

> Descartes' approach is more revolutionary, for it employs models, some of which deliberately relax the conditions, such as those of infinite speed, which the physical account had demanded; and in doing this, Descartes is further compelled to abandon the original hypothesis of stationary ether particles in favour of an emission theory of light particles moving through space.[10]

Descartes implied that what is true of the mechanical model (a ball struck by a racquet) will be true of light also, given a *bridging assumption*, in this case that the tendency to motion follows the same laws as motion itself. Worried by the seeming gratuity of this assumption, Descartes sought to vindicate his strategy in the *Discourse on Method*, which was written after the *Optics*:

> If some of my statements at the beginning of the *Optics* and the *Meteorology* seem shocking at first sight because I call them assumptions and am in no hurry to prove them, please read on patiently to the end and you will be satisfied. I believe that the arguments follow one another in such a way that the last are demonstrated by the first, which are the causes, and the first by the last, namely the effects. And do not imagine that I am making the mistake logicians call reasoning in a circle, for experience makes most of these effects quite certain, and the causes from which I deduce them serve not so much to prove as to explain them; indeed, it is the causes that are proved by the effects.[11]

---

[9] *Optics*, A.T., VI, p. 83.

[10] Gerd Buchdahl, *Metaphysics and the Philosophy of Science* (Oxford: Blackwell, 1969), p. 142.

[11] *Optics*, A.T., VI, p. 76.

This passage heightens rather than lessens our perplexity. Granted that Descartes managed to derive the sine law through reasoning round a model in geometrical fashion and by invoking the motion of projectiles, what causes, if any, have been *proven?* The knowledge of the truth of the consequences, i.e., the effect, is not axiomatic but empirical. What seems to be implied is the truth of the bridging assumption, namely, that the tendency to motion can be interpreted as following the empirically ascertained laws of motion. But even if this were granted, how does this procedure agree with Descartes' more rationalistic pronouncements, in particular his emphasis on intuitive clarity and mathematical rigor? If we look at the model, we cannot claim that the principles governing the motion of a tennis ball are intuitively identical with those that explain the transmission of light. All we have is an analogy derived from the fundamental laws of matter in motion; we cannot be said to have found the causal mechanism of the instantaneous transmission of light itself. In other words, the explanatory principles of optics have a purely hypothetical status. But all is not lost. At this point Descartes shifts his ground and claims that his explanation is ultimately deducible from higher principles. In a letter to Vatier, who had expressed surprise that Descartes should introduce assumptions without proving them *a priori*, he replies that *a priori* proofs would have involved an exposition of all his physics, something he had not proposed to do in his *Optics*. If required, he could deduce all his suppositions from the first principles of his metaphysics, although, he added, "they seem to me sufficiently demonstrated *a posteriori.*"[12] Elsewhere, he claimed that he had "demonstrated refraction geometrically and *a priori*";[13] but when Mersenne pressed him on this point, he replied somewhat impatiently: "to require from me geometrical demonstrations in physics is to ask what is impossible."[14] Descartes never squarely faced the tension between the requirement that an hypothesis be supported *a posteriori* by verified logical conclusions and the requirement of higher support at the metaphysical level.

As we have seen in this book, Descartes the rationalist was also a man who believed in revelation, especially when conveyed in the form of a threefold dream. Like the authors of Rosicrucian tracts, he was convinced that religion and science were not at enmity, and that he had been called upon to restore unity to human knowledge. This "marvellous" feeling never left him, but he was also never able to articulate it to his own satisfaction, let alone that of his readers. He repeatedly expressed the hope of showing "one day" that the principles of physics are demonstrated by metaphysics,[15] but his most serious attempt in the *Principles of Philosophy* ended with a fideistic rather than a rationalist argument for the validity of scientific reasoning:

---

12 Letter of Descartes to Fr. Antoine Vatier, 22 February 1638, A.T., I, p. 563.

13 Letter of Descartes to Mersenne, 1 March 1638, A.T., II, p. 142.

14 Letter of Descartes to Mersenne, 27 May 1638, *ibid.*, p. 142.

15 *Ibid.*, pp. 141–142.

If we only use principles that are clearly grasped (*evidentissime perpectis*) and only deduce from them what can be arrived at through mathematical reasoning, and, furthermore, if what is deduced is in perfect agreement with all the natural phenomena, then we would be making an injury to God were we to entertain the suspicion that the causes of things thus discovered are false, as if he had made us so imperfect that we err in the very process of using our reason correctly.[16]

At the very end of the *Principles of Philosophy*, and after explaining magnetism in terms of invisible microorganisms, Descartes briefly touches upon the legitimacy of reasoning in terms of unobservable entities. He claims that "from simple, obvious and naturally known principles" he had worked out the properties of motion for objects of any size. Nothing stood in the way of postulating entities below the threshold of experience, "especially," he adds, "when I could not think of any other way of explaining them."[17]

In reasoning from sensible objects to insensible ones, Descartes appealed not only to the general laws of nature but to human artifacts, such as clocks. The justification of this procedure is twofold: on the one hand, there is no essential difference between natural and man-made objects, and on the other, experience teaches us that those who are acquainted with automata can easily conjecture the way they are made, merely by being told what purpose they serve and observing some of their parts. But Descartes could not deny that a certain tentativeness had crept into his conclusions:

> This way we can perhaps understand how natural things could have been made, but we should not conclude that they were actually made in this way. The Supreme Craftsman could have produced all that we see in a variety of ways. I freely admit the truth of this, and I shall think I have done enough if what I have written is such as to correspond accurately to all the natural phenomena.[18]

The certainty that results from such hypotheses Descartes called "moral certainty" (meaning adequate for practical purposes), and he compared it to the assurance we would place in the decipherment of a cryptogram that accounted for each character and yielded intelligible words and sentences. That another key, providing a different solution, should be found is so improbable as to be "incredible" said Descartes. The problem is that Descartes was not satisfied with a mere "hypothetico-deductive" model whereby a scientific theory is considered satisfactory if it meets two conditions: (a) deductive inference from basic principles, and (b) agreement between these deductions and sensory experience. He required a third infinitely more stringent condition, namely, that the principles be self-evident. This appeared possible because the mechanical approach rested on concepts of

[16] *Principles of Philosophy*, Part III, art. 43, A.T., VIII–1, p. 99.

[17] *Ibid.*, Part IV, art. 203, p. 326.

[18] *Ibid.*, art. 204, p. 327.

extension and motion that were clear, distinct, and intuitively obvious. Hypotheses that employed these concepts were assumed to possess the same strength regardless of their inductive basis. At times, however, Descartes spoke as though the verified consequences entailed the incontrovertible truth of the premises. In actual practice, when he had no self-evident truth that could serve as a starting point, he chose a more or less convincing model by whose aid he proceeded to make deductions from a hypothesis, and to claim that the empirical confirmation of these deductions was a proof of the hypothesis itself.

The tension between Descartes' abstract ideal and his pragmatic achievements is obvious in the way he carried out his intention of purging physics from the occult and removing all organic features from science. At the programmatic level, Descartes often tells us that "motion, size, shape and arrangements of parts" are the only explanatory categories. All other properties, such as force of attraction and repulsion, sympathies and antipathies, and the like, are relegated to the rubbish heap of anthropomorphic conceptions. Descartes left no doubt where he stood when he was invited to Mersenne to comment on Roberval's *Aristarchus* in which two kinds of attractive force are invoked to account for the motion of the earth. To say with Roberval that the parts of the earth attract one another with a special property implied, according to Descartes, that these parts are animated by souls that are "intelligent and, indeed, divine, since they are able to know without intermediary what is happening in places far removed from them, and even to exercise their forces there."[19]

Roberval argued that without attraction many natural phenomena and specifically the solar system could not be explained. Descartes had to show that attraction was superfluous, and that a purely mechanical interpretation of motion accounted for all known facts. He saw his greatest triumph in the successful reduction of the most conspicuous case of attraction, the action of the loadstone, to the motion of invisible screw-shaped particles.[20] In the process Descartes virtually identified causal explanation by imaginary mechanism with the science of mechanics. Without precise mathematical laws to guide him in framing his micromechanisms, he assumed that they were miniature reproductions of those we know at the macroscopic level. Hence the man who had argued that physical reality differs from the world of experience could not help invoking a representational model as a requirement of a mechanical explanation. Descartes had a vivid imagination and readily imagined particles suited to the shape and motion of any desired phenomena. For instance, he claimed that the ease with which heat or wind drives water out of bodies shows that particles of water are long and flexible, or that the sharp taste of acids indicates that their particles have been

---

[19] Letter of Descartes to Mersenne, 20 April 1646, A.T., IV, p. 401.

[20] As early as 1628, Descartes wrote in the *Rules for the Direction of the Mind*: "there is nothing to be known in the magnet that does not consist of certain simple natures, known in and by themselves" (A.T., X, p. 411).

repeatedly battered by particles of fire until they acquired a flat and cutting edge. The absence of a criterion to judge the validity of postulated explanations of this kind did not strike him as a liability. He thought he had devised invisible mechanisms that would account for the most mysterious and allegedly occult forces in nature, such as showers of blood, milk, flesh, stones, and even animals from the air.[21] The French translation of the *Principles of Philosophy* even offers a mechanical explanation of why the wounds of a murdered man bleed when the murderer approaches.[22]

Purging matter of non-mechanical properties led to a deeper and more significant result. Cleansed of all organic features, hence of all internal forces, matter appears in several of Descartes' pronouncements as wholly inert. It is indifferent to motion or rest. It follows that bodies have no force to resist motion. The idea that matter contains such resistance is a prejudice "founded," as Descartes explained to a correspondent,

> on our preoccupation with our senses, and derives from the fact that, being accustomed since our infancy to move bodies that are hard and heavy, and having always experienced difficulty, we have been persuaded since then that the difficulty proceeds from matter and is therefore common to all bodies. It was easier to suppose this than to realize that it was only the weight of the bodies we tried to move which prevented us from lifting them, and the hardness and unevenness of their parts which prevented us from pulling them and, hence, that it does not follow that the same thing must happen with bodies that have neither hardness nor weight.[23]

A consequence of the indifference of matter to motion is drawn by Descartes when he states that bodies have to move with a finite velocity. Motion and rest are discontinuous, and a body starting to move does not pass through all the degrees of speed as Galileo maintained. In practice, however, Descartes was faced with the fact, as he himself recognized, that "size is always opposed to speed."[24] But if matter is wholly inert, how can size oppose velocity? The problem was not raised in *Le Monde*, but it was thrust to the fore in the *Principles of Philosophy* when Descartes sought to formulate the rules that govern motion. We have seen in Chapter Twelve how he tried to develop a comprehensive system of mechanics based upon the single relation of collision between moving bodies. His laws of impact describe the redistribution of velocities when two objects collide, but they are fundamentally vitiated because Descartes divorces change of direction from change of speed. In other words, he does not recognize the essentially vectorial nature of motion.

---

[21] *Meteorology*, Discourse VII, A.T., VI, p. 321.

[22] *Principes de la Philosophie*, A.T., IX–2, p. 309.

[23] Letter of Descartes to Morin, 13 July 1638, A.T., II, pp. 212–213.

[24] *The World*, Chap. 8, A.T., XI, p. 51.

Since Descartes treated change of motion as instantaneous, the resistance that he admitted cannot be reconciled with the inertness that he considered an essential property of matter. The resistance he attributed to matter had to be resistance to motion itself and not merely to change of motion. The fact that this incompatibility escaped Descartes gives us an idea of the magnitude of the conceptual change involved in his ontological identification of motion and rest. In his *First Law of Nature*, Descartes affirmed that motion like rest is a state, not a process, and hence that motion continues uninterrupted unless compelled to change by some outside agent. Combined with his *Second Law of Nature*, "that all motion is of itself straight," we have—in all appearance—a clear statement of the principle of inertia. That this is not the case can be seen in the way Descartes did not focus on change of motion but on steady motion. Whereas after Newton we think of free fall as a model of force, namely, a paradigmatic case of an external action changing a body's inertial state, Descartes thought of force in terms of the model of the collision of two balls.

We have seen how Descartes called upon God to vouchsafe the reliability of our knowledge of the external world. Likewise he appealed to the simplicity and immutability of God's action to justify his laws of nature. The Second Law, for instance, "only depends on God conserving each thing by his continuous action, hence at the very instant that he conserves it. It so happens that among motions, only straight motion is entirely simple and such that its nature is comprised in an instant."[25] I believe that it is in passages such as these that we gain our best insight into Descartes' deeply entrenched belief in the basic unity of science, metaphysics, and natural theology. Whatever change is brought about in the world, it is caused by mechanical action, but this does not make it less marvellous. God implants simple and self-evident notions of matter and motion in the human mind at the very instant that he creates it. Likewise God produces and sustains the motion of bodies at each and every instant that they are moving. Without these God-given notions, we would be unable to perceive motion, and without God's direct intervention, there would be no motion to be perceived. The magic of numbers and motion is rooted in the transcendental rationality of the Ultimate Mind.

---

[25] *Ibid.*, Chap. 7, p. 45.

Appendix

Chronology of Descartes' Life

1596. 31 March	Birth of René Descartes at La Haye in Touraine (since 1802 the town is called La Haye-Descartes). His father, Joachim Descartes, was a Counsellor of the Parlement in Brittany.
1597. 13 May	Death of Descartes' mother, Jeanne Brochard.
1597–1606	Descartes is brought up by his maternal grandmother and a wet-nurse to whom he remained attached all his life.
1606–1615	Studies at the Jesuit College of La Flèche.
1616. 9 and 10 November	Receives the baccalaureate and the licentiate in law at the University of Poitiers. He will never practice.
1618. January	Enlists as a volunteer in the army of Maurice of Nassau in Breda in the Netherlands.
1618. 10 November	Makes the acquaintance of Isaac Beeckman for whom he writes the *Compendium Musicae* and several short essays on physics.
1619. 30 April	Sails from Amsterdam for Copenhagen. He plans to

	travel to Danzig and reach Bohemia after crossing Poland and Hungary.
1619. 20 July–9 September	Festivities in Frankfurt to mark the coronation of the Emperor Ferdinand. Descartes attends part of the ceremonies.
1619. 10–11 November	Descartes quartered in a small town, probably Neuburg in Bavaria. Has three dreams. Becomes interested in the Rosicrucians.
1620–1621	Nothing is known of Descartes' life during these years.
1622. April	Descartes is back in France. He sells some of the land he had inherited.
1622–1623	Probably spends the winter in Paris.
1623. March	Leaves for Italy. Visits Venice. Makes a pilgrimage to Loretto. Reaches Rome.
1625. May	Crosses the Alps and returns to France after an absence of more than two years.
1625–1628	Sojourns in France, mainly in Paris. Drafts the *Rules for the Direction of the Mind*.
1628. 8 October	Calls on Beeckman at Dordrecht. Settles in the Netherlands but changes lodgings frequently.
1629. 6 April	Registers at the University of Franeker.
1629. October	Moves to Amsterdam.
1630. 27 June	Registers at the University of Leyden.
1630–1631	Lives in the Kalverstraat in Amsterdam. Does dissections.
1632. May	Moves to Deventer to be close to Reneri, his first disciple.
1633. November	Hears of Galileo's condemnation and decides not to publish the *World*, which he had completed.
1634.	Returns to Amsterdam and lodges in the Westerkerck Street.
1635.	Moves to Utrecht or a neighbouring town.
1635. 9 July	Birth of Francine, the natural daughter of Descartes and a servant girl. She was christened in the Protestant Church of Deventer on 28 July.
1636. March	Descartes goes to Leyden to supervise the printing of his first book (*Discourse on Method*, the *Optics*, the

	Meteorology, and the *Geometry*). Stays until Spring 1637.
1637. 8 June	Anonymous publication of the *Discourse* and the three accompanying treatises.
1637. Summer	Lives near Alkmaer.
1639. Autumn	Moves to Haderwick between Deventer and Utrecht.
1640. April	Moves to Leyden.
1640. 7 September	Francine dies at Amersfort.
1640. 17 October	Death of Descartes' father.
1640. November	Descartes sends Mersenne the manuscript of the *Meditations*.
1641. April	Moves to Endegeest, just outside Leyden.
1641. 28 August	Publication of the *Meditations* in Paris.
1642.	Publication of the *Meditations* in Amsterdam. A seventh set of objections and replies is added along with the *Letter to Fr. Dinet*.
1643. May	Publication of Descartes' *Letter to Gisbert Voët*.
1643. 1 May	Descartes moves to Egmond op den Hoef near Alkmaer.
1644. May–November	Trip to France.
1644. 10 July	Publication in Amsterdam of the *Principia Philosophiae* and the Latin translation of the *Discourse on Method*, the *Optics*, and the *Meteorology*.
1644. November	Moves to Egmond Binnen near Alkmaer.
1645. 16 June	Descartes sends a *Letter to the Magistrates of Utrecht* (published in 1656) attacking Voët.
1646.	Publication of the Latin translation of the *Geometry*.
1647. June–October	Second trip to France. Meets Pascal.
1647.	Publication in Paris of the French translation of the *Meditations* and the *Principia*.
1648. January	Publication of the *Notae in Programma Quoddam* against Regius.
1648. 16 April	Conversation with Burman.
1648. May–August	Third and last trip to France.
1649. February	Queen Christina invites him to Stockholm.

1649. September	Descartes leaves for Sweden.
1649. November	Publication of the *Treatise on Passions* in Amsterdam.
1650. 11 February	Dies in Stockholm.

Bibliography

THE LITERATURE ON DESCARTES IS VAST, and the purpose of this bibliography is merely to indicate the works that have been found most useful in writing this book. For a bibliography up to 1960, see G. Sebba, *Bibliographia Cartesiana*. The Hague: 1964. For 1970 onwards, see the "Bulletin Cartésien," published annually in the *Archives de Philosophie* since 1972.

The standard edition of Descartes' Works is:

Oeuvres de Descartes. Edited by Adam, Charles and Tannery, Paul. 13 vols. (vol. 12 contains the bibliography and index; vol. 13 a biography of Descartes by Charles Adam). Paris, 1897–1913. The first 11 vols. were revised and reprinted, Paris: Vrin, 1964–1974.

There is an excellent annotated edition of the *Discours de la méthode* by Etienne Gilson, 4th ed. Paris: Vrin, 1967.

Particularly useful French editions

Règles utiles et claires pour la direction de l'esprit et la recherche de la vérité. French trans. of the *Regulae ad directionem ingenii* by Jean-Luc Marion with mathematical notes by Pierre Costabel. The Hague: Martinus Nijhoff, 1977.

Exercices pour les éléments des solides. A critical edition of the Latin text and a French trans. of *De Solidorum Elementis* by Pierre Costabel. Paris: Presses Universitaires de Frances, 1987.

English translations:

Cottingham, J., Stoothoff R., and Murdoch, D. *The Philosophical Writings of Descartes*, 2 vols. Cambridge: Cambridge University Press, 1984. This was meant to replace:

Haldane, Elizabeth S. and Ross, G.R.T. *The Philosophical Works of Descartes*, 2 vols. Cambridge: Cambridge University Press, 1911, frequently reprinted.

Individual works:

Discourse on Method, Optics, Geometry, and Meteorology. Trans. with an intro. by Paul J. Olscamp. Indianapolis: Bobbs-Merrill, 1965.

The Geometry of René Descartes. Facsimile edition with a trans. on facing pages by David Eugene Smith and Marcia L. Latham. Lasalle, Ill.: Open Court, 1925. Reprinted New York: Dover, 1954.

The Principles of Philosophy. Trans. with notes by Valentine Rodger Miller and Reese P. Miller. Dordrecht: D. Reidel, 1983.

Treatise of Man. French text with trans. and commentary by Thomas Steele Hall. Cambridge, MA: Harvard University Press, 1972.

Secondary Literature:

Adam, Charles. *Vie et oeuvres de Descartes.* Paris: Léopold Cerf, 1910.

Addison, Joseph. "Nova Philosophia Veteri Praeferenda Est," in *Works*, edited by Richard Hurd. New edition, 6 vols. London: George Bell and Sons, 1889–1890.

Aiton, Eric. *The Vortex Theory of Planetary Motions.* London: Macdonald, 1972.

Aristotle. *On the Soul. Parva Naturalia. On Breath.* Trans. by W. S. Hett. Loeb Classical Library. London: Heinemann, 1975.

Armogathe, Jean-Robert. *Theologia Cartesiana: l'explication physique de l'Eucharistie chez Descartes et dom Desgabets.* The Hague: M. Nijhoff, 1977.

Arnold, P. *La Rose-Croix et ses Rapports avec la Franc-Maçonnerie.* Paris: C. P. Maisonneuve et La Rose, 1970.

Aubrey, John. *"Brief Lives" Chiefly of Contemporaries, Set Down by John Aubrey, Between the Years 1669 and 1697.* Edited by Andrew Clark. 2 vols. Oxford: Clarendon, 1898.

Bacon, Francis. *Works.* Edited by J. Spedding; R. L. Ellis; *et alii.* 14 vols. London, 1857–1874. Reprint, Stuttgart-Bad Cannstatt: Frommann, 1963.

Bacon, Roger. *Opera quaedam hactenus inedita.* Edited by J. S. Brewer. London: Longman, 1859.

Baillet, Adrien. *Abrégé de la vie de M. Descartes,* Paris, 1692. Reprinted in the collection "Les Grandeurs." n. p.: La Table Ronde, 1946.

Baillet, Adrien, *La vie de Monsieur Des-Cartes.* 2 vols. Paris: Daniel Horthemels, 1691. Facsimile reprint, Geneva: Slatkine Reprints, 1970.

Baron, M. E. *The Origins of the Infinitesimal Calculus.* Oxford: Pergamon Press, 1969.

Beck, L. J. *The Method of Descartes. A Study of the* Regulae. Oxford: Clarendon, 1952.

Beck, L. J. *The Metaphysics of Descartes: A Study of the Meditations*. Oxford: Clarendon, 1965.

Beeckman, Isaac. *Journal*. Edited by Cornélis de Waard. 4 vols. The Hague: Martinus Nijhoff, 1939–1945.

Bélaval, Yvon. *Leibniz Critique de Descartes*. Paris: Gallimard, 1960.

Blackwell, Richard J. "Descartes' Concept of Matter." In *The Concept of Matter in Modern Philosophy*, edited by Ernan McMullin, pp. 59–75. Notre Dame: University of Notre Dame, 1978.

Blackwell, Richard J. "Descartes' Laws of Motion." *Isis* 57 (1966), pp. 220–234.

Bos, H. J. M. "Arguments on Motivation in the Rise and Decline of a Mathematical Theory; the 'Construction of Equations', 1637–ca. 1750." *Archive for History of Exact Sciences* 30 (1984), pp. 331–380.

Bos, H. J. M. "On the Representation of Curves in Descartes' *Géométrie*." *Archive for History of Exact Sciences* 24 (1981), pp. 295–338.

Boyer, Carl B. *The Rainbow, From Myth to Mathematics*. New York: Thomas Josehoff, 1959.

Buchdahl, Gerd. *Metaphysics and the Philosophy of Science*. Oxford: Basil Blackwell, 1969.

Burton, Robert. *The Anatomy of Melancholy*. 3 vols. London: Dent, 1932.

Carter, Richard B. *Descartes' Medical Philosophy*. Baltimore: Johns Hopkins University Press, 1983.

Carteron, H. "L'idée de force mécanique dans le système de Descartes." *Revue philosophique de la France et de de l'étranger* XCIV (1922), pp. 243–277, 483–511.

Cicero. *De Senectute. De Amicitia. De Divinatione*. Trans. by W. A. Falconer, London: Heinemann, 1923.

Chastel, André, *Marcile Ficin et l'art*. Geneva: Droz, 1954.

Clarke, Desmond M. *Descartes' Philosophy of Science*. Manchester: Manchester University Press, 1982.

Clarke, Desmond M. *Occult Powers and Hypotheses: Cartesian Natural Philosophy under Louis XIV*. Oxford: Clarendon Press, 1989.

Cohen, Gustave. *Ecrivains français en Hollande dans la première moitié XVIIe siècle*. Paris: Champion, 1920.

Cohen, H. F. *Quantifying Music. The Science of Music at the First Stage of the Scientific Revolution, 1580–1650*. Dordrecht: D. Reidel, 1984.

Cohen, I. Bernard. *The Newtonian Revolution*. Cambridge: Cambridge University Press, 1980.

Cohen, I. Bernard. "*Quantum in se est*: Newton's Concept of Inertia in Relation to Descartes and Lucretius." *Notes and Records of the Royal Society of London* 19 (1964), pp. 131–155.

Cohen, I. Bernard. *Revolution in Science*. Cambridge: Harvard University Press, 1985.

Copleston, Frederick. *A History of Philosophy. Vol. 2: Medieval Philosophy. Part II, Albert the Great to Duns Scotus.* Garden City, N.Y.: Doubleday, 1962.

Costabel, Pierre, *Démarches originales de Descartes savant.* Paris: Vrin, 1982.

Costabel, Pierre. "Descartes et la Mathématique de l'Infini." *Historia Scientiarum* 29 (1985), pp. 37–49.

Costabel, Pierre, and Martinet, Monette. *Quelques savants et amateurs de Science au XVIIᵉ siècle.* Cahiers d'Histoire et de Philosophie des Sciences, nouvelle série, no 14. Paris: Société française d'histoire des sciences et des techniques, 1986.

Crombie, A. C. *Robert Grosseteste and the Origins of Experimental Science, 1100–1700.* Oxford: Clarendon, 1953.

Debus, Allen C. *The Chemical Philosophy,* 2 vols. New York: Science History Publications, 1977.

Dee, John. *The Mathematical Preface to the Elements of the Geometrie of Euclid of Megara.* London, 1570. Facsimile with an introduction by Allen G. Debus. New York: Science History Publications, 1975.

de Solla Price, Derek J. "Automata and the Origins of Mechanism and the Mechanistic Philosophy." *Technology and Culture* 5 (1964), pp. 9–42.

De Vrijer. *Henricus Regius, een "Cartesiaansch" hoogleeraar aan de Utrechtsc-Ohe hoogeschool.* The Hague: Martinus Nijhoff, 1917.

Dhombres, Jean. *Nombre, Mesure et Continu. Epistémologie et Histoire.* Paris: Nathan, 1978.

Dibon, Paul. "Clerselier, éditeur de la correspondance de Descartes." In *La Storia della Filosofia come Sapere Critico,* pp. 260–282. Milan: France Angeli, 1984.

Dobbs, Betty Jo Teeter. *The Foundations of Newton's Alchemy.* Cambridge: Cambridge University Press, 1975.

Drake, Stillman. "Free Fall from Albert of Saxony to Honoré Fabri." *Studies in the History and Philosophy of Science* 8 (1975), pp. 347–366.

Drake, Stillman, "Impetus Theory Reappraised." *Journal of the History of Ideas* XXXVI (1975), pp. 27–46.

Drake, Stillman, *Galileo at Work.* Chicago: University of Chicago Press, 1978.

Dreyer, J. L. E. *A History of Astronomy from Thales to Kepler.* Cambridge, 1906. Reprint New York: Dover, 1953.

Duker, A. C. *Gisbertus Voetius,* 4 vols. Leyden: Brill, 1897–1915.

Eastwood, Bruce S. "Descartes on Refraction: Scientific versus Rhetorical Method." *Isis* 75 (1984), pp. 481–502.

Federico, P. J. *Descartes on Polyhedra. A Study of the* De Solidorum Elementis. New York: Springer-Verlag, 1982.

Flourens, Philippe. *De la Phrénologie.* Paris: Garnier, 1863.

Funkenstein, Amos. *Theology and the Scientific Imagination from the Middle Ages to the Seventeenth Century.* Princeton: Princeton University Press, 1986.

Gäbe, Lüder. *Descartes' Selbstkritik. Untersuchungen zur Philosophie des jungen Descartes.* Hamburg: Meiner, 1972.

Galilei, Galileo. *Le Opere di Galileo Galilei*. Edited by Antonio Favaro. 20 vols. Florence: Barbèra, 1899–1909.

Galison, Peter L. "Model and Reality in Descartes' Theory of Light." *Synthesis* 4 (1979), pp. 2–23.

Galison, Peter L. "Descartes' Comparisons: From the Invisible to the Visible." *Isis* 75 (1984), pp. 311–326.

Galuzzi, Massimo. "Il Problema della Tangenti nella *Geométrie* di Descartes." *Archive for History of Exact Sciences* 22 (1980), pp. 37–51.

Galuzzi, Massimo. "Recenti interpretazioni della *Géométrie* di Descartes." In *Scienza e Filosofia*, pp. 643–663. Milan: Garzanti, 1985.

Ganguilhem, Georges. "Organisme et modèles mécaniques. Réflexions sur la Ibiologie cartésienne." *Revue Philosophique de la France et de l'étranger* CXLV (1955), pp. 281–299.

Garasse, François. *La doctrine curieuse des beaux esprits de ce temps*. Paris: Sébastien Chapelet, 1623. Facsimile in 2 vols. (but with continuous pagination), Westmead, Farnborough: Cregg, 1971.

Garin, Eugenio. *Vita e Opere di Cartesio*. Bari: Laterza, 1986.

Gassendi, Pierre. *Opera*, 6 vols. Lyon, 1658. Facsimile, Stuttgart-Bad Canstatt: Frommann, 1964.

Gaukroger, Stephen (ed.). *Descartes: Philosophy, Mathematics and Physics*. Brighton: Harvester Press, 1980.

Gilbert, William. *De Magnete*. Trans. by P. Fleuray Mottelay. New York: Dover, 1958.

Gilson, Etienne. *Etudes sur le rôle de la pensée médiévale dans la formation du système cartésien*. 3rd ed. Paris: Vrin, 1967.

Gilson, Etienne. *Index Scolastico-Cartésien*. 2nd ed. Paris: Vrin, 1979.

Gouhier, Henri. *La pensée religieuse de Descartes*. Paris: Vrin, 1924.

Gouhier, Henri. *Les premières pensées de Descartes*. Paris: Vrin, 1958.

Granger, G.-G. *Essai d'une philosophie du style*. Paris: Armand Colin, 1968.

Grene, Marjorie. *Descartes*. Minneapolis: University of Minnesota Press, 1985.

Guéroult, Martial. *Descartes' Philosophy Interpreted According to the Order of Reasons*. Trans. by Roger Ariew. 2 vols. Minneapolis: University of Minnesota Press, 1984.

Guéroult, Martial. *Leibniz, Dynamique et Métaphysique*. Paris: Aubier-Montaigne, 1968.

Guéroult, Martial. *Nouvelles réflexions sur la preuve ontologique de Descartes*. Paris: Vrin, 1955.

Hatfield, Gary. "First Philosophy and Natural Philosophy in Descartes." In *Philosophy, its History and Historiography*, edited by A. J. Holland, pp. 149–164. Dordrecht: D. Reidel, 1985.

Heath, Thomas. *A History of Greek Mathematics*. 2 vols. Oxford: Clarendon, 1960 (reprint of first edition, Oxford, 1921).

Heath, Thomas. *Mathematics in Aristotle*. Oxford: Clarendon, 1949.

Heilbron, John. *Elements of Early Modern Physics*. Berkeley: University of California Press, 1982.

Hoppe, Marie-Luise. *Die Abhängigkeit der Wirbeltheorie des Descartes von William Gilberts Lehre vom Magnetismus*. Halle a S.: C. A. Kaemmerer, 1914.

Huygens, Christiaan. *Oeuvres Complètes*. 22 vols. The Hague: M. Nijhoff, 1888–1950.

Hyman, John. "The Cartesian Theory of Vision." *Ratio* XXVII (1986), pp. 149–167.

Kästner, A. G. *Geschichte der Mathematik*, 4 vols. Göttingen, 1796. Facsimile Hildesheim: Georg Olms, 1970.

Keats, John. *Complete Poems*. Edited by Jack Stillingfleet. Cambridge: Harvard University Press, 1978.

Kenny, Anthony. *Descartes: A Study of His Philosophy*. New York: Random House, 1968.

Kepler, Johann. *Gesammelte Werke*. Edited by Max Caspar; Volker Bialas, *et alii*. 20 vols. to date. Munich: C. H. Beck, 1938–1988.

Knowlson, James. *Universal Language Schemes in England and France 1600–1800*. Toronto: University of Toronto Press, 1975.

Korteweg, D. J. "Descartes et les manuscrits de Snellius d'après quelques documents nouveaux." *Revue de métaphysique et de morale* 4 (1896) pp. 489–501.

Koyré, Alexandre. *Entretiens sur Descartes*. New York: Brentano's, 1944.

Koyré, Alexandre. *From the Closed World to the Infinite Universe*. Baltimore: Johns Hopkins University Press, 1957.

Koyré, Alexandre. *Galileo Studies*. Trans. by John Mepham, Atlantic Highlands, New Jersey: Humanities Press, 1978.

Koyré, Alexandre. *Newtonian Studies*. Chicago: University of Chicago Press, 1965.

Lachèvre, Frédéric. *Le procès du poète Théophile de Viau*. 2 vols. Paris: Honoré Champion, 1909.

Laporte, Jean. *Le rationalisme de Descartes*. Paris. Presses Universitaires de France, 1950.

Leibniz, Gottfried Wilhelm. *Die Philosophischen Schriften*. Edited by C. J. Gerhardt. 7 vols. Berlin, 1875–1890. Reprint Hildesheim: Olms, 1978.

Lenoble, Robert. *Mersenne ou la naissance du mécanisme*. Paris: Vrin, 1943.

Leurochon, Jean. *Recréation Mathématique*. Pont-à-Mousson: Jean Appier Hanzelet, 1626.

Lindberg, David C. *Theories of Vision from al-Kindi to Kepler*. Chicago: University of Chicago Press, 1976.

Lindberg, David C. "The Science of Optics." In *Science in the Middle Ages*, edited by David C. Lindberg, pp. 338–368. Chicago: University of Chicago Press, 1978.

Lynes, John W. "Descartes' Theory of Elements from *Le Monde* to the *Principes*. *Journal of the History of Ideas* 43 (1982), pp. 55–72.

Mahoney, Michael S. "Changing Canons of Mathematical and Physical Intelligibility in the Later 17th Century." *Historia Mathematica* 11 (1984), pp. 417–423.

Malebranche, Nicolas. *The Search After Truth*. Trans. by T. M. Lennon and P. J. Olscamp. Columbus: Ohio University Press, 1988.

Manuel, Frank E. *The Religion of Isaac Newton*. Oxford: Clarendon, 1974.

Marion, Jean-Luc. *Sur la théologie blanche de Descartes*. Paris: Presses Universitaires de France, 1981.

Marion, Jean-Luc. *Sur le prisme métaphysique de Descartes*. Paris: Presses Universitaires de France, 1986.

Marion, Jean-Luc. *Sur l'ontologie grise de Descartes*. Paris: Vrin, 1975.

McMullin, Ernan. *Newton on Matter and Activity*. Notre Dame: Notre Dame University Press, 1978.

McGuire, J. E., and Tamny, Martin. *Certain Philosophical Questions: Newton's Trinity Notebook*. Cambridge: Cambridge University Press, 1983.

Mersenne, Marin, *Harmonie Universelle*. 3 vols. Paris, 1636. Facsimile, Paris: C.N.R.S., 1975.

Mersenne, Marin. *La Correspondance du P. Marin Mersenne*. Edited by P. Tannery; C. de Waard; A. Beaulieu; *et alii*. 16 vols. Paris: Editions du CNRS, 1933–1986.

Mersenne, Marin. *Vérité des Sciences*. Paris, 1625. Facsimile, Stuttgart-Bad Cannstatt: Frommann, 1969.

Milhaud, Gaston. *Descartes savant*. Paris: Félix Alcan, 1921.

Miller, Valentine Rodger, and Miller, R. P. "Descartes' *Principia Philosophiae*: Some Problems of Translation and Interpretation." *Studia Cartesiana* 2 (1981), pp. 143–154.

Molland, A.G. "Shifting the Foundations: Descartes' Transformation of Ancient Geometry." *Historia Mathematica* 3 (1976), pp. 21–49.

Mouy, Paul. *Le Développement de la Physique Cartésienne*. Paris: Vrin, 1934.

Muraro, Luisa. *Giambattista della Porta mago e scienziato*. Milan: Feltrinelli, 1978.

Nardi, Antonio. "Descartes 'presque' galiléen." *Revue d'Histoire des Sciences* 39 (1986), pp. 3–16.

Naudé, Gabriel, *Introduction à la France sur la Vérité de l'histoire des Frères de la Rose-Croix*. Paris, 1623.

Nazaria, Gio. Battista. *Della Tramutatione Metallica Sogni Tre*. Brescia: Pietro Maria Marchetti, 1955.

Newton, Isaac. *Opticks*. London, 1704. Reprint New York: Dover, 1952.

Niceron, François. *La perspective curieuse, ou magie naturelle des effets merveilleux de l'optique, catoptrique, dioptrique*. Paris: Pierre Billaine, 1638.

Nicolson, Marjorie H. *The Breaking of the Circle*. Revised edition. Oxford: Oxford University Press, 1960.

Osler, Margaret J. "Eternal Truths and the Laws of Nature: the Theological Foundations of Descartes' Philosophy of Nature." *Journal of the History of Ideas* 46 (1985), pp. 349–362.

Pappus. *Mathematicae Collectiones.* Edited by Federico Commandino. Pesaro: Apud Hieronymum Concordiam, 1588.

Pirro, André, *Descartes et la musique.* Paris: Fischbacher, 1907.

Porta, John Baptista. *Natural Magick.* Anon. trans. London: Thomas Young and Samuel Speed, 1658. Facsimile reprint, New York: Basic Books, 1957.

Rabuel, Claude, *Commentaires sur la Géométrie de M. Descartes.* Lyon: Marcellin Duplain, 1730.

Risner, F. (ed.). *Opticae Thesaurus.* Basel, 1572. Facsimile, New York: Johnson Reprint, 1972,.

Rochemonteix, Camille de. *Un Collège des Jésuites au XVIIᵉ et au XVIIIᵉ Siècle. Le Collège Henri IV de La Flèche.* 4 vols. Le Mans: Leguicheux, 1889.

Rodis-Lewis, Geneviève. "Machineries et perspectives curieuses dans leurs rapports avec le cartésianisme." *XVIIᵉ Siècle* no. 32 (1956), pp. 461–474.

Rodis-Lewis, Geneviève. *L'oeuvre de Descartes.* 2 vols. Paris: Vrin, 1971.

Rodis-Lewis, *Idées et vérités éternelles chez Descartes et ses successeurs.* Paris: Vrin, 1985.

Rosenfield, Leonora Cohen. *From Beast-Machine to Man-Machine: Animal Soul in French Letters from Descartes to La Mettrie.* New enlarged edition. New York: Octagon Books, 1968.

Rossi, Paolo. *Aspetti della rivoluzione scientifica.* Naples: Morano, 1971.

Rossi, Paolo. *Clavis Universalis.* Milan: Riccardo Riccardi, 1960.

Rossi, Paolo. *Immagini della scienza.* Roma: Editori Riuniti, 1977.

Rossi, Paolo. *I ragni e le formiche.* Bologna: Il Mulino, 1986.

Sabra, A. I. *Theories of Light From Descartes to Newton.* London: Oldbourne, 1967.

Sakellariadis, Spyros. "Descartes' Experimental Proof of the Infinite Velocity of Light and Huygens' Rejoinder." *Archive for History of Exact Sciences* 26 (1982), pp. 1–12.

Schneider, Ivo. "Descartes' Diskussion der Fermatschen Extremwertmethode—ein Stück Ideengeschichte der Mathematik." *Archive for History of Exact Sciences* 7 (1970–1971), pp. 354–374.

Schône, Albrecht. *Emblemata. Handbuch zur Sinnbildung des 16. und 17. Jahrhunderts.* Stuttgart: Metzler, 1976.

Schuster, John A. *Descartes and the Scientific Revolution: 1618–1644: An Interpretation.* Ph.D. dissertation, Princeton University, 1977.

Scott, J. F. *The Scientific Work of René Descartes.* London: Taylor and Francis, 1952.

Scriba, Christoph J. "Zur Lösung des 2. Debeauneschen Problems durch Descartes." *Archive for History of Exact Sciences* 1 (1960–1961), pp. 406–419.

Shea, William R. *Galileo's Intellectual Revolution.* 2nd ed. New York: Science History Publications, 1972.

Shea, William R. "The Unfinished Revolution: Johann Bernouilli (1667–1748) and the Debate Between the Cartesians and the Newtonians." In *Revolutions in Science: Their Meaning and Relevance,* edited by W. R. Shea, pp. 70–92. Canton, MA: Science History Publications, 1988.

Sirven, J. *Les années d'apprentissage de Descartes* (1596–1628). Albi: Imprimerie coopérative du sud-ouest, 1928.

Slaughter, Mary M. *Universal Languages and Scientific Taxonomy in the Seventeenth Century.* Cambridge: Cambridge University Press, 1982.

Smith, A. Mark. *Descartes' Theory of Light and Refraction: A Discourse on Method.* Philadelphia: The American Philosophical Society, 1987.

Smith, A. Mark. "Ptolemy's Search for a Law of Refraction: A Case-Study in the Classical Methodology of 'Saving the Appearances.' " *Archive for History of Exact Sciences* 25 (1982), pp. 221–240.

Smith, Norman Kemp. *New Studies in the Philosophy of Descartes.* London: Macmillan, 1952.

Thorndike, L. *A History of Magic and Experimental Science.* 8 vols. New York: Columbia University Press, 1923–1958.

Thyssen-Schoute, Cornelia Louis. *Nederlands Cartesianisme.* Amsterdam: N. V. Noord-Hollandsche Uitgevers Maatschappij, 1954.

Trevisani, Francesco. "Symbolisme et interprétation chez Descartes et Cardan." *Rivista Critica di Storia della Filosofia* XXX (1975), pp. 27–47.

Van Berkel, Klaas. *Isaac Beeckman (1588–1637) en de Mechanisering van het Wereldbeeld.* Amsterdam: Rodopi, 1983.

Van Helden, Albert. *The Invention of the Telescope.* Philadelphia: American Philosophical Society, 1977.

Van Helmont, J. P. *Ternary of Paradoxes.* Trans. by Walter Charleton. London: J. Flesher, 1650.

Vasoli, Cesare. *Profezia e Ragione.* Naples: Morano, 1974.

Vuillemin, Jules. *Mathématiques et Metaphysique chez Descartes.* Paris: Presses Universitaires de France, 1960.

Waard, Cornélis de. "Le Mansuscrit perdu de Snellius sur la réfraction." *Janus* 39 (1935), pp. 51–73.

Wagner, Jean-Marie. "Esquisse du cadre divinatoire des songes de Descartes." *Baroque* 6 (1973), pp. 81–95.

Wahl, Jean. *Du rôle de l'idée de l'instant dans la philosophie de Descartes.* 2ème édition. Paris: Vrin, 1953.

Walker, D. P. *Studies in Musical Science in Late Renaissance.* London: Warburg Institute, 1978.

Wallace, William A. *The Scientific Methodology of Theodoric of Fribourg.* Fribourg: University of Fribourg Press, 1959.

Watson, Richard A. *The Downfall of Cartesianism, 1673–1712. A Study of Epistemological Ideas in Late Seventeenth-Century Cartesianism.* The Hague: M. Nijhoff, 1966.

Westfall, Richard S. *The Construction of Modern Science.* New York: John Wiley and Sons, 1971.

Westfall, Richard S. *Force in Newton's Physics.* New York: Elsevier, 1971.

Whewell, William. "On Hegel's Criticism of Newton's *Principia.*" *Transactions of the Cambridge Philosophical Society* VIII (1849), pp. 696–701.

Williams, Bernard, *Descartes: The Project of Pure Enquiry.* Harmondsworth: Penguin, 1978.

Wilson, Margaret Dauler, *Descartes.* London: Routledge and Kegan Paul, 1978.

Yates, Frances A. *The Art of Memory.* London: Routledge and Kegan Paul, 1966.

Yates, Frances A. *The Rosicrucian Enlightenment.* London: Paladin, 1975.

Yates, Frances A. *The Theatre of the World.* Chicago: University of Chicago Press, 1969.

Zarlino, Gioseffo. *Dimostrationi Harmoniche.* Venice: Per Francesco dei Franceschi Senese, 1571.

Zarlino, Gioseffo. *Istitutioni Harmoniche.* Third edition. Venice, 1573. Slightly reduced facsimile, Ridgewood, N.J.: Gregg Press, 1966.

Index

Addison, Joseph 341–342
Aemilius, Antoon 333
aesthetics 74, 89, 90
Agrippa, Cornelius 98–99, 108
Aiton, E.J. x, 288, 295, 302
alchemists 100
Aleaume, Jacques 151
algebra 36, 49, 128
angle; division of 12; trisection of 37, 40–42, 54, 67
Anselm of Canterbury, St. 169
Apelles 203
Apollonius 45, 61; *Conics* 50
Aquinas, Thomas, St: *Summa Theologiae* 5, 134, 261
Archimedes 45, 62, 275
architecture 92
Aristotle 16, 23, 65, 76, 84, 90, 96, 113, 125, 130, 135–136, 204, 209, 211, 222, 230–237, 263, 267, 269–270, 277, 308, 310 *Categories* 5; *Metaphysics* 5; *Nicomachean Ethics* 6; *On Generation* 5; *On Interpretation* 5; *On the Heavens* 5; *On the Soul* 5, 134; *Physics* 5, 65, 229, 300; *Posterior Analytics* 5; *Prior Analytics* 5; *Problems* 75; *Topics* 5

arithmetics 44–45, 69, 73, 79, 128, 132, 180
Arminius 9
Armogathe, Jean Robert 8, 181
Arnauld, Antoine 171–172, 181
astrology 1, 104, 119–120
astronomy 7, 11, 69, 104, 146, 229, 318, 321, 343–344
atomism 81, 84, 125, 144, 262, 268
Ausonius 116
automaton 182, 184, 186, 309, 346

Bacon, Francis 82, 135, 188
Bacon, Roger 11
Bagno, Guidi di 99, 129, 320–321
Baillet, Adrien 2, 9, 94–97, 99, 110–112, 115–116, 118, 121, 123, 126–129, 150, 193, 325–326, 332
Baliani, Giovanni Battista 18–19
Balzac, Guez de 8, 102, 124, 126, 193, 198
Ban, François de 7
Ban, John Albert 90, 330
Barberini, Francesco 321
Baron, Margaret 65
Bavaria, Duke of 93
Beaugrand, Jean de 125, 292